BLOOD BROTHERS

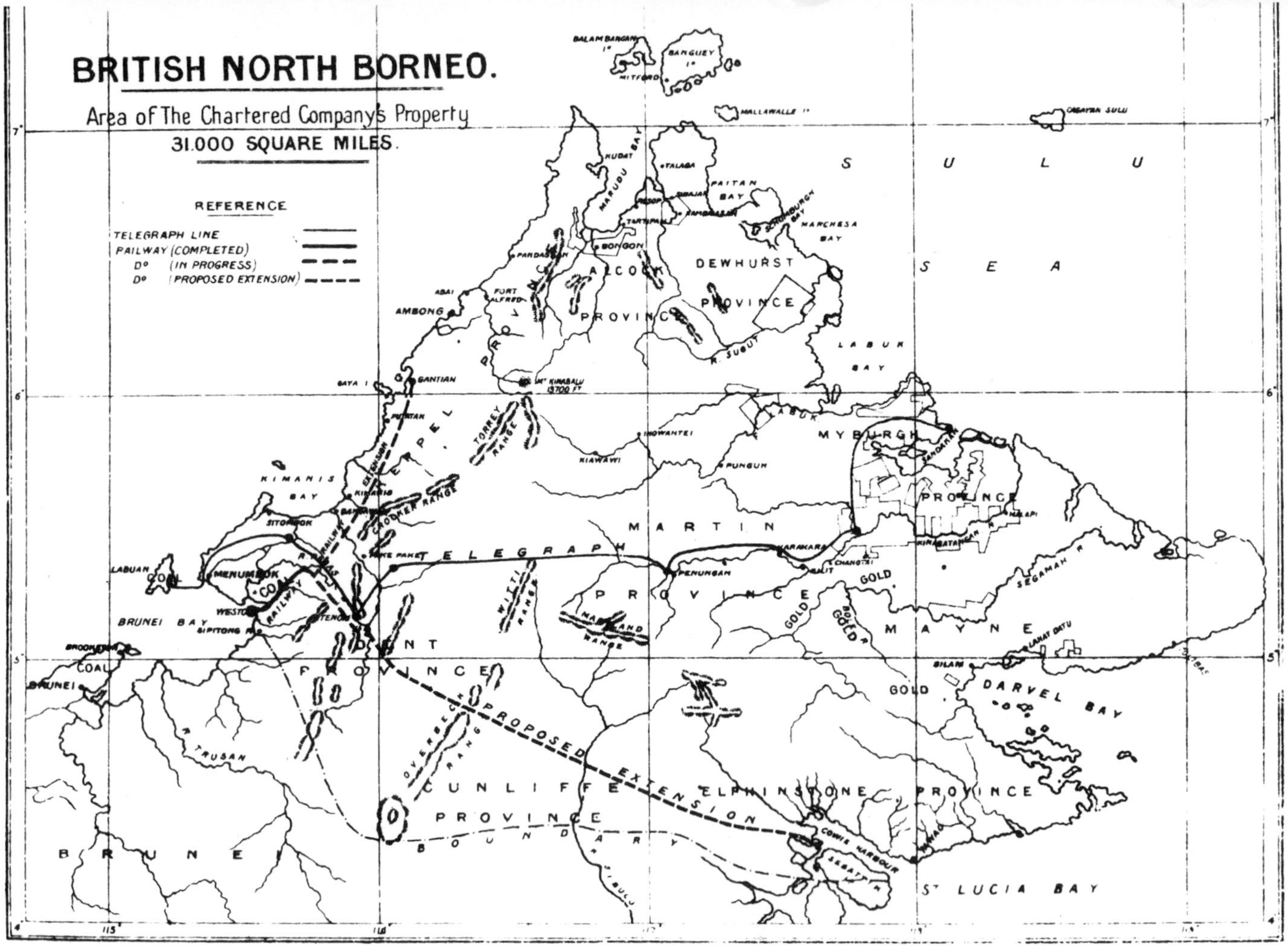

Map of British North Borneo

BLOOD BROTHERS

SABAH AND AUSTRALIA

1942–1945

Lynette Ramsay Silver

Opus Publications
Kota Kinabalu

2010

Published by

Opus Publications Sdn. Bhd. (183100-X)
A913, 9th Floor, Wisma Merdeka Phase 1,
P. O. Box 15566,
88864 Kota Kinabalu, Sabah, Malaysia.
Tel: +6088 233098 Fax: +6088 240768
e-mail: info@nhpborneo.com
Website: www.nhpborneo.com

Blood Brothers: Sabah and Australia 1942–1945
by Lynette Ramsay Silver

ISBN 978-983-3987-39-9

First published August 2010.

Printed in Malaysia.

CONTENTS

For all Sabah's unsung heroes

For their courage was of the rarest and highest order,
inspired not by the prospect of victory,
but by the reality of defeat and oppression.

Acknowledgements

The author gratefully acknowledges all those who so willingly provided information and photographs, particularly Aki Lagan, Datuk Irene Charuruks and Sabah Tourism Board, Sevee Charuruks, the late Chin Chee Kong (Sini), Daniel Chin, Michael Chin, Archdeacon Moses Chin, Catherin Chua, Valentine Fernandez, Reverend Clarence Fu, Martin Kong and the Management of Sabah Tea Gardens, Edward Kwan, Haji Kangawan Kulang, Kaingal (Suamin bin Gadalip), Kong Chong Yin, Lynnette Kong, Dr Lungkiam binte Dambul, Dr Osman Manudin, Ambrose Pang, Bart Pang, Alfred J. Pereira, Sabki Suhaili, James Sarda, Anup Singh, the late Mohamed Tahir Matusin, Jude Teo, Tham Yau Kong, Christine Willie, Michael Willie, the late Joseph Wong, Yumpil, and Zudin, all in Sabah; and in Australia, John Chapman, Josephine Chin, Justina Chin, Len Cottee, the late Eric Davis, the late Stan Davis, Rus Ewin, Mrs Fullford, Grace Funk, Melvyn Funk, Amos Hywood, the late John 'Lofty' Hodges, the late Roni Hodges, Jackson family, the late Carl Jensen, Veronica Keene, Warwick Macfarlane, Rosemary Maxwell, Elizabeth Moore, the late Ken Mosher and Imelda Mosher, Alice Ng, Pauline Patterson, the late Bill Rance, Stan Rance, Allan Russell, the late Ray Steele, Herb Trackson, Graeme Townes, Norm Wallace, Pam Wells and the late Rod Wells; George Stookes in France; Olga Puckett in New Zealand; and Bruce Blanche and Keith Andrews in the UK.

Special thanks also to Penny Williams, Australia's High Commissioner to Malaysia, Kathy Upton-Mitchell of the Office of Australian War Graves and Datuk C.L. Chan, who enthusiastically embraced the concept of this book; journalist Mary Chin for her assistance in locating local people; to my many staunch and loyal friends in Sabah and Australia, especially members of the 'Sandakan family'; to my friend Di Elliott and Andrew Cairns of National Archives of Australia for assistance with research; and my extremely tolerant husband, Neil Silver, whose financial, practical and moral support were so vital in seeing the project through to its completion.

Glossary of Malay terms

batu	stone/mile
bukit	hill
changkol	hoe
dhobi	laundry
kampong	village
kota	fort
kecil/kechil	small
kolek	wooden canoe
kompit	ocean-going boat (Filipino)
kuala	mouth of a river
mandor	overseer
merah	red
orang puteh	white man
orang tua	headman
padang	village green
panglima	warrior/headman
perahu	wooden boat
pulau	island
sulap	lean-to shelter
sungei	river or stream
Tamu	market
tanjong	cape
tuan	sir

Chapter 1

From small beginnings

The outbreak of World War II on 3 September 1939 caused barely a ripple in Sandakan, British North Borneo. Europe was far removed from the tropical languor of this peaceful corner of the world, so much so that news that had created banner headlines around the globe rated nothing more than a casual mention in the 'Notes Occasional' in the *British North Borneo Herald.* Far from rushing to enlist to help defend the Mother Country, there was little or no response from Britain's expatriate community, other than light-hearted suggestions from some members that perhaps they should give up alcohol for 'the duration'. For those who might be serious, it would not be too much of a sacrifice. The war, such as it was, would be over by Christmas – everyone said so.

And so, with barely another thought, the local population got on with the business of living in what, for the carefree Europeans and the well-heeled Asian inhabitants, must have been one of the most pleasant places on the entire planet. Administered by the British under a Chartered Company, Sandakan, as the capital of British North Borneo, enjoyed the best of both worlds – the modern conveniences of western civilisation set against the exotic backdrop of the Far East.

This tropical paradise had evolved from humble beginnings. Sabah, the Brunei name by which British North Borneo was originally known, had for centuries drawn traders from the Sulu Archipelago and places as far away as China, Spain and Portugal, attracted by the bountiful supplies of much sought-after edible birds' nests, pearls, sea cucumbers and bees' wax. Yet, apart from an ill-fated attempt by the British during the latter part of the 18th century to establish a trading post on the northern island of Balambangan, part of a vast expanse of territory granted to them in 1764 by the Sultan of Sulu, not one of the acquisitive European powers had shown any inclination to add Sabah to their expanding empires.

Unlike the flourishing British Crown Colony established by Britain on Labuan Island, off Sabah's west coast, the east coast was virtually uninhabited. The ravages of smallpox and cholera had further reduced its population, driven out by marauding pirates who constantly raided ships and villages in search of booty and slaves. On the Paitan, Labuk, Sugut and Kinabatangan rivers there was not a single village for 100 kilometres inland, while on the Muanad, Bongaya, Segama and Sebuco Rivers, all once well populated, not a soul was left. The pirate menace was so great that there was no European settlement anywhere in Sabah until 1872, when Scottish adventurer William Clarke Cowie appeared on the scene.

The manager of the Labuan Trading Company and a ship's engineer by profession, Cowie had secured a contract to run guns, ammunition and other contraband to the island of Jolo, in the Sulu Archipelago, to help fend off a blockade by the Spanish, who had already occupied the remainder of the Philippines. The cargo had scarcely been unloaded at its destination when a large Spanish gunboat arrived. However, there were no arrests. When Cowie produced papers, written in a mixture of Malay and Dutch, for a ship sailing under Malay colours, partly owned by German-born Carl Schomberg and navigated by a Scot with an English master's certificate, the Spanish captain, mindful of the possibility of international ramifications, gave Cowie two hours to quit the harbour.

Determined not to leave without his return cargo of valuable mother-of-pearl shell, still waiting on the docks, Cowie sailed about for some hours before nudging the vessel up a small waterway where it remained, out of sight, until word was received that the gunboat had departed. With the pearl shell successfully loaded, he headed for Labuan, only to run into a large pirate fleet, which gave chase in their heavily armed, 30-metre-long outrigger boats.

Having sold all his ammunition to the Sulus, Cowie may have come off second best during this altercation had he and his crew not cut up short lengths of chain, which they used for shot, fending off the attack and finally allowing them to escape. Realising that a secluded, local base was essential if he were to continue with his gun trade, Cowie obtained permission from the Sultan of Sulu to establish a depot among the mangroves on Pulau Timbang, twenty kilometres from the entrance of a large, sheltered harbour on the north-east coast of Sabah. The island formed part of a vast territory that successive Sultans of Sulu had controlled for 175 years, believing the land had been handed over in 1704 by the Sultan of Brunei in return for help with suppressing a rebellion.

Cowie named his new enterprise Sandakan, a name established locally for about 100 years and Sulu for 'the place that was pawned'. However, since the main promoter of the trade which soon developed was Carl Schomberg, and also since a good number of the dozen or so Europeans who lived on Timbang were also German, the Bajau and Sulu tribes people who dwelt in nearby kampongs referred to the settlement as Kampong German. Its inhabitants were called 'Orang German' (German person), a term used to describe Europeans in general and one that became part of the local dialect.

When his gun-running ceased to be profitable after a few years, Cowie, who had taken over the Labuan Trading Company from Schomberg and his partner J D Ross, formed a trading partnership with the Sultan of Sulu. Cowie, who was friendly with the Sultan, aspired to own lands in much the same way as the 'White Rajas' – the rich and powerful Brooke family in Sarawak – but a member of the European nobility, who had access to considerable financial resources, outmanoeuvred him.

In 1875 Gustavus Baron de Overbeck, the Austrian Consul-General in Hong Kong, had acquired concessions stretching from Kimanis Bay in the west, to the Kinabatangan River in the east, previously leased in 1865 to the US Consul General in Brunei, Claude Lee Moses, by the Sultan of Brunei. However, Moses had discovered there were problems with the grant: people living in the territory did not recognise Brunei's sovereignty; the islands of Balabac and Palawan were already occupied by the Spanish; and, to top it off, the Sultan of Sulu had already given the same tract of land to the British, a hundred years before. With the United States, which had just emerged from a civil war, expressing no interest in establishing Asian colonies, Moses sold the rights to his lease to Colonel Joseph Torrey, a diplomat and part-owner of the Hong Kong-based American Trading Company. Torrey established a small settlement at the Kimanis River which he named Ellena, but his attempts to obtain financial backing failed, and disease, death and desertion by immigrant labourers eventually led to its abandonment.

With the lease about to run out, Torrey found a buyer – Overbeck, who headed a small syndicate. Overbeck voyaged with Torrey to Brunei where, after checking on the validity of the lease, renegotiated it for a ten-year period. He then returned to Hong Kong where he found a wealthy backer in the person of Sir Alfred Dent of Dent and Company, a trading business based in Shanghai. In late 1877, with funds amounting to 10,000 pounds sterling, Overbeck and Joseph Torrey, along with Dent's employees Mr William Pryer, Mr Pretyman and Mr H L Leicester, set sail for Borneo on board SS *America*. The vessel, which had been especially outfitted for the voyage, attracted the attention of the Spanish and Dutch, who monitored her movements closely.

The party disembarked at the Sultanate of Brunei. On 29 December, after some difficult negotiations, which included settling the outstanding debts of the American Trading Company, Overbeck secured for himself and Alfred Dent a substantial portion of the Sultan's Sabah holdings in return for an annual payment of $16,000. The ship then sailed to nearby Labuan to collect Mr Cowie before continuing to the pirate-infested Sulu Archipelago, escorted by the British naval vessel HMS *Hart* on the advice of the Administrator of Labuan, William Hood Treacher. On 22 January 1878, on the island of Maibu, Cowie's friend the Sultan (who had been ousted from Jolo Island by the Spanish) relinquished his claim on all 'his' territories, in return for a payment of $5,000 a year – a bargain compared to his Brunei counterpart who was receiving $12,000 for practically the same land.

However, while the double payment ensured there would be no cross-claim, the leases did not transfer all of Sabah to the new owners. Some areas of the west coast, including several rivers controlled by Brunei chiefs of 'the blood royal', remained under the Sultan's jurisdiction. Nevertheless, over 70,000 square kilometres was in their hands and Sir Alfred Dent, already appointed Supreme Ruler by the Sultan of Brunei, now gloried in the titles of Maharaja of Sabah and Raja of Gaya, while his co-owner Overbeck became, courtesy of the Sultan of Sulu, Raja of Sandakan and Datu Bendahara. With the elevation in rank came the power of life and death over every inhabitant.

SS *America* then sailed for Kampong German, where Dent and Company's Mr A Hart Everett, and the new Maharaja of Sabah who commissioned Pryer as 'Resident', joined Overbeck and the others. Leaving Pryer, two other employees (a part-Indian known simply as Abdul and a West Indian named Anderson), two Chinese 'boys' and an agent appointed by the Sultan of Sulu to explain the change of ownership to the locals, the remainder of the party sailed for London on 11 February. On the way they dropped off another two Residents, Pretyman and Leicester, plus agents appointed by the Sultan of Brunei, at the west coast villages of Tempasuk and Papar. To protect the newly acquired interests, each of the three Residents had six rifles, a few ex-soldiers who had served under the British in the Indian Army, and Dent and Company's house

William Pryer

flag, the design of which was recognisable only to those with some affiliation to the organisation.

There were only ten villages all told along the entire eastern section of Sabah and just two short tracks leading inland. The first linked the Kinabatangan River to the Gomantong Caves which, along with their highly prized and valuable birds' nests, were fiercely guarded by a despotic chief; the other went from Madai to the Buturong Caves on Darvel Bay. The inhabitants, supposedly under the protection of the Sultans, were not particularly concerned that there had been a change of ownership. The river people kow-towed to any chief of any tribe who was sufficiently powerful to exert his authority, while the fierce headhunting tribes in the interior had no allegiance to anyone, least of all the Sultans. Everyone, however, was armed.

Despite Dent's and Overbeck's high hopes, obtaining official support from the British Crown for their venture was stalled owing to protests lodged by Spain, Holland and Sarawak, none of whom wanted to see the British in control of the territory. After a vain attempt to offload the land to Italy for use as a penal colony, Overbeck's syndicate withdrew from the partnership in 1880, leaving Dent in sole control.

Unable to obtain a Royal Charter until the various diplomatic claims were examined, Dent and five other influential men formed the British North Borneo Provisional Association which, with a paid-up capital of 300,000 pounds, allowed business to proceed. The Association's patience and faith was rewarded and, in November 1881, Queen Victoria granted the much sought-after Royal Charter – an announcement which outraged the Spanish, who considered they had a legitimate claim to the north and east coasts since their 'vassal', the Sultan of Sulu, had signed a treaty with them, six months after he had ceded the area to Dent and Overbeck.

There were further diplomatic protests from Raja Brooke in Sarawak, who had been given his territory by the Sultan of Brunei and had hopes of obtaining more, and the Dutch, who had colonised the remainder of the island of Borneo, or Pulau Kalimantan, as it was known there. The protests fell on deaf ears. The following May the Association was replaced by the British North Borneo Chartered Company, with Dent as Managing Director. The Company had a brand new flag to proclaim its presence, which featured the instantly recognisable Union Jack and a rampant lion in a yellow circle, against a blue background. The Company's men were now firmly in control, and would remain so for the next sixty years. However, they did not have an entirely free hand. Conditions laid down by the British Crown in return for the charter stipulated that the Company must remain British, could not transfer its territory without consent, must abolish slavery, and was to administer justice and law in concurrence with native laws and respect the religion and customs of the local people.

Despite this edict, there were some customs which the Company refused to tolerate. Headhunting, used by some tribes to test a young man's suitability for marriage, was completely outlawed, along with the slow torture and ultimate sacrifice of slaves in an attempt to communicate with the dead. The Company also refused to recognise the Muslim practice of cutting off the hair of a woman accused of adultery before flogging her, and the beheading of thieves.

The responsibility for overseeing these policies and introducing new ones lay with the official Residents. Pryer was progressing well at Sandakan but Pretyman was having a hard time coping with lawless, cattle-rustling and slave-dealing Illanuns and Bajaus in his area. Fortunately he had able assistance in the form of a former Austrian naval officer, Captain Franz Xavier Witti, who had been lured to Sabah by Overbeck. Unable to obtain a posting with the Company through the London office, he had worked his passage to Borneo on a merchant ship and, once on the scene, was immediately hired.

Franz Witti

Whenever a new settlement was established, a new Resident was commissioned. In time, appointments would be made for the West Coast, Interior, Kudat and Tawau Residencies which, in turn, would be divided into provinces or districts under the control of a District Officer. However, while these administrators wielded a considerable amount of power, the very top job went to William Treacher, a clergyman's son, former Government Secretary for Perak State in Malaya and Administrator of Labuan. In 1881, with the approval of the Crown, he was appointed by Dent and his colleagues to the exalted post of Governor of British North Borneo.

At the time of Overbeck's departure overseas in 1878, Kampong German, built out over the water, comprised seventeen atap (palm thatch) and bamboo houses. However, it was far larger than the Bajau village of Oopak, which was in the mangroves opposite and boasted only four dwellings. A few kilometres away, also on Pulau Timbang, was a Sulu village, headed by Datu Haji Mohammed Ansurudeen, while tucked away in a nearby bay was a community of Bajau boat people. Apart from a sole Chinese trader, there were no other inhabitants in the area.

Pryer, although previously employed as a bookkeeper with the Shanghai-based firm of Thorne and Company, had an adventurous streak and had explored a large portion of the Philippines. A man of great enthusiasm and energy, he was also blessed with what would be termed today 'great people skills'. Before long, after winning over the locals by responding to an urgent call from Datu Ansurudeen, whose village was in danger of attack by head-hunters, Pryer brought Sandakan Bay under his administrative control.

Once this was established he organised the local people to deal with the ever-present pirate menace, convincing them that strength lay in numbers and that, by imposing customs duty on goods arriving at the port, they could raise the revenue to do so. His next step was to set up a justice system, based on that used by the British in India, before departing with an armed escort in the Company's steam launch to wave the Company flag at scattered communities along the Kinabatangan River and then the Labuk. The only hostility he encountered was from Pangeran Samah, who controlled the lucrative birds' nests in the Gomantong Caves. Although previously compelled to pay a 'tribute' to the Sultan of Sulu, he was not at all pleased with the prospect of paying taxes on his ancestral property to a foreigner. Despite his threatening behaviour, the Pangeran was outfaced by Pryer, who took a firm stance.

He also outfaced the captain of a Spanish man-o-war, who arrived in September demanding that unless Pryer handed over the settlement to Spain the ship's cannon would pound Kampong German to pieces. Backed by his policemen and the bay's entire population, as well as Cowie who had arrived in his trading vessel *Far East*, Pryer stood his ground. Fortunately, Cowie, who had fallen out with Overbeck over the cancellation of a minor business deal and had plotted to have the Sultan of Sulu claim 'his' lands back, was now back on side: Dent and Overbeck had paid him a 'subsidy' to keep him happy. In the face of such obdurate determination, the Spanish commander Captain Lobe, and his colleague Captain Alejo, the commissioner, eventually weighed anchor and sailed for the Philippines in order to 'seek advice'. Although a ship was dispatched some months later to bombard the settlement in retaliation, the vessel was recalled when the Spanish, fearing a diplomatic incident, rescinded the order.

A few months after Captain Lobe's departure, pirates learned that the majority of the bay's population had departed on trading missions and blockaded the harbour entrance. However, before a situation developed, help arrived in the shape of a ship with six Somalis, all ex-Indian army, recruited in Singapore by Colonel Arthur Harrington, the Company's Police Commandant. As this news and stories of Pryer's accomplishments spread, the population swelled considerably with the arrival of Bajaus from the southern Philippines, who created a separate settlement on Pulau Timbang at Tronglit.

In June 1879, having survived external threats from pirates and the Spanish, Kampong German was razed when fire accidentally broke out. The blaze not only consumed almost every building, it also destroyed a fortune in trade goods and most of the rice store. Instead of rebuilding, Pryer decided to relocate. He chose a mangrove-and-jungle-clad site with deep water frontage on the northern shore of the mainland at a place called Buli Sim Sim, close to the harbour

'Elopura' (Sandakan)

entrance. On 21 June, six days after the disastrous conflagration, Pryer felled the first tree and, in so doing, became the founder of 'Elopura' (beautiful city). However, although the international press used Pryer's choice of name, it did not strike a chord with the local inhabitants and, within a few years, Elopura had reverted to the much older name, Sandakan.

With pirates still a very real threat, Pryer first secretly constructed a fort, screened by a dense patch of trees. Once it was completed and armed with three guns, one of which was a seven-pounder loaned by Cowie, the trees were chopped down and reconstruction of the settlement began. Owing to the shortage of flat land, many of the bamboo-and-atap houses were constructed on rickety piles out over the water. With Kampong German now defunct, the Bajaus at Tronglit created a new settlement at Kampong Bokara, a few kilometres west of Elopura.

By December 1879, less than six months after Pryer turned the first sod, there were 57 houses and 698 inhabitants. Now that he had a

Sandakan 1883

fort and an armed constabulary as well as the local population to back up his authority, Pryer went on the offensive. The pirates, having come off worst in a couple of skirmishes, no longer tried to harass the settlement, but word came that the Illanuns had joined forces with the Baligninis and had raided a Bajau village to the south: the 65 women and children had been kidnapped and sold into slavery, while the men who tried to defend them were slaughtered. The pirate chief Datu Kurunding and his band were reportedly holed up in their stronghold at Tungku, on Darvel Bay.

Meantime, a stand-off between Pryer and a would-be usurper from Palawan Island, who had ideas of taking over Sandakan for Spain, had just been resolved when an armed British naval ship, HMS *Kestrel*, unexpectedly sailed into port, putting paid to the aspirations of the challenger, later to become Sultan of Sulu. On hearing of the latest pirate outrage, *Kestrel*'s Captain E Edwardes, accompanied by Pryer and his local forces, set sail at once for Tungku where they accounted for sixteen armed and fortified vessels, killed many of the pirates and sacked their village. With the pirates no longer a worry, a period of prosperity set in, as people felt confident to move along the rivers and engage in coastal trade. Pryer was also on the move, setting up government stations along the Kinabatangan River.

By June 1881, Sandakan's ever-increasing population stood at 1,200. However, while the East Coast Resident had been busy looking after the Company's interests, Alfred Dent and his colleagues had also not wasted time in expanding their horizons and exerting their control over their estimated 150,000 'subjects'. With the uncharted territory in the interior recognised as a potential source of revenue for shareholders, professional explorers were engaged to venture forth.

The first of these was Captain Witti, who had been helping Mr Pretyman but whose primary task was one of exploration. Over a three-year period Witti, who became fluent in a number of Dusun dialects, organised expeditions to explore almost all of Sabah – from Marudu Bay to Papar, via the eastern slopes of Mt Kinabalu; from Marudu Bay to Sandakan; and, finally, in 1882, from Papar on Kimanis Bay in the west to the Sebuco River in the far south-east, via the upper reaches of the Kinabatangan and Nambunawan rivers. With a fierce Murut tribe (referred to by Witti as 'Tinggalum') using the wild Kuamut ('Quamote') River to access the Kinabatangan and terrorise local villagers, the explorer was keen for the Company to establish a fort at the junction of the two rivers to keep the marauders in check, as the area was rich in camphor, rattan and 'gutta'.

The latter was a huge rainforest tree, which provided easy-to-carve and durable timber, but it was the sap that interested Witti. Once dried, it formed an inelastic latex called gutta-percha (from the Malay getah perca, meaning percha sap), which was not only resilient but also an excellent electrical insulator, making it in great demand for coating telegraph lines and, more particularly, underwater cables, as it was also impervious to attack by marine plants and animals. A versatile, non-reactive material, gutta had many uses, including dentistry and in the manufacture of acid containers. Since 1848, it had also been giving golf balls their bounce.

While en route to his target area, Witti received a message from Governor Treacher, sent by a runner, to postpone his visit to the region and return at once to the nearest District Officer, at Papar. The reason for the recall was not given, but it is likely that as Pryer was already undertaking a journey up the Kinabatangan in order to establish a station at the river junction, perhaps the Governor felt Witti's expedition was redundant. Keen to complete his survey of Sabah, Witti rejected any suggestion that he return, citing the importance of his work, the success of which he hoped would excuse his disobedience.

Witti crossed the interior without mishap and was at the headwaters of the Sebuku River, which emptied into the sea south of Tawau, when disaster struck. He was now in an area occupied by a strange tribal group whose language he did not know. He and his men slept in the village and the next day prepared to depart downstream using boats obtained from their hosts, some of whom offered to act as guides. The eleven-man party set off, only to be stopped by shallow water. While Witti waded ashore to make some notes, his men prepared to drag the boat, into which all the rifles had been placed, further downstream. Without warning, the party was ambushed by a large force. Hit in the chest by a poisoned dart from a sumpitan, or blowpipe, Witti was mortally wounded, along with three or four others. He managed to fire his revolver, but four of the cartridges were affected by damp and failed to detonate. The remainder found their mark, killing two of the attackers. Witti and several of his companions were then overwhelmed by their adversaries and speared to death. Three of the party escaped and reported the massacre, news of which soon reached the outside world. It was believed by some that the attackers were head-hunters, possibly from the tribe that Witti had hoped to subdue. Others were of the opinion that Witti's party, having come from an area regarded as hostile by its hosts, had been regarded as the enemy and deliberately led into the ambush.

Unlike his unfortunate colleague, young Frank Hatton had encountered only friendly native people in his explorations. A brilliant scientist who had been made an Associate of Chemistry and a Fellow of the Chemical Society by his 20th birthday, he had turned down the offer of a posting at Guys Hospital in London in 1881 to accept an offer from Alfred Dent to undertake a mineral survey of Sabah. Not only did he learn to read and write Malay and various Dusun dialects, he also compiled a comprehensive Dusun dictionary, which he hoped the Company would publish.

Accompanied by Australian gold-miner Andrew Beveridge, Hatton undertook three journeys of exploration, the most important of which, in early 1882, involved his surveying the entire Labuk River and its tributaries, from the estuary in the east to Mount

Frank Hatton

Hatton and his Dusun friends become 'blood brothers'

Dusun women pounding rice

Sketch of Mt Kinabalu and the Kinuran River, by Hatton

Mt Kinabalu

Hatton, the explorer

Witti's death

Gold panning

Hatton's last expedition

Kinabalu in the west, before turning north to Kudat. Although during his four-month journey he found very little evidence of any minerals, apart from coal, he encountered no hostility from the local people. Indeed, the Dusuns embraced him with such friendship and cordiality that several of the tribes made him a blood brother, in ceremonies conducted with traditional rites.

Before returning to England on leave in 1883, after which he hoped to be appointed to the post of Interior Resident, Hatton was asked by Pryer to try and discover the source of the gold that locals had found in the south-east. After surveying the Kinabatangan River, Hatton planned to travel overland to the Segama and then follow it as far upstream as possible before striking out for Mt Salim, near Lahad Datu, passing through a considerable amount of territory that was simply a blank space on the map.

Unable to travel cross-country from the Kinabatangan owing to the wet season, Hatton and his party returned to the coast and proceeded up the Segama to access the interior. On 27 February, they had stopped for the night at 'Sugoon Tukol' (possibly present-day Litang), about 100 kilometres from the river mouth, when Hatton spotted an elephant on the opposite bank. He fired his gun but his aim, which was usually sure, was off, and he only succeeded in wounding

Hatton, shortly before his death

Hatton's grave, Sandakan, the first European burial

the animal, which headed off into the jungle. The party took chase, but the creature eluded them and, with darkness soon to fall, Hatton called off the hunt. On the return journey and finding his way blocked by thick vines, Hatton held up his heavy-calibre, repeating Winchester rifle by the barrel, using the butt like a club to try and clear a path. A rotting tree stump crumbled under his weight and, as he stumbled, vines caught in the trigger and the weapon discharged. Shot through the upper chest, and with two major arteries severed, he had no hope of survival. His 'boys' then paddled day and night to reach Sandakan,

270 kilometres away. A funeral service was held by Pryer in a room at his house, put aside as the Church of England (C of E) chapel. Hatton's remains were buried in a small clearing on the side of the hill, thereby giving him the distinction of being the first European to be laid to rest in the settlement. With his death occurring within a few short months of Witti's murder, both of which made international headlines, the Company decreed that the task of exploring new areas and adding new territory would be carried out in future by District Officers.

In 1883, the same year that Hatton died, the capital of British North Borneo (now the 'official' name for Sabah) moved from Kudat, on Marudu Bay in the far north-west, to the rapidly expanding Sandakan, where Pryer had begun importing Chinese, Sulu, Filipino and Javanese labourers to work on his agricultural projects, which included the cultivation of Manila hemp, coffee, cocoa and tobacco. The Company also expanded its western territory by obtaining the rights to the Pangalat, Putatan and Kawang Rivers along with the Mantanani Islands for an additional rent of $2950 to various chiefs. The following year, after prolonged negotiations, the Sultan of Brunei signed over the Padas and Klias rivers which, with the Tuaran and Bongawan Rivers, cost the company a further $3,100. However, the rental was by no means onerous, the original $16,000 paid to the Sultan having been reduced in March 1881 to just $5,000 with another $2,500 going to a minor chief.

The transition of territory to British rule was not always peaceful. To maintain law and order, the Company continued to recruit ex-Indian army personnel, mainly Sikhs and Sepoys, as the local population had exhibited no desire to join the ranks of the Constabulary. The Sikhs, being very tall men (even without their turbans), were very intimidating – which was just as well since the entire force, including British officers holding the most senior positions, amounted to fewer than 100 in 1882. Inspector de Fontaine was singularly unimpressed with the rank and file, describing them in 1883 as being 'scattered around the east and west coast stations, totally undisciplined, with arms of different types and six different uniforms'.

However, the Constabulary's alleged lack of discipline was not to blame for an incident that occurred on the west coast in May 1883, when an armed party was instructed to follow the course of the recently acquired Kawang River to access territory occupied by recalcitrant headhunters. While waiting for the Dusun carriers to sort out a slight disagreement with Bajau villagers regarding the

The quayside, Sandakan

Street in Sandakan, prior to the fire of 1886

ownership of a cow, the expedition halted and the police were stood down. While engaging in what appeared to be a perfectly amicable conversation with two Bajaus, Dr Fraser, the Government Medical Officer, was shot dead. Two Sikh policemen, resting under a tree, were speared. An outraged Inspector de Fontaine took off in pursuit of the culprits but tripped and was set upon. He was transferred to Sandakan in the Company's steam launch, but died a day or two later.

Over in the east, Pangeran Samah who controlled the Gomantong Caves was still a thorn in Pryer's side. After visiting the bay to make death threats, which he ultimately failed to carry out, in 1884 the headman decided to delay collecting the valuable birds' nests in order to avoid paying any duty. This move was ill advised. Sandakan's population had grown to almost 4,000, giving Pryer plenty of muscle to enforce Company rule. On learning that Pryer intended to counter his disobedience by organising the collection himself, the Pangeran threatened to set fire to the caves. To make sure he did not, a party of armed men from Sandakan was dispatched up the Kinabatangan, where Pangeran Samah's men confronted them, armed not merely with native-style weapons but also with guns in the form of old muzzle-loading muskets. The ancient firearms were no match for the guns carried by the police and, during the fifteen-minute skirmish that ensued, the Pangeran was killed and the caves, along with their birds' nests, confiscated.

In 1886, disaster struck for the second time when many of the bamboo-and-atap buildings in the settlement Pryer had worked so hard to establish went up in flames. To help preclude the possibility of it happening again, all new homes and shops were to be constructed entirely from sturdy planks or brick, with either tiled or corrugated-iron roofs. One of the first to be erected was a two-storey hotel, built by Sun Kwong Lung. Situated at the base of the escarpment known as Bukit Merah or Red Hill, it was an elegant brick building, with a wide shady verandah running the full length of the front facade. Although, by necessity, many of the streets were still on piles out over the water, they were built from durable wooden slats, with plenty of room for pedestrians to move along. Ponies and wheeled vehicles, including rickshaws, were prohibited from using these timber thoroughfares, but this did not create a problem as the boats moving in and out of the port could be loaded and unloaded virtually on the traders' doorsteps.

In December 1888, with their numbers increased, the police force in the West Coast Residency was sufficiently well trained to initiate hostilities in a military capacity in the Padas region, where a Brunei chief and his subjects were not taking kindly to being 'colonised'. Armed only with knives and swords, but with the protection of a stout fort, the defenders managed to repel the aggressors, who were armed with guns and cannon, and keep them at bay for the best part of five months. They won the battle, but not the war. The British declared them pirates (outlaws) and killed them one by one. The Company eventually took over the entire area and in 1895 renamed it Beaufort, after the then Governor. In 1888, to forestall possible complications which might arise from the unwanted attention of acquisitive or avaricious foreign powers, a British Protectorate was declared over Sarawak, Brunei and British North Borneo. The British Crown now assumed responsibility for Sabah's external affairs, while the Company retained its control of internal administration.

The effectiveness of their internal control was soon put to the test in a police action, this time on the east coast, which was now under the administration of a new Resident, Pryer having retired in 1886. A Murut chief, who had sold his beautiful daughter in marriage to Walter Flint, an English merchant who ran a trade store, reclaimed her and disappeared into the jungle, along with his wife and two grandchildren. The husband followed and, according to the local people, caught up with his family but unfortunately died from a virulent disease shortly afterwards. On learning of his brother's death, Raffles Flint (named for his uncle, Sir Stamford Raffles, founder of Singapore) obtained permission from the Governor in Sandakan to undertake an expedition of enquiry to the tribal village on the upper reaches of the Kalabakan River, which emptied into the sea near Tawau. Accompanying him were the Resident; a Dyak trader, whose wife was Murut, to act as a go-between; and thirteen men from Sarawak's headhunting Iban tribe, who had been recruited as constables to strengthen the police force.

According to every native they met, Walter Flint had died in the manner previously reported. The search party made its way slowly up the Kinabatangan, the Kuamut and then the Nasan, where they struck out across jungle-covered mountains to pick up the Kalabakan. It was not until they reached the village and discovered a freshly made grave holding the remains of Flint's headless, dismembered body, that any of the inhabitants was able to recall the violent scene which had resulted in the white man's death. Learning that the headman, along with his entire extended family, had fled the scene, the party sent off in pursuit.

It did not take long for the police scouts to locate the fugitives in a longhouse on a nearby tributary. Dawn was just beginning to

William Pryer with local inhabitants

break. The party, which was not spotted until within 100 metres of the longhouse, stormed the building, guns blazing. Anyone who managed to flee was cut down. In the twenty-minute battle that followed, 140 Muruts were killed. With the exception of Walter's wife and children, and two other women and a child – all of whom, though wounded, managed to crawl into the jungle – the entire family was wiped out. After the police took the heads, which they slung over their shoulders, the expedition returned to Sandakan. No European venturing into the region was ever troubled again.

Chapter 2

Achieving prosperity

While the massacre at the longhouse had a sobering effect on would-be lawbreakers on the east coast, it did nothing to quell the fires of rebellion that were now smouldering elsewhere. Problems arose in 1894 when younger relatives of the Sultans of Sulu and Brunei protested against the loss of their birthright. The most prominent of these dissenters was Datu Muhammad Salleh, generally known as Mat Salleh, who had married a Sulu princess. As the son of a Sulu father, who was leader of the Inanam people, and his Bajau wife, Salleh had spent part of his childhood in west coast villages at Inanam and on Gaya Island.

European investors were by this time buying land from the Company with the aim of transforming Sabah into a crop-producing region. More than 260,000 hectares had been leased for tobacco production and a profitable timber trade with China and Australia was also developing. With the introduction of cash crops and the move to abolish slavery, practised widely by some tribes, social and economic changes were inevitable. These were exacerbated during a worldwide depression in the 1890s, and overspending by Company administrators, who had not been nearly as stringent as the original appointees. William Cowie, who had re-entered the scene and was now General Manager, decided that a good way to raise revenue for the shareholders was to impose taxes on various items including locally brewed tapai (rice wine), cassava wine and beer, firearms and boats.

Although this initiative was backed by some of the shareholders, it was not welcomed by the local people or, indeed, by the Company's founder Sir Alfred Dent who, with several others, resigned in protest. It did them no good. Cowie made matters even worse by appointing Leicester Beaufort as Governor, a lawyer with no experience of the Far East, no administrative skills and who was later described as 'the most incompetent governor North Borneo ever acquired'. Believing he could expand Sabah's weakening economy, Cowie instituted two ambitious projects – a railway line from Brunei Bay in the west to Cowie Harbour in the extreme south-east, and a telegraph line from Sandakan to Labuan. To help pay for it all, new taxes were imposed, including on rice, the staple diet of the local people.

In 1895 a dispute arose between Mat Salleh and the Company, which was annoyed that he was collecting the long-established poll tax without approval. On the other hand, Salleh, who conducted a trading business along the Sugut River to the north of Sandakan, was most unhappy with the new taxes. With the 'independent' rivers still outside Company control, and wanting to stay that way, conditions were ripe for unrest, especially among the Inanam Bajaus when it was learned that Governor Beaufort had gone to Brunei to buy the rights to their territory.

Consequently, they were keen to join Salleh when he masterminded an attack in 1898 on the west coast settlement at Pulau Gaya, resulting in its complete and utter destruction. After sacking the village, Salleh and his followers put every building to the torch. The spectacular blaze could be seen quite plainly on the mainland where people rushed from their homes shouting 'api api' (fire fire). It is said that in 1899, when a new settlement was established on the coast opposite Pulau Gaya, the locals called it 'api-api' rather than Jesselton, named in honour of Company Director Sir Charles Jessel and a name which non-Europeans found difficult to pronounce.

Salleh's tactics were simple: carry out a raid and then retreat to one of his forts, only to reappear in some other part of the country. By promising to liberate the Kadazans and Dusuns from the British, Salleh, despite his different ethnic origins, was able to recruit them in large numbers to join his cause. With the police force still standing at only 200, and an appeal to Singapore for assistance refused, as the Governor there did not like either Cowie or the Chartered Company's rule, the European community took up arms and formed militia groups, including one led by Raffles Flint.

Following skirmishes near his hideout at Inanam and at Menggatal, Salleh and his followers moved inland to Ranau, where he ordered a massive fortress to be built, some 20 metres square and surrounded by sharp bamboo spikes. The British forces tried to capture it but met with heavy resistance. Believing that punitive action against the rebels was not the answer, Cowie travelled from England. In a face-to-face meeting with the rebel leader on 22 April 1898, Cowie offered to allow Salleh and his people, all of whom he promised would be pardoned, to live at Tambunan, which was south of Ranau and not yet occupied by a District Officer. Salleh agreed, and his fort at Ranau was burned to the ground. With the rebellion deemed to be at an end, Cowie negotiated the transfer to the Company of all the independent rivers and all land and bays north of the Padas River, previously under the Sultan's jurisdiction. The British North Borneo Chartered

Company now owned the rights to every square centimetre of land in Sabah in return for an annual rent of just $23,131 or 2,313 pounds sterling.

Despite its profitable outcome, the peaceful truce brokered by Cowie did not meet with the universal approval of the British. Many, including the Company Directors in London, considered the terms offered to Salleh were outrageous, so much so that the West Coast Resident, the Police Commandant and several District Officers resigned in protest. Salleh's followers were satisfied with the deal until the terms of the written agreement, presented to their leader for his signature, revealed that anyone who was an escaped prisoner was not eligible for a pardon, leaving the Bajaus, who had just lost control of their river communities, feeling that they had been double crossed.

However, having given Salleh autonomy over Tambunan, which he ruled from a new fort built at Kampong Toboh, the Company reneged on the deal the following year by telling him he must work side by side with the Keningau District Officer, Mr Fraser. Salleh refused and fighting recommenced. On 31 January 1900 the rebel leader, or freedom fighter, depending on one's point of view, was shot through the head at Kampong Toboh by a policeman, allegedly firing a machine gun from more than a kilometre away. Although with Salleh's death the rebellion was over, some of the less tractable Muruts continued the fight against taxation until 1915, when they were subdued after skirmishes in the Rundum valley.

Despite their dogged persistence, it was a battle that the local dissidents could not possibly have won. By the time the Empire welcomed a new century, and mourned the death of its long-reigning Queen, the British were well entrenched. Furthermore, there was now instantaneous communication from one side of the country to the other, via a telegraph line running from Sandakan to Labuan. Finished in 1897 at a cost of over $170,000 and linked by several relay stations, the 700-kilometre-long line followed a series of valleys. After running west from Sandakan for about fifty kilometres, it turned due south to the Kinabatangan to more or less follow the river's headwaters to Pinangah. Continuing west, the route then skirted the northern end of the Witti Range before diverting in a more south-westerly direction to Tenom, where it cut through the Crocker Range to follow the Padas and then the Klias rivers to Mempakul, near Menumbok, on the northern tip of Brunei Bay. The final link, to Labuan, was via underwater cable. Unfortunately, as the line passed through difficult, jungle-clad terrain, communications during the early years were often interrupted, resulting in elaborate celebrations for the 1902 coronation of King Edward VII, postponed due to the King's illness, being held on the original date.

Administratively, British North Borneo was now split into ten provinces (districts), all with British names and with a principal settlement in each – apart from the very remote Cunliffe province on the Dutch Borneo border. Sandakan was in Myburgh province while Jesselton was in Keppel. Doubtless in deference to her Majesty, Queen Victoria, whose Diamond Jubilee in 1897 was celebrated in Sabah with great festivity by her loyal subjects, Balmoral, the name of her much-loved Scottish castle, was assigned to a settlement on the Labuk River, at a place which today appears to be identical with that of Beluran.

The Company flag now flew at settlements along the coast at Mempakul, Putatan Gantian (Gaya Bay), Ambong, Kudat, Sandakan, Sugut, Lahad Datu, Tawau and, in the interior, at Penungah, Tambunan, Keningau, Tenom, Bukau and Beaufort. The Company had also taken over the administration of Labuan Island, which had an annual coal output of 50,000 tonnes, making it an important refuelling stop for vessels as well as a trading centre. Coal had also been found in Sabah at the Bengoka and Sugut Rivers, Cowie Bay and Sandakan. Owing to the influx of immigrants, Sabah's population stood at around 200,000, of whom 20,000 were Chinese. Besides tobacco and timber, trade had been developed across a large range of commodities, including atap, beeswax, birds' nests (worth in excess of $25,000 a year), blachan (a type of strong-tasting shrimp paste), camphor, coconuts, copra, coffee, cotton, fish, gold, gutta-percha, ordinary or India rubber, ivory, iron ore, opium, pearls, pepper, rice, rattan, sago and sago flour, sea slugs, sharks' fins, shells, sugar, and tortoise shell.

To facilitate the transfer of many of these commodities, a railway line from Weston on Brunei Bay to the Padas River, begun in 1896, had already been completed, with an extension to Jesselton and another from Beaufort to Tenom due for completion in 1905. Much of the route had been surveyed by a New Zealander, Ernest Alfred Pavitt. Born in the South-Island town of Akaroa in 1856, Pavitt, the son of a magistrate, was said to have been lured to Sabah by a spirit of adventure. However, in order to accept a posting with the Company, evidently some time in the mid-to-late 1880s, he had left his young wife Rose, aged 23, behind. In 1888, while he was away, she died of typhoid fever. He remained in Borneo and by 1897 held the post of Supervisor of the Public Works Department, by which time his much younger brother Frank had joined the Company as Government

Surveyor, Labuan. In 1896, at the age of forty, Ernest fell in love with Kwai, a beautiful Kadazandusun girl. Her father, the headman of Limbahau village, near Papar, made it quite clear that if Pavitt wanted her, he would have to make her his wife. They were married according to village custom, but in 1898 he abandoned Kwai, their small son and baby daughter, and went to Australia, where, in June that year, he married a woman from Pontville, Tasmania. Three years later he was back in Borneo, where he became involved with the construction of the Beaufort–Jesselton railway. Evidently unencumbered by any family considerations, either in New Zealand, Tasmania or Sabah, Ernest dabbled in coal mining in Sandakan and Labuan, gold mining at the Australian-owned mine at Raub in Pahang state, Malaya, and explored much of that state as well as Kelantan. The Beaufort–Jesselton rail line was completed satisfactorily, but Cowie's overly ambitious plan to push a rail line through the mountainous jungle to Cowie Bay, in the far south-east, did not ever come to fruition. However, this did not impede development as the eastern rivers provided good transportation, with numerous estates near Sandakan established to the north and south of the town and on the Sugut and Labuk rivers.

Sandakan itself was a thriving metropolis, with a population of 7,000 — only a small number of whom were Europeans. The remainder, apart from the Sulus and Bajaus who continued with their traditional way of life, were mainly Chinese. The rest were a mixture of Arabs, Indians, Sikhs and Somalis. The settlement now stretched for three kilometres along the harbour foreshore. Although much of the development was still out over the water, the shoreline being very narrow, a large reclamation project was underway which would greatly increase the amount of flat land. There had been no lifting of the strict building code, so houses and shops were still of a high standard.

Jutting out over the sea was the fish market, flanked by a variety of shops of all shapes, sizes and colours, which sold fruit, vegetables, cakes, salted fish and many other commodities. The Government Wharf, constructed from almost indestructible belian timber, extended for the best part of 200 metres, with a fine Customs House about half way along and a coal godown (storage facility) at one end. With ponies and wheeled vehicles restricted to the land, goods were transported to and fro along the timber-slatted streets by coolies, carrying large loads strung onto long bamboo poles which they balanced, seemingly with ease, on their shoulders.

At the eastern end of the settlement, where the Company flag fluttered proudly, was Fort Pryer – its guns, which had yet to fire a shot in anger, used only for saluting purposes. Also occupying this small hill were two-storey barracks for the 300-strong police force and a large, sturdily constructed gaol of three storeys, with the Commandant's house immediately behind on the lower slopes of the escarpment. Justice was dispensed by the Police Magistrate who presided over a Sessions Court, convened when and if required. The Governor, who was also responsible for confirming death sentences and issuing the warrants, heard appeals. Execution, as was the case in Britain, was by hanging.

In the centre of town were two hotels, including that built by Sun Kwong Lung and now renamed Sandakan Hotel. Nearby were substantial, colonial-style government offices, in front of which was a sizeable white marble cross, erected in memory of the explorers Witti and Hatton, Inspector Fontaine, and Sikh police who had died in the Company's service. Towering over both the cross and the offices was a handsome clock tower, unveiled in 1897 in honour of the Queen's Diamond Jubilee. Although the tower was a distinctive landmark, the clock itself was possibly even more distinctive in that the hands on each of the four faces often showed a different time. The erratic time-keeping of the clock aside, normal office hours were from 10 am until 4 pm, after which members of the white community often met for drinks at the nearby Sandakan Club. This substantial wooden building, tucked against the side of the hill on a parcel of land between Daly Street and North Road, overlooked the town square and harbour and was the centre of European social life. Founded in 1884, the club was a whirl of constant activity, providing not only food and beverages, but also a venue for dances, cabarets, fancy dress parties and performances by the dramatic society, as well as billiards, croquet and tennis. As was the case with Europeans throughout the Far East, money rarely changed hands at the club, or anywhere else, 'chits' being used instead of cash. The Company issued its own currency, with one Borneo dollar being on par with one Singapore Straits dollar (pegged at two shillings and four pence sterling) but the chit system extended even to visitors, who would sign for all kinds of goods and services and then settle up on the wharf with their creditors, just prior to departure.

The evenings, if not spent at home or at the club, were a time for socialising with friends or perhaps attending one of the vice-regal functions at Government House, where black tie was mandatory. With servants to cook, clean, shop, garden, look after small children,

Memorial to Witti, Hatton and others who died in the service of the Company, outside the Administrative buildings

Sandakan Hotel

run messages and wash and iron, there was plenty of time for women to engage in leisurely pursuits such as needlework, shopping and letter writing. Although the telegraph line to the west coast had been completed, the delivery of mail and overseas newspapers was dependent on steamships, which plied between Sandakan, Hong Kong and Singapore.

One of the highlights on the annual calendar was Chinese New Year, which was celebrated by everyone. After being ushered in with a salute fired by the guns at the fort, the traditional festivities began. The Europeans' contribution was the 'Flower Show'. Instituted by Pryer in 1880, it had evolved into an exhibition showcasing all manner of things, from needlework and embroidery, to geese, fowls and monkeys, coal, coffee, sugar cane, fruit and vegetables. To further liven up proceedings, there were kite-flying contests, boat races in which the Bajau men and women participated, and aquatic sports.

Charter Day on 1 November was marked by a public holiday, but by far the most spectacular annual event was the Dragon Boat Festival, held around June. To drive out evil spirits and ensure continuing prosperity for the town, magnificent dragons, covered in green and gold scales and measuring up to thirty metres in length, made their way through Sandakan's streets, to the accompaniment of noisy fire crackers and gongs. Once the various Chinese celebrations were over, it was back to more mundane forms of entertainment provided by sporting and recreational clubs.

Of these, horse racing was by far the most popular, with meetings held on a racecourse at William Pryer's Beatrice Estate. By this time, the tobacco plantations were returning good profits, allowing the 'Tobacco Kings' and wealthy Chinese merchants to place extravagant wagers on their fancied ponies. Race days were not to be missed, so much so that the District Magistrate made sure that his cases were either dealt with, or adjourned, by 11 am. Horse racing was also a great social event, allowing ladies to turn out in their best finery, every detail of which was faithfully reported in the press.

The spacious, elevated bungalows in which the privileged European community lived were dotted about on the small hillocks around the town, or on the slopes of Bukit Merah, to take advantage of the sea breezes. Government House sat in splendid isolation on its own small hill, described by the recently widowed Mrs Pryer as 'a slight eminence'. Irrespective of size, these well-appointed homes were surrounded by lush gardens, with carefully tended lawns, graceful palms and a riot of multi-coloured tropical plants.

Dominating the scene, however, was the Church of England's St Michael and All Angels' Church. Built from dark grey stone quarried at Buli Sim Sim by convicts sentenced to hard labour, it was well on its way to completion. Like William Pryer, St Michael's Reverend William Henry Elton was a man of vision. By 1893 the church/school building, which had replaced the spare room at Pryer's house, needed to be upgraded and, with Sandakan evolving as the showplace of South-East Asia, Elton concluded that his new church should be worthy of a town that would one day be a cathedral city.

Having already obtained possession of the highest hill in town, situated just to the west of the government buildings and later named Elton Hill for him, Reverend Elton had removed the entire summit in order to create sufficient flat land. After marking out the dimensions of his new church, he engaged the services of Mr Benjamin Mountfort, a prominent and talented architect living in New Zealand, and a devout member of the Church of England. Although almost 70 years of age and retired, Mountfort accepted the commission. The pair had met in Christchurch, on New Zealand's South Island, where Elton's previous post had been Precentor at the Cathedral. Apart from insisting that the Sandakan church must have shades over the windows and incorporate 'verandahs' to cut down the heat, the Reverend gave Mountfort a free hand.

The Gothic Revival design, for which Mountfort was famous, with its steeply pitched roofs, towering walls and shady side arcades, was based on Christchurch Cathedral but on a smaller scale. It exceeded William Elton's wildest dreams. Initially, the building was to have been constructed from belian timber, a plan that was scrapped when the building contractor advised that there were not enough skilled workers to undertake such a large project. When brick was also rejected as the only available bricks from Hong Kong and Singapore were of inferior quality, Elton announced that he would use stone, forcing Mountfort to draw a third set of plans. However, the church committee now backed away, informing the priest that he must take sole responsibility if he wished to build in stone. Undaunted, and taking out personal loans to help cover the costs, the clergyman went ahead. It was a slow process. He was away a great deal attending to the pastoral needs of his far-flung flock, so building work could only be carried out when he was there to supervise it. However, he persevered and both he and the town were rewarded by the sight of a beautiful stone church, rising majestically from the top of the hill.

Besides organising and overseeing the construction of both the church and a large rectory alongside, Elton had established a book

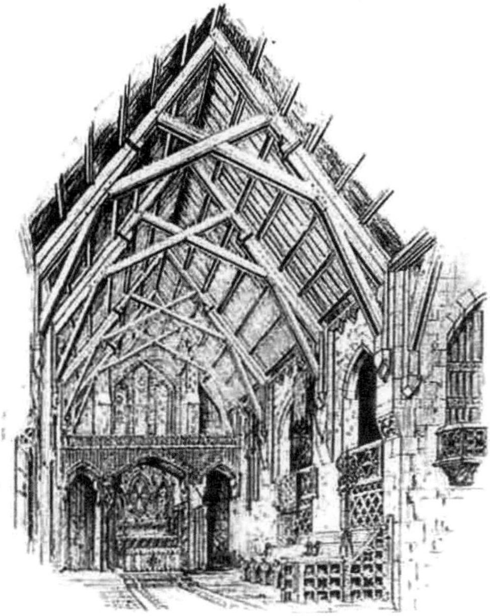

Architectural drawing of chancel and sanctuary of St Michael's Church

Exterior of St Michael's, circa 1930s

club/lending library, which operated from a building behind the rectory. He was also responsible for St Michael's School, which had opened with one pupil in 1888 and now catered for both boys and girls. His Roman Catholic counterpart Father John Byron, who presided over the nearby and far more modest wooden St Mary's Church, also attended to the educational needs of Sandakan's youth at a mission school founded in 1887. As well as teaching, the Catholic nuns assisting him cared for unwanted and abandoned babies.

The non-Christian population was also well served. Tucked against the hillside and facing Dhobis' Green, a patch of swampy grassland where the dhobis (laundrymen) hung their washing and where cattle previously roamed, was the Sum Sing Kung (Three Saints) Chinese temple. Its construction in 1887, which made it the oldest place of worship in Sandakan, had been organised by the Cantonese, Hakka, Teochew and Hainanese Chinese communities and funded by public subscription, $100 of which had been donated by Governor Treacher. There was also a mosque near the government offices and a Sikh temple conveniently located near the police barracks. In keeping with conditions laid down by the Charter to respect the customs of local people, the Company also employed a Muslim cleric to dispense law according to his faith and to preside over the Islamic divorce court.

Despite these progressive measures, slavery had not yet been completely abolished, although children born to slaves since 1883 were free. The form of slavery still practised in Sandakan, however, was more like a benign indenture, with no stigma attached – far from it. Indeed, when Pryer had tried to hire a paid labour force, the men he approached were most upset, much preferring that he 'bought' them. With the world recession now over, there was no shortage of paid jobs for those willing to work. The Public Works Department (PWD), a major employer, was responsible for roads, bridges, drainage, the government wharf, the police barracks, and all government offices, buildings and living quarters, including Government House, the Residency and the homes of civil servants. The PWD was also responsible for ensuring that the kerosene lights, which lit the streets at night, were kept in good order and the wicks well trimmed.

Other major employers were two sawmills to the west of the town and the hospital, which sprawled across the side of a hill. A series of light, airy buildings, Sandakan's hospital consisted of a ward for Europeans and another mainly for Chinese, as most of the local people preferred to place their faith in their own traditional medicines. There was also a dispensary for outpatients and accommodation for the government medical staff.

Over the next four decades, Sandakan went from strength to strength, building on the foundation stones so carefully laid by William Pryer. St Michael's Church, completed in 1908, still dominated the town. Besides separate schools for boys and girls, with boarding facilities, there was now a very active Boy Scout Troop, the first in Borneo, founded by Canon Alexander who had succeeded William Elton in 1912. Following the general emancipation of women following World War 1, a Girl Guide Company had also been formed. However, although there were also similar groups established at St Mary's, there were few, if any, European children among the ranks. As was the custom, white children were sent 'home' to boarding school at about seven or eight years of age. The C of E, Catholic and Chinese schools, which offered education to secondary level, had healthy enrolments among the Chinese and Eurasians. Pupils attending the government-run Malay-speaking primary schools were required to undertake a bridging course in English before they could progress further. However, there were few applicants as many indigenous children did not attend school at all, and only a very small percentage went beyond three years of schooling.

Clubs of all kinds now abounded – golf, croquet, squash, bridge and rugby, polo, soccer and, of course, that sport so beloved by the English – cricket. Tennis was immensely popular and by 1935 there were four lawn courts on the town square, bordered on three sides by the Sandakan Club, Albany Mansions (old offices converted into flats), the Sandakan Hotel, the Law Court, Administrative Offices and Secretariat. Private tennis courts were also dotted about the estates. To cater for the more theatrically inclined there were also dramatic and musical societies, as well as Malay operas and the very popular Chinese street opera, known as 'wayang'. The Sandakan Club remained the hub of European social life, with functions arranged to celebrate anything and everything, including St Andrew's Day, when gentlemen claiming Scottish heritage turned out in kilts. Those who did not, and the ladies, wore formal evening dress.

Citizens flush with funds had replaced sedan chairs with sedan cars, and slow-moving horse- or buffalo-drawn vehicles with trucks. The first car had appeared in 1912. Within ten years there were many more and Sandakan reported its first motor accident. After some resistance, a petrol station was opened on Jalan Tiga (Third Street). Buses also arrived on the scene and the PWD became the proud possessor of earth-moving machines and a steamroller, imported from England. As motor vehicles had became more common, the ponies all but vanished, along with the Sandakan Turf Club.

The timber industry, which had started up by accident, was the biggest money earner. It was pioneered by Baron de Lissa who had bought and cleared 100,000 acres (40,000 hectares) of land in the early 1880s with the intention of planting sugar cane, when the world's sugar price collapsed. Faced with bankruptcy, he salvaged the situation by exporting the lumber from his felled trees to Australia in 1885, and then to China and Hong Kong. The timber industry was dominated by four firms until 1920, when the Chartered Company and Sabah's leading trading firm, Harrison and Crosfield, formed the British Borneo Timber Company, which was given total monopoly over all timber cut and exported. Wherever valuable hardwoods were accessible, the BBT, as it became known, built a network of light rail lines to transport the huge logs to the nearest river, where they were floated to logging pens at the sawmills along the harbour. Also associated with the timber industry was 'cutch' – the extraction of tannin from mangrove-tree bark for use in the tanning industry. The largest company in Sandakan was the Bakau and Kenya Extract Company, whose processing factory was on the foreshore near the timber mills.

The 1920s also saw an increase in the amount of rubber under cultivation – an industry that, at a time of growing world economic hardship, would prevent Sabah from sliding into total depression. One of those involved in the burgeoning industry was Englishman Herbert James Walker, known as Bert. The son of a quartermaster-sergeant serving with the British Army, Bert was working as an accountant in London when he concluded that there must be more to life than the four walls of his office. In 1912, attracted by advertisements appearing in the London *Daily Telegraph* he successfully applied for a job with the Beaufort Rubber Company. A couple of years later, and now fluent in Malay, he decided to move on. After a brief stint with a boring desk job in Jesselton he accepted an offer from the North Borneo Trading Company as an Assistant Head Tapper on their rubber estates. Having claimed he could ride a horse, which was integral to the job, he spent many painful hours in the saddle, suffering in silence until he was appointed manager of the Tenghilan Estate, between Tuaran and Kota Belud. While working there he mastered the local dialect, a feat that so impressed the headman of Kampong Suhaman, who had never before heard an 'orang puteh' (white man) speak his language, that he made Walker a blood brother. After toying with the idea of forming a partnership to buy his own estate, Walker accepted a job as an estate manager with Harrison and Crosfield, which owned substantial rubber plantations near Sandakan.

Mangrove bark awaiting collection

Sandakan, looking west, 1911

Rubber in this area had been confined originally to the Labuk River but, as more land came under cultivation, an all-weather vehicular access, known as Labuk Road, had been constructed to the north-west, with a branch road leading to the Batang and Manila rivers. As was the case in most British colonies, Labuk Road was marked every mile with a concrete 'stone' or 'batu', a Malay word which was also used for 'mile': a British concept totally alien to local people. Harrison and Crosfield, having combined their estates at Mile 5 and on the Batang River, now wanted to expand. After selecting and clearing a suitable site, Walker established a 400-hectare estate at Mile 11, at the same time managing Batu Lima (Mile 5), where he enjoyed a typical bachelor's existence: hard work, hard play, and occasionally hard drinking with his other unmarried friends – the preferred planters' tipple being either beer or gin-and-tonic.

By the time Walker arrived, Sandakan had developed into a very cosmopolitan town. Observer and writer Owen Rutter recorded that:

> *'For its size perhaps no city in the world has such a medley of inhabitants as Sandakan. Its streets are always busy and alive with all sorts of conditions of men: Chinese, from wealthy merchants in European clothes to coolies with no clothes at all save a battered hat and a waist-cloth of brilliant red; Malays in coloured sarong and round velvet caps; stalwart Sikh policemen in khaki uniforms and Pathans with legs as thin as sugar canes; olive-skinned Dyaks, Arab traders with distinguished noses and shifty eyes, and Philipinos, with beautifully laundered suits – their womenfolk are the best washer women in the world; Japanese ladies in bright kimonos, their shrill voices and the clatter of geta making the most noise of all; Dusuns from the jungle; Javanese from the estates; Indians; and – most picturesque – Sulus with coloured head-cloths, long tight breeches and closely fitting embroidered coats, purple, orange and deep blue, often be-sprinkled with sequins and fastened with thirty-four buttons of silver gilt.'*

The Resident by this time had been provided with a substantial new home, while the Governor and his Lady now occupied a magnificent mansion on the high ground behind the town, approached by a sweeping drive and surrounded by vast green lawns and beautiful gardens. Any visitors to Sandakan who signed the book at the entrance to Government House could be assured of an invitation to a vice-regal dinner, which they were expected to accept, provided they owned or could obtain the obligatory formal wear. These occasions were not infrequent, especially if the Company President was in town on his annual inspection, triggering a round of cocktail parties,

The Sandakan Club

Sandakan and the harbour, 1935

Chinese women bringing produce to the town market

Pongholo 'Pedro' Dominic

dinners and receptions. Visits by Royal Navy ships also provided a good opportunity for the Europeans to offer their hospitality. The formal events were conducted with much pomp and ceremony, with the ship's band playing on the padang, followed by sporting contests organised between the sailors and local teams.

The growth of the civil service, which now employed non-Europeans in positions of responsibility, was reflected in the size of the new administrative buildings and an improved standard of living for a number of local people. Pongholo Stanislaus Dominic, known as Pedro, had come to Sandakan from the Philippine island of Palawan with his family as a young child in the 1880s. Adopted by William Pryer, he had risen steadily through the ranks of the civil service to become Assistant Deputy Commissioner for Customs, a most prestigious and well-paid post. He and his wife with their eight girls and four boys lived very comfortably in a substantial two-storey timber home, situated in Happy Valley, near the civil hospital. With four bedrooms, two bathrooms and interior furnishings which included Persian carpets, cabinets full of curios, two pianos, two harps, a radio (always tuned to the BBC), and two brass cannons positioned decoratively in the lush, spacious garden, the Dominic family's 'Rose Cottage' rivalled many of the European-owned houses. The family also owned rubber estates and orchards along the Labuk Road. As well as being well educated and musically gifted, Pedro was a voracious reader, a good footballer and a fine cricket player. Described as a natty dresser, he always wore a jacket, crisp white pants, starched shirt, bow tie and hat, and was never seen without a pipe or walking stick, of which he had quite an array. In many ways, probably due to the influence of William Pryer, Pedro Dominic was more British than the British. A leading light in the social and recreational scene, he was well known for his outgoing personality, his collection of rare orchids (for which he won prizes at the Flower Show) and his English-style hospitality and cuisine, which featured traditional breakfasts and dainty afternoon teas served on fine English china, roast dinners, crusty pies, hams, and, at Christmas, a rich plum pudding.

The hard-working Chinese, in particular, had also prospered and many owned thriving businesses and estates. The most prominent company was that established by former immigrant Kwan Woon Kwong, who had borrowed $500 from his sister to set up business in 1882 in a prefabricated, iron-roofed store. A Chinese Chamber of Commerce had also been formed, replacing the Kapitan Cina who had acted as liaison officer between the Company and the Chinese community. Gradually, as land was reclaimed, the wooden streets in the town centre had given way to paved thoroughfares lined with two-storey shop houses, and comfortable bungalows had sprung up to the west of the business area.

In 1902, with the creation of a town padang on reclaimed land, the Sandakan Recreation Club had opened at the northern end with thirty-one Chinese, Dutch, English, Japanese, Filipino and Indian members. With the profits from their lucrative trading enterprises, Harrison and Crosfield had erected a most impressive two-storey edifice, complete with hexagonal tower and pillared colonnades, on a prime site between the padang and the wharf. A cinema and theatre were also built, along with a wireless station, electric light and power station, waterworks, ice works, a nipapalm alcohol distillery and a State Museum. The former manual telephone exchange, opened in 1896, had been replaced in 1923 by an automatic exchange, the first in the Far East. The telegraph network now linked Sandakan to Lahad Datu, Tawau, Jesselton and Kudat, as well as Labuan.

Although, during the 1930s, the town's population stood at 15,000, the white male population hovered around forty, and the female, roughly twenty. The imbalance between the sexes was due to the Company's policy of not allowing male employees to marry until they had served for a minimum of eight years. In the absence of suitable European-born partners, many of the bachelors formed liaisons with local women. In 1940, there was only one unmarried white woman on the entire east coast – Matron M North, an Englishwoman in charge of nursing at the hospital.

Consequently, European weddings in Sandakan were rare so, when the seemingly confirmed bachelor Bert Walker became engaged at the age of forty-six, after a six-week courtship, and announced that the marriage service would be at St Michael's, there was great excitement. Bert was popular with everyone, so his friends were overjoyed to learn that the couple would remain in Sandakan, where

The Burling-Walker wedding party, 1929

a brand new house was being built for them at Mile 11. Alice Burling, Bert's Australian bride-to-be, had met him in Sandakan in mid-1928 while staying with an old school friend and it had been love at first sight. On learning on her return that she was not only to be married in Sandakan, but also actually live there, her friends in Sydney decided that she must be either 'mad' or 'very brave'.

The wedding date was set for 2 April 1929. All was on track when the bride's ship, SS *Arafura*, was delayed, forcing a postponement of fifteen days. The service was rescheduled for 3 pm on Friday the 17th, but any inconvenience to guests because of either the day or the hour was of absolutely no consequence. With the Right Reverend Logie Danson, the Bishop of Labuan and Sarawak, assisting the officiating priest, the Reverend S M Collier, and just about every European and Chinese person of note in Sandakan in attendance, including the Governor, two 'honourables', a judge and a knight of the realm, the wedding was the social event of the year, if not the decade. The *British North Borneo Herald* certainly thought so, reporting everything in minute detail over two editions of the paper. Nothing was missed: the flowers in the church; the hymns that were sung; the music the organist played; what the bride and her attendant wore; the flowers they carried; who was present; the gifts received and who gave them; and the toasts proposed at the lavish wedding breakfast held at Pelawan House, the home of The Honourable F W Pinnock, who had given the bride away. After the reception, the

Bert Walker's house at Mile 11

happy couple departed on their honeymoon, showered in confetti. They were not going far – only to Mile 11 – but this did not stop the bride from changing into a stylish 'going away' outfit, the details of which were also faithfully reported in the press.

The major event of the following decade was the Silver Jubilee of the reigning monarch, King George V, held in 1935. To celebrate the occasion, Sandakan streets were decked out in patriotic red, white and blue bunting and an elaborate street pageant organised, as well as a service of thanksgiving at St Michael's Church, attended by the Scouts, Girl Guides, as many local citizens as could be accommodated and, of course, His Excellency the Governor and other dignitaries. In keeping with any special occasion, the gentlemen with the means to do so wore white cotton-drill suits, hats and ties, with the occasional pair of spats putting in an appearance, while the ladies were decked out in their best finery, including silk stockings, gloves, ropes of pearls and elaborate headwear. The Governor, as was expected, was in full ceremonial attire, which included an immaculate white uniform, sword, various medals and a white pith-helmet, complete with ostrich feathers. He and his entourage, as always, sat in specially designated pews, which had clamps attached to the sides to hold the Union Jack and the Company standard. To further commemorate the Jubilee, the town padang, festooned with 'illuminations' or coloured lights, became the focus of a fireworks display by night and a vice-regal military review by day, featuring a parade by the Constabulary and a detachment of Royal Marines from one of the visiting British warships. The chiefs and headmen of various ethnic groups, dressed in their colourful traditional costumes, added a touch of the exotic to the festivities, to which they were all invited. The Flower Show, opened by the Governor, was bigger and better than ever, with a Beautiful Baby Contest among the attractions.

Another exciting event in the October of 1935 was the arrival of an American couple, Osa and Martin Johnson, film makers and adventurers, who had visited Sandakan in 1920 to film the wildlife and local tribes. For their return trip, they arrived by flying boat from Kuching, making history by being the first people to fly across the interior of Sabah. Although a very excited *British North Borneo Herald* journalist had reported their impending visit well in advance, the arrival of their Sikorsky aircraft, *The Spirit of Africa and Borneo*, created a sensation in Sandakan, and an even bigger one when they landed on the Kinabatangan River. After establishing a substantial base for their explorations on a sweeping bend of the river

Street parade, King's Silver Jubilee

The Governor departs, following the King's Silver Jubilee service

Girl Guides outside St Michael's, following the Jubilee service

The BNB Volunteers and visiting military personnel on parade, at the padang

The Governor inspects the parade

Visiting Naval personnel and BNB Volunteers on parade

Local chiefs attending the Jubilee celebrations

The Governor opens the Jubilee Flower Show

at Abai, which they named Johnsonville, they spent many months filming from their plane, or along the river, sometimes travelling in a motorised dug-out canoe or Chinese junk, but more often being towed along in an extremely comfortable houseboat, complete with a large kerosene refrigerator. It had been loaned to them by Mrs Agnes Keith, an American journalist who had married the head of the Department of Agriculture and Forest Conservation, Harry Keith. The tribespeople fascinated the Johnsons, and the Johnsons fascinated the tribespeople. Not only had the glamorous white strangers come out of the sky inside a great metal bird, they also had a magical machine that made ice, and even better, ice-cream – the first that the people of the Kinabatangan had ever tasted.

On their first trip, members of the Constabulary had escorted the Johnsons. Fifteen years later, they came and went as they pleased. Although Indians, especially Sikhs, still formed the backbone of the North Borneo Armed Constabulary, local people had now joined the ranks. A small police post had been set up at Mile 8, not far from the Agriculture Department's Experimental Farm, established in the 1920s. On the outskirts of town, jungle now gave way to a number of coconut plantations and rubber estates, some of which covered many square kilometres. Labuk Road was sealed as far as Mile 15, where it degenerated into a dirt vehicular track. Four miles further on, this narrowed to a dry-weather footpath leading to Beluran. However, apart from a small, well-maintained local network around town, there were no other roads. The only access into the interior was by river, interspersed with native trails.

The year of 1936 saw the death in January of King George V, whose Jubilee had just been celebrated, and the ascension of two new Kings – Edward VIII, who abdicated on 11 December after a reign of just 325 days, and George VI, who was crowned on 12 May the following year. The Coronation, which took place with great pageantry in Westminster Abbey in London, was celebrated with enormous enthusiasm in Sandakan. The guns at the fort and on board the British cruiser HMS *Adventure*, dispatched especially for the event, opened proceedings with a seventeen-gun salute. This was followed by a sumptuous Garden Party at Government House, to which anyone whose name appeared in the Visitors' Book had been invited, along with native chiefs from all over Sabah, some of whom had travelled for three days by boat down rapids to attend. Everyone, from the most snobbish European ladies who had ordered gowns specially from 'home', to the lowliest chief, were dressed in their finest clothes. The garden party concluded that same afternoon,

St Andrew's Night, 1940, at Sandakan Club. (Note thistle light fittings)

Alice Walker (foreground, left) judging the Beautiful Baby Competition

but the celebrations continued unabated, with private parties held in mansions and small servants' quarters, jam-packed with relatives from the interior. The festivities went on well into the night for an entire week, with the skirl of bagpipes from the band of the visiting Seaforth Highlanders mingling with the sound of Chinese drums, Malayan gongs, native chants and proud Company families singing 'Land of Hope and Glory', as glasses were raised again and again to the new King and Queen, for a long and glorious reign.

In 1941, those fortunate enough to live in Sandakan were enjoying a most enviable lifestyle. In just over six decades, Kampong German had blossomed from a tiny, primitive settlement, beset by headhunters and pirates, into a modern crossroads where East met West with ease and people of many races, colours and creeds lived in harmony, all against a background of stunningly natural beauty, so very far removed from war-torn Europe. Life, especially for the close-knit white community, was close to idyllic – that is, until the Imperial Japanese Army arrived.

Chapter 3

Paradise Lost

It was the fifth day of January 1942. Four-year-old Anup Singh was walking along the road that led to Buli Sim Sim when it happened. The three, single-engine fighter-aircraft, with bright red circles painted on their wings and fuselages, came roaring in from nowhere. With machine guns blazing they strafed the waterfront and central market area, including the Post and Telegraph Office, before disappearing out to sea. Petrified, Anup ran to the Sikh Temple, the closest place of refuge that he knew, and hid. Others close to Elton Hill scurried inside the stout stone walls of the church, designated as an air raid shelter just four days previously. One British customs officer, who was large and overweight, heaved himself into a drain and tried to hide, unaware that, since half his body was showing and he was wearing a white suit, he made an enticing target, had he been spotted. He and the others were safe enough for, although the Government Printing Office was subjected to heavy fire, and machine-gun bullets peppered the roof of the King's Theatre, no bombs were dropped and there were no deaths. Casualties were limited to just three, but only two were attributable to the Japanese: a couple of boatmen slightly wounded on a launch approaching the wharf from nearby Berhala Island. The other was a Chinese motorist who, in his panic to get away, crashed his car.

The *Borneo Post* advised readers, in the event of future attacks, to seek shelter in the culverts along Elopura Creek (checking of course to make sure the creek was not in flood), or in the large monsoon drains near the padang and in town. It was suggested that, in the 'unlikely' case of bombing, that citizens should throw themselves flat on the ground, wherever they might happen to be, 'in order to avoid the blast'. News on the war, including an update on Dutch Borneo, Malaya, the Philippines, China, Russia and Libya, filled just one page – the same space denoted to 'Ration Recipes'. Cooking hints included how to substitute honey for sugar (now severely rationed), improve the taste of tinned butter, and substitute sweet potato for rice when necessary. The virtues of coconut, breadfruit and corn were also described at length. The remainder of the paper was filled with social jottings; a lengthy article about the joys of sailing, headed 'Life's Not So Bad'; letters to the editor; the Almanac for January (English Chinese and

Islamic calendar); the usual advertisements; and a belated Yuletide message from the Court of Directors of the Chartered Company in London, received at Government House on 14 January: 'Court sends cordial greetings for Christmas. May New Year bring better times for you all in North Borneo'. The overall reaction to the war situation, as well as the recent air raid, appeared to be one of inconvenience – an opinion shared by Anup's father, Jemadar Ojagar Singh of the North Borneo Armed Constabulary, who believed the lightning raid had been nothing more than a terrifying, and very effective, show of strength, just in case there were any thoughts of resistance.

There weren't. The attack by the enemy planes had come without warning, but it was not unexpected. In fact, the adult population had been anticipating the worst for two or three weeks. Up until then, believing that ships at the mighty naval base in heavily fortified Singapore were ready to defend Britain's Far-Eastern empire, interest in the war by Sabah's Europeans had been confined to raising money to pay for a Spitfire in England's fight against Germany – a fund also generously supported by the very pro-British Pedro Dominic, the Chinese community and, surprisingly, Dr K Yamamoto, who was Japanese. Although China had long been engaged in a struggle against Japan, most people did not seriously consider the possibility that the Japanese might become acquisitive enough to take on the mighty British Empire.

Despite the war, Australians and Americans who went home on leave returned to Borneo, confident that all would be well. Although Sabah's Principal Medical Officer, Dr Jim Taylor, thought it best that his wife Celia remain in the family home in Sydney, where their young daughter Elizabeth was enrolled at boarding school, she decided otherwise and returned to Sandakan in early 1941. On 8 December, before the year was out, the Japanese had invaded Malaya and bombed Singapore and several key places in the Far East and the Pacific, including Hawaii and the US fleet at Pearl Harbor. The Japanese military, having gained a strong foothold in northern Malaya, began rapidly pushing its way south.

There was barely any time to reinforce Singapore, let alone less important outposts such as Sabah, although Sarawak did have some troops. When the possibility arose in late 1940 that Japan might flex its muscles, the British government, concerned about the rich oil fields at Miri in Sarawak, and Seria in Brunei, had stationed at Kuching a battalion of Indian Army soldiers, a heavy gun battery from Hong Kong and some Royal Engineers. Raja Brooke had also raised a force of 1,500 men, mainly Iban and Dyak tribesmen, who formed the Sarawak Rangers.

Although no troops at all had been sent to Sabah, the British had taken the precaution of surveying a large tract of land, already stripped of its heavy timber, for a proposed air base. As the policy at the time was for airfields to be guarded by soldiers, wooden barracks to accommodate them, along with a water and electricity supply, had been completed on land belonging to the Experimental Farm at Mile 8.

Apart from the Constabulary (a well-established military/police force that was trained to fight), Sabah's only potential defenders were members of a part-time militia unit. Formed in 1937 and known as the North Borneo Volunteer Defence Force, it comprised two companies – Company A in Jesselton and B in Sandakan. The Sandakan group had started out with just one platoon but in 1938 this was increased to three: one of English-speaking Europeans, Indians, Malays and Chinese, under the command of Lieutenant H F Hunt; another of Malays, commanded by Lieutenant Bert Walker; and the third of Chinese, under Lieutenant Kong Su En, the Chartered Company's Chief Clerk, now aged thirty-six and an 'old boy' of St Michael's School. The Constabulary's Ojagar Singh and Lieutenant Michael Edge were the drill and weapons' instructors. The Volunteers all had normal day jobs but, being purely part-time, were not sufficiently trained to engage in all-out warfare.

Lieutenant Bert Walker, B Company, BNB Volunteers

At the end of November 1941, following a warning issued by the United States that there would be an attack in the Asia-Pacific area, the Volunteers were ordered to report immediately to the Drill Hall, alongside the Customs House. Their Commanding Officer was Captain Henry Rupert Parnell, an Australian who had served in the

Walker inspecting the Volunteers

Great War. Harry, as he was known to his friends, informed the men that, as they had all been mobilised under the Army Act, they were now on full-time duty and had been placed on the payroll. Each of the rank and file was to receive 35 cents a day, plus meals. They were not permitted to return home, and must sleep at the Drill Hall. Their tasks for the present were to guard vital installations and important buildings and establish a coast-watching station.

Despite the mobilisation of the Volunteers, the suggestion that Borneo might be attacked was not taken seriously by many of the civilians, for, as the British were so fond of saying, 'who would want all this jungle? Only the mosquitoes.' The announcement also came as a great surprise to Lieutenant Walker, who was about to depart for Sydney to visit his wife and daughter Pauline on the next ship, due to sail for Singapore in just a few days.

However, as an added precaution, Charles Robert Smith, the Governor and Commander-in-Chief, dispatched a small party, under Corporal Khoo Siak Chiew, to Tawau, where a steamer from Japan called regularly. It was suspected that this vessel collected far more than rubber and Manila hemp from the estates, controlled by a large Japanese consortium and whose workers, one way or another, were believed to engage in spying. As was the case in every Far Eastern territory under the control of the Dutch and British, the Japanese had for many years been establishing a comprehensive spy network. The agents, who worked in a variety of industries and professions, from fishing to rubber planting to photography to diplomatic postings, reported anything which could be of the slightest interest: the condition of roads, the positions of bridges, the amount of rolling stock on the railway system, the number of Volunteers who mustered every week for training, the size and quality of the Constabulary, the depth of water in various harbours, the suitability of shorelines for landing craft, the length of airfields and the relationship between local people and the colonial powers. As long as a state of hostility did not exist, there was little the British or Dutch could do to counter this mass of intelligence gathering – not even when it was blatantly obvious what was going on. In October 1940, the Japanese consul at Sandakan had made a tour of his consular district, an area that took in all of Sabah, Brunei and Sarawak, for the sole purpose of assessing landing places for invasion forces. To gather other information, Japanese agents only had to read the local newspaper. Somewhat naively, the Governor allowed the *British Borneo Herald* to publish the names of everyone who contributed to the Spitfire Fund, along with the amount.

Ten days after the Volunteers had been mobilised, Japan, using information gathered by its expatriate and loyal subjects, entered the war. In Sandakan, stunned citizens who owned radios heard the chilling announcement that Malaya had been invaded and the US Fleet sunk at Pearl Harbor. When the news broke, Chin Piang Syn and his fellow senior students were partway through their Junior Cambridge Examinations at St Michael's School, as were Pedro Dominic's youngest daughters, Rosalind and Flora, who attended the nearby St Mary's Convent. Some candidates were so shocked that they had to be persuaded to stay and finish. Their efforts were wasted – the exam papers never reached England.

With no air force or navy to protect the oil fields at Miri and Seria, and no possibility of any being sent, Sarawak's reaction was swift. Within hours of receiving news that Malaya had been invaded, staff at the oil fields, as well as at the refinery at Lutong, pre-empted any invasion attempt by blowing up the plant and installations, firing the oil reserves and rendering the airfields inoperable, before evacuating the town. If the Japanese wanted oil they would have to drill for it themselves. Neither Sarawak nor Sabah had yet been attacked, but there was a bit of excitement at Sandakan when Anthony Robert, who was carrying out coast-watching duties with the Volunteers, reported that two large ships were heading towards the harbour. Fortunately for the vessels, which proved to be Chinese junks, the members of the machine-gun section, who had been placed on alert, held their fire. However, the very next day a Japanese fishing boat, obviously unaware that a war had started, sailed blithely into port, resulting in the detention of the crew and the confiscation of the vessel.

At twelve o'clock that night, the ship on which Bert Walker had hoped to sail weighed anchor, right on schedule. Despite urgings that women and children should leave Sandakan and much heart-wrenching over what was the best thing to do, there were very few passengers on board.

The following day, believing that the fishing boat which had been impounded had come from Pulau Si Amil, Walker and twelve armed men set off on *Baynain*, a small steamer of about 650 tonnes, owned by the Bakau and Kenya Extract Company. Also on board was a detachment of the Constabulary to reinforce Lahad Datu, which they reached at 4 pm that day. After disembarking the Constabulary and taking on board four Japanese arrested by the local police, *Baynain* set sail for the island of Si Amil, sixteen kilometres to the south-east of Semporna. Its large fish-factory, run by the Japanese-owned Borneo Fishing Company, had long been suspected of being a cover for subversive activities.

Apart from the crew of a fishing boat that had been out to sea and, on seeing the armed Volunteers, dumped its catch and attempted to flee, Walker's men rounded up the island's 347 workers without incident. Before they left with as much food and medical stores as they could move in the time available, they destroyed thousands of litres of fuel oil, immobilised two motorised fishing vessels undergoing repairs and beached the boat which had tried to escape. They then sailed for Semporna where Walker, aware that *Baynain* was nearing capacity, commandeered a large timber barge from the BBT Company, before towing it to Mostyn, where there was a large Japanese-owned hemp estate employing over 200 workers. After arranging for Japanese carpenters to construct an atap shelter over the barge, to which he now transferred many of the fishermen, Walker loaded 240 prisoners onto *Baynain*, along with four Chinese coolies arrested for looting. As Walker had received instructions that the estate was to be left intact, in the care of the European manager and one Japanese assistant, *Baynain*, with the barge in tow, sailed on the evening of 14 December for Sandakan.

On arrival three days later, the Volunteers handed over their 587 prisoners to Lieutenant Edge, who was expecting to receive around

300. Japanese rubber estate employees, shopkeepers and workers, as well as local citizens who had been spreading anti-British rumours, were already occupying the 2nd class (Asiatic) ward at the hospital so space was at a premium. To take the massive overflow, additional internment camps were established in run-down buildings at the old Quarantine Station on Berhala Island at the harbour's entrance, and at the unoccupied British barracks at Mile 8, where additional atap accommodation was being hastily constructed. Although the accommodation provided was basic, the British made sure that all internees were issued with mattresses, bedding, and good, nourishing food.

While Walker and his Volunteers were away, the citizens of Sandakan had been waiting for the Japanese military to put in an appearance, which they must surely do, as the war situation had become steadily worse. The great British warships *Repulse* and *Prince of Wales* had been sunk by enemy action in the Gulf of Siam with tremendous loss of life; the US base at Guam had been lost; Shanghai occupied; the Gilbert Islands invaded and the American bases on the nearby Philippines under constant attack. And then, on 16 December, had come the worst news possible. The enemy had landed at Miri.

Three days later Kuching was bombed. On receipt of this news, the Volunteers were told that British North Borneo was no longer to be defended and all machine guns and ammunition were to be returned to the store. In addition, one machine-gun post was to be demolished and the other camouflaged as an air raid shelter so as not to attract unwanted attention from enemy aircraft. Once these tasks were completed the Volunteers were to continue with their guard duties and also assist the police, as there had been several cases of looting and one murder. Since a number of Chinese shopkeepers had abandoned their stores or only visited during the day, making them a soft target for thieves, dusk-to-dawn patrols were organised, which effectively put a stop to further outbreaks of lawlessness.

As Bert Walker made his way to Police Headquarters at Victoria Barracks to collect the axes to demolish the wooden machine-gun post, he met a visibly distressed Ojagar Singh, devastated by the thought that they were to give up without a fight. The tall Sikh was a proud man, and fiercely loyal to the British. So was his father, Pal Singh, who had come out to British North Borneo with his brother Chanda from their home village of Mannan, in India. Both men had joined the Constabulary in Jesselton, where Pal had married Sant Kaur, the daughter of another policeman, Sadhu Singh, whose son,

B Company Volunteers. Jemadar Ojagar Singh (inset)

Dial, was also in the police force. Pal's second son, Ojagar, born in Mannan where he spent his childhood, arrived in Borneo at the age of ten. By the time he was eleven he, too, had joined the Constabulary, as a bugler. Now a Jemadar (Senior Warrant Officer), he was the father of eight children, five daughters and three sons, the youngest of whom was Anup, the small boy who had run for his life the day the enemy fighters attacked the town.

Raised in a family with a highly developed sense of duty, Ojagar would have wished for nothing more than to be able to fight for the King and to defend the country and the Empire that he loved. But the war news confirmed that this was not an option. By Christmas Day the enemy had occupied Kuching and captured the nearby airfield. The troops stationed there fought back but, on finding themselves hopelessly outnumbered, were eventually forced to flee into the jungle, retreating into Dutch territory where those who survived the arduous trek were finally captured in April. Although many civilians and troops had been killed and injured in the bombing and subsequent fighting, Japanese casualties stood at just 40 dead, mostly from drowning due to amphibious operations.

Panic buying now broke out in Sandakan. With Borneo importing almost all its rice from Thailand and Burma, and the likelihood of any more ships arriving zero, the price skyrocketed. Who won the war did not concern the local people overly much; the question of food was far more important. When a rumour ran round town that all the shops would close, Lillian Funk, wife of Johnny Funk, a signaller serving with the Volunteers, ordered two bags of rice and stocked up on as much milk, sugar and medicine as she could obtain. She had let her stocks run down as her husband had resigned his position as an engineer with the Public Works Department over a pay dispute and was about to take up another job with the Johor Water Works in Malaya, when war broke out.

With it becoming increasingly likely that it would only be a matter of time before Japanese aircraft attacked Sandakan, streets were now unlit and no light was permitted to spill from buildings. The Europeans discussed the situation amongst themselves, and the Governor issued orders for calm. Unlike the European population, some local people were anxious to meet the Japanese, who had broadcast a propaganda message assuring listeners that the role of the military was simply to liberate the oppressed from the domination of the white man. The Japanese also appealed for everyone to remain calm and warned people not to damage any property belonging to the private or government sectors.

Two days after news reached Sandakan that Kuching had fallen, every European woman in Sandakan received a letter from Governor Robert Smith, advising that *Baynain* was sailing for Tarakan Island in Dutch Borneo at noon the following day and would take any women and children who wished to leave. From Tarakan it was hoped to trans-ship the passengers to Java and then to Australia. Intending

Sandy Young, Alice Walker, May Young and Bert Walker

travellers were required to submit their names to the Commissioner of Customs by 6 pm and report to the ship next day with bedding, food and clothing for the journey and at least seventy-five pounds in cash.

As there had been reports that oil-rich Tarakan had been bombed on Christmas Day, the decision on whether or not to go was difficult. In the end, there were only four passengers: May Young, whose husband William 'Sandy' Young was manager of the Bakau and Kenya Extract Company, the firm which owned the ship; their small son, Alan; Clare Parnell, wife of the Volunteers' commanding officer; and Norma, their grown-up daughter. The others either refused to leave their husbands, decided they had left it too late or, torn between going and staying, could not make up their minds by the 6 pm deadline. Among those electing to remain behind was Mary Baldwin, aged in her 60s and married to the ship's Chief Engineer. With just four passengers to be accommodated in the two available cabins, there was now no need for bedding, allowing May Young to take additional clothing and food, plus a few toys and books.

Early the next morning, after May attended Communion at St Michael's where Reverend Reuben Henthorne offered prayers for the safety of the ship, the passengers made their wills, checked that their passports were in order and withdrew whatever funds they had available. They also had lunch – the time of departure having been put back until 4 pm. On reaching Tarakan safely, they learned that they had been extremely lucky. Japanese bombers normally made a run over the harbour each morning and afternoon. The ship had arrived too late for the first, and poor flying conditions had put paid to the second. However, as the Dutch had sensibly evacuated all their women and children some time before, further travel south was a problem. Any movement by sea was near to impossible and a plane dispatched from Balikpapan to try and rescue them had turned back after spotting enemy aircraft. After weathering constant air raids for ten days, the women had almost given up hope when they were offered a ride to Balikpapan on a Dornier bomber ferrying nine American airmen whose Catalina flying boats had been shot down while defending the Philippines. From here the evacuees made their way to Surabaya on the last available KLM plane and then to Australia by Qantas flying boat. Others were not so fortunate. A week later the Qantas plane was shot down over the sea by Japanese aircraft. With their vessel sunk on 11 January, *Baynain*'s master, Captain Dooley, and Mary Baldwin's husband, David, were trapped on Tarakan. Baldwin did not survive captivity and died in July 1943.

Those who had elected to remain behind at Sandakan had no hope of escape. On New Year's Day the Japanese were on Labuan Island. Furious that the stocks of aviation fuel had been destroyed, the senior Japanese officer vented his rage on the Resident, Hugh Humphries, hitting him repeatedly with a sword scabbard before exhibiting him for twenty-four hours in an improvised cage. In Sandakan, where life proceeded as normal, a Watchnight Dance to welcome in the New Year was held at the Recreation Club. Among the guests were the Chinese Consul General, the Honourable Mr Robertson and other leading Europeans, along with members of all the well-known Eurasian, Chinese and Filipino families. Party games, described by the Editor of the *North Borneo Herald* as 'hilarious', kept everyone occupied until midnight, when they all joined hands to sing the traditional 'Auld Lang Syne'. Lillian Funk, who did not want to attend as Johnny was on guard duty, spent the evening glued to the wireless.

From Labuan the invaders moved to Weston on Brunei Bay and inland along the Klias River to Beaufort, where they released Japanese from the internment camp and armed them. Part of the force then returned to Brunei, taking the West Coast resident, Richard Evans, and the Commandant of the Constabulary, Colonel W C Adams, with them. Next stop was Jesselton, which was surrendered without incident on 9 January. However, it was not until 13 January that Governor Robert Smith actually issued orders outlining procedures to be followed in the event of capitulation. These orders were far too late to be of any use to the west coast Residents who, in the absence of any direction from above, had been forced to do what they thought was best.

The inhabitants of Sandakan were informed that they were to follow a policy of denial and passive resistance; to meet the enemy but not to co-operate; to remain at their posts and to destroy all resources, which included the dumping of thousands of litres of fuel stored at Mile 2 onto the nearby golf course, sinking launches and boats, wrecking industrial and plant machinery, burning stocks of rubber and timber, and dismantling the sawmills, where the huge saws were thrown into the sea for good measure. To make sure no one had any wild ideas about resisting the enemy, all firearms and ammunition were to be handed in and placed in a central store, guarded by Volunteers.

The war was now the only topic of conversation in town, where people gathered in coffee shops to discuss the latest news. On the advice of Mr M S Patel, the pharmacist at the Sandakan Dispensary, Lillian Funk stocked up on quinine, calcium tablets and other vitamins, spending far more than she normally would: Patel had also predicted that, if the Japanese arrived, money would devalue and there would be nothing to spend it on. On 17 January, worried that her house would be ransacked, Lillian packed her most treasured possessions, the silverware, bedding, medicines, foodstuffs and other precious goods and chattels into a truck and moved to a rubber estate at Mile 7 on the Labuk Road, owned by her father-in-law, John Simon Funk. As Johnny was on duty, the Funk family thought it best that she and their small son Melvyn should be out of town when the Japanese arrived. Others who had country properties also left.

At about this time a small, native-style boat sailed into the harbour, carrying five Americans who had escaped from Manila on 31 December, just one hour ahead of the advancing Japanese. The party comprised Dr Ashton Laidlaw (a dentist who had been attempting to return home from Shanghai via Manila) and two engineers involved in the construction of defences, Harry Webber and George Colley, plus their wives. After resting and recovering from the seasickness that had plagued all of them, they set off towards the south, hoping to put some distance between them and the Japanese, now off Kudat. Any Sandakan citizens still clinging to a prediction made by the British top brass that Sandakan Harbour was far too shallow for an invasion force had their hopes dashed. On Sunday the 18th, the Agricultural Department's Harry Keith received reports that two small steamers were just off the north-east coast, battling heavy monsoonal weather.

It poured with rain all day, reducing visibility to almost zero. Water was everywhere, with rivers swollen, small streams overflowing and bridges washed away. Fallen trees blocked roads and brought down telephone lines, and landslides were reported in many areas. In spite of the terrible weather, Lillian Funk attended Mass at St Mary's. Like St Michael's, it was packed for the morning service. At six pm, after a day of intense apprehension, a call went out for all European women and children to report immediately to one of three previously designated centres: Government House; the Mitchells' house on Trig Hill; and Leila Lodge, home of Mr Phillips on Leila Road at Kampong Gelam, near the sawmill. All white government male employees were ordered to proceed at once to their respective posts.

Gathering up her small son George, Harry Keith's wife Agnes, whose book about life in Borneo, *Land Below the Wind,* published in 1939 and now a best-seller, headed for Government House, just a five-minute walk away. Up on Elton Hill, Reverend Henthorne and his congregation continued with their Evensong service before dispersing. Sister Irene, one of two English nuns belonging to an order known as The Companions of Jesus of the Good Shepherd, handed the School Log Book to St Michael's assistant priest Sung Khi Fong, who buried it in a sealed tin in his garden, along with some church valuables. They and the rest of Sandakan then waited anxiously all night, but there was no sign of the Japanese. Unfortunately, they were not far away. They had anchored off-shore, ready to make their triumphal entry bright and early at seven o'clock the next morning.

Waiting on the wharf to receive them stood the solitary figure of Owen Rutter, now the East Coast Resident. Standing in the bow of the first steamer was his west coast counterpart Richard Evans and the commander of the Jesselton's North Borneo Volunteers, Colonel Adams, both brought along to act as a human shield. Behind them, but out of the line of any fire, was Major Suga Tatsuji, a very short, well-turned-out officer, wearing campaign medals from the First World War, when Japan was an ally of Britain. With him were Captain Takakuwa Takuo, in charge of all internees; Kobayashi, a senior officer in the dreaded kempeitai (secret military police) and three of the town's former Japanese citizens – the manager of the cordial factory, a doctor from one of the Japanese-owned rubber estates and a humble 'cake seller', who had peddled his wares door-to-door while collecting information and was now resplendent in full Japanese uniform and samurai sword. Ranged along the decks of the two vessels were 400 occupation troops. To the intense disappointment of the thirty Volunteers, assembled in the nearby Drill Hall, there was no resistance. The Governor had made it quite clear that they were to surrender their arms and equipment and be disbanded. However, not all arms had been handed in. Johnny Funk's brother, Alex, in defiance of the order, had retained a pistol, a .303 rifle, and ammunition, all now safely hidden on the family property at Mile 7.

As Major Suga stepped ashore a shot rang out. Believing that Owen Rutter had been murdered, those within earshot, including everyone waiting at Government House, were most alarmed, especially when panic-stricken local people started to stream along the road heading out of town. However, the Resident was safe. The shot had come from the pistol of Mr Pillipson, the manager of the Bode Rubber Estate, who had taken his own life. As he was a German national, and therefore an ally of Japan, the reason for his premature suicide remains a mystery.

It was not long before Japanese soldiers were swarming across the sweeping lawns of Government House and taking up residence in the building itself. Although they bullied the current occupants and relieved them of anything of value, including fountain pens and watches, no one was physically harmed. The women also managed to forestall any untoward incidents by quickly pouring the entire liquor stock down the drain, before the troops could get hold of it. In the meantime, Robert Smith was summoned to town, where the very angry Major Suga, furious that so many valuable resources had been destroyed, confronted him. At the conclusion of this rather tense and uncomfortable meeting, Smith instructed all senior civil servants to remain at their posts and to carry on with their normal duties. The Volunteers, after being stripped and detained for two days, were released. However, a few days later the kempeitai recalled Chinese baker Lim Kuan Poh, who had been guarding Japanese internees. Roped by the waist, with his hands bound, and with a white card denouncing him as a 'traitor to the Japanese' hung around his neck, he was paraded round the streets and along Leila Road as far as Kampong Tanah Merah. After threatening to behead him, and encouraging him to consider changing his loyalties, the kempeitai sent him on his way. Shattered by this experience, Lim and his wife left town and lived in the jungle, where they felt much safer. Lieutenant Kong and the more senior non-commissioned officers were required to report to the kempeitai periodically for 'interrogation', a process which involved torture and beatings.

Although the Volunteers had been disbanded, the Constabulary remained on duty to preserve internal law and order, as was usual under the rules of international warfare. One member of the Constabulary who was not involved in peace-keeping duties was Lance-Corporal Koram bin Andaur, a proud member of the Murut tribe, renowned for their fighting qualities. On 9 January, the Governor had given him new orders. He was to remain behind the lines and report to Allied forces if, and when, possible. As the Japanese at that time were already at Jesselton, he headed for the west coast. While enemy troops were making their way further north, Koram and ten members of the Constabulary built a fort between Langcon Estate and Kota Belud where, on 21 January, they were attacked by a force of 500 Japanese. During the fighting, many enemy troops were killed or wounded. Four days later, under the protection of a flag of truce, a Japanese officer informed the defenders that the District Officer, John Dingle, had advised that all of British North Borneo had now been surrendered. The men were taken into custody and sent to Kudat, where they were beaten up and imprisoned. Koram was then sent to Sandakan, where he was subjected to a round of severe face-slapping and confined for the time being to the Mental Hospital at Buli Sim Sim.

Dr James Taylor

An uneasy calm settled over Sandakan, while the Japanese considered what to do next. They began by placing the Chinese consular staff and their families under house arrest and confining almost all the European males (including Dr Laidlaw and the two American engineers whose boat had been intercepted off the coast) in the 2nd class ward of the hospital, recently vacated by the Japanese internees. One of the exceptions was Resident Owen Rutter who, against the wishes of the Governor, had made a decision to co-operate with the Japanese, believing that he could be of some use by acting as a buffer between the occupying forces and his local community, otherwise left leaderless. As the Japanese permitted freedom of religion, Reuben Henthorne, his assistant priest Denis Brown and Sisters Irene and Alison (along with the Dutch and English Catholic priests, Mother Rose and Sisters Frances Mary and Clitus from St Mary's Church) were also allowed to go about their normal business. So were Sandy Young and his staff at the Bakau factory; planters on various estates outside town; and the hospital medical staff, Doctors James Taylor, Hugh Wands and Matron North.

James Taylor, born in 1897 in the country town of Yass in NSW, Australia, had visited Sandakan as a ship's surgeon in 1922. While in port, he had met Irish-born Dr Conyngham, who invited the young doctor to join his large and busy practice. The appointment was supposed to be for only one year but, just as Taylor was to leave for home in 1924, he was offered a job as medical officer at Manau, between Membakit and Lumut, on Sabah's west coast, a post he held for six years. While on twelve-months' home leave in 1930, he took time out to further his studies and conduct a whirlwind courtship with Celia Ryan, whom he had known in his younger days. They were married in July that year, just before Jim was due to return to Sabah. In 1936, after a five-year posting in Jesselton, where their daughter Elizabeth was born, Jim was appointed District Surgeon. The family moved to Sandakan, where Jim was responsible for the 100-bed Sandakan Civil Hospital, the Mental Hospital at Buli Sim Sim, the inmates in the gaol and a large Leper Colony, on the opposite side of Berhala Island from the Quarantine Station. In 1940, he was appointed Principal Medical officer for all of British North Borneo.

Dr Val Stookes, on enlistment in the British army, 1914

Also free was a dentist, Dr Fritz Peter Laband, a German Jew who had fled the Nazis and taken up the post of Government Dental Surgeon in 1938. In 1939, when the war began in Europe, the Company cancelled his contract and ordered him to Jesselton where, being a German national, his movements were restricted by the British. However, after a considerable delay he was permitted to go to northern Sarawak, to fulfill a private contract with an oil company before moving to Sandakan and setting up private practice. Realising that war with Japan was inevitable, in early 1941 he sent his wife to America. The Japanese allowed him to remain free and continue with his private practice, but another German-born medical practitioner, Dr Sternfeld, who was also Jewish, was detained, along with his friend, forty-eight-year-old Dr Valantine Alexander Stookes.

Born in Liverpool, England, in 1893, Val Stookes was in his final year at medical school at Edinburgh University when World War 1 rudely interrupted his studies. In 1915 he was commissioned into the Scots Greys as a lieutenant but, as it was believed that a good horseman would also be a competent airman, he was subsequently seconded to the Royal Flying Corps. Despite his ability to handle a horse, he did not make the grade as a pilot and became a navigator/ observer instead. In 1916 he was awarded a Military Cross for 'conspicuous gallantry and skill' by engaging the enemy with rifle fire and shooting two of them, while the pilot photographed the ground from an altitude of 200 feet. During this incident Stookes was shot in the back and returned to England for treatment. Once he had recovered, he qualified as a pilot, gaining an early discharge in October 1917 to resume his medical studies. In 1921, now a fully fledged medical practitioner, he took up a posting in Singapore, where he spent two years before relocating to Miri. In 1927 he bought the medical practice in Sandakan owned

The Stookes' home, on Bukit Merah

Dora Stookes

by Dr Conyngham, who was retiring. The practice, where Jim Taylor had first started out, was a large one, covering six rubber and tobacco estates owned by Harrison and Crosfield, as well as European and Asiatic patients in the town itself. Local people were treated at his small private hospital. Europeans went to Stookes' house on Bukit Merah.

In 1935, with a failed marriage behind him, Stookes and his new partner Dora Sherman, a Japanese-American, bought 'Letak Liman', a twenty-hectare farm situated 100 kilometres up the Kinabatangan River at Bilit. The family, who raised cattle, pigs and vegetables, lived part-time on the farm, to which Stookes commuted by boat at weekends. During the week they stayed at the town house, which was just across the road from the Keiths' bungalow. Val Stookes had little time for the European social scene in Sandakan, refusing invitations to Government House and elsewhere because Dora, being Eurasian, was not accepted. A compassionate man, he would often send patients who were experiencing hardship to have a holiday on the farm, where Dora, who held the position of Matron at his hospital, looked after them until their health recovered. Among the grateful guests were prostitutes, whom Stookes sent in the hope that Dora could give them some basic education to help them enjoy a better life.

At the weekends, Stookes also gave people living along the Kinabatangan River the benefit of free medical advice. Frustrated by the amount of time it took to move up and down the tidal rivers, even in his 25-knot motor launch (which Sandakan's conservative Europeans predicted would result in his early demise), he had often thought about buying a plane to help him in his work, but was always deterred by the cost. In 1936 he was inspired to take up flying again after meeting the adventurous Americans, Martin and Osa Johnson. Encouraged by Martin Johnson, and after dispatching many telegrams to assure the manufacturers that floats, not wheels, were definitely required, Stookes imported a kit plane – an Aeronica – which he then proceeded to assemble with the help of the Johnson's pilot and engineer, Jim Laneri. After a successful test flight at 500 feet over Sandakan Harbour, Val Stookes, the flying doctor, was in business.

His critics were eating humble pie after his first medical flight, when he flew to a group of men cutting mangrove bark, treated them, and returned home by lunchtime – a journey that had previously taken him two days and a night. His next trip was to a rubber plantation on the Segama River, so isolated that no doctor had visited for at least six years. After that, enquiries came in thick and fast, asking if he could land on this bay, or on that river, and before long the waterways

Stookes' plane, on its test flight

Stookes and local people, following the test flight

were sprinkled with home-made buoys and windsocks. To protect his precious flying machine during the monsoon, a hangar and ramp were constructed in a sheltered corner of Sandakan Harbour, and the services of a mechanic engaged. Within a year Stookes was making regular rounds every Thursday, with occasional visits on Tuesday. His weekends, as usual, were spent at the farm after a flight that took about fifteen minutes, a vast improvement on the four-hour boat trip. In November 1937 he noted that his journey back to town on Sunday evening, laden with a week's supply of fruit and vegetables, was 'still a source of amusement to everyone'.

Elderly Dr Sternfeld, formerly an obstetrician from Vienna, was one of three doctors fleeing Nazi persecution who had come to Sandakan in the late 1930s to work with Stookes. Doctor Ernst Kratzenstein (Cranston) was now in Mostyn, where he was being badly treated, and Dr Linck had also moved on, but Sternfeld, until his internment, was employed as medical officer with the North Borneo Trading Company. A gentle man with refined ways, his nationality did not help him in his dealings with the Japanese, whose treatment of German nationals, supposedly their allies, was haphazard. On the other hand, Dr Taylor and his wife, who for some reason had not been required to report to a safe house with the other women, were free, but had been evicted from their comfortable two-storey home by a Japanese officer and allocated a small cottage in the hospital grounds. Before he left his house, Taylor managed to stow some of their more precious belongings in the roof and bury the rest in sealed kerosene tins in the brush behind the house.

Bert Walker had also been allowed to retain his liberty after the Volunteers were disbanded. After spending the night with Captain Parnell, he returned to his home at Mile 11, where he organised his workers, or at least those who had not fled, to begin planting food crops. On 24 January, with his colleague Pillipson dead, he applied for, and received, permission to travel to Bode Estate where he organised a similar programme. Two days later, just as it appeared that the Japanese might have forgotten all about him, he was summoned to Sandakan and arrested for his 'volunteer activities' by Major Suga, who was not at all pleased to learn of the destruction wrought at Si Amil Island. However, despite being under arrest, Suga allowed him to return to Mile 11 to hand over the management of the estates to his deputy Mr Maw, who was also still free, and to arrange for the transfer to town for safekeeping of two boxes of linen (wedding presents from his family) and a pair of ivory tusks from an elephant Walker had shot on the estate a few years before. In return, he had to promise that he would communicate with no one else, and report back to Suga's office the following morning at 8 o'clock.

When Walker reported the next day, 27 January, Suga informed him that, as he was to become a prisoner of war, he was to await further orders at the Sandakan Hotel, soon to become the Japanese officers' barracks. It was all very civilised. Walker was given breakfast and lunch at the hotel, before being driven to The Hut, a large bungalow belonging to the Chief Justice, Mr C Macaskie, where the white male civil servants had been interned. Their wives were also confined, in the home of Mr G L Gray, a senior civil servant. Although the men were under house arrest, they did not find it onerous. The Hut was very spacious, the beds comfortable, the company good, there were plenty of books to read, and the food supplied was generous.

At about the time that Walker was losing his liberty, European males engaged in essential services or food production were released from the 2nd class ward, along with their wives and children. This included Bert Walker's close friend, Scottish-born Gerald Mavor, Superintendent of the Sandakan Power and Light Company, whose key workers Ng Ho Kong and Chan (Ah) Ping were now forced to work for the Japanese administration. Ng's family, alarmed by his detention, sensibly fled town to take up residence on a relative's rubber estate on Trig Hill, where they had had the foresight to build a small hut.

Also released were Sandy Young and his staff; the clergy; Mr A E Phillips, Manager of the North Borneo Trading Company; and Mr and Mrs Cohen, who owned a large emporium in town. Although Phillips had allowed Leila Lodge to be used as a muster centre for women and children, and headed the company whose machinery and sawmill had been laid waste, the Malay community had vouched for him, as his wife was a local woman. Sandy Young had sabotaged his company's factory, but the Japanese had overlooked this transgression as they were keen to get it up and running again. The wealthy Cohens probably owed their liberty to the fact that they had the necessary funds to ensure their freedom, ran a business essential to the local economy, and were practising Jews who only ate kosher food. The elderly Mr Cohen, who had diabetes and was suffering from systemic poisoning, also needed special care.

Dr Stookes was liberated for the time being, but the rest of the white population remained in detention – the women at Leila Lodge, the civil servants at The Hut, and the other men at a Government

House annex known as 'The Cottage', the main building having been appropriated for the new Governor of the East Coast Residency, Tanuke Kumabe. On returning home, those newly released found that their possessions had been looted, not only by the Japanese but also by Asiatic civilians: with the sawmills, the town's greatest employer, wrecked, there were now hordes of hungry, idle workers about. To protect the remainder of their goods, householders took to sleeping with a golf club handy, all weapons having been surrendered. In the Rectory on Elton Hill, where all the clergy now spent the night, Reuben Henthorne kept a parang (jungle knife), as well as a stout stick, beside his bed.

On 18 March, Walker and the civil servants were transferred from The Hut to The Cottage, where they discovered that the Japanese had indulged in some 'home improvements' by constructing sleeping platforms around the walls. Although they no longer had the luxury of individual beds, only mattresses, they had a fine view of the ocean and had plenty of space to exercise. The only downside was that Captain Takakuwa insisted on giving lessons in Japanese every morning and afternoon, which his pupils felt were entirely unnecessary since the latest rumour was that they would be released within a few months.

With almost all the radios confiscated, news from the outside world was limited to the brave souls who had managed to hide a short-wave set. One of those who tuned in each night was Simon Chong Yew, a staff member of St Michael's School, who lived near the church. A keen member of the Scout Troop, he had received the Chief Scout's Order of Merit from the Governor on Charter Day 1939, the first Scout decoration ever awarded in Sabah. Although Denis Brown, the Scout Leader and school principal, was still free, along with Reuben Henthorne, a sentry had been placed at the church to monitor their movements. Despite the obvious risks, this did not stop the pair from crawling through the grass at night to Simon's house to listen to the ten o'clock BBC news.

In March, Sandy Young and two of his three employees at the Bakau factory also lost their freedom. Apart from some Japanese civilians who came at intervals to inspect the premises, the four men were enjoying a peaceful existence when they were taken to the kempeitai's main headquarters, just out of town on the Labuk Road. The Japanese, who planned to obtain new belts for the machinery, which had been burnt, and recover the tubes from the evaporators, now lying in the sea beyond the jetty, invited each man, in turn, to work with Japanese civilians to resume production. Young, who believed that co-operation with the enemy was another word for collaboration,

Pisang (banana) money

refused. So did Matt Allen and Mr D S McLeod. Mr Hunt, formerly Lieutenant Hunt of the Volunteers, agreed. The dissenters were then escorted to a car and driven to the gaol, where they were placed in solitary confinement.

For the four months following the arrival of the Japanese, the remainder of Sandakan's British and pro-British rubbed along with the conquerors as best they could. Life was now very different. The Japanese had split Sabah into two administrative zones. The West Coast, Kudat and Interior Residencies were now combined to form a single West Coast Residency, named Seikai Shiu. The East Coast Residency, which occupied the remaining territory, was renamed Tokai Shiu. Jesselton was Api and Sandakan, once again, Elopura. Labuan became Maedashim or Maeda Island, named in honour of Marquis Maeda, the Commander-in-Chief who was killed in an air crash in 1942. As the Japanese Empire ran on Tokyo time, all clocks were wound back two hours and the year altered to conform to the Japanese calendar. It was no longer 1942. It was either 'Showa 17', the 17th year of the reign of Emperor Hirohito, or 2602 (Japan's reckoning being 660 years ahead of the Christian calendar).

The Japanese also printed their occupation money in dollars. It was supposed to be on a par with the local dollar but inflation quickly set in. Before long, a box of Japanese matches cost $10 in occupation money – 100 times the local equivalent. By May 1942, the currency was virtually worthless, giving rise to the derisive term 'pisang' or 'banana' money, a reference to the bunch of bananas featured in the design on the bank notes.

Anyone who still had gold, or any type of non-occupation currency, kept quiet about it. The Japanese had not been in control for a month when orders were issued to deposit all funds in excess of thirty shillings (about 13 local dollars) in the new Yokohama Specie Bank, which occupied part of the Treasury Building in Humpreys Street. All gold and silver had to be surrendered and merchants were obliged to give a full account of their cash resources. Estate owners were no better off. Any rubber produced had to be sold to the Japanese at a price so low that it did not cover production costs.

Although Japanese propaganda was still promising a 'new Asia' under their much vaunted 'co-prosperity sphere', these plans did not include Chinese now living in their supposedly Utopian empire. For years, Chinese outside China, Japan's long-term and traditional enemy, had been donating large sums of money to the China Relief Fund to support their homeland in the struggle against Japanese aggression and occupation. Anyone who had contributed was a marked man. In Singapore, where the spy network was extensive, there were wholesale executions. However, at this stage any physical punishment in Sandakan was restricted to imprisonment of those known to be leaders in the Relief Organisation.

Nevertheless, the Chinese as a race were made to pay dearly. The new masters set the tone by issuing a proclamation that all Chinese-owned property was to be confiscated. This was followed with a demand for donations to support the Japanese war effort. The amount levied on Sabah was one million dollars: $600,000 from the West Coast Residency and the remainder from the East. Leading merchants and traders were very heavily assessed, and those unable to withdraw money from the bank were forced to borrow at high rates of interest in order to discharge their liabilities.

To meet the levies, dispossessed land owners were often compelled to borrow from those who had managed to work within the new regime and had cash to spare. Recognising that here was an opportunity to make even more money, black-marketeers flourished, especially anyone who had managed to find favour with the Japanese. One very wealthy merchant became so stressed by the mental torture inflicted by financial demands on his fortune that he was admitted to hospital, where he died in 1943. In order to protect the Chinese community from further harassment, $100,000 of the deceased's estate was donated to the compulsory fund. In a further attempt to extort money, the Japanese demanded a poll tax of $6 from every Chinese male. However, this scheme aroused such general ill-will that it was abandoned after one year.

Taking a seemingly softer line, the Japanese invited merchants to dinners and other entertainment. Although the guests despised the hosts, the invitations were at first openly accepted. However, while the dinners were promoted as a means of fostering co-operation, the real aim was to record the names of those who attended, some of whom subsequently found themselves in prison. Despite the obvious danger, invitations were still accepted by some, the promise of a sweet 'take home' present, such as a kati of sugar, being too hard to resist.

As the Japanese also believed in education, as well as freedom of religion, the church-run schools, which had closed down in December, were reopened to day students by the C of E and Catholic nuns with the help of faithful local teachers. However, in keeping with every school in the occupied areas, Japanese was now a compulsory subject. At St Michael's the classes were conducted by a Mrs Richardson and a Japanese parishioner.

Ever since 19 January, the European community had borne the humiliation of defeat and daily irritations with stoicism. However on 12 May, everything changed. At very short notice, all Europeans not in detention were ordered to report to the Japanese Military Administration Headquarters (formerly The Secretariat) at 3 pm. After keeping them waiting until 4 pm, Suga announced that everyone, apart from the previously nominated medical staff, Mr Phillips, the Cohens and Gerald Mavor, was to leave for a prison camp within the hour. Baggage was restricted to one suitcase per person and the men and women were to be segregated.

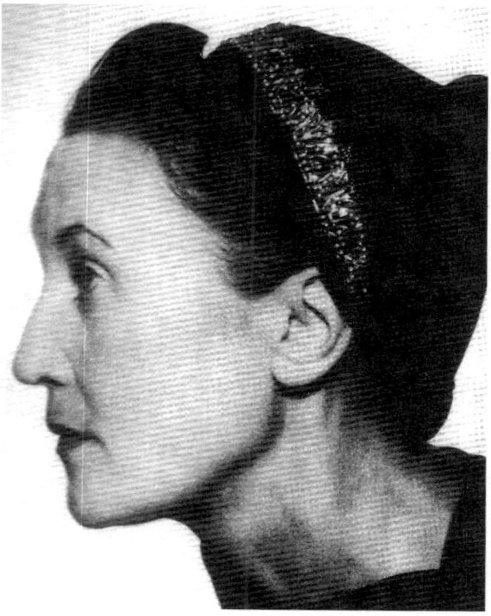

Agnes Keith

Hurrying back to St Michael's, Reuben Henthorne managed to remove the sacraments from the tabernacle behind the altar, say a final prayer for deliverance and pack a small bag, before the truck arrived. As he closed his front door for the last time, he might have taken some comfort in the knowledge that his home would not be occupied by rampaging Japanese troops. Instead, it became the Japanese Lending Library, stocked with 20,000 books, a good number of them undoubtedly from the Book Club. One of St Michael's teachers, Samuel Phui Koo, was fortunate enough to land the job of librarian. However, as there was no transport, he had to leave his home at Mile 10 at 3 am each day to walk the sixteen kilometres into town, arriving back at eight o'clock in the evening.

What the internees were permitted to take on board the vehicles, and what they were not, depended on the escorting officer. To Agnes Keith's distress, she was allowed only a small bed roll, a mosquito net and a suitcase each for herself and her son. A folding stretcher wrapped in a thin mattress, a box of food for young George and a case containing medicines were unceremoniously dumped onto the road. However, at the next house, Mrs Hill and her daughter Susan were permitted to bring not only suitcases and bed rolls, but baskets of food and a large red rocking-horse.

The men who had been interned at The Cottage were far worse off. They were about to depart in two buses, with their baggage stowed in a couple of trucks, when kempeitai chief Kobayashi appeared on the scene in a towering rage. The men were ordered to take all their luggage off the lorries and to repack what they needed into one suitcase which, according to Kobayashi, they would be expected to carry to the next camp, sixteen kilometres away. As a further inducement to travel lightly, he declared that anyone offering to help carry another's bag would be beaten up. As a result, a great deal of clothing and canned food, as well as all the bedding, was left behind. With their transport now nowhere to be seen, the men were then marched off down the hill, under guard, to the waterfront. Waiting there were the three Bakau staff, released from solitary confinement, and also Mr Hunt who, with his services no longer required by the Japanese, had been made redundant.

On reaching the government wharf, everyone was searched and any money found was confiscated. They were then crammed into small launches and transferred in relays to the old Quarantine Station. Because the Japanese guards had no experience in boat-handling, what should have been a twenty-minute ride for the women took the best part of five hours. By the time they arrived it was 10 pm.

After struggling along the jetty with their assorted bundles and tired children, they were reunited with the group that had been confined to Mr Phillips' house and had arrived earlier in the day. Conditions were worse than the newcomers could have possibly imagined. The crude wooden huts were set on a small flat area about 100 metres from the beach. Originally built to quarantine Asiatics, they had been recently occupied by Japanese internees and were in a filthy, derelict state. Confined by ten-metre-high timber fences on two sides and multiple strands of barbed wire on the other two, the building assigned to the women had shuttered openings in place of windows and no interior or exterior lighting. The roof, infested with rats whose droppings littered the rotting floorboards, leaked like a sieve. There was no plumbing – just a large concrete tank holding water, which had to be boiled for drinking. Nor was there anything remotely resembling bathroom facilities, and no latrines, apart from a couple of concrete holes which had no removable containers nor any type of drainage to empty them. In the interests of sanitation, the Japanese agreed to supply two galvanised-tin buckets which, when full, were hauled down the jetty and emptied into the sea. Unless the wind was favourable, the contents floated right back in on the next tide to the beach, which was used for bathing.

The two buildings comprising the men's camp, separated from the women's by the wooden fence with an empty hut to act as a further buffer, were in a similar condition. However, there were no toilet facilities at all for the men, who were forced to dig their own urinal trenches and latrine holes, using nothing more than sharpened sticks. Both camps were also put to work. The men had to cut the tall native grass surrounding the camp with table knives and clear prickly lantana and scrub with their bare hands, while the women tackled their grass with their hands or, if they had the foresight to pack them, sewing or nail scissors.

Food consisted of rice, mainly low grade 'sweepings' into which lime had been mixed to deter weevils, and boiled green vegetables, usually kangkong, a type of wild spinach. This was sometimes enlivened with a small amount of salted fish or dried prawns which, until Western stomachs became accustomed to it, resulted in bouts of vomiting. There was also an abundance of tea, delivered in a bucket with the leaves floating on top, as the water had not been boiled, and usually with additional vitamins in the form of various bugs lying on the bottom. Exercise was limited to a one-hour walk along the beach each day, and performing various tasks around the camp. There was no medical officer in the women's compound but, if the situation demanded, a guard could call Dr Sternfeld or Dr Stookes from the adjoining men's camp, to offer medical advice and assess if hospitalisation were necessary.

Shortly after the Sandakan internees arrived at Berhala, they were joined by civilians rounded up from Kudat earlier that month. The only exemptions were a Dr Blaauw and his family, who remained with Dr Taylor at the hospital until September, when they were sent to Mostyn, near Lahad Datu, at two days' notice. The one positive aspect for those at Berhala was that the Japanese guards, who were rotated on a weekly basis, regarded the posting as a kind of holiday camp and were often very lax. This enabled women prisoners to burrow under the fence to fraternise with their men and, while taking their exercise, to receive eggs and other delicacies from Mohamet Salleh bin Madang, the island's caretaker/night watchman who lived with his family in a small shack at the end of the wharf. The path leading to the spring, which was Salleh's water supply, passed by a screen enclosing the latrine buckets, allowing him also to slip small parcels through the wire. Food, which the male internees obtained from the leper colony on the seaward side of the island, was also smuggled to the women's camp. With only a low saddle separating the camp from the colony, the men had no trouble slipping out at night. Using money obtained from selling desirable items to the new inmates from Kudat, who had not been searched and still had their cash, they were able to purchase peanuts, sugar, dried fish and eggs.

Major Suga also came to inspect the camp. Introducing himself as 'Major Sugar, the Commandants of all the Borneos', he assured them that all Japanese officers were 'honourable' and that as long as the internees worked hard, didn't complain, behaved themselves, kept well, stayed happy and kept up their morale, they would be fine. However, Captain Takakuwa was a notorious womaniser and far from honourable. The women internees, who generally regarded Japanese as figures of fun, loathed and detested him. Fortunately, he visited only on a weekly basis and as his transport was a decrepit launch with a very noisy engine, there was plenty of time for the women to make sure they were decently clad, and for anything incriminating to be hidden.

On 15 June, help came from the outside in the form of Dr Fritz Laband, the dentist, who had been a reluctant employee of the Japanese since 1 April, when he had been compelled to treat Japanese troops in return for a salary of $150 a month. He had visited Berhala in a professional capacity in May, just three days after the internees arrived but, as no teeth required his attention, the visit had been more social than otherwise. Having learned that the food situation on Berhala was precarious, he used his next visit to work out a way of getting supplies to the island.

Using a strategy devised by Laband, and with Salleh the watchman acting as a go-between, the interned Sandakan civilians were soon sending money to their Asian friends and staff, who obtained whatever was wanted. Local people posing as fishermen then rowed out to the island and left the goods at a pre-arranged pick-up point, either outside the wire or in a coconut plantation, about 1.5 kilometres away. As contacts on the mainland became better organised, food supplies began to arrive in increasing quantities, helped by loyal members of the police force who had been rostered on sentry duty to assist the Japanese guards. The prisoners assigned for the pick-up slipped under the wire after dark and returned hours later, laden with as much as they could carry – eggs, meat, fruit and potatoes – which was then shared with the women's camp. The degree of friendship between the races astounded the Kudat internees, who had been accustomed to keeping Asiatics at arm's length.

An unprecedented opportunity for smuggling presented itself in October when Dr Sternfeld arranged for Agnes Keith and George, who were extremely ill with malaria, to be transferred to hospital. They were admitted to the 2nd class ward, the superior ward being reserved for Japanese soldiers undergoing treatment for venereal disease.

About two weeks after Agnes' admission, a very drunk Captain Takakuwa swaggered through the hospital. As his extra-curricular activities had left him with hefty dose of syphilis, he was on his way to the venereal disease ward for treatment. He was not too drunk, however, to notice that Berhala internees occupied six of the beds in the 2nd class ward. The American woman and small boy were ill with malaria but since, in his opinion, the other four were fit, he ordered their immediate discharge. An hour later they left under guard, and on foot, for the wharf that was well over a kilometre away: a 75-year-old man; Dr Laidlaw, encumbered by a broken foot in a heavy plaster cast; a woman suffering from gallstones and a stomach ulcer; and Mrs Li, wife of the Assistant Chinese Consulate, who had given birth just ten days before. She was now ill with milk-fever and running a temperature of 103 Fahrenheit.

In a further demonstration of power, Takakuwa also organised a Day of Humiliation in Sandakan for the Berhala internees. The men were set to work grading and mending roads, clearing weeds from monsoon drains and public spaces and performing other community work. Before they returned to their camp they were paraded on the padang so that the locals could see just how far the once-proud white tuans (bosses) had fallen. Meantime the women had spent their day at the rear of the Japanese officers' barracks, washing and mending soldiers' clothes. This laundry and repair service was on a strictly 'while you wait' basis: the more modest soldiers stripped down to their loincloths and waited. The others stood about, stark naked.

Although Dr Taylor had warned Agnes that internees admitted to hospital were prohibited from having any contact with outsiders, this did not prevent local people who were visiting their relatives and friends from stopping by her bed with small gifts of food. Nor did it prevent George's amah, Ah Yin, from somehow sneaking in. Dr Laband, who was supposed to be attending solely to dental matters, also dropped by, as well as Dr Stookes, who had been detained, released, detained again and then re-released. As he was the only person who could fly his idiosyncratic aeroplane, and as the Japanese had no aircraft of their own, Major Suga let him out to fly the Japanese around, despite the plane's deteriorating mechanical condition, there now being no spare parts available. Stookes' latest release, in September, appeared to be permanent and had been sparked by the birth of his son George. As Dora was at the farm, without medical assistance, Major Suga had allowed her husband to deliver the baby. The spirits of both Agnes and George Keith were also lifted by visits from Mrs Cohen, who was in hospital for about a week, receiving injections for a skin complaint.

Moselle Cohen was undeniably Sandakan's most colourful identity. Born in Palestine, she and her husband had been in Sandakan for some years, after fleeing Hitler's Europe. A many-chinned, well-endowed woman, her ample proportions were always enveloped in flowing, flamboyant clothing, for which she had an absolute passion. She was kindness personified, generous in spirit and worldly possessions, dispensing practical assistance and comfort to anyone who was in need of it – Eurasians, Chinese and Malays, housemaids, amahs, market sellers and prostitutes. Enfolding them to her bosom, she would wipe away tears, murmur words of sympathy and slip bank notes into hands and pockets. Despite her size, she was light on her feet and, with her dancing partner Pedro Dominic, won many dancing competitions. Larger than life, she was a driving force in Sandakan's Asian community; the core of Eurasian society, commerce and business – and no wedding, funeral or celebration was complete without her.

She was still undergoing treatment when she received an urgent summons from her husband, who was having trouble coping in her absence. Soldiers coming into the shop were demanding goods at half price and, when he refused, were beating him up. The Japanese may have been able to intimidate poor Mr Cohen, but they were no match for his wife. Using a mixture of coercion, apparent collaboration, flattery and bribery, she had gained and maintained the upper hand from the very beginning by concealing the best stock, selling them inconsequential items for whatever they were prepared to pay, handing out worthless trinkets, plying them with coffee and lending a sympathetic ear to their troubles.

Despite the ban on visitors, for the six weeks that Agnes was in hospital her Asian friends neatly circumvented this rule by timing their visits to coincide with the two-hour rest period each afternoon. With the nursing staff either sleeping or playing bingo in town, there was plenty of time to hide anything incriminating. As she started to recover, Agnes received a constant stream of visitors. Some were well known to her. Others were not. But all came bearing gifts of food and money, and requests for cash to be delivered to other internees.

They were, in fact, part of an underground assistance group now headed by Dr Taylor who, as principal medical officer, moved between the hospital, the gaol and the leper colony. The group's existence was due partly to Dr Laband and partly to Ernesto Lagan, an ex-employee of Harrison and Crosfield and member of the Volunteers, who was married to Pedro Dominic's granddaughter, Katherine Neubronner. As Lagan was now working as a 'detective' for the Japanese, he was closely connected to the police. Shortly after the civilians were sent to Berhala, he had received a message from the Constabulary's commanding officer, Major A Rice-Oxley, seeking financial assistance for himself and two other officers, Captain H B Rowland and Lieutenant M G Edge. The note had been passed from Salleh to Sergeant Ikes and Corporal Koram, who had been released from the mental hospital after agreeing to 'help' the Japanese and was now posted to Berhala to guard the internees. On receipt of the note, Lagan canvassed those whom he was sure he could trust and appointed Sergeant Yusop Basinau to begin collecting whatever money anyone could spare. The sergeant had no trouble finding contributors, with Inspector Samuel Guriaman, Sergeant Major Yangsalang, Sergeant Abin and Corporal Koram willing to donate on a weekly basis, along with Privates Kai, Damudaran, Lumatop, Kassiu, Gorokon and Mohamed Tahir Matusin.

Mohamed Tahir had not been a policeman for very long. Although he was 25 years old, he was attending school in Tuaran as a mature student in early 1941, hoping to start teacher training in two years' time. However, with war clouds looming, he had quit school and joined the Constabulary. Policing was in his blood: his father was a retired sergeant and his grandfather had served during the Mat Salleh campaign. After finishing his training at Victoria Barracks in

Jesselton, Tahir was posted to Sandakan, where he was put to work filling sandbags and building pillboxes and other simple defence structures at Sungai Kayuh, Buli Sim Sim and Mile 2. Despite the promises of a better life under the Japanese co-prosperity sphere, Tahir had remained loyal to the previous regime: a decision based on his family's fine tradition of service and the savage beating he had witnessed of an elderly Chinese woman who was carrying a load of vegetables to market and had neglected to bow to a sentry.

Another policeman who could not wait to give his financial and practical assistance was the handsome and fiercely pro-British Jemadar Ojagar Singh, who had been so distressed at not being allowed to oppose the Japanese landings. He and others involved in these activities had to take great care. While most of the Constabulary were loyal, some were not. Police Constable Masakup was working as a spy on the Bilit Estate, where Dora Stookes was taking note of his activities. Lance-Corporal Amat bin Yusop, a 39-year-old Bajau from the west coast, was not simply content to collaborate with the Japanese. He also ill-treated villagers while searching their boats and bodies and robbed those whom he met at sea, aided and abetted by a friend, also in the employ of the Japanese – Baduah bin Juli, of Kampong Sambulan, near Jesselton. Aware that not all the police could be relied upon, Ojagar Singh and Sergeant Major Yangsalang made sure that only the most trustworthy of their men were rostered for guard duty at Berhala.

When pleas came from other Berhala internees for help, the circle of helpers expanded, and so the assistance group was born. Lagan was the principal player in the drive for extra funds, to which Taylor, Stookes, Phillips and the town's civilians willingly contributed. Although money sent to adults was now shared among them all, Celia Taylor earmarked her donations to be spent on food for the children. As the nest-egg grew, the money was given into the care of Mrs Cohen, a major donor, whose flowing dresses allowed her to secrete large amounts of cash around her ample person. As the internees were in dire need of medicine, the medical staff at the hospital was also drawn in. Although the group's initial aim had been to supplement the poor rations provided to the internees by working through the food controller and Salleh, the latter also became a conduit for messages passing between Taylor and Governor Robert Smith. Others involved in maintaining lines of communication with the Governor were Richard Low, who worked as a dresser (a nursing assistant) in the hospital, Koram and Ojagar Singh. It was this close-knit network, which was now responsible for sending the food, drugs, money and other necessities to Berhala.

Throughout all this, Dr Taylor, who had taken on the role of chairman of the assistance group, carried on as usual, checking on the health of inmates in the gaol and attending to his various hospital patients, only one of whom, apart from the occasional Berhala internee, was European. She was the mother of civil servant Mr Gray, and she was terminally ill. When she eventually died, Jim Taylor conducted the funeral service, as all the English-speaking priests were interned.

In November, four more civilians also went into custody – Mr James Smart Abernethy, his wife Winifred and their very small daughters Fenella and Fiona, who had been hiding in the jungle for months. On the outbreak of war, Mr Abernethy (who had held the post of Legal Adviser to the Commissioner of Lands and Protector of Labour from 1937) had been appointed Food Controller for all of North Borneo. However, his wife and the girls were staying at the Stookes' farm at Bilit and, rather than go into captivity, the entire family had fled by boat to Pitagan, further up the Kinabatangan River, where they created a jungle hide-out. However, as they were not self-sufficient they were reliant on the nearest native store for basic commodities. With the Japanese offering a bounty for 'escapees', they were betrayed by 'an Arab' by the name of Murana, one of a growing band of informants and most likely an employee of Borneo Shokusan Kaisha, which had a hemp estate at Bilit, opposite the Stookes' farm.

When Taylor finally discharged Agnes Keith from hospital in December, she left with far more than her health restored. Sewn in to the hem of her slacks was $350 in occupation money, with another $325 concealed in a pouch attached to the inside of the waist band, or sandwiched between two brassieres that she had stitched together. In her suitcase were 4.5 kilograms of sugar, two tins of butter and two tins of powdered milk, bundled up inside her clothing.

To try and smuggle this contraband past the guards and into the camp was going to be hazardous enough, but it was nothing compared to the other risk she was taking. Secreted inside George's toy panda bear was a document which, if discovered, would cause her a great deal of trouble, possibly death. It was a letter, addressed to Major Rice-Oxley. The sender was Captain Lionel Matthews, an Australian prisoner of war.

Chapter 4

Dangerous liaisons

Isolated at their camp on Berhala, the internees were unaware for some time that Australian prisoners had arrived at Sandakan. Following Singapore's unconditional surrender on 15 February 1942, all Allied troops there had been placed behind barbed wire, jammed into barracks at Changi previously occupied by the British garrison. Overwhelmed by the tens of thousands of POWs whom they now had to feed and accommodate, the Japanese decided to make use of their labour. Some were sent to sub-camps around the city to clear away bomb damage or to load tonnes of commodities from warehouses along the wharves onto ships bound for Japan. Others were sent further afield.

On 4 July, the Japanese announced that 2,000 Australians were needed for an overseas draft in three days' time. The announcement was not unexpected, as a force of 3,000 Australian and British prisoners had already been transferred in May 'somewhere up north'. There was no trouble filling that quota. The Japanese had painted such a rosy picture of life in the new camp that there were plenty of volunteers.

Mindful that a time might come when it could be possible to stage a revolt, the senior officers had compiled this draft, known as A Force, with great care. By ensuring they had a balanced command structure and a good mix of combat troops, they were able to form a mini-brigade with three 'battalions' (A, B and C), a headquarters team, and a commanding officer. Should the opportunity arise, it was hoped that the men chosen would be able to form a composite fighting unit.

However, by the time orders were issued to draft another force, various sub-camps had reduced the number of Australians at the main Changi camp from 15,000 to 3,800. This included all hospital and administrative staff, the sick, the convalescing, those on light duties and the less-well disciplined, along with a large number of officers, who were not required to work. When the Japanese realised that the target of 2,000 could not be reached, the quota was reduced to 1,500. Since they also insisted that the prisoners were going to a 'rest' camp with plenty of nourishing food, more than enough medical supplies, and only light duties, the convalescents and officers were encouraged to go. To take care of the sick, many ambulance men also volunteered.

There were also a number of 'non-volunteers' – troublemakers whose names had been added by senior camp staff, anxious to be rid of them.

Although this group, known as B Force, was divided into D, E and F battalions, its ability to function as a fighting unit was questionable. Only forty per cent of the men were from combat units and, while many of the infantry soldiers selected were young, there was a large number of 'old men' (anyone over the age of 35), mostly drawn from non-combatant units. The number of officers was also disproportionately large: 143, or one for every ten men. While many officers were not frontline troops, there were some battle-hardened soldiers among them, including Captain Ken Mosher, a stern disciplinarian but a good commander who had the respect of his men. Also with the officers were Captain Lionel Matthews, a signaller whose bravery in battle had earned him a Military Cross; his brilliant young colleague, wireless expert Lieutenant Roderick Wells; and Lieutenant Norman Sligo, the group's intelligence officer. New Zealand-born Sligo, who was originally a dentist in country NSW, had moved to Malaya pre-war, where his occupation was described as a 'river boat captain'. However, it is far more likely that he was an undercover agent, working for British intelligence. At the outbreak of war with Japan, he was given a commission in the Royal Naval Reserve, a common 'cover' to protect secret agents in the event of being taken prisoner. However, just as B Force was about to depart Sligo was 'transferred' to the Royal Australian Navy on the direct command of the most senior Allied officer, Lieutenant-General Percival, British Army, who sanctioned his move to Sandakan as the B Force intelligence officer.

At the other end of the scale from Matthews, Wells and Sligo was 18-year-old Eric Davis. Although he had taken part in the battle for Singapore, he had not been sent to Sandakan because of his fighting qualities. Discovering that his working party was to help construct a shrine to honour Japanese war dead, he had decided not to report for work – an action that saw him sent back to the main camp as punishment. As he was still there when orders were received to form B Force, he found himself on the list.

There had been no announcement as to where they were going, but the current rumour was that it was a place in Borneo called Sandakan. No one knew where it was, but one of the younger soldiers thought that, since Borneo was closer to Australia (only fifteen centimetres away on his map), he might have a better chance of escaping.

On 8 July, confident that a brighter future awaited them, the Australians formed ranks before dawn to march to the docks, twenty-five kilometres away. Most had not seen the city since the surrender, and it was a sobering experience. Although the prisoners had heard rumours of terrible atrocities perpetrated against the local people, they were unprepared for the sight of scores of freshly severed heads, rammed on sharp metal stakes at intervals along the streets, and displayed on tables either side of the Anderson Bridge spanning the Singapore River.

All had been hoping to board a hospital ship so, when they saw that their transport was *Yubi Maru*, a rusting tramp-steamer of about 2000–3000 tonnes, their hearts plummeted. Morale dropped even more when they were herded down vertical iron ladders to their accommodation in three cargo holds, one of which was covered in coal dust fifteen centimetres deep. There were no portholes.

It took ten hideous days to reach Sandakan. Dysentery broke out, there was very little water, hardly any ventilation, the sanitation facilities were crude 'over the side' platforms, and food consisted of unwashed, heavily limed rice. Finally, just as dawn was breaking on 17 July, *Yubi Maru* rounded the huge red cliffs of Berhala Island. As the ship made her way slowly towards the government wharf, the prisoners on decks looked at the town with disbelief. With its palm trees and bougainvillea a perfect foil for neat white bungalows nestling among the dark green foliage, and fishing boats tied up along the waterfront, Sandakan looked like something out of a romantic South-Seas film. For a fleeting moment Lieutenant Rod Wells fantasised that he had reached paradise; a place where there was peace, tranquillity and no Japanese. Then he saw the flags – blood-red suns upon white, fluttering from every official building in town.

It was not until late afternoon that an order was given for the prisoners in the first and centre holds to disembark. Those remaining in the small third hold were to sleep on board or on the nearby padang. As the men filed down the gangplank, their feet and legs were sprayed with phenyl, a common toilet disinfectant which, according to the Japanese, would cure the dysentery that had broken out. Once on the wharf the prisoners were counted and recounted under the watchful eye of Lieutenant Hoshijima Susumi, a tall, quite handsome, but arrogant-looking officer, who had just been appointed as camp commandant. As soon as Hoshijima was satisfied that the head count was correct, the prisoners were escorted under guard to the padang.

The local residents, informed of the prisoners' arrival in advance, had turned out in force to take a look, but not too close a look. After ten days at sea with no washing facilities, the heat, humidity and dysentery had combined with the pungent smell of the phenyl to create a powerful stench. Those who welcomed the Japanese as liberators

from imperial colonialism waved their red and white flags dutifully and looked smugly satisfied at seeing the white tuans humbled, but others, especially the Chinese, were visibly distressed.

Hoshijima had issued strict orders prohibiting any contact with the locals, but some of the POWs were able to edge their way to the side of the padang where they exchanged a few words with some of the braver spectators. Before the guards put an end to the fraternisation, the Australians, using a mixture of broken Malay and English, revealed that they had come from Singapore. This news came as a surprise to the onlookers, who had been told by the Japanese that the prisoners were from Japanese-occupied Australia.

The POWs had only just lined up to receive their evening meal of putrid, limed rice when a rain squall moved in from the sea. As no one had been able to wash since leaving Singapore, some stripped off their filthy clothing and rubbed the worst of the grime from their bodies, much to the amusement of the local people, who were not accustomed to seeing orang puteh (white people) behave in such a fashion. After eating their meagre meal, the prisoners were formed into groups of 44 and marched up Church Road, the winding track leading to Elton Hill.

Among the sick and lame bringing up the rear was Sergeant Walter Wallace, who was hobbling along with the help of a stick as he was recovering form a recent appendix operation. These stragglers were accompanied by a small, plump guard. Realising from the guard's attempts to converse that he was trying to be friendly, Wallace made signs that he was thirsty. While the guard obligingly waited outside, Wallace went into a nearby house. When he re-emerged he had valuable

Bungalows in Sandakan town, before the war (Photo: Kwan Yau Moi)

Walter Wallace

information about the countryside and local conditions stored in his head, and a map of Borneo and Sandakan hidden in his pocket.

By the time the bulk of the men reached St Michael's at the top of the hill, it was dark. Using the light cast by hurricane lamps hanging from the stone walls of the church, the men found a place to sleep. The more fortunate stretched out along the heavy wooden pews; others were in the organ loft, vestry, around the altar, curled up inside the pulpit, in the aisles or in the open arcades running along each side of the nave. Most of the officers bedded down on the floor of the school hall, next door.

They were all woken next morning at about four o'clock, counted and recounted, and marched back to the padang where breakfast was distributed. Although hungry, they had to force themselves to eat what was on offer – the previous night's leftovers. Since they were about to undertake a thirteen-kilometre march to their new camp at Mile 8, Dr Yamamoto Koji, the medical officer responsible for POWs in Sandakan (possibly the same Dr K Yamamoto who had given money to the Spitfire Fund), ordered about twenty of the sick to wait for a truck to transport them and the heavier baggage. Despite the early hour, nearby residents, alerted by the noise of 1,500 men assembled on the padang, emerged from their homes to see what the commotion was about. Most looked on admiringly as the prisoners, hoisting whatever they could carry to their shoulders, straightened their backs and marched off, the strong supporting the weak, to the rousing strains of a much-loved Australian folk song, 'Waltzing Matilda'.

The all-weather route they were following (at that time named Beatrice Road) wound to the top of the escarpment, where roads branched to the hospital on the left and, on the right, to Government House and to the home of Harry and Agnes Keith, recently appropriated by Hoshijima, along with Harry's large Buick sedan. At this point the main road (named North, then Kebun Cina and then Labuk Road) continued down the hill, past a large government bungalow now occupied by senior kempeitai. On reaching Mile 3, the prisoners were allowed to have a short rest and a smoke. They were pleased to stop for a while. Although all had started out well enough, most found the going difficult. The first part of the route passed through fern-banked cuttings with trees forming a canopy overhead. However, by the time they reached more open country the sun was high in the sky and the men, after days at sea sustained only by a minimum rice ration, exhausted. As the pace slackened the guards moved in on the stragglers, beating them with sticks and rifle butts and chasing away local people trying to hand out food and water. One prisoner, who stepped off the road to take some fruit being offered, found himself being shot at.

On reaching Mile 8 where Sergeant Abin, a Dusun policeman who was in charge of the police post, lived with his wife Bintang binte Udung, the column turned off to the right to follow a dusty vehicular track cutting through the Experimental Farm. About 400 metres from the turn-off, at the foot of a small hill, were the power plant and boiler house, where a galvanised-iron pipe ran from an orange-coloured steel tank to larger concrete storage tanks on the crest of the hill, about 100 metres away. Another pipe snaked away in the direction of the nearby Sibuga River. To the left of the tanks was a small cottage belonging to the farm, while on the right there was a grove of mature palms. Although the farm's purpose was to grow experimental trees and crops, much of the land was under vegetable cultivation as part of a food-growing programme, instituted by Harry Keith in December 1941. This had since been greatly expanded by the Japanese, who had also introduced pigs and cattle.

From the boiler house the track swept around to the right, skirting a swamp; previously an elephant watering hole and now a buffalo

Sketch of the Mile 8 Camp, Australian B Force Compound

The Big tree, B Force Compound

Model of the B Force Camp, showing The Big Tree and huts

wallow. On reaching a multi-strand, barbed-wire fence, the road turned sharply to the left, following the fence line to the top of the hill and two large gates. Hanging in the centre of one of the gates was a wooden sign, identifying the site as 'No 1 Prisoner of War Camp, British North Borneo' and advising that the POW Administrative Headquarters were in Kuching.

There was no mistaking that the two-hectare site, completely encircled by two runs of barbed-wire fencing, had been laid out according to British military regulations. The area was small and the terrain irregular, yet the layout was orderly and use of the available space efficient. On the crest of the hill, parallel to the fence and on either side of the gate, were three neat rows of atap-roofed wooden huts and a few other assorted buildings, all supported on stout wooden piles. The six huts on the right, and another six on the left, measured roughly 13 metres by 6 metres and had been constructed from milled hardwood planks. Each was split into three distinct rooms, which opened onto a covered verandah. The window openings were fitted with strong wooden shutters. Nearby was a small louvered weather-station and a huge Mengaris tree, about seventy metres tall and looking decidedly the worse for wear from repeated lightning strikes.

This was the original barrack area, constructed before the outbreak of war with Japan. Running at right angles, and down the slope, were the huts erected to take the overflow of Japanese arrested by Bert Walker and his men. This new wing occupied part of an area set aside for the farm's water buffalo, including a swampy area at the foot of the hill. It was obvious that the newer buildings had been put up in a great hurry. Unlike the strong hardwood supports used for the other barracks, these twenty-four huts, fashioned completely from atap, were perched on stilts made from the trunks of rubber trees. The internal framework was of roughly hewn poles while the atap used for the walls and roof had been made in such haste that the nipah palm had not been properly dried. It had now shrunk and there were gaping holes everywhere, letting in rats, snakes and the rain.

The entire compound was in a filthy state as no attempt had been made to clean up after the previous occupants. The split bamboo sleeping platforms were infested with bed bugs, and cockroaches scuttled off into every corner. The well-constructed communal latrines had been fitted with removable pans, but as these had not been emptied they were swarming with maggots and overflowing.

The area beyond the accommodation area had been cleared, apart from a small patch of rubber, and three or four larger trees. Some distance away, to the right of the compound and occupying part of a low ridge, was a small timber house. It was the home of 43-year-old Mr (Joseph) Wong Yun Siew, one of Harry Keith's employees, and his wife and daughter. At the time of the Japanese occupation, Joseph Wong, who spoke Chinese, Malay and English, held the post of Officer in Charge of the Agricultural Research Station, also at Mile 8. However, as Japan's priority was food production, not research, he was now appointed to oversee the Experimental Farm.

On the other side of the compound, down on the flat and just outside the wire, was a cow shed and a small piggery, while a kilometre or two beyond the Wongs' house a large area had been cleared of all timber and undergrowth. This was the site of the airstrip that the British had proposed and which the Japanese now intended to implement, using forced labour provided by the unsuspecting prisoners of war and 4,000 Javanese civilians, who had not yet arrived. Since Hoshijima, the engineer in charge of construction, was not ready to start work on the airstrip, the Australians spent their time trying to make the camp habitable. The Japanese, who were fairly relaxed, left them in relative peace. With no large movements of prisoners in or out of camp, the inexperienced guards, who were rotated from the town garrison on a daily basis, were satisfied to stroll along the outer perimeter. For those looking for a chance to escape, the temptation was too great. On 31 July, just twelve days after they arrived at the Mile 8 Camp, eleven prisoners went under the wire.

The first six went in two groups: one with two men, and the other of four. While the third party would manage to stay at large for more than five months, the others were not as lucky, even though their unit's Warrant Officer Bill Sticpewich had provided them with some rations, anti-malarial drugs and a compass. Taking advantage of a severe storm, and with Sticpewich and their senior officer promising to cover for them at the 9.30 pm roll call, Herb Trackson and Matt Carr departed first, followed by Drivers Shelley, Allen, Jacka and Harrington. Although the general consensus was that their chance of success was not good, none of the men was prevented from leaving.

When the Japanese finally realised that prisoners were missing, the repercussions were less than expected: lining up in the broiling sun for an extended period while everyone was counted and recounted; enduring a pep talk on their responsibilities from Ozawa, Hoshijima's Formosan interpreter; and no fish, vegetables or smoking for a week. In addition, no one was allowed outside the camp for the rest of the day to gather wood and, in an attempt to smarten up security, all prisoners were issued with a POW number stamped on a piece of cloth, which they were required to attach to their hats.

Meanwhile, the six escapees were well away from the camp. While Trackson and Carr headed towards Sandakan, the other four moved roughly north-west across fairly open ground and plantations for about five kilometres, where they hit the Sungei Batang Road, linking Mile 11 to the Manila River. Bert Walker's rubber estate, now being managed by his assistant Mr Maw, lay on the far side, and small-holdings owned by local people bordered the other. Having no idea of which way to go, or what to do, the escapees hid in an abandoned timber-cutters' hut in the jungle, until hunger forced them to seek help from Chu Li Tsia, a Chinese farmer, at around 7 pm one night. His house was a good fourteen kilometres from the road junction, so Chu was surprised to see anyone at that hour, let alone four hungry white men dressed in military uniforms. He supplied them with food for the next three days, when they decided to move back towards Sandakan.

Gabriela Lai, who assisted the escapees

It was not long before they ran out of food. Fortunately, they were found by seventeen-year-old Peter Raymond Lai (also known as Lai Kui Fook), a member of the underground. Left motherless at the age of six, Peter and his brothers had come to Sandakan from their hometown of Papar to attend boarding school at St Mary's. Apart from the Japanese occupation, Peter's year had been most eventful – he had left school, obtained a job as a dresser (nursing assistant) at the hospital with Dr Taylor and, despite misgivings from both families, married Gabriela Lobos, a beautiful Spanish/Filipino girl.

With the prisoners in dire need of food and shelter, Peter took them home where Gabriela, once she recovered from the initial shock, helped her husband provide them with food, clothing and medical care. They were keen to reach the Philippines. Apparently acting on information given to them by Peter, they set off for Leila Lodge, unaware that they were about to place in jeopardy the entire underground organisation, whose subversive activities now incorporated the Mile 8 Camp.

The Australians had become involved in the underground a few days after their arrival, when Hoshijima agreed to a request from the senior Australian officer, Colonel Walsh, to allow officers to work in the vegetable gardens outside the wire. It was not considered necessary to send a guard with them, so the prisoners went unescorted. Taking advantage of the situation, Dick Majinal, a Malay, had told Matthews about Dr Taylor, the assistance group and the internees on Berhala. Lieutenant Sligo, as intelligence officer, accepted Majinal's offer to establish a link to Sergeant Abin at the nearby police post and, through him, to Taylor and the Governor.

With one of the prisoners in extreme pain with a stomach ulcer, others suffering from dysentery and with more cases expected, Colonel E Shepherd, the senior Australian medical officer, was very anxious to meet Taylor in order to secure a supply of drugs, especially morphine. On the pretext of needing to borrow a stethoscope from the hospital, Shepherd pleaded his case before Hoshijima, stating that the B Force medical officers had been assured in Singapore that everything would be provided in the new camp. Hoshijima agreed to Shepherd's request, unaware that the sceptical Australians had brought basic medical supplies with them. He also agreed to allow Sligo, the recently appointed 'canteen officer' (his latest undercover role), to walk the thirteen kilometres into town with the Colonel, so that he could arrange the purchase of goods from Goto Sang, a Japanese shopkeeper, using funds which the Japanese had advanced for that purpose. Arriving in Sandakan, they went straight to the hospital where Taylor promised to send whatever drugs he could, and to also try and organise supplies of morphine through Mr Patel, the pharmacist at the Sandakan Dispensary. He also made a further undertaking to ask the local administration to allow him to supply the camp with basic drugs (particularly quinine, used in the treatment of malaria) from the huge amounts that were stockpiled – enough to treat all of North Borneo for the next two years. Before he left, Shepherd handed over a letter from Matthews formally requesting medical supplies. This appears to have been a rather naive move, as he was only supposed to be borrowing a stethoscope. The note was passed in full view of the guard, who reported the incident to Hoshijima. However, apart from delaying the establishment of the canteen for two weeks, the commandant took no further action and, with the guards not bothering to accompany the vegetable or wood-collecting parties, Sligo was able to explore the possibility of making further outside contacts. He was still working on this when the eleven men escaped.

The day before the escape, while the medical staff were waiting for drugs to arrive, Lance-Corporal Frank Armstrong, the soldier suffering with the ulcer, died. There was no cemetery at the camp, so his body was transported to the Sandakan Civil Cemetery, near the hospital, for burial. Dr Frank Mills, one of the Australian medical officers, accompanied the burial detail. A Japanese sergeant escorting the group, who claimed to be a medical student, had some rudimentary medical knowledge – enough to be dangerous. He understood that certain drugs could alleviate pain, but not enough to know the correct dosage. When Mills told him that one of the prisoners was in great pain, he agreed to allow the Australian to buy some morphine from the pharmacy recommended by Taylor, provided it was only 'one dose'. In a loud voice, Mills asked Mr Patel for 'one dose of morphine – about half an ounce' (fourteen grams). When the pharmacist handed over the requested amount, enough for at least 500 doses, he refused to accept any payment.

Patel, who was Indian, was pro-British, but many of the Malays and a good number of Indians, who supported the Indian Independence Movement, were not. Had the four escapees heading for Mr Phillips' house informed Sligo that they intended to make a break, they would have had a better idea of the degree of caution necessary when moving about inhabited areas. Unfortunately, although the men found Leila Lodge without any trouble, Phillips knew that an informant had seen them enter his house. His unexpected visitors placed him in a most difficult situation, especially since the kempeitai's interrogation centre was directly across the road, in the Bakau and Kenya Extract Company's spacious bungalow, formerly the residence of Sandy Young. Phillips knew the consequences, once the Japanese learned that he was harbouring escaped prisoners: he would be arrested and interrogated by the kempeitai, whose methods of extracting information were extremely effective. One little slip of the tongue and the entire underground network could be lost. Faced with the agonising choice of turning in the men himself, or waiting until the kempeitai came to call, Phillips took the only option open. On 8 August, a day that the Chinese considered to be extremely lucky, the four Australians found themselves in gaol.

Seventeen days later, on 25 August, Herb Trackson and Matt Carr joined them. Unlike the other four, they had been quite well-prepared, carrying ground sheets, knifes, matches, cooked rice and some rice cakes in small haversacks. Leaving their hut at the height of the storm, they had made their way across the buffalo swamp and then under the wire. On the far side of a patch of jungle they found a pipeline, which they followed. As it was the camp water supply line, it led them back towards the Experimental Farm, where they helped themselves to a few ears of corn and some tapioca tubers before crossing the Labuk Road. From here they made their way through secondary jungle and a rubber plantation to Trig Hill, just above the town. A reconnaissance soon revealed they should move further west, so they began their descent well beyond the town limits. Apart from one woman who gave them some rice and asked a boy to show them the best way down, the Chinese they met were too frightened to offer assistance. After scouring the shoreline for two days without success, they finally found a canoe stowed under a house. As soon as night fell, they paddled across the harbour to Pulau Bai and fell into an exhausted sleep among the mangroves. They awoke late next morning to discover their canoe was gone. After finding a replacement, they made their way along the web of waterways near Tanjong Aru to the sea. However, they were unable to handle the flimsy craft in the open water and abandoned it.

After walking south along the sandy beaches for some days, feasting on crabs and fish stolen from traps, and coconuts and vegetables foraged from native gardens, they met a group of Chinese salt-makers who told them that a reward was being offered for their capture. The Chinese suggested they go to Tawi Tawi with the next salt boat, due to arrive from the Philippines at any time, but when it turned up the Australians didn't like the look of the crew and decided to keep on walking. Several days later, near the mouth of the Kinabatangan, both men were both stricken with malaria. A Malay took them to a hut, promising to bring them food, but he brought Japanese troops instead. Handcuffed and placed under arrest, the fugitives were put in a boat and taken back to Sandakan, where they spent three days in gaol before being transferred with the other four to Kuching, to face trial.

Accompanying them were their unit's two most senior officers, who were held responsible for the escape: the absconders had stated that their officers had told them, quite correctly, that it was the duty of every prisoner of war to try and escape. Fortunately, after another bout of interrogation by the kempeitai and a short spell in Kuching Gaol, the officers, accused of inciting prisoners to escape, were sent to the main POW Camp at Batu Lintang Barracks, about seven kilometres from town. The other six, brought before the court on 25 October, were found guilty of trying to escape and were sent to Singapore's Outram Road Military Prison to serve their sentences. The escape attempts had little effect on the rest of the camp, apart from a slight tightening of security and a farcical attempt to have the prisoners sign a 'no escape agreement', or 'oath', which interpreter Ozawa referred to constantly as 'ze oase'.

While Trackson, Carr and the others had been on the run and in the Sandakan Gaol, the activities of the underground had expanded. In mid-August, another of the Australian doctors, Captain Don Picone, obtained permission to collect palm oil seeds as he wanted to extract the oil to counter eyesight problems in some of the men caused by vitamin A deficiency. Lionel Matthews nominated himself and three lieutenants for the task. The nearest oil palm grove was on a rubber estate that backed onto the Experimental Farm, just to the east of the police post. Here Matthews met Matusup bin Gungau, a former government vaccinator in Taylor's medical department, who now worked as a watchman/ cow herder at the Experimental Farm. He introduced Matthews to Abin, who agreed to carry letters to Dr Taylor and Governor Smith when he went into town to deliver his weekly police report. To facilitate the process, a 'post box' was established in a large tree. Using the new postal service, a letter was sent to the Governor and another to Dr Taylor, asking for supplies of vitamin B to help ward off beriberi. As Matthews also belonged to the gardening party, which collected dung from the cow shed for fertiliser, he and Matusup had no trouble meeting.

The seed-gathering lasted only two weeks, but in that short space of time many new contacts were made. The post-box was on a property owned by John Simon Funk, a retired magistrate and father of Johnny and Alex, the Volunteer who had failed to surrender his weapons. The Funk family had a long and loyal association with the Chartered Company and was highly respected in the Sandakan community. John Simon, born in Hong Kong in 1886, was just one year old when his family arrived in Kudat as political refugees. His father was born in China as Hung Yung Meng, but the missionaries in Kudat gave him a new name, Thomas Paul Funk. Thomas, who is thought to have been related to a revolutionary leader, the great Hung Xiuquan (Hung Hsiu Tsuen, known as 'Heavenly King of the Tai-Ping Tien Kuo'), was a distinguished scholar and had served as a magistrate in Hung's revolutionary government.

When John Simon was quite small the family moved to Sandakan. An academically gifted child, he attended St Mary's Mission School, where his father became a teacher. He was educated in both English and Chinese and was fluent in Chinese Hakka, Malay and English. In 1901, at the age of fifteen, he joined the Sandakan Treasury as a learner (clerk). Climbing his way up the bureaucratic ladder, he served in almost every government office in Sandakan, Jesselton and Beaufort until 1925 when, after further study, he became the first non-European to qualify as a First Class Magistrate. Apart from being a

Captain Lionel Matthews

Alex Funk

Johnny and Lillian Funk

Magistrate John Simon Funk, in court

well-known horse trainer and jockey, a brilliant billiards player and a member of the Recreation Club, John Simon excelled in middle distance running, was captain of the Sandakan soccer team and played cricket.

The Funks' palatial eleven-room town house, filled with beautiful furniture and furnishings, had been taken over by the Japanese, but on their rubber estate, where Lillian Funk had retreated when the Japanese arrived, there was another fine bungalow. John, a widower, was married to a Eurasian woman: Helen, the daughter of New Zealander and Company man, Ernest Pavitt, and Kwai, the beautiful daughter of the Kadazandusun headman. Although the relationship had lasted a scant two years, Pavitt had paid for the education of his two children, who attended boarding school at St Mary's, in Sandakan, where he had coal mining interests. However, in 1918, disenchanted with their father's overall lack of parental attention, Helen and her brother Jules changed their name to Stephens. On his retirement in 1923, Pavitt moved to Tasmania.

A gracious hostess who enjoyed her superior position in the Sandakan social scene, Helen entertained lavishly at both her homes and was accustomed to the good things in life, as were all the members of the family. Between them, the couple raised ten children: five from John's first marriage to Agnes Wise, four from the second, and an adopted daughter. After completing school at St Mary's, three of the boys, Johnny (John Simon Junior) and Paddy (Patrick), with their younger half-brother Alex, had all undertaken further education in Singapore before joining the Public Works Department. Johnny, his previous resignation now null and void, had been rehired by the Japanese, so all three were once again working for the PWD.

Through Alex, who had married Maggie (Magdelene) Neubronner, a granddaughter of Pedro Dominic, the Funks were also connected to the large Dominic clan and to Ernesto Lagan, who had married Maggie's sister, Katherine. Paddy, like his two brothers, was a family man. When Johnny, hailed as Sandakan's most eligible bachelor, had married Lillian, the stunningly beautiful daughter of an independently wealthy Suluk princess and a handsome American, the Nuptial Mass at St Mary's Church, and the reception that followed, rivalled the wedding celebrations of Alice and Bert Walker. As the Japanese were now occupying their house, Johnny and Lillian lived with their close friends, Val and Dora Stookes, on the farm at Bilit. The arrangement worked well. Lillian, who had worked as a nurse for Stookes, could assist in this capacity at weekends, while Johnny commuted with him in the plane to Sandakan. Once in the air, the pair took every opportunity to spy on the Japanese.

It was at the jungle post-box that Matthews renewed his acquaintance with Alex, whom he had previously met via Matusup at the cowshed. When Matthews asked for assistance in obtaining medicine and food, Alex recruited Johnny, known locally as Jonil, who was only too eager to help. During the meeting, Matthews learned that members of the Chinese community were in contact with a Filipino guerrilla unit operating in the Sulus under the auspices of the United States Forces in the Philippines (USFIP) and under the command of Lieutenant-Colonel Alejandro Suarez, son-in-law of the Sultan. He also learned that Lillian Funk's father was Guy Strattan, an American army officer and veteran of the Spanish-American war, who was Deputy Governor of the Sulu Archipelago. In January that year, on the direct orders of the United States President, Strattan had been given the task of welding various factions in the southern Philippines into a cohesive fighting force. Consequently, he was closely allied to Suarez. Since many members of the Funk family, one way or another, were involved in the underground network, Lillian's American and Filipino connections made her a vital link in the chain connecting Sandakan to Tawi Tawi.

Her husband was also an invaluable member of the organisation. Johnny had trained as a civil engineer but, as he was not European, his qualifications were not recognised by the British who classified him as a 'technical assistant' or foreman – part of the reason for the pay dispute. His job working under the Japanese administration allowed him to move about freely, 'inspecting' roads, bridges and water works and providing excellent cover for his clandestine activities. Disguised as coolies, he and Alex were able to meet Matthews on a regular basis. During one of these meetings, Alex gave Matthews his .38 pistol and ammunition, and told him that he had a .303 rifle and ammunition buried at the farm.

As Matthews was contemplating escape, Alex also handed over a fountain pen, which was as good as hard currency when it came to trading, and some forestry survey maps and information about inland tracks supplied by Filipino-born Lamberto Apostol. Aged in his thirties and an ex-forestry employee, Apostol was now supervising agricultural production on the Experimental Farm. He had learned about the underground when Abin, who was unable to read English and could not decipher Matthews' notes, had asked Apostol to help him. The seed-collecting party had no trouble getting Alex Funk's gifts back into camp: Matthews' fellow officer, Lieutenant Rus Ewin, slipped the pen into the fly of his shorts, while Matthews, blessed with nerves of steel, simply walked back through the gate with the pistol in his haversack, hidden under the oil-palm seeds.

On 31 August, Lieutenant Sligo, who had been stricken with dysentery, died. Dr Taylor, who now made it his business to attend every funeral, slipped money and drugs to Padre Albert Thompson, who was accompanying the burial party. With four men now dead, Dr Shepherd was particularly anxious to receive the medical supplies that the Japanese had promised but, despite Taylor's best efforts, none had arrived. The response from the civil administration was that any application concerning POWs must come through Hoshijima, who in turn assured Dr Taylor that the supplies would be flown in. Fortunately, since none would ever appear, Taylor came to the rescue himself. The Japanese had made a full inventory of the hospital's drugs which the doctors were authorised to dispense and sell to patients. Unable to simply take what was wanted without the loss being noticed, Taylor, Stookes and Wands, along with Dr Liu Tse Shia, a Chinese colleague, entered fake sales in the register for the drugs, which Taylor then paid for, out of his own pocket.

The precious bundles were then smuggled to the camp by hospital workers Richard Low and Peter Lai, who peddled out to the camp on his bicycle, where, with Matusup's help, he left the parcels in bushes near the wire for retrieval by the prisoners. No opportunity to deliver supplies of food and medicine was missed. Jenny bin Sarudin and Dr Stookes' nurse Phoebe Lai, who had no idea that her boss was involved in the underground, slipped medicines and food to the prisoners sent on occasional working parties to Mr Phillips' sawmill. Dr Liu's wife, Mabel, was also lending her assistance by donating large sums of money to the Berhala internees and the POWs, as were Lo Hoi Tshi, manager of a gambling syndicate; leading businessmen Lau Bui Ching; Wong Wei Ming, a former Volunteer and manager of the King's Theatre; and Kwan Ming Ming and Kwan Choo Ming. Chan Tian Joo was the treasurer of the fund, which would continue to be supported by many people, ranging from the most affluent to the poorest coolies, who gave what money they could spare.

Following Sligo's death, Matthews took over as intelligence officer and appointed Rod Wells as his deputy. With little to fill in his time, other than gardening, and with the boiler requiring vast amounts of timber to keep the lights blazing all night, Lieutenant Wells had no trouble obtaining permission to form a permanent wood-collecting party. As was the case with the gardening and seed-gathering teams, the wood party was not under guard, enabling Wells to forge close contacts with Chan Ah Ping, a middle-aged engineer detained with Ng Ho Kong to keep the Sandakan Power and Light Company running and now in charge of the Mile 8 power plant.

Believing that Chan Ah Ping might be able to help secure enough parts to make a radio, Wells received permission to stay with the wood party on a permanent basis. The young lieutenant soon learned that Ah Ping was a close friend of Joseph Wong, who was a good friend of Dick Majinal, Matthews' contact. Wong, whom the younger prisoners called 'Pop' because of his 'advanced' age of 43, also knew Matthews, whom he had met at the cow shed on one of the dung-collecting visits. When Wong, who had a stockpile of salt for the cattle, discovered that the POWs were suffering from salt depletion, he gave a sack to Matthews, who smuggled it into camp under the pile of dung.

Shortly after the prisoners arrived at the camp, Hoshijima had issued orders for all prisoners to assemble beneath the *Mengaris* tree which the Australians, not knowing what species it was, simply called The Big Tree. Although Hoshijima had a good command of English, he insisted on speaking through Ozawa, even though his own English was superior and he interrupted constantly to improve on the translation. After reminding them that they were all prisoners of the Japanese, the commandant launched into a long-winded speech extolling the wonders and benefits of the Japanese Co-Prosperity Sphere. After winding up his oration with the prediction that 'Japan will be victorious even if it takes one hundred years', he dropped a bombshell. Sandakan was no rest camp. The prisoners were to build an aerodrome.

Lieutenant Boundy, an Australian engineer, went out to inspect the site. Worried that they might be forced to work on a project which was intended for military use, the prisoners were relieved when they heard Boundy's verdict: even if they worked for ten years, the airfield would never be finished. Reassured, some of the prisoners began road construction to the site, confident that the war would be long over before the aerodrome was even started. The work was not too hard, the guards kept a low profile and there was no shortage of food: 750 grams of rice, per man per day, for anyone engaged in manual labour, and 550 grams for the others.

August came and went. At the beginning of September, just as the camp's inmates were beginning to think that Sandakan might not be such a bad place after all, Hoshijima, recently promoted to Captain, ordered everyone on parade. Mounted on a small dais, and once again using his interpreter, he declared:

> *You have been brought here to Sandakan to have the honour to build for the Japanese Forces an aerodrome, For this you will be paid ten cents a day. You will work. You will build this aerodrome if it takes three years.*

His announcement certainly shattered any hopes that work would not start on the airstrip but, as the Australians were certain the war could not possibly last three years, ripples of laughter ran along the ranks. Hoshijima became so enraged that, forgetting he had an interpreter, he bellowed out angrily, 'I tell you. I have the power of life and death over you. You will build this aerodrome if you stay here until your bones rot under the Borneo sun.'

He meant what he said. An aerodrome would be built and the prisoners, along with the Javanese coolies already at work, plus a large number of local people (including all government employees and Volunteers not already engaged in an essential service) would provide the necessary labour. Their first task was to clear the entire area. The trees had long gone, but the stumps had not, and scrubby undergrowth had sprung up. All of this had to be removed, either with bare hands or with the help of a changkol (hoe) or axe. It was back-breaking labour. Once the vegetation had been cleared away and dumped into depressions as fill, work began on levelling the area by scooping blindingly white earth from the hillocks into small woven baskets and dumping it in hollows. It was not until the Japanese, in an effort to speed up the work, brought in skips, which ran on the BBT's light rail network, that the prisoners had some respite.

With an increase in the speed of construction, Lieutenant Okahara, the tough and usually merciless guard commander, allowed some of the locals to sell or trade food from a roped-off area alongside the aerodrome, during the noon break. One of those who made his way to the trading area, disguised as a cake-seller, was Heng Joo Ming, a young Singaporean Chinese whose house adjoined the airstrip. For the past six weeks he had been supplying food to Rus Ewin who had contacted Heng through his live-in girlfriend, Siti binte Jakariah. Heng had heard that Ewin had been beaten after returning back late to the camp after one of their meetings and was anxious to find out if he had been compromised. To his relief, he learned from Warrant Officer Wallace that Ewin had managed to hide the food and all was well. While chatting, Wallace discovered that Heng, a geologist previously employed by British Petroleum, had been offered a job as mandor, to oversee the coolie labourers. Realising that Heng might be a very good contact, Wallace urged him to accept the post.

Usually, the working parties were composed of the same men, but occasionally prisoners were sent to help with wood gathering, rice collecting or, best of all, gardening at the home of Mr Joseph Wong, where they might catch a glimpse of his beautiful daughter. These excursions away from the camp provided a wonderful opportunity to gather local intelligence for Matthews, whose underground network continued to grow. As there was now a constant stream of messages between the camp, Berhala and the hospital, Matthews and Taylor had adopted the code names of Roslyn and Geebung. Celia Taylor, who also took care of the organisation's clerical work, decoded the more confidential messages sent by Matthews to Taylor and the Governor.

However, even with the skips, work at the aerodrome was not proceeding fast enough for Major Suga, who raised the daily quota of earth to be moved. A four-man 'basher team', under the command of Lieutenant Moritake, was brought in to make sure the target was reached. Any prisoner who failed to meet his quota, stopped to catch his breath, wiped his brow, had a sip of water or leaned momentarily on his changkol, was at their mercy. Armed with heavy pick handles, the bashers, all heavy-set Formosan conscripts, would move in. By way of variation, they attacked groups in rotation, for no apparent reason, and imposed 'group punishment' where prisoners were forced to hit each other, hold heavy rocks above their heads, or stand with arms outstretched, looking directly at the sun. The resolve of anyone whose spine even looked like sagging was stiffened by a hefty whack.

Pleas for clemency were useless. The strip had to be operational for a trial landing by aircraft before Christmas, no matter what. To meet this deadline, more skips were brought in and the sick were forced out, along with a party of more senior officers who were told that rations to the entire camp would be cut unless they were prepared to form a working party. Even Warrant Officer Sticpewich was sent out to work one day. A jack-of-all trades who could fix just about anything, he was not required to work on the airfield as he had made himself indispensable to the Japanese, who allowed him to live in a hut outside the wire. Fifteen Borneo natives, bare-footed and with tattooed necks and pierced body parts, were recruited to act as guards for the increased numbers of workers, but they were quiet and inoffensive and did not cause the POWs any grief.

As the Japanese had decided that drainage was not necessary, no drains had been dug. This was not a problem in the dry season, but as the wet season began the effects of this faulty line of reasoning became evident. The Japanese sent for the only two pieces of

Australian POWs at work on the airstrip and being punished with 'flying practice'. (Drawings by Bill Young)

equipment available to rectify the problem – a fairly new excavator and an ornate, ancient steamroller, both belonging to the PWD. The excavator, a tracked-machine, was making quite good progress digging drains, but after only one day it developed a mechanical problem. It was coaxed to the boiler house, where Lieutenant Wells instructed Sergeant Stevens, one of two POWs detailed to help Ah Ping, to fix it permanently by putting sand in the sump. Not at all anxious for the Japanese to discover this sabotage, the mechanically minded Australian corporal who was sent to 'repair' the excavator kept up the pretence that it was fixable. He spent many pleasant days tinkering with the engine, to no avail. As an extra precaution, at Wells' request sand was also added to the sump of the farm's Fordson tractor. Mr Felix Azcona Senior, a Filipino who owned a radio shop in town, and one or two other members of the underground volunteered to undertake this useful bit of sabotage.

With the 'official opening' looming ever nearer, the Japanese now pinned their hopes on the magnificent, ancient steamroller, which they were certain could 'squeeze' water from a very boggy patch in the middle of the proposed runway. The results were spectacular, but not in the way the Japanese intended. On reaching the boggy area, the heavy, ornate machine slowly sank gracefully into the mire. With all mechanical solutions now exhausted, Suga, who arrived the following day to inspect the progress, issued fresh orders – box drains would be dug, by hand, and the prisoners would not have a single day off until the work was complete.

They didn't. With men now working seven days a week from dawn until dark, more and more reported sick each morning. Some were ill with dysentery, others with malaria, beriberi (vitamin B deficiency), appendicitis, tropical ulcers, severe tinea and nasty skin complaints. As the quota for the working parties had to be filled, doctors and medical orderlies, as well as those suffering with leg ulcers so severe that shinbones were exposed, were forced out, leaving 250 bed-ridden patients to fend for themselves. By mid-November another ten men had died, an amazingly low death toll, considering the hardship being encountered. All were buried in the Sandakan cemetery where Taylor, now the self-appointed 'grave digger', had ample opportunity to hand out coffee and sandwiches to the burial party and pass on much-needed drugs, messages and information. Meanwhile, work continued at the aerodrome at a frantic pace. There was a great incentive to keep going. Hoshijima had dreamed up a new form of punishment – confinement in a small wooden cage, which the guards called 'Esau'.

By some miracle, enough of the strip was completed by the deadline to enable a plane to land on what the Japanese called the 'Yasuo Air Port'. No effort was spared to celebrate the occasion. An enormous archway of jungle vines and brilliantly coloured flowers, put together by the coolies, was erected at the entrance to the airport, with small ones at various intervals. Red and white Japanese flags were handed out with strict instructions for the locals to wave them. The prisoners, like the local people, were forced to attend and were ordered to make themselves presentable – a difficult instruction to obey since few owned any decent clothing or boots, and razor blades were scarce. Looking anything but smart, they lined up along some very well-turned-out fellows: Chinese and Malay coolies, dressed from top to toe in Australian uniforms taken by the Japanese from army supplies in Singapore. To the prisoners' great disappointment, the planes landed safely and the dignitaries alighted. After much bowing, waving of flags and speech making (all in Japanese) the Yasuo Air Port was declared open for business.

The airport was open, but the lines of communication between the camp, hospital and Berhala had been seriously curtailed. Koram, who had been arrested on suspicion of carrying messages for the POWs and gaoled for a fortnight, had been warned that next time he would be shot. With Koram lying low, delivering Matthews' most recent message to the Governor may have been a problem had it not been for Agnes Keith, who was about to be discharged from hospital.

She managed to smuggle all her contraband into Berhala, including the letter inside the toy panda, but there were a few heart-stopping minutes when George, in a tantrum, threw his bear over the wire. Fortunately, it was retrieved by a kindly guard, who tossed it back without a second look, allowing its dangerous contents to be delivered without any further trouble. The bear was an ideal place for hiding forbidden material, but Agnes was worried that if George had a similar tantrum at some other time she might not be so lucky. She solved the problem by telling her son that his panda had an operation and must rest quietly in the suitcase to recover.

While catching up with her friends after her six weeks' absence, Agnes discovered that while she had been away there had been a new and exciting development in the camp. The internees were receiving news from the outside world. The Australian prisoners had a radio.

Chapter 5

Beyond the call

A wireless had indeed been made. Its construction was a remarkable feat, made possible to a great extent by one of the young prisoners, whose high-spirits had often landed him in trouble. Assisting Sergeant Stevens and Chan Ah Ping at the camp power plant was Private Eric Davis, who had scored a much-sought-after job at the boiler house when the camp administration discovered he had worked as a boilerman on the troop ship *Queen Mary* while serving in the Merchant Marine.

All three men lived at the power plant and the Japanese guards took absolutely no notice of Davis going in and out of the compound. However, although they were accustomed to seeing him and Stevens wandering about outside the wire, protected by special symbols inscribed in red on their cloth POW number tags, the conspirators still had to be very careful. The full-time boiler attendant Ali Asar was also a known Japanese collaborator, and the loyalties of Chun Ah Teng, who worked in the engine room during the day, were highly suspect.

With Ah Ping, Stevens and Davis acting as go-betweens, wireless expert Rod Wells had received a crystal detector and a headphone

Private Eric Davis

Lieutenant Rod Wells

from Dick Majinal, which signaller Lieutenant Gordon Weynton used to make a basic crystal set. As it was only able to pick up local stations, Wells asked his contacts to try and locate more sophisticated components with which to build a proper set. Ah Ping did not have access to parts, but he was able to supply diagrams showing the layout of all Sandakan's electrical and telephone lines. However, through Pop Wong, Wells obtained valves from Lamberto Apostol and a telephone receiver from Abin. Due to Pop Wong's efforts, a variable condenser, one of the most difficult parts to locate, was eventually provided by Gerald Mavor, who entrusted delivery to his chief engineer, Ng Ho Kong. Ng and Ng Peng Keong, a former Volunteer, were also helping smuggle food to the internees at Berhala and the POW camp.

Samuel Aruliah, Simon Young, Alex and Johnny Funk, and Mr Phillips also supplied parts. Once they were located, the precious components were passed along the line until they reached the engine-room staff. More often than not, the final link in this chain was Eric Davis, whose job of checking and maintaining the water-inlet valve on the pipe running to the Sibuga River enabled him to meet secretly with Apostol, Pop Wong or some other courier. The parts were smuggled to Wells when Davis made his daily trip into the camp to collect his rations.

However, in October, although Wells was able to make some parts, he realised that unless other vital components could be obtained, he would not be able to build a radio capable of picking up shortwave broadcasts. A breakthrough came a few days later when Heng Joo Ming accepted the job of mandor at the airfield. He was yet to become a member of the underground but, as he had developed a good rapport with Wallace during the lunch-time trading, he agreed to try and obtain a complete radio set or, failing that, enough spare parts to make one. Within a day or two he had broken into a storage shed and stolen a battery-operated set, minus the batteries. After taking it apart, Wallace smuggled it into the camp, bit by bit. However, instead of delivering the parts to a senior officer, Wallace, aware that he now had a highly valuable commodity, sold them for $20 to Corporal Rickards who had brought a large amount of money with him from Singapore. As Rickards could not reassemble the radio himself, he was compelled to confide in another signaller, who informed Matthews. Using these components, and others already collected, Wells and Weynton, with the assistance of one or two other signallers, began work.

The penalty for listening to a radio, let alone owning one, was very severe, so the small band worked in great secrecy, in either Wells' or Matthews' cubicle or in an unoccupied hut. After each working session, the part-assembled set, which was screwed to a wooden base, was wrapped in a waterproof groundsheet and lowered on lengths of wire to the bottom of a disused latrine pit.

By late October, Wells and Weynton, with the help of Corporals Small and Mills, had successfully constructed a 'regenerative receiver', powerful enough to pick up transmissions from England, the United States and Australia. With many of the parts unprocurable, the inventive Wells had made them from scratch. Wire wrapped around a glass bottle created a coil. The grid leak condensers were made from metal foil, paper and coconut oil. The resistors were from string, with the impurities from burnt coconut husks or bark from the cinnamon trees, growing just outside the wire, providing the necessary resistance. Wire stolen from Japanese beehives outside the compound and coated with baked-on coconut oil and flour provided insulated wires, while a pair of chemical cells made from test tubes supplied the valve filament voltage. To remove some of the high voltage hum, a choke coil was made from beehive wire wrapped around a small piece of steel fish plate, stolen from the railway lines at the airfield, and cut into three pieces by Ah Ping, while the filter condenser consisted of an oiled sheet of newspaper, sandwiched between two pieces of foil and rolled together to form a tube, 45 centimetres long. The completed radio was a testament to Wells' ingenuity and determination, and the underground network, whose members had helped make it possible.

However, without sufficient power, the radio was useless. When a determined search for fresh batteries proved fruitless, Wells further demonstrated his inventiveness by making a chemical rectifier, using two medical test tubes, silver foil from the lining of a tea chest in which the rice was delivered, and two common chemicals from the first aid supplies. Using this apparatus, he was able to convert the camp's electricity supply from alternating current (AC) to direct current (DC). The problem of an aerial was soon solved – a length of wire attached to a wire clothesline, strung between the huts.

The next problem was how to obtain sufficient voltage to operate the set. The electricity generated at the power plant was delivered to the huts via raw copper wires strung between bush poles, but by the time it reached the camp it had dropped from the required 110 volts to just 90. Wells needed an output of at least 130. Ah Ping agreed to increase raise the electrical output, provided he could listen to the 'Chungking news', the Chinese overseas equivalent of the BBC. As it was calculated that he would need an extra .25 tonnes of timber each night to stoke up the boiler, the wood party ensured there was an adequate supply. The first attempt was very nerve-wracking. In his eagerness to tune into the Chungking news, Ah Ping raised the voltage so quickly that light globes all over the camp suddenly became very much brighter. The next day, terrified that a repeat performance would alert the Japanese, Wells explained it must be raised very gradually, one volt at a time.

On 4 November, after a great deal of trial and error, Wells and Weynton heard the sounds of London's Big Ben chiming, and an unmistakably English voice announcing 'this is the BBC'. Unfortunately, the programme that followed was on growing hops (a vital ingredient in the brewing of beer) in the county of Kent. The next night when they tuned in, it was in time for the news. The Japanese noticed that the lights became brighter after dark and stayed that way until midnight (by which time the radio had been disconnected) but they put it down to Ah Ping's diligence in making sure that the compound and the perimeter fencing was well lit until after the prisoners had settled down for the night, when he reduced the power output to conserve the wood supply.

To avoid detection, the radio was operated only in short bursts at night, in an atap hut near the cookhouse, with sentries on the lookout for guards who might be lurking about. The listener (generally Rickards, who had a proprietorial interest in the radio as he had paid for most of it) sat in total darkness, the sole earphone strapped to his head, as he took down notes on the back of a recycled signal pad, keeping his writing more or less straight by using notches cut along the left hand edge of the pad as a guide. The notes were then rewritten onto a single sheet in a more journalistic style for circulation among the officers as *Sandakan Ausso* – a title chosen to counter the Japanese propaganda sheet, *Sandakan Nippo*. After about two weeks, the rank and file was fed small news items in the form of rumours.

Every Friday, special weekly news summaries, compiled by Wells, were sent to Berhala and Dr Taylor. Wells used a simple numerical code whenever possible and eliminated all non-essential details, but the contents could still be understood by anyone familiar with idiomatic English. He then rolled the news sheets tightly and hid them in a pair of spare socks, until it was time for the power house workers, through Rus Ewin or Eric Davis, to pass them to Ah Ping, who gave them to Abin. As Wells had given up the wood party to concentrate on the radio, passing and collecting the regular 'mail' to and from Abin was now the responsibility of Rus Ewin. As the forty men assigned to the wood party were now working further afield, they and their guard travelled by lorry, which had an open-sided cabin. While the guard in the vehicle was busily returning Abin's salute at the police post, Ewin dropped the notes, rolled tightly and secured with wax, onto the ground. Collecting the mail was more risky. On the pretext that he needed to return to the farm workshop to replace a broken axe or sharpen a saw, Ewin made his way to the police post where Abin handed over a Players' cigarette tin containing messages and whatever contraband Taylor had managed to provide.

Wells and Matthews also spent a good portion of their time compiling detailed camp reports and intelligence summaries. Wells passed his paperwork to Abin, who hid it in his house behind a loose rock in the kitchen hearth. Matthews secreted his material in the camp. Only he knew where.

While Wells had been busy with the radio, the underground's Finance Department, begun by Lagan, had expanded and, with the connivance of wealthy Chinese merchants, was now changing substantial amounts of Australian currency into occupation dollars. Money was sent to and from the camp in sealed tins. The rate was set at a favourable $6.40 to the Australian pound, which Taylor then subsidised to an even higher $7. Maggie Funk, wife of Alex, whose grandfather Pedro Dominic was a money changer, and Ngui Ah Kui, one of Mavor's employees, were among those who assisted in these transactions, which eventually totalled 800 pounds in Australian currency. A commission of $2 in every pound exchanged was used to buy food for the camp hospital.

An increasing number of Chinese now belonged to the organisation, their traditional hatred for the enemy having escalated sharply by general ill-treatment and atrocities carried out against their local community. The Japanese, who had posted notices advising that 'the Chinese must always remember that the Japanese commander holds power of life and death over them and at the word of the Japanese commander, they can be killed instantly', regarded all Chinese citizens as fair game. Failure to raise a hat or bow to soldiers whom they encountered anywhere, any time, would result in several hits across the head with a rifle butt. At the airfield, where large parties of men and women were forced to work, a pregnant woman was beaten badly and left in the sun for six hours, while other women were beaten for begging for food or trying to give fish or fruit to the prisoners. At the camp, a man was tied to a post for an entire day for trying to sell food to the camp canteen, for which Goto, the Japanese shopkeeper, had the monopoly. While he was trussed up and helpless, the guards ashed their cigarettes on his bare skin. In town the kempeitai had executed a man accused of looting by stringing him upside down from the padang's soccer goal posts, with lengths of wire passed in front of his Achilles' tendons. This atrocity, which resulted in a slow and agonising death, was followed by an unprovoked attack on a pregnant Chinese woman, whose abdomen was cut open by Japanese soldiers for no other reason than to determine the sex of her unborn child. As no instructions were issued to Japanese troops regarding the molestation of women, all females in Sabah, irrespective of race, age or creed, had no protection whatsoever.

It wasn't just the Chinese who were suffering. The Japanese co-prosperity scheme had not been embraced by any of the locals as the Japanese were the only ones prospering. People were offered less than half the value of the crops or merchandise produced and, when they were paid, it was in worthless occupation dollars. Mostly, they were not paid anything at all. The Japanese simply took what they wanted, including people for enforced labour. As time wore on, villagers watched in despair as soldiers shot their pigs, buffaloes, cows, pigs and goats, stole their chickens and cut down entire coconut palms to harvest the fruit. Anyone who protested was badly beaten, forced to stand in the hot sun for extended periods, or imprisoned.

Consequently, many Chinese left the towns to shelter on small landholdings in the interior, while local tribespeople retreated further into the jungle, where they lived on whatever wild animals they could trap, wild tapioca, sago and wild yams. Farmers who stayed reduced their rice harvest to the bare minimum by storing supplies in the jungle or behind false walls in their houses, and turned their cattle loose. Fishermen caught only what they needed, and hid their small boats so that they could not be stolen. Taxes also became more onerous, with lists drawn up of every occupant in every house in every town and village. Headmen, forced to collect the taxes and make sure all regulations were obeyed, were summoned by the Japanese to attend meetings, the real purpose of which was to intimidate them sufficiently to extract promises of co-operation. To ensure that they did, spies were placed in every village and town. If there were no willing collaborators, or not enough, the Japanese could often persuade 'recruits' to change their minds by confining them to gaol.

However, before the increasing number of collaborators became a problem, a Chinese-Filipino by the name of Wong Mu Sing had offered his services to the underground. A sandalwood trader who shuttled back and forth between Sandakan and the Philippines, Mu Sing had been recruited in early 1942 by Lagan, shortly after he began 'working' as a 'detective' for the Japanese. Since then, Mu Sing had carried a number of messages from Taylor to the guerrilla forces. Unbeknown to Isumi, his Japanese trading partner in Sandakan, Mu Sing was now an undercover lieutenant for the United States Forces in the Philippines (USFIP) and was using his numerous kompits (ocean-going wooden vessels) and two wooden power boats to move far more than trading goods between his home base on Sitangkai Island, on the southern tip of the Sulus, and Sandakan, which his vessels visited every ten days or so.

In October, after Mu Sing had received details from Matthews, through Koram, of the Australian POWs, he relayed the news to his commander at Batu Batu, near Tawi Tawi Island, who in turn passed the information to American submarines supplying the guerrilla forces. By the end of December, a report of the POW situation in Sandakan was in Allied hands. Soon they would have photographic evidence: somehow, Matthews had managed to get hold of a camera. The exposed film was passed to Alex, who arranged for the developed prints to be smuggled to the Filipino forces. From Suarez, Matthews received a map of Tawi Tawi and details of the guerrilla organisation, prompting Major Fleming to establish a chain of command, should the opportunity arise for the prisoners to assist in a local uprising or Allied landing. Major Rice-Oxley nominated Matthews to take over as chief of police, while Captain Ken Mosher was appointed to command four platoons of the most able men, with other officers appointed as quartermaster and chief medical officer.

Captain Ken Mosher

Once regular contact between outside American forces and the guerrillas was well established, it was possible to stockpile weapons for Mosher's platoons. Early in the new year, with the assistance of Corporal Alberto Quadra of the USFIP, the Tawi Tawi force sent two machine guns, 27 rifles and 2,500 rounds of ammunition to Sandakan with Mu Sing, to be hidden by the two Funk brothers and others at a secret location near Mile 15. In the event of an uprising, these arms would be supplemented by those held by the police.

The underground was lucky that any weapons arrived at all as the kompit had been stopped and challenged by a Japanese patrol boat after leaving Tawi Tawi. Realising that their vessel would be boarded and searched, Mu Sing's men opened fire with a concealed cannon and deck-mounted machine-gun, blasting the patrol boat to bits and annihilating the entire crew. Fortunately, the Japanese assumed that Moro pirates, who frequented the area in search of food and commodities, had attacked the vessel (hence the need for Mu Sing's armament). While the engagement may have been an adrenalin-pumping incident for the aggressors, the underground movement was no longer just a collector of intelligence. It had moved into very dangerous territory.

Matthews' appointment as Police Chief had been precipitated by the announcement on 10 January that the 47 women and 15 children on Berhala Island were to leave in two days for an unknown destination. There was no statement made regarding the men. The guards knew no more than the internees, but they had plenty of suggestions: the women were going to Kuching to a new camp with electric lights, beds and furniture; they were to be repatriated; or, most worrying of all, they were to work for the Japanese in a brothel. There was no disagreement regarding the fate of the men – all would be executed. Not one of these rumours was true. The men remained at Berhala for the time being, and on 12 January the women and children departed on a small steamer for Kuching, to be interned in the main camp at Lintang Barracks where Suga had his headquarters. Accompanying them was a contingent of guards and the much-loathed Captain Takakuwa.

While Takakuwa's departure brought some relief to the civilians still in Sandakan, there was no respite for the prisoners at the airfield, where the same mindless brutality prevalent before the short Christmas break continued. Not only had the punishment schedule been stepped up, but Hoshijima also had announced that stage two of the aerodrome must be completed as soon as possible. To meet the deadline, the daily quota of men required to work was increased and the sick forced to make up the numbers. Always hoping that an opportunity might arise to overpower the Japanese, 'force commander' Ken Mosher spent more time at the aerodrome, overseeing the work, than any other officer. Normally, if the officers were required to supply a working party, those nominated were junior lieutenants.

It was at about this time that Chin Piang Syn who, such a short time before, had been sitting for his Junior Cambridge examinations at St Michael's School, joined the underground. In 1933, at the age of 13, he had emigrated with his mother from Kwang Tong Province in China to Sandakan, where there was a large Chinese Hakka community. His father had deserted the family, so, in order to help support himself and his mother, he worked as a grass cutter on a rubber estate. The opportunity to attend school did not come until Piang Syn was fifteen, when the principal of St Michael's offered him a place and allowed him to put his age back by three years. Fortunately, the new 'standard one' pupil was short of stature and slightly built. His mother, who earned $12 a month as a servant, paid the $5 monthly fee. However, when her younger son arrived from China and became chronically ill, she could no longer afford to pay. Unable to qualify as a 'mission pupil', Piang Syn worked his way through school, paying for his board and tuition by cooking meals for St Michael's boarders and washing dishes.

When the Japanese arrived, the school's hostel closed down, forcing Piang Syn, whose mother had moved to Jesselton, to accept the offer of a job on a small rubber and coconut plantation at Sungei Manila (Manila River) owned by the family of one of his school friends. Part of his job also included tapping rubber at another property at Mile 7, not far from the airstrip. The work was not difficult, but his employer's father was a hard taskmaster and no matter how diligently Piang Syn worked, the old man was never satisfied. In January 1943 he quit and took a job as a labourer at the nearby aerodrome. However, although Piang Syn could see the Australians toiling away and wanted to help them, the local coolies were not allowed anywhere near the prisoners, let alone attempt to speak to them. It was probably just as well, as the kempeitai were about to install a spy in the camp.

While some of Sandakan's citizens had volunteered to work for the Japanese almost at once, even to the extent of joining the secret police, others were recruited by the kempeitai. Among them was Lo Ah Fuh, a gunner with the Volunteers and Deputy Assistant Commissioner of Customs, the post once held by Pedro Dominic. Fluent in Chinese, Malay, Japanese and English, he was infiltrated into the Mile 8 Camp. Known as Jackie Lo to the prisoners, who soon detected his true role, he was attached initially to the wood party, and on more than one occasion his presence prevented the dispatch of messages to Taylor and Berhala Island.

Despite the presence of Lo, the underground's intelligence section was able to send out streams of information, using the three-way flow between Matthews, Taylor and Tawi Tawi. Johnny Funk, with his unlimited access to the entire area, compiled up-to-date reports, to which Alex also contributed, on roads, rivers, bridges and public utilities, while Lagan provided details of enemy movements and the location of defences such as machine-gun emplacements, gathered while carrying out his 'investigations' for the kempeitai. PWD contractor Soh Kim Seng, Peter Leong and Felix Azcona Junior, whose father owned the radio shop, prepared maps. Felix Junior, an accomplished draughtsman, had worked as a survey officer, drawing maps for a Japanese-owned agency, Three Diamond, based in the Labuk area. Aged twenty-three, he was married to Tasiana, sister of Peter Lai's wife, Gabriela.

Through Matusup, Alex Funk sent Matthews two maps of the Sandakan area on which he had marked the position of the Japanese barracks, the machine-gun posts and communications facilities, including the wireless transmission station at Mile 2. As information gleaned by the police and prisoners working outside the camp came in, the maps were updated. Information regarding dates, local news and the like were tabulated by Matthews and Wells, each man keeping half of the information to prevent either portion being complete in itself. Matthews buried his inside the camp while Wells, as was his custom, handed his section to Abin for safekeeping.

Despite their caution, Matthews found himself under close scrutiny when Jackie Lo saw him talking to Matusup's wife, Halima binte Binting, about the delivery of food purchased in town by her husband for the camp. Claiming they had simply been chatting about inconsequential matters, they refused to comply with Lo's demands to accompany him to Hoshijima's office, so Lo called a guard to escort them. Not satisfied with their explanation, Hoshijima hit Halima about the head with a stick. When she stuck to her story, she and Matthews were tied to a post and left in the sun for over an hour. When further interrogation failed to break them, Hoshijima eventually let them off with a stern warning.

With Lo very much on the alert, the need to rebuild the radio came at a bad time. However, the efficiency of the valves had decreased to such an extent that reception was no longer possible. Fortunately, by this time the Japanese, pleased with Wells' management of the wood party, had given him the job of supervising the power house workers, allowing him to move about freely. This unrestricted movement enabled him to call at the police station, where he made direct contact with Alex Funk and other pro-British locals who were allowed to sell food to the wood collectors. By delegating the responsibility of the wood party to Corporal McMillan, and then to Corporal Roffey, Wells was able to add their names to the growing list of prisoners ferrying messages between the camp and the post box.

With the assistance of Khoo Siak Chiew, former Volunteer and a senior official with the Department of Communications, Wells and the wood party were able to smuggle in new parts to rebuild the radio. Valves, resistors and condensers were provided by Heng Joo Ming, Samuel Aruliah (an Indian ex-customs examiner) and Amigau bin Hassan, a Malay working at the Post and Telegraph Department. However, construction was held up for some time when some of the laboriously collected components, hidden in a false-bottomed onion box in the vegetable hut, were stolen. This theft, coming on top of a previous incident when atebrin had been stolen and sold to locals working at the airstrip, so enraged Matthews that he set up a court of enquiry. Ken Mosher, who was already investigating the disappearance of the drugs, was asked to assist Lieutenant Draney in the investigation. While they concentrated on bringing the culprits to justice, Weynton began rebuilding the set, using duplicate parts Wells was fortunately able to obtain from his underground suppliers.

Meanwhile, the Japanese had discovered that one of their Chinese coolies, Chin Piang Syn, could not only read and write. He could also speak English, Malay and Chinese. He was promoted immediately to storekeeper and given the job of distributing tools to the workers. This put him into constant contact with the prisoners, who called him 'Sini'. Because he was small, and looked so much younger that his real age of 21 years, the Australians believed him to be about fifteen or so. So did the Japanese who, regarding him as just a youth, allowed him free access to pedal about the place on his bicycle.

Foo Seng Chow

With conditions at the airstrip as gruelling as ever, Walter Wallace, who had long harboured ideas of escape, approached his friend Heng on the best way to go about it. Heng, in turn, asked

Chin Piang Syn (Sini), in his Scout uniform

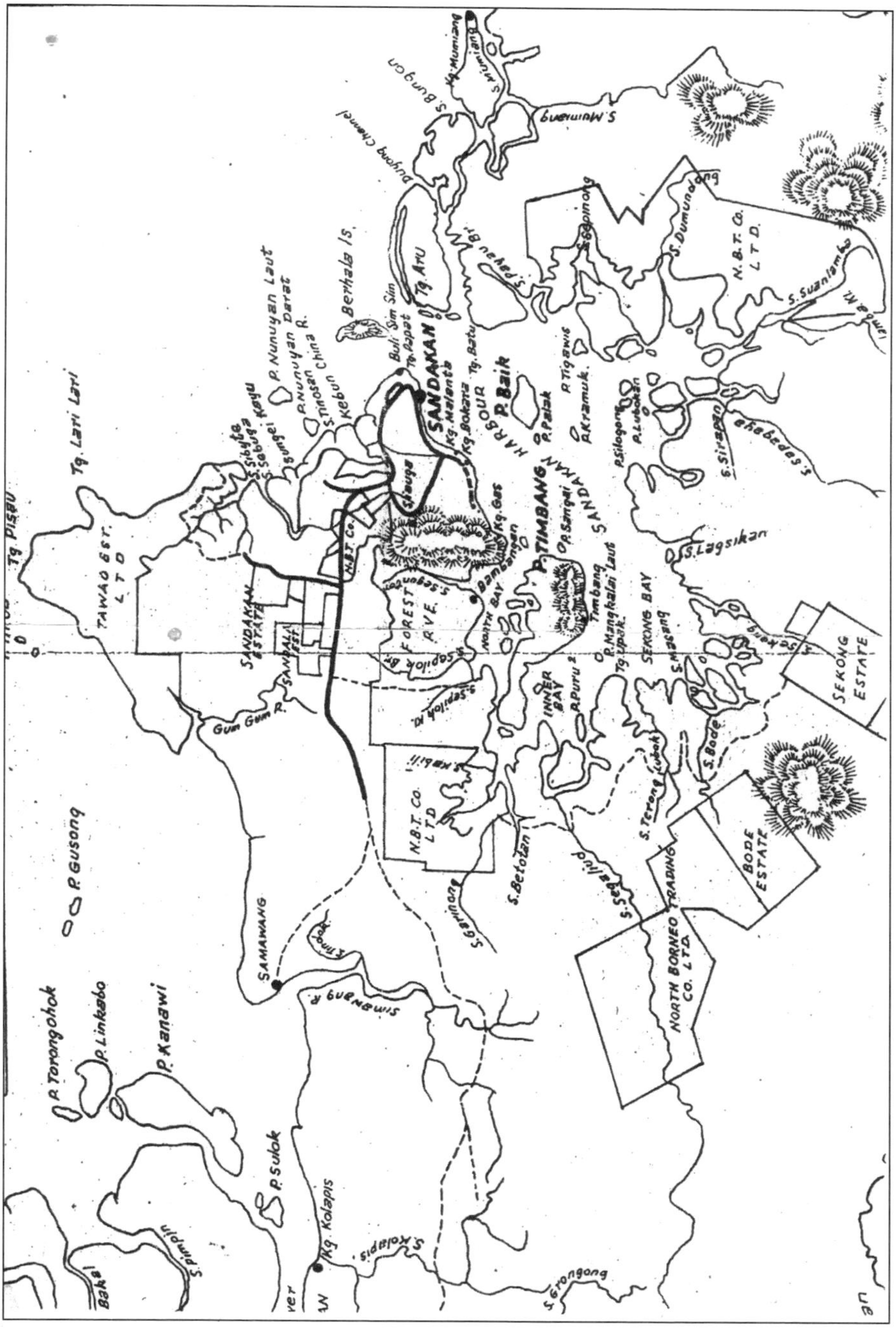

Map of Sandakan area

Sini, who rejected Heng's suggestion that the jungle might be the best option and promised to investigate some other means. On 27 January, before he had a chance to do so, the town and camp were abuzz with news. The five infantrymen who had escaped the previous July had been captured.

They had started out with the right idea. After moving away from the camp, Private Alan Minty and his four friends had made their way to the Sungei Batang road at Mile 11, where they had hidden in a tract of jungle adjoining a tobacco farm owned by Foo Seng Chow. When he found them stealing vegetables from his garden, Foo offered to help and contacted a wealthy Chinese named Sin Tshau who owned a nearby estate. On discovering through Taylor's network that they had not moved on, Abin made contact with the group through a fellow policeman, Kassiu. Kassim bin Jumadi and his brother Surat Min, who had a farm nearby, took the fugitives some food, while quinine was sent from the camp to help stave off malaria. Using money from a POW escape fund organised by Taylor and the Governor, Foo and two of his neighbours, the Goh brothers Tiek Soong and Tiek Tshi, who ran a general store nearby, kept the men supplied with food and ensured they had enough materials and tools to build a hut. To supplement their rations, the men filled in their time hunting for tiny mousedeer (about the size of a rabbit) and non-poisonous snakes.

After six months, with their physical condition deteriorating, they asked their Chinese friends to help them obtain a boat so that they could try and sail to Australia. The Goh brothers advised that the monsoon season was not the best time to put to sea, while Foo warned that the prevailing currents and winds could be dangerous. When the Australians shrugged the warnings aside, replying that they were good navigators, Foo moved them to a hut on a six-hectare farm owned by Puloro Mananai, Paddy Funk's father-in-law. As the Manila River flowed right through the property, it was an ideal departure point. For the ten days that they were in hiding, they were fed by Puloro, his wife Agnes, and their daughters Dimitria (Dimit) Funk and Monica Pastor. Meanwhile, Foo began negotiations to purchase a boat moored nearby. On discovering that the vessel was not seaworthy, the POWs, on Foo's advice, went further down the river and located an ocean-going junk, which was in much better condition. Clad in Chinese clothes, and armed with a map and provisions for two months, the Australians, accompanied by Foo's son, headed downriver. After seeing them safely onto the junk and out to sea, he returned home in his kompit.

Foo was right. The winds and currents were tricky and the Australians were blown onto a mudflat near Bongon Kecil, a small headland south of the harbour. They swam ashore without difficulty but were seen by Sin Kee Seng, a 50-year-old Cantonese and his friend Chong Mew Lee, also known as 'Kecil' ('Shorty'). They reported the sighting to Chong Fong, a prosperous gardener who, aware that 'POW hunting' was a potentially lucrative source of income, formed a gang with Sin, Chong and five other locals. They informed the kempeitai, who imprisoned the fugitives in Sandakan Gaol.

All five were in poor shape, suffering from beriberi, malaria and various skin diseases. Dr Stookes and Mr M Damudaran, a clerk at the gaol, attended to them, while Taylor arranged for Richard Low and Peter Lai to obtain extra food, smuggled in by Warder Number 15, a kindly disposed Indian named Mohamed Zamen. On hearing of the prisoners' arrest, their Chinese friends at Sungei Batang were extremely worried. They were even more worried when Lagan, the 'Japanese detective' arrived on their doorstep to seek details of their involvement, having been informed of their identities by Stookes. Having no idea who Lagan really was, the Chinese said nothing. However, worry turned to terror when the food contractor at the gaol delivered a note from the prisoners, seeking a loan of $25. Once again, they said nothing.

They breathed a sigh of relief when, in late March, the escapees were sent to Kuching with two others who had attempted to escape in February, and another who had struck a Japanese guard. After spending three months in wire cages at the Kuching Camp, the Australians, along with five Chinese accused of subversive activities, were put on trial. The Chinese were all condemned to death. The Australians, sentenced to varying terms of imprisonment, remained in the cages until mid-August, when they were transferred to Outram Road Gaol.

As the capture of the five men had not deterred Wallace in the slightest, Sini continued with his discreet enquiries about possible ways to escape by sea. In early March he met up with his old friend, Soh Kim Seng, who had prepared maps for Wong Mu Sing to take to Tawi Tawi. When Soh asked about conditions at the camp, Sini told him that some of the prisoners wanted to escape but he was having difficulty in finding anyone to help. Soh asked Sini if he would like to join the underground. A keen Scout for the past six years, Sini had a well-developed sense of duty and a love of Empire, fostered during his time at St Michael's. Without hesitation, he agreed. It was then that Soh confided that Lagan, too, was investigating avenues of escape and had been in touch with Mu Sing, who had just arrived from the Philippines with instructions from a United States officer to find out how many Japanese were in the Sandakan area, and where they were stationed. While Ojagar Singh prepared this information, having managed somehow to acquire a detailed plan of the town from the government offices, Mu Sing took time out to marry a local girl, Halima binte Amat.

Mu Sing was keen to help, and Wallace wanted to escape at once, but Sini was more cautious. He advised the Australian to wait a little longer, to make sure that Mu Sing (a foreigner) and Lagan (supposedly working for the Japanese) could be trusted. To determine if they were trustworthy, he intended to sail to Tawi Tawi with Mu Sing or, failing that, follow him. However, Mu Sing had no problem in taking Sini along. On 15 March, with letters from Wallace, addressed to the Internal Affairs officials of the South-West Pacific area, hidden inside his shoes, Sini set sail for Sitangkai, about 240 kilometres away, with Mu Sing and his new bride. They were in a very small boat, so when they were waylaid by Moro pirates who stripped them of their money, food and spare clothing, they could offer no resistance. They reached Sitangkai Island safely on 21 March, but two days later Japanese arrested them and asked why they had landed there. Their story that they had put into the island for protection after the pirate attack was accepted and they were released. By this time they had discovered that it was impossible to go to Batu Batu, their intended destination, due to fighting between the guerrilla forces and the Japanese, so Sini handed Wallace's letters to Mu Sing, who gave them to the Secretary for Sitangkai who, in turn, gave an undertaking to get them into Allied hands.

On his return to Sandakan, Sini reported to Taylor, Matthews, Heng Joo Ming and Wallace. Although Wallace did not believe Sini had been to the Philippines and back, he nevertheless confirmed that he was anxious to escape as soon as possible. Sini told him he must wait until the escape organisation was properly established. Wallace, impatient to move things along, composed a letter to Suarez with the help of his friend Frank Martin. Bypassing Sini, they gave it to Heng Joo Ming for delivery. Wallace then reported what they had done to Major Fleming, who reprimanded him sternly for putting lives in danger by acting without authority. He had scarcely finished his lecture when Wallace announced that he would try to escape. When Frank Martin, who had taken Fleming's advice seriously, told

Wallace he was no longer interested in joining him, Wallace began canvassing the rank and file for a new escape partner.

Meanwhile, in early April, Sini had received a message from Rod Wells, asking if he could obtain some specialised wireless parts. They were not for the radio receiver, which was still being overhauled, but for a Morse-code transmitter, which Wells now wanted to make. Inspired by Sini's successful visit to the Philippines, and aware of the progress the guerrillas were making against the Japanese, he was hopeful that when and if the time came to revolt, he could be in touch with the US Forces. This hope strengthened a week or two later when Koram had an unexpected encounter with an American submarine.

He was out fishing when it suddenly surfaced beside him, and Corporal Alberto Quadra, USFIP, emerged. Neither man knew the other, but Quadra was no stranger to Mu Sing, nor was his name unknown to Matthews. However, he was not delivering weapons this time, but a letter for Matthews which Koram was instructed to give to any white man he saw. Quadra also gave instructions that any future messages to and from the camp from the USFIP were to go through Mu Sing, Felix Azcona Junior or Abin.

The letter, delivered to the jungle post box by Abin, was from Colonel Suarez, asking if Matthews and Wells wished to join the guerrilla forces, or if they wished to be extracted by submarine. Suarez also advised that if they, or any escapee, wished to take up this offer, arrangements for a pick-up could be made through Mu Sing, whose trading vessels were still calling at Sandakan every ten days. Wells and Matthews asked Major Fleming to consider the proposal but, after some deliberation, Major Fleming decided that, in view of the work they were doing, they should remain in the camp.

News that guerrillas were operating in the nearby Philippines had by this time filtered down to the rank and file, who fantasised that rescue and liberation might be possible. While such a notion gave them a hope to cling to, the reality was somewhat different. Even if the guerrillas had the resources at hand to feed and house the fittest of the prisoners, to effect an evacuation they would need hundreds of submarines, or a fleet of well-armed ships and a large strike force, all of which were beyond their resources and capabilities.

With any thought of evacuation effectively quashed, at least for himself and Matthews, Wells turned his attention to his transmitter, for which he needed two huge 6L6G valves to make a 'push-pull' amplifier. Despite their scarcity, the ever-dependable Heng located the valves and passed them to Lieutenant Pascoe-Pierce at the airstrip.

Gerald Mavor who, up until this point had only been indirectly involved, now came to the fore. He was well aware of the success of the radio, as Chan Ah Ping and Ng Ho Kong, who also forwarded the news bulletins, kept him up to date. In the ensuing weeks, Eric Davis and Stevens smuggled in a power transformer that Mavor had made in the power station workshop, rectifier valves and condensers. While most parts came via Ng Ho Kong and Ah Ping, Mr Phillips delivered some directly to Abin. Stevens, who was making the final delivery, nonchalantly strolled past the guards with the parts under his arm, in a rolled up shirt. Anything else that was unprocurable, Wells made.

While the radio receiver was being rebuilt, there had not been any news distribution, which was probably fortunate. The Japanese, aware that war news was circulating in the town, suspected that Dr Stookes, his wife and their friend Johnny Funk were involved. In late April they arrested Dora Stookes for allegedly helping to spread war news obtained from her husband. When they failed to elicit any hard evidence or the whereabouts of the radio, which the Japanese were sure was in town, she was allowed to return home. Johnny Funk, who was still living at the farm, was also interrogated and released. It appears that they did not catch up with Val Stookes who, the following month, was transferred to Kuching, along with his plane.

Although he had not been taken in for close interrogation, Dr Taylor had also become aware that he was also 'a person of interest'. The Japanese had been visiting him at the hospital on a regular basis, asking questions on many subjects, the nature of which was making Taylor uneasy. He was also becoming increasingly concerned that a close watch was being kept on his movements. Meanwhile, while Weynton looked after the now-rebuilt radio, Wells continued to concentrate on the transmitter, his determination to contact the outside world strengthened by the news that another 1,200 prisoners of war had arrived in Sandakan.

Chapter 6

The Escape Route

The first to arrive were about 700 British POWs, captured in Singapore. Split into two parties of 200 and 500, they had come from Jesselton where they had been working on an airfield since the previous October. While in Jesselton, they were accommodated in the gaol at Batu Tiga (Mile 3), built to hold forty prisoners: forty officers in pairs in comparatively roomy stone cells, and non-commissioned officers in wooden warder's barracks. The rank and file were squashed into atap huts, which had been squeezed between the main buildings and the three-metre-high outer wall. The remaining space, on an incline to the rear of the buildings, was taken up with inadequate trench latrines, which overflowed every time it rained.

The commandant could do nothing about the overcrowded and unsanitary conditions, or contain the dysentery that broke out. After six months, with an alarming forty-eight prisoners dead and another three dangerously ill, the camp was shut down and orders issued to move the prisoners to Sandakan. One soldier no longer with this group was Johnny Funk's brother Eddie (Edward), who had joined the Royal Army Medical Corps in Singapore. Once back on his home soil, he had escaped.

Senior officers at both the Sandakan and Jesselton camps had been aware that the other existed for some months, though a message relayed from Wells by Mrs Anna Wales, the Chinese wife of Cyril Wales, an interned English planter. Anna, a nurse at the Sandakan Civil Hospital, was a friend of Dora and Val Stookes and a member of the underground network. She and Wells had met at the Mile 8 police post, shortly after he had started to supervise the workers at the power plant.

Although the Australian message had been delivered safely, the British had not responded. Having witnessed several beheadings in Java, their senior officer, Squadron Leader Hardie, was wary of reprisals and, despite several overtures from Jesselton agents, had resisted all invitations to become involved in subversive activities. Consequently, Wells knew only what Anna Wales had told him: that the British imprisoned in the Jesselton Gaol were army and air force personnel. As there had been no chance to make any further contact, the Australian officers did not know much more – only that the prisoners, who had arrived in two groups on 12 and 18 April 1943, were quartered in huts near the airstrip.

Another remaining 500 prisoners were Australians. Known as E Force, they had arrived from Singapore via Kuching on the *Taka Maru,* a rusty hulk of a ship, six days after the advance British party, and were now occupying the huts at the Quarantine Station. There had been no contact with them either, as the lines of communication to Berhala, shut down following the transfer of the male internees to Kuching the previous month, had yet to be restored.

Two days after E Force arrived at Berhala, an influx of 43 new guards, under Captain Nagai Hawara, took up duties at the Mile 8 Camp. Unlike the previous guards, who came out every day from town on a truck, the new contingent lived in recently constructed barracks, for which some of the camp's electricity wires and water pipes were being removed and recycled. The newcomers were Bushido Youth Corps' conscripts and all were Formosans. Aged between sixteen and twenty years, they were young and slightly built, but they made up for both with a swaggering aggression that rivalled that of the basher gang. Drunk with power, and commanded by an officer who let them do as they pleased, these young bullies, called 'kichi' (kecil) guards by the prisoners because of their small size, were far worse than the old Japanese soldiers who had previously guarded the camp.

The arrival of the kichi guards may have been the reason why, towards the end of April, MacAlister Blain and Joe James informed Wells that they wanted to escape. Unlike other escape attempts, where senior officers had been noncommittal, Major Fleming sanctioned this one. He believed that 47-year-old Blain, a former Independent Member of Parliament who had also served in the war of 1914-18, could perhaps organise some kind of assistance if he reached Australia. As Wells and Matthews were not keen on the idea of anyone escaping at this time, Blain wrote a letter seeking assistance to Frank Forde, Minister for the Army. The letter, sealed inside an envelope bearing a parliamentary crest, was sent to Dr Taylor with Blain's gold parliamentary pass, via Driver Scott who worked on the wood party. Taylor returned both items and told Blain to wait. Undaunted, he contacted Wallace's friend Frank Martin, who was working at the airfield. He and Joe James approached Sini, thinking the gold pass would impress him. It didn't. He kept the letter, sent back the gold pass and told them to wait.

While they were waiting, Warrant Officer Wallace and two other prisoners escaped. Although Wallace had told Frank Martin and Heng Joo Ming that he was going, no one else had any idea that he had escaped until the alarm was raised at roll call the next morning. Sini, stunned to learn from Frank Martin that the 'white tiger', as he called Wallace, had left before any outside support had been finalised, went immediately to Wong Mu Sing and Lagan. They had been co-ordinating Wallace's escape and were as astounded as Sini to learn he had already gone. Perhaps the only person not surprised by the sudden departure was Captain Ken Mosher, who was about to arrest Wallace for stealing the atebrin tablets and the precious radio parts, sold to finance his escape.

He had left with two signallers – Howard Harvey aged 21 and Theodore Mackay (also known as Donald MacKenzie), aged 32. Heng had considered joining them but, as his wife and children were in Singapore, he was fearful of reprisals against them if he were caught. On the night of 30 April, the Australians had hidden beneath the vegetable hut, slipping under the wire at about 9.30 pm. Wallace, who had a pistol, a home-made parang, maps, $200 in cash from the sale of the stolen goods, and food supplied by Heng, planned to head south-west to Seroi and follow the Lokan River down to the Kinabatangan. From here he could either strike out across the northern part of the Brassey Range to the Segama River, or follow the Kinabatangan downstream and then move cross-country to the Segama. At the mouth of the river was Lahad Datu, where he hoped to find a boat to take them to Tawi Tawi. The total distance from Sandakan to Lahad Datu, as the crow flies, was about 160 kilometres. The routes Wallace would have to follow were considerably longer.

Wallace had a compass and had read a book on Borneo's geography lent to him by Heng, but he seriously underestimated how tough the going would be. After just a few days' battling through snake-infested jungle, interspersed with slimy, foul-smelling swamps, they abandoned the plan to go to Lahad Datu and headed back towards the camp. They found the main road, where a group of Malays told them they were near Mile 15. Despite a warning that Japanese patrols were about, the three men turned towards Sandakan before heading north again, so that they could skirt the aerodrome. Following the Sungei Batang–Manila road from Mile 11, they stopped off at a small house to ask for food. Although the penalty for assisting prisoners of war, especially escapees, was very severe, the occupants gave them fresh fruit, fish, eggs and fruit.

The next day they took to the jungle again, wading through deep, sago-palm swamps and thick mangroves, before finally merging onto the banks of the Sungei Manila. Fearful of crocodiles, they hailed a boatman paddling towards them but he took fright and went off in the opposite direction. Deciding to risk it, they swam the river with their gear wrapped in a groundsheet, and then pushed on through more swamps until they came to an even wider waterway – the Sibuga. To their joy, a Bajau boatman saw them and stopped. After giving them food, water and cigarettes, the boatman, who spoke good English, warned that search parties were out and that the most wanted person was a man named Wallace. He then took them downstream to a better hiding place, instructing them to stay well back from the river while he went off to collect more food. He returned shortly with rice, fish and, amazingly, hot coffee.

After hiding out for another day, Mackay became dissatisfied with their slow progress and suggested they should swim down the river to Heng's house. Wallace disagreed, pointing out forcefully that, apart from the danger posed by crocodiles, they should stick to the jungle, as the Japanese would be watching the river during daylight hours. After a very protracted argument, Mackay convinced Harvey that his idea was best. The pair left the next morning, 8 May, taking advantage of a strong out-going tide.

Wallace continued on until he, too, became fed up and took to the river. Supported by logs, he drifted with the current for some distance, before running aground on a mudflat. He swam ashore, but failed to tie his bundle of belongings securely and lost everything, including his compass, spare clothes, pistol and money. Once on dry land, he was alarmed to see discarded cigarette packets lying about the bank – evidence, he felt sure, that Japanese sentries had the river under surveillance. Taking care to avoid the aerodrome, he headed for Heng's house and hid in the hen house, where he managed to attract the attention of Heng's girlfriend, Siti, who was astonished to see Wallace among the chickens, holding a stout stick and wearing only his under-shorts. An all-night discussion ensued about what to do next. That morning, just before dawn, Heng took Wallace to a secure hideout in the jungle, where Koram and two other policemen built him a small shelter. As the entire area was swarming with search parties, the fugitive was instructed not to venture out until after dark. Siti would bring whatever food and water he needed, while Sini would see what arrangements could be made to get him away to Tawi Tawi. The following day when Heng returned from work at the airfield, he brought the sobering news that Harvey and Mackay were dead.

They had made it downstream without any trouble but, after going ashore near Kampong Sibuga, were spotted on 11 May by five pro-Japanese Malays, identified by Koram as Awang, Imam Mualin, Tamborok, Salani and Supahat. Two feigned friendship and went off to 'arrange' for a boat, leaving three to stay with the Australians, who busied themselves collecting coconuts for their journey. When the other two returned, Jackie Lo and two truckloads of Japanese accompanied them.

The prisoners, who tried to fend off the Japanese with stones, had no hope of survival. Under Japanese law, all those who tried to escape, after signing the so-called 'no escape' agreement, could be imprisoned for a minimum of one year, provided the guards had not shot them first. However, many Japanese officers considered that, as POWs were part of the Japanese military, escape was the same as desertion and was therefore punishable by death.

Late that afternoon, the two men were bound and taken to a secluded spot where two of the soldiers fired a full clip of cartridges into Harvey, who died instantly, and another into Mackay, who did not. After finishing him off with their rifle butts, the search party 'blooded' their bayonets on the corpses. Prisoners at the airstrip heard the gunfire, but it was not until Lieutenant Pascoe-Pierce identified the bodies that they realised its significance. Wallace, now alone on the outside, was terrified he would be next. He sent messages begging Matthews to let him back in, but it was out of the question. Wallace was too well known and there were now surprise roll calls and head counts every day.

Meanwhile, as the underground had re-established communications with Berhala Island, Matthews had received a message from Captain Ray Steele, E Force's second most senior officer, along with a report of the POW situation in Singapore and some radio parts. The E Force men had planned to build a radio, with various officers carrying in the vital components, but as Wells already had one in operation and was sending out the news, there was now no need.

The newcomers had no trouble making contact with the underground. With the Constabulary responsible for patrolling the camp's perimeter fences, Ojagar Singh and Yangsalang, who were in charge of the roster, made sure that only the most trustworthy men were assigned. Among this select group, which included Mohamed Tahir, was Corporal Koram who, a few months earlier, had been punished by the Japanese for passing messages to civilian internees. His misdemeanour had been forgiven, as he had seen the error of his ways and had 'agreed' to act as a 'spy' for the Japanese. When Koram appeared on duty, displaying police number 142 on his armband, Private Jock McLaren knew exactly who he was.

Before arriving at Sandakan, SS *de Klerk* had called in at Kuching to discharge 500 British prisoners at the main camp. The Australians, having spent the last few days at sea enduring appalling conditions, were pleased when they, too, were ordered to disembark. It was just a transit stop while some of them unloaded a cargo vessel. They were billeted at the Batu Lintang Camp, and it wasn't long before the more daring men were wriggling their way under the wire of their compound and across the vegetable patch to the barbed-wire barricade surrounding the women's camp about 400 metres away. Some made the risky journey to investigate the possibilities of escape, while others simply wanted to chat. Private Howard Hewitt, a notorious black marketeer who had tried to escape from Singapore, was keen to make use of the compass concealed in his water bottle, but decided to combine business with pleasure. To the delight of Agnes Keith and Australian missionary Mary Bewsher, who had responded to Hewitt's appeal for information, he tossed them a tube of lipstick and cigarettes, both highly valuable black market commodities.

Sapper Don Marshall and friends Ted Keating, Carl Jensen and Joe Weston, who had also tried to escape from Singapore, were eager to try again, so Marshall was delegated to crawl over to the men's camp. Luck was with him, for the male internees had just arrived from Berhala. Marshall was able to meet the senior members of the underground – Harry Keith and his assistant Mr Brown (Apostol's immediate boss) and Major Rice-Oxley – who gave him maps of British North Borneo, a Forestry Department Survey chart, notes from Brown to Apostol and Paddy Funk (who had been employed at one time by Brown), and details of two possible escape routes: one through the Celebes (Sulawesi) and the other through the western Philippines, via Jolo Island.

Private Jock McLaren was also on the lookout for any useful information. He had escaped from Singapore into Malaya shortly after the surrender, only to be recaptured after serving with Chinese guerrillas for some months. He had been looking for a chance to escape ever since and had hidden a small map, plus a pistol and twenty rounds of ammunition stolen from the Japanese, in the collar of his gas cape. During his stay in Kuching, one of the B Force officers, transferred to Kuching the previous October, introduced him to Governor Robert Smith. McLaren's best chance of escape, he said, was through Mata-mata (police boy) Number 142 – Corporal Koram.

On 21 April, after a further five-day voyage, this time in the holds of *Taka Maru,* a rusting cement-carrier of just 1500 tonnes, E Force reached Sandakan, where the prisoners were transferred to timber barges for the short journey to Berhala. Waiting for them on the wharf near Salleh's hut was Captain Hoshijima, looking his immaculate best. After a superficial search by the guards, who failed to find an amazing amount of smuggled goods, including an anti-aircraft shell, the POWs lined up on the small parade ground for Hoshijima's welcome speech. As this was the third time he had delivered it in less than two weeks, Ozawa, who was translating, as usual, should have been word perfect. They were prisoners of Japan; they were there to build an airstrip; they would work until their bones rotted under the tropical sun; escape was futile because if the Japanese didn't capture them the jungle would; and any escape attempts would result in bloody reprisals, as would any attempt to communicate with any other POW camp. The war could still last 100 years, but this time Hoshijima added 'we will win'.

The Quarantine Station, with its three wooden huts designed to hold a maximum of 150, was far too small for 500 men, many of whom slept under the buildings or out in the open. However, there had been some major improvements: plunge baths and proper latrines, built out over the water. The hospital/quartermaster's store was outside the wire in the former women's compound, now minus its wooden fence. The guardhouse, to which half a dozen Japanese soldiers had been assigned, was still at the shoreline, not far from the new latrines, which jutted out over the sea at high tide. The officers protested about the overcrowding in the huts, but the Japanese were not interested in hearing any complaints. As soon as enough timber had been felled to build a new camp, all would be shifted to the mainland.

They had only just settled into their new surroundings when Ted Keating, who had firmed up plans to escape with Marshall, Jensen and Weston, approached Captain Charles Wagner, the E Force intelligence officer. Wagner agreed not only to join the party, but also to lead it, so they handed over copies of all the material they had been given by Harry Keith. When Howard Hewitt and his friend Nelson Short heard about the plan, Hewitt gave Wagner his compass as a gesture of good faith. However, when Short later pressed him for details of how and when they would escape, Wagner was very vague, saying only that any escape must be organised from the mainland. He didn't offer to return the compass.

The six men who had put such faith in Wagner were unaware that he was already a member of an officers' escape party. It had evolved in Singapore when three artillery officers, Captain Ray Steele and Lieutenants Rex Blow and Miles Gillon, formed an alliance which they called the 'Dit Party' – 'dit' being the way of describing the short tap on the Morse-code key signifying the letter 'E', and ' E' standing for 'escape'. When Rex Blow, who had a pistol and 40 rounds of ammunition, discovered just prior to leaving Singapore that Private Jock McLaren also had a weapon and twenty rounds, he was invited to join the Dit Party.

When it became clear to Blow and Wagner, after a series of cautious conversations with Koram, that Mata-mata 142 could be trusted, they told him they wished to escape. Knowing from his recent encounter with the submarine that this could be arranged, he sent a message to Matthews to set the wheels in motion. On Dr Taylor's instructions, Koram also relayed Quadra's message to Wagner and the other members of the Dit Party, who had already reconnoitred the island for a possible escape route while gathering wood. Although the three officers believed their duty to escape was greater than their obligation to remain with their men, it was not a viewpoint shared by their commanding officer Captain Richardson. His misgivings about potential reprisals were also so great that he threatened to tell the Japanese of any planned escape attempt but, after some effective counter-arguments, he had backed down reluctantly. While Koram began making arrangements for the pick-up, the Dit members concentrated on building their fitness levels and stockpiling rations. The police guards inadvertently assisted the get-fit programme by allowing the POWs to play baseball and swim in the sea twice a day, while Koram helped the food situation by smuggling dried fish and prawns, fruit and potatoes. Using money provided by Mrs Cohen, these rations were organised by Taylor with the help of Chan Tian Joo, manager of a local merchant firm, Kwang Teo Heng. However, before the Dit party had a chance to formulate any plans, Wallace, Harvey and Mackay escaped, throwing the mainland into an uproar.

Three weeks later the Japanese were still searching for Wallace, who was still hiding at Heng's house. Concluding that the only option was to get him to Tawi Tawi by boat, Sini, Lagan and Mu Sing had met with Taylor on 14 May. They agreed to meet again the next day to finalise the arrangements so, before he left town, Sini collected three letters for delivery to Dr Taylor. As he walked home, a military bus stopped and the Japanese invited him to hop on board. Unable to refuse without arousing suspicion, he did so. Sure that he was being watched, and terrified that he might be followed and searched, Sini lurched unsteadily down the aisle to the front of the bus as it neared his house and, in an apparently inebriated state, pitched himself head first out the door. By falling from the bus, he had only intended to get away from the Japanese but as he had knocked out two teeth he was taken to hospital – where he handed the letters to Taylor.

With Sini in hospital for a week recovering from his facial injuries, an attempt to evacuate Wallace by kompit to Tawi Tawi was made on the night of 17 May. Accompanied by Heng, Wallace made his way down jungle trails to the river, where Mu Sing and Lagan were waiting with a small, ocean-going sailing boat. They waited all night at the appointed place, hoping that the fishing lines they dangled over the side would fool any enemy patrols, but there was no sign of the kompit. With dawn approaching, they returned Wallace to his hiding place, where he remained with the support of Dr Taylor, who sent in clothing, toiletries, money and messages of encouragement. However, with each passing day, the situation became more dangerous and Wallace, who was placing unreasonable demands on Taylor to hurry things along, more of a liability. Eventually, after another lengthy conference at Heng's house, the conspirators decided to move Wallace to Berhala Island, where Salleh and Koram could hide him until the Dit Party was ready to leave. Before Wallace left the hideout, Sini gave him the letter written by Blain, with instructions to deliver it to Frank Forde.

Mohammed Tahir

On the night of 26 May, Siti's father Jakariah and his fisherman friend, Sidek, rowed Wallace in a small boat down the Kaya River to Sandakan Harbour and then out to sea, where Koram, Mu Sing and Mohammed Tahir had arranged to row out and meet them. When they failed to arrive, Wallace was returned once more to the mainland. For the next attempt, four days later, Heng took him directly to Berhala, where Koram had built an excellent hideout. As there were no firm arrangements for the escape, Wallace was instructed to remain hidden until the time came for the others to leave the compound. He didn't have long to wait. In the early hours of 4 June, Koram advised that he, Tahir and the other members of the Constabulary were to return to their barracks at Buli Sim Sim, as E Force was about to be transferred to the main camp. Later that day, when a large barge arrived to transport the prisoners up the Sibuga River to the camp, the guard was doubled and orders issued for the next day's transfer. With the move confirmed, the Dit Party would have to make its break that night.

Captain Ray Steele

Corporal Koram

The original five-man group had swelled to seven when McLaren discovered that two of his friends, Jim Kennedy and Rex Butler, were also intending to escape. With Wallace, the party of eight was now far too big, so it was split in two. The four officers and Wallace were to remain in hiding on the island, where Salleh could look after them until a kompit arrived. The others were to paddle a kolek kelebat (a large fishing canoe with a sail), which the lepers used for offshore fishing, to a rendezvous point off the coast where Koram would be waiting with a larger vessel to take them further south. As the paddles for the kolek, which was to be taken without the lepers' knowledge, were stored separately, two of the men had shaped a rough set from wooden planks: it was far too risky to rely solely on the small sail for propulsion.

To make the Japanese believe that they had all left together, in one boat, the lepers gave permission for a party, led by Salleh and Koram, to dismantle their large, ocean-going perahu (wooden boat) and hide it in the jungle. Unaware that they would soon be without any fishing craft at all, the lepers had also agreed to tell the Japanese that the white men had sailed away in their perahu. But that was only part of the plot. The kolek kelebat could only hold three or four at the most, so, to convince the lepers that everyone really *had* gone, Blow and Wagner, who were strong swimmers, were to take a second canoe and sink it in deep water.

Nelson Short and Howard Hewitt knew nothing of the planned escape bid. Neither did Keating, Jensen, Marshall or Weston.

Confident that Wagner, who had copies of all their escape data and Hewitt's compass, would keep his part of the bargain, they waited patiently to be told it was time to move. Hearing that a transfer to the mainland was imminent, Keating went to Wagner and asked if he were ready to make a break. His response was to wait until they reached the mainland. A few hours later, he and the rest of the Dit Party escaped.

They had no trouble leaving the compound. At about seven o'clock, just as the main gate was due to be closed for the night and shut off access, the men made their way to the latrines. Dropping through the holes, they landed on the sand below. A quick dash through the mangroves and across a strip of sand and they were in the jungle. They met up with Wallace, who had shifted their gear, secreted outside the wire earlier in the day, along a jungle trail leading up the hill. While Gillon, Steele and Wallace continued up the slope, the other five followed a small path leading down the saddle to the sleeping Leper Colony. Leaving the other three to wait on the beach, Blow and Wagner swam out to the koleks, one of which was anchored with blocks of lead, linked with wire. As they heaved the makeshift anchor from the water and into the boat, the metal clanged loudly, waking the lepers. On reaching the shore, Blow and Wagner were confronted by an angry crowd, outraged that the prisoners were making off with their only fishing boats. McLaren, Kennedy and Butler brushed aside their protests and paddled off. Wagner and Blow headed after them but, once they were out of sight around the bluff, sank the boat. They then swam ashore to a spot where the cliffs were less sheer, and, without too much trouble, joined the others.

Once free of the Leper Colony, McLaren, Kennedy and Butler headed south and, at about 9 pm, met up with Koram and his perahu, which took them and their kolek about sixty kilometres down the coast to Kuala Kinabatangan. Although the perahu arrived there well before the appointed time of 3 am, the submarine was unable to surface, owing to Japanese torpedo boats operating in the area. As dawn was less than three hours away, Koram remained in position in case the submarine eventually arrived, while the escape party headed further down the coast towards the Segama River. They were prepared, if necessary, to continue on even further south to make the final run across the Sibutu Channel to Sanga Sanga, the most southerly of the Tawi Tawi group. Depending on their navigational skills, they would have between 43 nautical miles (80 kilometres) and 30 nautical miles (55 kilometres) of open sea before the next landfall.

Cliffs on Berhala Island. Leper Colony is to the right

The submarine failed to surface before dawn broke but Koram finally made contact the following night. It searched for the kolek without success, but the Australians, after running onto mud banks and encountering delays caused by stormy weather, were helped by locals along the way and arrived safely at Sanga Sanga on 14 June. They were later transferred to Batu Batu to meet Suarez before being taken to their billet for a well-earned rest, in a beautiful house normally occupied by Guy Strattan, Lillian Funk's father.

Meanwhile, the remainder of the Dit Party were still on Berhala. Despite being double-crossed, the lepers had not reported the theft of their koleks, so it was not until the early morning muster that the Japanese discovered that anyone was missing. Even then, it was not immediately apparent. When the guards, instead of conducting a head-count, ordered the assembled POWs to number off, the prisoners called out their numbers at random, instead of in numerical order. However, eventually the Japanese realised they were seven men short.

When the lepers, who stuck to their half of the bargain, reported that the prisoners had made off in a northerly direction with their ocean going vessel, the Japanese immediately dispatched a fast motor-launch to look for them. They did not, at that stage, suspect that any of the absconders, least of all Wallace, was still on the island. Salleh certainly gave no hint of it, not even when Hoshijima, who arrived at Berhala at 7.30 am, an hour after the prisoners left for the Mile 8 Camp, offered him a $1000 reward for information leading to the arrest of the escapees. Hoshijima, who had no doubts about Salleh's loyalty, was confident he would report any sighting immediately, especially given the size of the reward: a fabulous sum for a man as poor as he. Three times a day search parties called at the wharf to see if Salleh had anything to report, and three times a day Salleh replied, 'I am sorry that I have not seen the white men. I wish I could. I would love to have the reward'.

Wong Mu Sing's trading vessels were in port at the time of the escape, waiting for the signal to move, but were thwarted when the Japanese, on discovering that prisoners were missing, ordered all boats to leave Sandakan immediately. When the fast motor-launch had failed to find any trace of the escapees out to sea, search parties of Japanese and members of the Constabulary, including Tahir and Koram, were ordered to scour the island and nearby mainland, forcing the prisoners to keep well out of sight as they moved into areas which the Japanese had already searched. They were safe enough, as long as they were careful. Berhala was quite a large island, with many small caves and a great deal of dense bush and jungle, which the Japanese were not overly keen on entering.

To convince the Japanese, and the lepers, who had only seen five men leave the island, that there were no prisoners still in hiding, on the third night of the search Koram took a small boat and paddled out to Berhala, where he stole two of the lepers' dinghies and sank them in deep water. Creeping ashore, he then used a pair of large-sized army boots to create a confusion of footprints on the sand. The following day the lepers reported the theft to the Japanese who, like the lepers themselves, were now convinced that all the prisoners had fled.

For ten days Koram dared not visit the hideout, in case he were followed. When he did, it was in broad daylight and with the full approval of the Japanese. They had agreed to his giving a blowpipe demonstration at a forthcoming sports' day, for which he needed a supply of a paralysing drug, the only local supplies of which, he assured the Japanese, were on Berhala Island. He brought with him some welcome provisions of dried fish and prawns, noodles, rice and some bananas.

While waiting for Mu Sing's kompit to arrive, the Australians remained undetected due to the steadfastness of Salleh, the assistance of Koram and the generosity of Taylor and Mrs Cohen, who donated the sixty dollars needed to buy enough food to keep them going. Lagan, with the help of Mr Chan Tian Joo, also opened an appeal for additional funds, to which many of the local people contributed, ignoring the possibility of future reprisals. With E Force gone and the guards withdrawn, the fugitives were now solely reliant on Salleh to deliver the food, and Koram to make sure it was ready and waiting for him when he made his usual trips to the mainland. Once Salleh returned to Berhala, he left the food and other supplies in one of five designated spots, signifying his presence by mewing like a cat.

The port was still closed to outgoing vessels when Alberto Quadra arrived from the Philippines, ostensibly on a 'trading mission' to visit his brother Bernard, a Sandakan resident. With the prisoners still at large, the Japanese remained on the alert, and it was not until Abdul Cani and a fellow customs' examiner vouched for the visitor that suspicions were allayed. Once Alberto was no longer under surveillance, he, Mu Sing, Lagan, Ojagar Singh, Koram, Heng and Sini busied themselves making the final arrangements.

On the afternoon of 23 June, Mohamed Tahir met Salleh's son at the Sim Sim water village to borrow his dinghy, ostensibly for a fishing trip. The next morning he went to the market, where he bought fruit for the escapees and a fishing net for himself. At about 7 pm, he began casting his net. As soon as it was completely dark, Alberto and Koram joined him. Using their hands as paddles, they made their way to Berhala. At 11 pm, when they met Steele and the others in Salleh's hut, they handed over the food, the money collected by Lagan and Chan and written instructions from Taylor. Alberto then broke the good news that the waiting was over. As the Japanese launch was no longer patrolling the island, he would pick them up at 8 pm in one or two days' time, on his way back to Tawi Tawi. Tahir wanted to go with them, but his request was refused.

For the next two nights the Australians kept watch at the small, secluded beach below their hiding place. At about four o'clock on the afternoon of 26 June, Mohamed Tahir went to Ojagar Singh's house on Bukit Merah, where they watched Quadra's two distinctively black-sailed kompits slowly make their way down the harbour and out the entrance. While one sailed for Tawi Tawi, the other waited off shore until it was dark. Shortly before 9 pm the escapees heard the faint splash of oars and the sound of a sail, slapping against the mast as Quadra's seven-metre-long kompit, crewed by four Moro sailors, neared the beach. Guided by the glow of the evil-smelling native cigars on which the Australians were now puffing madly, Quadra expertly steered the craft to the pick-up point. Within ten minutes, all five men were on board and on their way to Tawi Tawi. The only person to see them leave was Salleh, who watched the vessel disappear into the darkness towards Tanjong Aru with a certain tinge of regret.

Quadra, who felt only relief, was keen to put as much distance between himself and Sandakan before dawn. The three-day voyage was not without its incidents. The first, running aground on a sand bank, was only a minor irritation and the vessel, having a shallow draught, was soon free. The second arose after they passed Tambisan Island which was not, as Rex Blow thought, the closest point from which to make the run across the Sibutu Channel to Tawi Tawi. It was actually further south, between Dent Haven and Labian Point. As the helmsman, who navigated by the stars and sun, tacked south-west before turning the boat to the east, Rex Blow, convinced he was returning to the mainland, pulled a pistol on him. Unaware of the real reason for the course alteration, Blow dined out on his version of the story for years.

The third incident occurred the following day in the Sibutu Channel, when they were all but becalmed. Spotting smoke on the horizon, Quadra ordered his passengers to take refuge under a false floor, especially installed for such an emergency. The approaching vessels were two Japanese transports and a cruiser escort. Lying prone on the bottom of the boat, with heavy rice bags stacked on top of them, the Australians were kept informed of what was happening topside by Quadra, who calmly kept up a running commentary. Unlike his passengers, who were all sweating profusely, Quadra was confident that with their sail lowered, the pointed atap roof over the cargo space giving the impression of living quarters, and the crew rowing along at a leisurely pace, the kompit looked like a native fishing boat going about its normal business. The Japanese officer on the cruiser, who had them under surveillance through his binoculars, certainly thought so. After returning the friendly waves from the Moros, the ships continued on their way. A day later, having made good progress before a stiff westerly breeze, Quadra pointed to three small bumps on the horizon and announced, 'Tawi Tawi'. The new arrivals were soon reunited with their fellow escapees, who had given them up for dead. On 1 July, the entire party was formally inducted into 125 Regiment, USFIP.

Suarez informed the Allied military that the prisoners had made a successful escape and also sent a note to Matthews. On reaching Sandakan, the message did not go via Abin and the Mile 8 post box, but to Sini who, with his youthful looks and bicycle, enjoyed great freedom of movement. Now an integral member of the network, he had been entrusted with new tasks, one of which was to facilitate the delivery of messages between the town and the camp. His contact was invariably Ken Mosher who, with more weapons due to arrive from the Philippines, was out at the airstrip most days.

After signalling to Mosher to meet him in the tool repair shop, Sini handed him the note, which said: 'Delighted to report safe arrival of escape party of eight from Berhala Island. Operative 23, USFIP'. This was indeed wonderful news but, worried about Sini's involvement in the underground and his apparent youth, Mosher asked if he realised what would happen if he were caught carrying messages like this. Sini replied, 'Yes, Tuan. The Japanese will execute me.' When Mosher expressed his admiration at Sini's bravery, he said 'I am not brave, Tuan, but I must do my duty. I am British, and also a Boy Scout.'

Another member of the underground stationed at the airfield and also doing his duty was Chang Ting Kiang, known as Henry Chang. Although Henry's family was too poor to send him to school, he had taught himself basic mechanics by pulling apart bicycles, and then motorbikes, finally becoming proficient enough to land a job as Dr Stookes' mechanic. With Stookes and his aeroplane in Kuching, Henry was now 'employed' by the Japanese to service their military aircraft. Henry, with his wife, mother, and young niece, lived in a house at Mile 7 owned by John Simon Funk. While working at the camp, Henry managed to exchange a few words with Frank Martin and some of the other prisoners, who asked for news of the outside world and handed him letters, photos, messages and personal effects, hoping he could get the items away to the Philippines and then home. Although, like Sini, Henry was well aware of the penalty, he agreed to help, smuggling their precious papers and mementos from the camp to his house, in a tin.

Townspeople who were not members of the underground were also taking risks. Pedro Dominic's son-in-law, Andrew Pereira – a government printer who had been allowed to keep his job – was among those fortunate enough not to have attracted the attention of the Japanese. The family had moved from their large bungalow on the reclamation ground to another property, further along the bay near Tanah Merah, which had more land on which to grow food. One day, while Andrew was cycling to work at the printing office, situated near the town mosque, a POW cutting grass along the Leila Road tossed him a watch, indicating that he wanted to trade it for cigarettes. Pereira not only returned the watch, with the requested cigarettes, but also, from that day on, always made sure he carried a packet to give to any prisoners he saw.

With conditions deteriorating at the camp following the escapes, the POWs valued acts of kindness such as this. Riled by punishments meted out by Hoshijima for not being vigilant enough, the guards were now taking out their ill humour on the Australian prisoners. Security was tightened considerably. To prevent any fraternisation between the two groups, the 500 E Force men had their hair shaved off and all prisoners were issued with a new POW tag, which not only identified individual prisoners but also their Force: B Force being numbers 1-1500, with E Force following on. The wooden tags, which replaced the cloth variety, had to be worn at all times. Hoshijima also increased night surveillance by introducing guard dogs, which were kept in a yard behind the main guardhouse during the day and tied beneath the perimeter sentry boxes at night. However, it didn't take long for the prisoners to befriend them, and several ended up as stew. The Australians told the guards that crocodiles, which they claimed frequented the buffalo swamp at night, must have eaten the missing dogs. From then on, the guards gave the swamp a wide berth.

The British, who had not made a single escape attempt and tended to be much better behaved than the Australians, were not subjected to the same degree of brutality. However, neither did they have the benefit of drugs and additional food which, because of the Australians' close relationship with the local underground, continued to flow into the camp. As the two Australian groups and the British were kept segregated from each other at the airstrip, any communication had to be by hand signals, scrunched up notes or clandestine meetings in the tool shed. Unfortunately, although the Australians successfully passed the radio news to the British via the tool shed for about a month, the meetings came to an abrupt end when Hoshijma became suspicious.

News of the successful escape from Berhala now encouraged other Australians to try and escape. Ted Keating's party, whose fury over Charlie Wagner's duplicity had increased tenfold with the news that he was free, was now more determined than ever. So were Blain and James, who had been joined by Driver Scott. However, Blain no longer had his gold pass. Realising that, if the Japanese found it, it might create more trouble than it was worth, he had wrapped it in a gas cape and buried it, along with two handguns and a compass, until such time as he might need them. Others were also keen to make a break – E Force's Privates Stan Davis and Tom Rumble, and Sergeants Ray Holly and Colin Lander.

When E Force had first arrived at the airstrip in early June, Keating and Stan Davis were delegated to drive a couple of recently acquired road rollers. As he manoeuvred his machine past the area assigned to the local labour force, Davis managed to speak to Henry Chang, who contacted Mu Sing. However, since at this stage there had been no word of the fate of the Berhala escapees, Mu Sing told Keating to wait and on no account to escape into the jungle. This was not what Keating, who still had Mr Brown's letters of introduction to Apostol and Paddy Funk, wanted to hear. He wrote a note, signing himself as 'Carter' which, with Brown's letters to Apostol and Paddy Funk, he gave to Henry for delivery. Apostol sent money and cigarettes, but the response from Paddy, now part of the underground, was low-key. He simply offered the same advice already given by Mu Sing to Stan Davis. Wait. However, with news arriving in early July that the Berhala group was in Tawi Tawi and serving with the guerrillas, Taylor authorised Sini and Mu Sing to advance the escape plans for the Keating and Blain groups.

Wells had made great progress with his transmitter, but May had not been a good month for the internal camp network. Gordon Weynton had been arrested when the Japanese intercepted a message he had thrown from a truck, advising the British that medical supplies could be sent over from the Australian camp. Beaten up by Hoshijima, he was left in a water-filled pit for the night and then sentenced to fourteen days in the cage. On 4 May, two days later, Eric Davis, infuriated by taunts made by Ali Asar that Australia was finished and that Japan would win the war, lost his temper and punched the detested collaborator on the jaw. Ali, who had been knocked out, wasted no time in reporting the incident. When Davis was hauled in for questioning, he soon realised that his interrogators – Hoshijima, Suga and two members of the kempeitai – were not the slightest bit concerned about the fight. They were only interested in his comings and goings at the boiler. Ali, out for revenge, had told Hoshijima that he suspected the prisoner was in contact with locals outside the camp.

Fortunately, since Ali had no hard evidence, the interrogation was exploratory, focusing on whether Davis knew various people whom the kempeitai and Hoshijima named. Some, of course, were only too well known to him. Asked about his relationship with Apostol, Davis replied that he waved to him when he saw him and had once asked about a cure for dysentery. Pop Wong, he said, was also a 'waving' acquaintance, but he had no idea who any of the others were. He was dismissed for the time being but Matthews, worried that a follow-up interrogation would not be so benign, added Davis's name to a list of prisoners being transferred to Kuching: seventeen officers and four of the younger prisoners, who were ill-disciplined and constantly in trouble.

With Eric Davis transferred to Kuching, and Ali Asar openly spying at the power plant, smuggling in parts for the transmitter to replace those which had been stolen was not as easy as was the case previously. Neither was it as easy to move outside the camp at night, as rolls of barbed wire had been placed between the two perimeter fences. When no one was available for a pick-up, Wells himself took the risk and wriggled through the wire. However, one night his shirt caught on one of the barbs of the inner fence, creating a loud pinging noise. The floodlights came on. Unable to get free, he flattened himself against the ground as bullets from the machine gun mounted near the front gate whizzed past his outstretched hands. However, after that one burst, the gun fell silent and the lights went off, allowing him to gradually ease back from the wire. Although badly shaken by the experience, Wells' determination was rewarded when he advanced the construction of the set, although not yet complete, to a stage where he was able to send two test transmissions. It would not be until after the war that he would learn that his messages had been picked up by United States personnel monitoring signal traffic in the south-west Pacific.

While Wells was occupied with his transmitter, Sini, Heng and Mu Sing, who were doing their best to assist the prisoners, had become embroiled in a plot to overthrow the Japanese. It was to be a joint operation involving Suarez's guerrillas, the local civilian population, the Constabulary and the Australian POWs, and appears have been part of a much larger movement to co-ordinate armed rebellions in Jesselton and Sandakan with Dutch-led insurrections in the south. The Jesselton group was under the command of Kwok Fen Nam, known as Albert Kwok. A well-known Chinese medical practitioner, he had been made an intelligence officer by the Chinese government while studying traditional medicine in Shanghai. Well aware of the atrocities and bloody massacres that accompanied Japanese occupation in China, he had returned to Sabah in 1940. The public notices in 1942, warning that all Chinese citizens could be seized and put to death by the Japanese High Command had a profound effect on Kwok. This terrifying edict, coupled with the recent news that the entire population of Long Nawan in neighbouring Dutch Borneo had been massacred, was a defining moment. Kwok decided it was now time for him to actively oppose the enemy.

He had been laying the foundations for rebellion for some time. In February 1942, he had tried to make contact with the Long Nawan group, but had been forced to turn back at Pensiangan on the Dutch border after discovering that any further movement by river was impossible as the Japanese had complete control of the area. The following year he met Jesselton businessman Lim Teng Fatt, who was a partner in Ban Guan and Company, a well-known merchant firm, and a most active member of the Overseas Chinese Defence Association. He was also an officer in Suarez's army. Through Fatt, Kwok was introduced to Imam Murajukim, a Muslim cleric based in Inanam who, in peacetime, was in charge of a mosque in the Sulus. The Imam was also a Filipino guerrilla agent who wore Western clothing and passed himself off as sugar trader, working out of Jesselton in much the same way as Mu Sing in Sandakan. Following a trip to the Philippines in early 1943, Kwok returned to Jesselton, where he formed the Kinabalu Guerrilla Defence Force, based at Menggatal. In June, accompanied by the Imam, he again visited Suarez, taking with him medical supplies and a donation of $11,000 to assist the Filipino guerrillas. When Kwok returned he was not only the North Borneo Guerrilla chief but also Lieutenant, United States Forces in the Philippines.

Very few officers in the Australian camp knew of Sandakan's role in the planned uprising, or that Sini and Mu Sing were laying the groundwork, paddling to Nunuyan Laut Island, five kilometres from the entrance to the Sibuga River, to organise hiding places for arms, as well as secreting rifles and machine guns brought from the Philippines in strategic spots close to the POW camp and in the Batang River area. According to the locals, co-operation from the civilians was guaranteed when Matthews, now the Police Chief, promised that if they took part in the uprising they would be assured of much better treatment. It was planned that as soon as word was received that an invasion was imminent a whistle would be blown to alert Mosher and his men. Before too long, Wells hoped that his transmitter, which was nearing completion, would be brought out of hiding and put to use.

Isolated on the north-eastern coast of Sabah, the Sandakan underground had no idea that a similar planned revolt in the south had ended in disaster. Dr B J Haga, the former Dutch Governor, had formed a group committed to the overthrow of the occupying forces in Kalimantan. However, in June the kempeitai discovered a radio transmitter and arms cache in the southern coastal town of Banjarmasin. Governor Haga and his wife were arrested at Pontianak, on the north-west coast. A further 257 people, accused of being implicated, were rounded up and tortured. Not a single one, the Hagas included, survived the purge.

There had also been activity much closer to Sandakan. Sometime in June, a mixed force of American and Filipino guerrillas from Palawan Island had raided Cagayan Sulu Island, which lay off the north-eastern tip of Sabah. Soldiers were dispatched from Sandakan to deal with the incursion, and Dr Taylor, who was still being closely watched, questioned. When this raid was followed by other, smaller raids along the coast, the Japanese began to suspect that arms were being smuggled from the Philippines and gravitating towards the POW camp.

In Sandakan, where it was business as usual, the conspirators in the camp were about to send the Blain and Keating escape groups on their way. Oblivious to the disastrous fate that had befallen those in the south and completely ignorant of the raids to the north, they were completely unprepared for what happened next. On the morning of Thursday 22 July, while most of the prisoners were working at the airstrip, the Japanese swooped on the Sandakan Number 1 POW Camp.

Chapter 7

The Sandakan Incident

The lightning nature of the raid gave the few prisoners rostered on camp duties little time to hide anything. They and the sick were herded outside the wire while the searchers, led by Hoshijima, almost tore the place apart. They collected a mountain of prohibited material, including pistols belonging to soldiers Tom Graham and Roy Davis, two pieces of paper with the latest news summaries tucked inside a pair of unidentified socks, and a map of the south-west Pacific, belonging to Lieutenant Rae. Late that afternoon Matthews, Rae, Davis and Graham were all placed under arrest.

A petty falling-out among friends was to blame. For some time Heng and his friend Dominic Koh had been buying rice from small neighbouring islands for resale in Sandakan. However, on one of these excursions a disagreement had arisen. It was over a business deal involving, of all things, singlets. Worn by coolies throughout the Far East, singlets, like rice, were in short supply. At the airstrip, POWs exchanged them for food with local people, who then offered them for sale in town at a good profit. Heng, who had promised to obtain singlets for Koh, had failed to deliver the goods. A deal was a deal, and Koh was feeling resentful. As he knew Heng had hidden Wallace and was mixed up in some kind of resistance organisation, Koh decided to blackmail him – not directly, but through his Indian friend Bah Chik, who worked at the aerodrome with Heng. Offered a half-share in the payout, Chik threatened to expose Heng unless he paid up. When Heng called his bluff, Chik and Koh told Jackie Lo, who informed Hoshijima. On 17 July, five days before the POW camp was raided, about twenty Japanese, together with Bah Chik and Lo, arrested Heng Joo Ming.

Heng was taken to the kempeitai interrogation centre on Leila Road, where he was subjected to a long and painful interrogation. When a jujitsu expert failed to extract any information of interest, he was given the water treatment. This hideous and highly effective torture, previously unknown in Sandakan, involved pinning the victim to the floor and then forcing as much water as possible down his throat with a length of hose. A member of the interrogating team then jumped from a chair onto the suspect's fully distended stomach. When Siti's father Jakariah, who had helped in Wallace's escape, was also arrested and subjected to this treatment, it did not take long for names to be named.

In the early hours of the next morning, 18 July, the kempeitai descended on Sini's house. He was arrested and taken to a building at the airstrip where he joined Siti, her mother Mrs Jakariah and Apostol. Shortly afterwards, they were taken into town where the kempeitai, in the mistaken belief that the youthful, slightly built Sini would be the weakest link in the chain, began an immediate interrogation. For the next four days Sini endured diabolical torture. After a dose of the 'water treatment' he was suspended by his wrists and beaten severely with wooden sword scabbards before being subjected to repeated jujitsu throws by a team of experts, operating in relays. He was then forced to kneel on a piece of sharp-edged timber, with a second plank passed behind his knees. Two Japanese, sitting at either end of the plank, then used it as a see-saw. Despite the excruciating pain, Sini told them nothing.

Siti, Heng's girlfriend, was also beaten up. Heng pleaded with the Japanese to release her, which they did about a fortnight later, by which time many others had been brought in for questioning and undergone extreme torture. As Siti left, she was able to snatch a few words with Heng who vowed that, should he ever be free again, he would be going after Dominic Koh. 'If not', he declared, 'my friends will also know how to deal with him.'

However, many of Heng's friends were also under interrogation. At seven o'clock on the morning of Monday 19 July, the day after Sini's arrest, a car had pulled up at a house on Bukit Merah, where Ernesto Lagan lived with his wife Katherine and four young children. The kempeitai drove him to the hospital where, in his capacity as a detective, he was forced to arrest Doctors Taylor and Wands, and dresser Peter Lai, before being arrested himself.

Taylor, a prime suspect, was interviewed by Sergeant-Major Ehara Kesao, head of the kempeitai. Their first encounter was benign but chillingly formal, with Taylor denying all knowledge about drugs supplied to the Australians. After offering to allow him and his wife to go free if he confessed, Ehara brought the interview to an end. As Ehara had no hard evidence against them as yet, he locked Taylor and Wands in a downstairs room to await further interrogation.

There was no preliminary interview for Lagan, who was subjected to immediate and prolonged torture. Unable to hold out completely, he gave up some information and admitted he had a diary. A week after his arrest, the Japanese returned his bloodstained clothing to Katherine Lagan who, fortunately, had burned the diary immediately after Ernesto was arrested. She denied all knowledge of it and stated that she knew nothing about any of his affairs. Infuriated, the kempeitai pushed her around the room shouting that, as she was his wife, she must know something. Unable to break her, they returned the next day and ransacked the house, finding incriminating documents hidden between the atap layers on the roof. The searchers then moved outdoors where, watched by Lagan's eldest son, seven-year-old Alban, near the latrine they unearthed a box, containing papers, various small bundles, a camera and a gun.

Katherine Lagan

The next day they were back again. After drawing the blinds, they herded Katherine and the four children into the darkened room, telling her that this was her last chance. Unless she told them everything she knew, she would suffer. Once again, Katherine stood firm. Keeping Alban with them, the kempeitai sent her and the three youngest children downstairs. Although Alban was promised chocolate and presents, the boy had been well-schooled by his mother and told them nothing, stating only that he was always busy playing and did not see his father bring anything home, at any time. Unable to coerce Alban into revealing anything at all, the kempeitai departed, leaving a 24-hour guard rostered at the house. For the next fifteen nights, the guard on duty woke Katherine from her sleep and fired off questions, promising that, if she told the Japanese what she knew, she would be rewarded and her husband set free. When she still refused to say anything, the kempeitai switched tactics: she could see her husband, provided they only spoke of domestic matters. However, not even the sight of Ernesto, thin and pale and seemingly devoid of any strength, weakened her resolve.

Meanwhile, Wong Mu Sing and Dick Majinal had been taken into custody, along with Gerald Mavor, Corporal Koram, Paddy Funk and Henry Chang, who were all rounded up on the day of Lagan's arrest. Paddy Funk and his entire family had been under close scrutiny. Alex, along with several others, had been taken in for questioning some weeks earlier. Although all had been released, Paddy knew it would not be long before he, too, was called in. At dusk on 19 July, the Japanese arrived at his home in the PWD quarters built out over

Dick Majinal

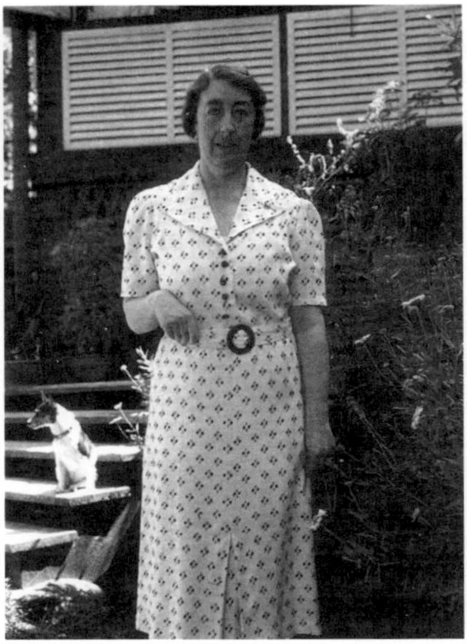

Mrs Mavor

the sea between the sawmill and Tanah Merah village. He was just sitting down to a meagre meal of ubi kayu (tapioca) chips with his wife Dimitria (Dimit) and children Gabriel and Olga when there was a loud bang on the door, followed by a hefty kick. A truckload of soldiers, bayonets drawn, waited by the side of the road. As Paddy unlocked the door, a kempeitai officer and two burly soldiers pushed their way inside. With Paddy's distressed wife and children looking on, the officer slapped Paddy across the face, kicked him in the stomach and forced him out the door and onto the truck. Terrified that the house would be searched, Dimit tore up all incriminating papers and slipped them through the cracks between the floorboards and into the sea. She then snapped into small pieces their collection of playing records featuring English songs and disposed of them in the same way.

The next suspect on the list was Henry Chang who, as he lived in a Funk-owned house at Mile 7, was an obvious target. Both he and Paddy were taken to the interrogation centre, where they were badly beaten. Paddy was subjected to the water treatment, twice. He fainted, but it brought no respite: the Japanese injected him with a stimulant so that they could continue. Meanwhile, a posse of soldiers had returned to raid Henry's house. His mother, wife and young niece, Theresa, were ordered to stand in the corner of a room while the entire building was ransacked. However, not comprehending the seriousness of the situation, Theresa followed the soldiers into Henry's room. When one wrenched out a drawer of the writing desk, a tobacco tin, which had been attached to the underside, came free and rolled across the floor, unnoticed by the search party. The design on the lid caught Theresa's eye so she grabbed it and hid it under the rag doll she was cradling.

As she cuddled her doll, the soldiers continued their search – slitting pillows and mattresses; tossing aside rugs and furnishings; searching behind pictures, in trunks and boxes and under beds. They even dug up the garden. Finding nothing, they eventually left.

Theresa had what they wanted. In the tin were a list of people involved in the underground network, the plan of escape, names of Australians who had absconded, pictures of various POWs, letters addressed to their families, and medals from the Great War. Theresa's aunt fainted when she saw the contents of the tin. Fortunately, the grandmother was more practical. She burnt the documents and buried the medals before hurrying away to Mile 9 to warn other relatives. Three hours later, the Japanese were back. They arrested Theresa and her aunt, who were forced to walk in the pouring rain to the interrogation centre. The aunt denied all knowledge of any documents or weapons and, after three days, they were released. Luckily, the Japanese had not bothered to question Theresa who, a few days before her uncle's arrest, had seen Paddy Funk hand Henry a hessian sack, which they hid under the chicken coop. Fortunately, this was the one place not searched. Inside the bag were two pistols.

Koram, however, was in deep trouble. Three collaborators named Gurisman, Wah Singh and Burrong, sent to question the lepers, had discovered he had been seen with the escapees. Although badly beaten, he denied everything, but his stoicism was in vain. Lagan, under torture, revealed that Koram had helped the Australians escape. Of all those arrested to date, Lagan's interrogations had been the most brutal: the Japanese were furious that he had 'betrayed' them. Taking advantage of a break in his own interrogation while the kempeitai concentrated on the unfortunate Lagan, Koram climbed out the lavatory window and escaped. Although the guards gave chase and fired at him, he did not keep running but remained close by, so close that he stole food from the kempeitai's pantry. After about a week he moved to the town reservoir, where fellow policemen Apuk and Gatua kept him supplied with food. A fortnight later, recovered from his injuries, he made his way to the jetty at Sandakan, where he set fire to the Japanese storage tanks and a fuel tender moored at the dockside. He then travelled to the Japanese office at Beluran, where he informed the local administration that he had come to take a census of the local population. Using this ruse, he resumed the role assigned to him by Rice-Oxley before the surrender – to stay behind the lines and gather information for the Allies. When Koram finished taking his 'census' at Beluran, the Japanese obligingly gave him food and cigarettes and supplied three coolies to carry his belongings to the next destination, which he said was Keningau, hundreds of kilometres to the south-west. However, Koram headed instead for Kota Belud, on the north-west coast, a journey that took almost three weeks. Here he met up with two old friends from the Constabulary, Dado Siniong and Jemadar Gubud, who invited him to join Albert Kwok's Kinabalu Guerrillas.

Kept in solitary confinement for a week after his interrogation, Paddy Funk had no idea that the rooms at the torture house were filling rapidly. Bernard Quadra, brother of Alberto, was arrested on 20 July, along with Matusup, lured into the arms of the kempeitai by a Chinese collaborator. Within two days, the Australians arrested began to arrive.

When the Japanese swarmed into the Mile 8 Camp on 22 July, most of the B Force officers were working in the vegetable garden, where Matthews, named by Heng and Lagan, was arrested. When Tommy Graham discovered, on his return from the airfield, that his pistol and ammunition (souvenired from the body of his senior officer who had been killed during the fighting in Singapore) were in Hoshijima's office, he voluntarily turned himself in. On the advice of a senior officer, Graham 'confessed' that, although he had the pistol in his possession, he was not the owner. The real owner, he claimed, was an officer who had been killed in 'an honourable battle', and he was taking it home to the dead man's relatives, in much the same way as swords of Japanese officers killed in action were returned to their families. While this 'confession' did not save Graham from being arrested, it would go some way towards mitigating any punishment.

The kempeitai had yet to recognise the significance of the news summaries compiled by Wells, but anyone who had any contact with the underground was in danger. Fortunately for Matthews, his pistol and ammunition were not discovered. One of his fellow officers, confined to the camp with illness, had hidden them in the bottom of a cupboard. As he was able, Rus Ewin arranged for them to be smuggled to Abin's house, where they were hidden in the chimney, along with Ewin's diary and some nominal rolls.

Although Wells' intelligence reports were safely with Abin, it was bad luck that the Japanese had found the news summaries. Friday was collection day, and in another twenty-four hours they would have been gone. Although he had written them in an abbreviated form of code, Wells knew it would not take the kempeitai long to work it out. And when they did, they would be back.

He was right. Two days later, there was another, more thorough search of the camp. The Japanese did not find the radio in its hiding place at the bottom of the latrine, or the transmitter, wrapped in oiled paper and buried between the officers' huts. However, they found some very incriminating evidence. The three maps drawn for Matthews, showing buildings, troop dispositions and military information, were still in the camp. They also seized a very small black notebook, said to have been found hidden among the buttress roots of The Big Tree.

That afternoon, when the working parties returned, they were assembled on the road outside the gate. Climbing onto the back of a truck, Hoshijima called for POW 124 to step forward – Rod Wells. Hoshijima produced the news summaries from his pocket, which Wells admitted were his. Enraged, Hoshijima yelled 'You have radio', punching the lieutenant about the head and face and trying to throttle him with the sweat rag tied around his neck. Under interrogation in Hoshijima's office, the Australian denied all knowledge of any radio, until presented with a list of parts, extracted from civilians undergoing torture. Wells then took Hoshijima on a wild goose chase through the camp, pretending to look for the radio, until he accepted that the charade could not continue indefinitely. Thinking, quite rightly, that the Japanese would not know one piece of wireless equipment from another, he decided to sacrifice the transmitter to save the receiver. At about 6 pm he handed it over. A gloating Hoshijima, believing he had the prize in his hands, paraded Wells before the other prisoners before sending him off to the kempeitai. Like most of the other Australians, he was not interrogated immediately, but held instead in a cell beneath the main building, where the cries of the tormented being interrogated in the room above were clearly audible.

With or without the news summaries, Hoshijima had been certain there was a radio in the camp. On 22 July, the day the POW camp was first raided, the number of arrests had escalated. Heng admitted passing wireless parts to Wallace, while Lagan, unable to endure the appalling torture, signed a confession that implicated many. On 23 July Mohamet Salleh, Samuel Aruliah and Sergeant Abin were all arrested. The following day, the Japanese arrested Celia Taylor and Mrs Mavor. They were detained in a downstairs cell for some weeks where, in spite of close questioning and being beaten with a riding whip, they revealed nothing of their husbands' activities.

The Japanese were exerting considerable pressure. The kempeitai not only had Lagan's signed confession, a list of wireless components and the names of those who had supplied them, they had also extracted a confession from Ng Ho Kong. He had been arrested after his name, along with that of Chan Ah Ping, had been mentioned by their elderly boss, Mr Mavor.

The next day, 25 July, the Japanese escorted a badly beaten Ng to Ah Ping's house at Mile 8. On seeing the terrible condition his friend was in, Ah Ping came out of hiding and, within the hour, he, too, was behind bars. Brought in for immediate interrogation, he denied he had anything to confess: a response which resulted in being struck around the face and head with the sole of a wooden sandal, which had been rubbed in wet sand. He was then thrown to the floor, brutally kicked and belted thirty times with a stick before being taken to Sandakan Gaol, where he was placed in a cell alongside Ng Ho Kong. Ng confided that, as he had admitted to everything, it would be wise for Ah Ping to do the same. The following morning, 26 July, when dragged before the kempeitai for reinterrogation, Ah Ping also signed a statement.

On the strength of this confession, Lieutenant Moritake immediately confronted Sergeant Stevens who, admitting his complicity under questioning, was bashed and kicked before being tied up and taken into town. The next day he was joined by two other links in the line of communication – two members of the wood party, Corporals Roffey and McMillan. Other officers and men thought to be implicated in what the Japanese would later term 'The Sandakan Incident', were put on short rations and confined to the cage, some of them for well over a week. Anyone associated with Matthews or the underground waited in trepidation, none more so than Rus Ewin, who had not only been actively involved but slept in the bunk next to Wells. Although Captains Brown and Harold St John, who shared a cubicle with Wells, were taken away, Ewin need not have worried. There was no way the kempeitai were going to get anything out of Wells.

Meanwhile, Matthews and Taylor, who had been severely flogged, had been removed from solitary confinement and placed in a large room, measuring about eight metres by eleven metres. Lieutenant Rae, Graham and Davis, who had been arrested with Matthews, had been moved to Sandakan Gaol, where Ng and Ah Ping were being held. Staffed by members of the Constabulary, it was a holiday camp compared to the interrogation centre, where all inmates, except when being questioned, were forced to sit cross-legged and at attention from 7.30 am until 9.30 pm. The only movement permitted when not being interrogated (when there was far too much physical activity) was during a five-minute exercise session each morning and afternoon. Anyone not performing the exercises to the satisfaction of the guards was beaten or made to 'freeze' in awkward positions for up to ten minutes at a time. At night, the prisoners slept on the floor, but remained under constant surveillance, with a light kept burning. As interrogations could occur at any hour of the day or night, it was often a disturbed sleep, punctuated by the cries of agony of those undergoing the latest round of questioning. In all, well over 100 people were arrested. Anyone who came under the slightest suspicion was held, beaten, interrogated and then either released or detained for further questioning. No communication with the outside was permitted, but local people were allowed to have meals sent in by their families, enabling Apostol's wife to smuggle in 400 dollars in cash. Through her father's Japanese friend Simuda, a storekeeper of many years standing and now an interpreter with the Japanese Civil Administration, Gabriela Lai was able to send in a gold chain to her husband, concealed in a water flask. Sometimes, if the guards were not too vigilant, the local people were able to pass messages and additional rations to the Europeans, whose food consisted of a small cup of rice, with a small amount of vegetables or a cubic centimetre of rock salt or salt fish, served twice a day.

Six other attempts to escape via the lavatory window failed. However, messages were smuggled in and out, and from one prisoner to another, in the bottom of the food containers brought in by relatives. Matthews, who had not met Taylor face-to-face until their imprisonment, also managed to communicate with him by using his fingers to trace out words on his thigh. Later, when Matthews' signallers and members of the Constabulary and Volunteers joined him, they devised a method of using finger movements to communicate in Morse code. Although they were all seated, with arms folded and all facing the same way, the rows were staggered, enabling those behind to see the finger movements of those in front. Although the guards noticed that Matthews was constantly moving his fingers, they put it down to some kind of mental instability or anxiety.

Meanwhile, the investigations ground on. When Sergeant-Major Yangsalang, who was also severely tortured, declined to make a statement, the kempeitai gave him three days to think about it. During this period, he was confined to a room close to the interrogation chamber and was able to hear information, which incriminated him, being dragged out of fellow policemen Gorokon, Abin and Kassiu. When Lagan, who was undergoing another bout of torture, was brought in for re-interrogation, Yangsalang was left in no doubt that the kempeitai knew everything. Believing there was absolutely no point in holding out any longer, he agreed to make a statement. As punishment for not telling the truth the first time, the kempeitai beat him up again.

Because of his height and the respect he commanded from both the Constabulary and the civilian population, Jemadar Ojagar Singh was especially targeted. Although police friends had warned him that his name had been revealed by others under interrogation, he had refused the entreaties of his wife to escape, believing that, if he did, the Japanese would harass his family and possibly hold them to ransom. Shortly after Ojagar's arrest the Japanese, acting on further information, escorted him to his house. Ojagar, who remained perfectly calm, told his wife to look after the children. The Japanese then ordered his daughter, Biba, to show them the chicken coop, further up the hill. The searchers, who knew exactly what they were looking for, retrieved letters sent by Rex Blow seeking assistance for his escape. They then searched the house, moving gold jewellery, cash, and a pistol and ammunition. As the family had no means of support, Mrs Singh, who was pregnant, moved into the police barracks.

The Japanese seemed to delight in brutalising prisoners who were physically larger than they, or who were leading members of the community. Unfortunately, the tall Sikh fitted into both categories. During his violent interrogations, his jaw was broken and his elbow shattered. Dr Taylor tried to help ease his pain but, as the steadfastly loyal policeman would reveal nothing, the Japanese denied him medical treatment as an additional punishment. Mrs Singh was not permitted to visit and it was only through police friends that she was able to find out anything. As she washed her husband's clothes, soaked with blood and pus, she would pray, tears rolling down her cheeks, certain that she could hear Ojagar 'calling' to her that he would die and that she must look after their children.

Salleh, another suspect targeted for 'betraying' his Japanese employers, revealed Mohamed Tahir's name while under torture. The police constable was on his usual beat around town when he was told to report back to the barracks, as he was wanted by the kempeitai. Denying everything, he was stripped to his underwear and, with hands tied behind his back, was taken to the interrogation centre, where the Japanese beat him night after night in an effort to make him confess. One of his Australian cellmates, who spoke Malay, encouraged Tahir to admit nothing, as he was only accused of collaboration, not of being involved with the resistance organisation. However, the kempeitai kept up the pressure, flogging him senseless with a thick rope and exhorting him to avoid execution by confessing.

When he finally did, he was flogged again for his trouble. Like all those arrested, he spent the next two months or so sitting at attention.

On 27 July, Chan Tian Joo was brought in. With interrogations among those already detained continuing, one name was leading to another. Heng mentioned Frank Martin's name, resulting in his arrest four days later. Flogged severely, Martin's face and body were so badly mutilated that he found it difficult to move for some time. As an additional punishment he was transferred to the POW camp, where he spent several days in the cage.

As July passed into August, the members of the underground fell like ninepins. Abin, who, despite his stoicism was unable to withstand the prolonged and brutal bouts of interrogation, had let other information slip, resulting in the arrests of Dr Laband and Mr Phillips, along with Mrs Cohen, who was placed in the downstairs cell with Celia Taylor and Mrs Mavor. Soh Kim Seng, Wong Wee Man, Lo Hoi Tshi and Lau Bui Ching were all imprisoned in early August, along with Alex Funk.

Alex, who, following his earlier interview, was being pressured by the kempeitai to become a spy, had been working at a timber camp with Felix Azcona Junior and Johnny on an island in the Labuk under a forced labour programme. He had told his step-mother Helen that he would not collaborate with the Japanese and would run away, but an informant alerted the kempeitai, who were also told that Alex had a weapon. He and Felix were caught at Kemansi, on the far side of the river, and arrested. Alex was taken to the Sandala Estate, another Funk property at Mile 14, where other relatives, including his wife, were grilled regarding the conversion of Australian currency and the whereabouts of Alex's .303 rifle, believed to be buried close to the Mile 8 Camp. With no information forthcoming, Alex was taken to Sandakan and handed over to the kempeitai, along with Felix Junior. After four days of torture, he confessed that he had buried his rifle.

When Alex arrived at the Mile 7 house, escorted by the kempeitai's Ehara and Kuno, part of his ear was missing, his clothing was soaked in blood and his face badly swollen. His father and his youngest bother Ernie were now forced to accompany him, under guard, to Henry Chang's house. Young Theresa watched as Alex, dressed in filthy, torn clothing, his face grotesquely swollen from repeated beatings, dug up the precious rifle and ammunition. John Simon and Ernie were then allowed to return home. While they had been absent Helen Funk, alarmed at her son's condition and by the unexpected arrival of the kempeitai, burnt letters and photographs belonging to Matthews which were hidden in the house.

At the interrogation centre, Lagan and Taylor were having a very difficult time. In about the second week of August both men saw their wives. Taylor had just been subjected to three hours of continual flogging. Ehara, with three members of the kempeitai, had handcuffed him before punching him about the face, beating his head with a wet, sand-covered shoe and kicking him repeatedly about the body. For good measure, they also banged his head repeatedly against the walls of the interrogation room. With his face swollen and raw; his chest, back and stomach black and blue; and blood saturating his shorts and running down his legs, he was escorted downstairs to his wife. Although Ehara yelled for her to 'Tell your husband to tell the truth, or he will die', Celia responded only with a whispered 'Oh my God, Jim. What have they done to you?'.

Katherine Lagan was permitted to see her husband again on the condition that they spoke only of family matters. She had brought a change of clothing with her and remained while he put them on. It was only now that she saw a large dark blue bruise running down the entire side of his body, and a deep wound across his back, which had been stitched. In answer to her distressed questions, Lagan said only that he had fallen down, mentioning nothing of the suffering he had endured. Devastated that he had been unable to hold out under the torture, he asked her to send in extra food for the Australians imprisoned with him. When she replied that she was short of funds, he told her to 'sell all my clothes and shoes, and buy more food with the money'.

Before the week was out, Sergeant-Major Ehara was confronting Joseph Pop Wong. At 10 am on 13 August, the kempeitai chief appeared without warning at a rice field at the experimental farm, calling out Pop's name. With him was Lamberto Apostol, who had let Wong's name slip during interrogation. On arrival at kempeitai headquarters Wong was slapped across the face twice and asked where the radio valves were. Although Apostol, who was brought in, stated that he had given Pop two valves, Wong's repeated denials earned him the log treatment, followed by the water torture. A good half-hour of face slapping with a wooden slipper was next, interspersed by repeated requests to divulge the whereabouts of the valves. Wong replied that while he had never had any valves, he did have two light globes, given to him by Apostol, which he had thrown away as they did not fit the sockets. Ehara did not believe him. For the next six days he was subjected to the log treatment, water torture and wet sandal slap, beaten with a heavy stick, lacerated with a sword scabbard, had chilli rubbed into his genitals, and was threatened with decapitation. When the prospect of losing his head failed to achieve the desired effect, he was spreadeagled on a table and beaten mercilessly.

When finally released from his bonds an hour later, Pop Wong was taken to a nearby room, where Dr Taylor, Mr Phillips, Gerald Mavor, Apostol, Chan Ah Ping, Abin, Lionel Matthews, Sergeant Stevens, Alex Funk, Paddy Funk, Felix Azcona and Wong Mu Sing were all being held. Recalling that the Japanese were said to be compassionate towards the mentally afflicted, Wong began campaign to have himself declared insane. When Ehara beat him, he laughed; when given food, he threw it away; and when ordered to sit at attention, he threw himself down the stairs with a wild-eyed look, or sang. He even drank his own urine: not because he thought it would help his charade but because he had heard that it was beneficial in healing internal injuries. The Japanese, convinced he was certifiably insane, ceased the interrogations and sent him to the mental hospital.

Pop Wong kept up the pretence for three months. At the end of this period, having convinced everyone that he was an 'orang gila' (madman), he was fined and released. Once outside, he put on quite a show, by removing his trousers, urinating, and then walking along the Buli Sim Sim Road with his trousers in his hands, laughing and shouting all the way. It was all too much for the Japanese. They returned his fine and instructed him to buy some medicine. Once out of sight, Wong slipped quietly away and hid on a plantation near Mile 15 until the Japanese had forgotten all about him.

Unfortunately, they had not forgotten about Wong's accomplices. On 29 July, Gordon Weynton had been arrested and thrown in the cage at the camp where he spent he next sixteen days. For the first fourteen he was not interrogated. However, while Hoshijima was not aware that the radio set handed over by Wells was a transmitter, by 12 August he knew from information extracted from the locals that 'another' set (actually the rebuilt receiver) had been made, and that Weynton had something to do with it. Parading Weynton in his office, Hoshijima demanded that he reveal the location of the second radio. When Weynton pleaded his innocence, he was returned to the cage, during which time food, water and visits to the latrine were denied. On the morning of 14 August, bound hand and foot, he was thrown into a lorry and taken to the interrogation centre.

That same day, Rod Wells, who had spent the previous three weeks in solitary confinement in a downstairs cell, was escorted to the interrogation room. Attached to the wall was a large flow-chart showing the progress of the investigation, and who was linked to whom. It was obvious to Wells that, to wrap up their case, all the kempeitai required were signed confessions. In an effort to obtain his, the interrogators subjected Wells to terrible torture.

On 14 August, when the usual whippings, floggings and beatings did not produce the desired outcome, Wells was passed to Ehara, who rapped him repeatedly on the head with a hammer, before tapping a thin bamboo skewer into his ear canal, perforating his eardrum and destroying the nerves in his middle ear. When Wells regained consciousness after this excruciating ordeal, and still refused to confess, Ehara forced him to eat three cups of raw rice, washed down with large amounts of water. As the rice absorbed the water, it swelled, distending Wells' stomach and intestines so greatly that loops of his lower bowel were forced from his body. Far from admitting anything, Wells simply pushed his intestines back.

Two days later, while trying to force him to confess that Major Fleming was involved in a planned insurrection, Ehara used a version of 'the rack': a torture device which stretched the joints to breaking point and not seen in the Western world since the sixteen century. Handcuffed, Wells was suspended by his wrists from one of the verandah rafters, so that his knees dangled fifteen centimetres from the floor. A long heavy piece of timber, about ten centimetres square, was then positioned behind his knees. When two men stood on either end of the plank, the upper body of the victim was effectively 'racked'. When the plank was placed across Wells' heels, the flesh was torn from his ankles, causing him to pass out. He called out for his mother in his agony, but never once did he tell his tormentors what they wished to know.

The sight of Wells' ruptured bowel and his racking helped strengthen Gordon Weynton's resolve. Like Taylor and his fellow officers, Weynton had no intention of caving in, no matter how dire the punishment. He had spent the first two days at the kempeitai headquarters sitting cross-legged in the main holding room but, on 16 August, the day of Wells' racking, was removed to the interrogation room where Ehara, believing he could extract information on Matthews, Wells and the radio, beat him about the head and shoulders with a riding crop and pressed burning cigarettes into the tender flesh of his armpits. Weynton said nothing: not even when Ehara put him through it all again three days later, with a jujitsu session thrown in for good measure.

On 28 August, Weynton was moved from the main room, subjected to another round of torture and reinterrogated. When he still refused to admit anything, the kempeitai showed him statements by the locals naming him as one of those who had obtained radio parts. As a trump card, they produced Dick Majinal's updated list of radio components and the little black notebook. When Weynton realised it referred to activities in which he, Small and Mills had taken part, he had no option but to admit the existence of the second radio, resulting in its recovery from the camp on 30 August, and the arrest of its custodians, Rickards, Small and Mills.

With all those involved in the transmitter and receiver now identified, the kempeitai increased the pressure. For the next four to five days, suspects were interrogated and re-interrogated, including Samuel Aruliah, who had been released in July, only to be re-arrested on 11 August. Every time one of them differed on a detail, all would be beaten until agreement was reached. Once the second radio was found, attention turned to Weynton in an effort to gain more information on Wells and Matthews. When tacks hammered under his fingernails failed to break him, he was racked. When that also failed, Ehara turned his attention to other victims.

As no British prisoners were involved, none was brought in for questioning. However on 16 August, evidently in an attempt to make sure that British POWs were not led astray by more senior ranks, the Japanese transferred all but nine of the forty officers to Kuching. Two days later, the remainder were moved from the airfield to a new compound adjoining the E Force Camp, where a closer watch could be kept on them.

However, it was the Australians who remained in the spotlight. The arrest of Blain and James on 8 September was followed two days later by that of Keating, who was implicated by Henry Chang and also by the note to Apostol. When local people were brought out to the camp to identify prisoners with whom they had been in contact, the rest of Keating's group joined him: Weston, Rumble, Lander, Jensen, Marshall and Holly on the 19th, and Stan Davis on the 25th. Suffering from dysentery and scarcely able to walk because of a huge leg ulcer, Keating was beaten unmercifully by Ehara for passing a note to Weynton, while the others were given a variation of the log treatment. Marshall and Stevens, considered to be 'serious' cases, were burned with cigarettes. Although ambulanceman Bill McDonough was not involved in any escape plans, the Japanese discovered he had supplied chemicals (for what, they were not quite sure), resulting in his arrest on 15 September. As Abin had confessed to carrying messages to E Force on Berhala, Matthews was forced to name Poole and Morrison as the two lieutenants who were the recipients.

Abin did not, however, reveal the hiding place in the chimney. Had he done so, Wells would have been finished. Even then, the

Australian lieutenant escaped by only the most slender of margins. The kempeitai were on their way to search Abin's house when they hit a water buffalo, greatly delaying their arrival. This gave his wife, Bintang binte Udung, who was warned by some sixth sense, time to dispose of the pistol and all the documents hidden in the chimney before the search party arrived.

By early September, just about everyone connected to the underground was behind bars: Ngui Ah Kui; the Goh brothers and Foo Seng Chow who had helped the escape party at Mile 11; Damudaran, who had helped smuggle food and medicine to them in the gaol; contributors to the escape fund; Jakariah's friend, Sidek; and Inspector Samuel Guriaman and other loyal members of the Constabulary, all of whom had pledged unswerving allegiance to Matthews.

The Goh brothers, whose names were mentioned by Lagan, were rather portly gentlemen. Deciding that they could not stand up to much in the way of torture, they admitted only to having given the escaped prisoners small quantities of food on a couple of occasions. Although Puloro Mananai had allowed them to hide in the jungle hut and had given them food, his name had not been mentioned, so he was safe for the time being. Damudaran, who had been arrested with Inspector Guriaman in August, signed a confession after being severely thrashed with a Malacca cane around the face and head, and brutally kicked.

Sergeant-Major Yusup was attending a Japanese School of Instruction in Kuching at the time of his arrest in September. On searching his house, the Japanese had found a pencil drawing of Matthews and pictures of King George VI and Queen Elizabeth, as well as Winston Churchill, the British Prime Minister. As Yusup was not there when these items were discovered, the Japanese took out their fury on his wife, who was beaten so badly she was vomiting blood.

In early September, the kempeitai also caught up with Johnny Funk. He had been working at the timber camp on the Labuk with Alex and Felix Azcona but had returned to Bilit where Lillian, with the help of Dora Stookes, had recently given birth to a baby girl. Shortly before the Japanese arrived, Johnny took his small son Melvyn to the far side of the farm to shoot a large eagle that had been causing problems for local farmers. When they returned to the house, a Japanese officer armed with a sword was waiting, along with six or seven soldiers, bayonets drawn. Standing on the porch, facing this terrifying invasion and intimidating display of power, was the tiny figure of Lillian Funk, restrained but fearless. After relieving Johnny of his shotgun, the officer slapped him viciously, while the soldiers kicked and belted him with rifle butts until he fell to the ground. He was then securely trussed and dragged to the small motor launch, which headed down the river to Sandakan.

Now that Johnny had been arrested, it was far too dangerous for Lillian to remain at the farm. With her every move monitored by collaborators on the Japanese estate opposite, she put into train a contingency plan that she and Johnny had agreed upon some months before. Packing up as much as she could carry, and with baby Doreen on her back, she and Melvyn followed Johnny to Sandakan, where they joined the extended Funk family, now living in John Simon's house at Mile 7.

To Melvyn's delight, this included his fun-loving Uncle Ernie. Now aged in his early twenties, Ernie was in Singapore with his brother Eddie, studying engineering when war had broken out. As a member of a machine-gun company with a local defence force unit, the Straits Settlement Volunteers, Ernie had been mobilised and was on guarding the approach to Robinson Road when Singapore fell. A few weeks later, in keeping with a policy known as 'Operation Cleanup' – to exterminate any Chinese with British affiliations, Western leanings or supporting the China Relief Fund – Ernie was ordered to leave his house at 118 Killiney Road, just behind Fort Canning, and report to a concentration centre on Arab Street. Anyone with an English name, who wore Western clothing or glasses, was educated, or spoke English, was segregated for subsequent execution.

Ernie Funk

Fortunately, Ernie managed to fool the Japanese checking identities by changing his name to Fung Loi Fook, which was simple to write in Chinese characters. Believing he was harmless, the Japanese military gave him a 'chop' (Japanese symbol) to wear on his shirtsleeve. As one of many Chinese labourers, he was then sent to work on a rusting cargo ship which was bound for Borneo. Like Pop Wong, Ernie knew that the Japanese were compassionate to those who were affected

Johnny and Paddy Funk

mentally in some way. For the entire voyage to Miri he put on a great show of being poorly coordinated, by dropping and breaking various items. When hit with rifle butts and fists as punishment, he sang and danced about. Believing he was definitely intellectually handicapped, and therefore nothing more than a strain on their resources, the Japanese ordered him from the ship at Miri.

After working as a labourer for Mr Saga, an Indian, Ernie managed to obtain leave. Aware that the lives of his brothers, being Volunteers, and, indeed, the lives of the entire pro-British Funk family were at risk, he returned immediately to Sandakan. He had arrived home shortly before Alex, Johnny and Paddy were placed under arrest.

With the three Funk brothers now in custody, the investigation against Alex began in earnest. Johnny and Paddy were then given a dose of the same treatment in an attempt to discover if they, too, had weapons secreted anywhere. During his interrogation Johnny had his jaw broken and was subjected to five types of torture: the log treatment; jujitsu; slipper slapping; spine bashing with wooden scabbards; and face whipping. Nothing the Japanese did to him made the slightest difference. Matthews, who had not divulged anything, had managed to advise Johnny to remain silent. The older man recognised in Johnny an iron will and determination to survive. He also knew that Johnny, a trained signaller, could read Morse code, so he entrusted him with the full story of the organisation, which he tapped out with his foot. Lionel Matthews then added a very personal plea: 'If anything happens to me, Johnny, and if you ever happen to met my wife, or any Australians, tell them that I have died for my country.'

John Simon Funk and his wife Helen had also been questioned by the kempeitai, who suspected them of collaborating with their three sons, and knowingly assisting the prisoners of war, by allowing their property to be used as a staging post for meetings between the underground and the camp. However, despite a lengthy grilling, insufficient evidence could be brought against them and they had not been arrested. Their daughters-in-law Maggie, Dimit and Lillian had also been interrogated and beaten, but none had given up any information. Although the entire Funk family was under suspicion, John Simon decided to visit Kempeitai headquarters to plea for the release of his sons. Far from showing any mercy, the kempeitai gave him a severe thrashing for his trouble.

By mid-September the kempeitai had finished their investigations. Not only had the principal ringleaders 'confessed', they had confessed most satisfactorily – mainly because Ozawa and Miura Isawu had 'translated' the confessions. The Australians believed that these mistranslations were deliberate. Although Miura, a 37-year-old ex-pupil from St Michael's School was also later accused of beating prisoners, he went out of his way to help fellow 'old boy', Sini.

With the confessions secured, all that remained was to ship the 52 civilians and 20 POWs to Kuching to stand trial for crimes ranging from insurrection to money changing. While the key personnel would face the most serious charges, Lamberto Apostol had the longest and most diverse list: supplying milk and eggs to the camp hospital; trafficking in chickens and salt; sending Christmas cakes to the internees at Berhala (with the help of his Japanese friend, Goto Sang, the food contractor); acting as a news courier; passing notes; procuring radio parts; and helping POWs escape.

With 72 criminals behind bars and awaiting transfer to Kuching, Ehara and his gang had good reason to feel satisfied, especially when they heard that another uprising in Dutch Borneo, bigger than the last, had been thwarted. During September, acting on a report that resistance fighters connected to Dr Haga's Banjarmasin group were planning to overthrow Pontianak, the Japanese had rounded up 1500 suspects, almost all of whom had been tortured and killed.

On 15 October, most of those still held by the kempeitai were transferred to the Sandakan Gaol. The exceptions were Ojagar

Singh and several others, who remained at the interrogation centre; Keating, who had been admitted to hospital with his leg ulcer; and Felix Azcona Senior, who had been released, along with Dr Wands. Captains Brown and St John, with Lieutenants Rae, Morrison and Poole, and also Sergeant Weston, were given the good news that, although they would be shipped to Kuching, they would not be tried.

Lillian and Maggie Funk made the trip into Sandakan from Mile 7 every day with food for Johnny and Alex. Standing outside the prison wall with their children, they and Paddy's wife Dimit shouted at the tops of their voices to let their men know that they were there, and that food parcels were on the way. Other families also brought along food, but none of it went beyond the two surly Japanese guarding the prison door. Inspector Samuel Guriaman received no messages or food parcels from his wife. She had died of a broken heart a week after his arrest.

While the prisoners were still languishing in gaol and the Sandakan kempeitai basked in the glow of their successful investigation, some startling news arrived from Jesselton. Albert Kwok and the Kinabalu Guerrillas had staged a massive revolt.

Chapter 8

Retribution

After Kwok's return from his meeting with Suarez in Tawi Tawi on 10 September, he had expanded his guerrilla organisation to include ex-Volunteers and members of the Constabulary, Koram among them, as well as Suluks and other islanders. The Jesselton A Company Volunteers were integral to his cause, with training organised by several members, including Lieutenant Tet Phui and Sergeant Jules Pavitt Stephens, Helen Funk's brother.

The Dusun farmers and Murut tribespeople of the interior, worried about losing their traditional lands if they supported an uprising, were still making up their minds about joining the guerrilla forces when there was a shocking new development. Evidently concerned about the unrest in Dutch Borneo, the Japanese announced that, in order to release regular soldiers for combat, 2,000 young Chinese men from the west coast area were to be conscripted into the Japanese army to act as garrison troops.

Kwok was extremely concerned. Enforced conscription would not only deprive him of recruits, it would also increase the number of enemy soldiers available to oppose his guerrillas. Even worse, the Japanese had decreed that local Chinese girls were to work in Japanese brothels as 'comfort women', while all former Volunteers were to report for immediate duty. Kwok had to mobilise now, ready or not.

The opposition his guerrillas faced was formidable. Besides regular troops stationed at Pensiangan and Ranau in the interior, and Jesselton and other centres along the coast, there were numerous kempeitai detachments, Japanese-controlled police garrisons at Jesselton, Menggatal and Tuaran, and paid informants known as Jikidans in the villages. At the time of the announcements, Kwok's forced numbered about 100 Kinabalu Guerrillas and roughly 200 other volunteers, mainly islanders. Some of his men had military training, but the majority were raw recruits.

Unlike Sandakan, there were no POWs on hand to give possible further assistance; until arms pledged by Suarez arrived from the Philippines, Kwok would have to rely on a groundswell of resistance to keep the Japanese at bay. As soon as his men were properly armed, the guerrilla leader planned to harass the enemy with hit-and-run attacks in the style of Mat Salleh until the Allies could mount an invasion force and drive out the Japanese.

After a great deal of deliberation, the date for a co-ordinated uprising at various locations around Jesselton was set for the night of 9 October – the eve of the Double Tenth festivities, held on the tenth day of the tenth month, to celebrate the anniversary of a successful Chinese revolution in the 1930s led by Dr Sun Yat Sen. It was Kwok's belief that, if Jesselton's Chinese could celebrate this day as free people, they would be motivated to continue the fight against the occupying forces.

In spite of their well-organised spy network, the Japanese in Jesselton had no idea that an uprising was underway until a Formosan informant arrived from Menggatal, by which time it was too late; the guerrillas had attacked the police posts to obtain the necessary arms. Instead of coming to the aid of the police, the kempeitai hid in their heavily fortified interrogation centre at Victoria Barracks, allowing Kwok's men to gain the upper hand. With their objectives secured, the guerrillas sounded a bugle – the signal for the islanders, who had come from as far as Pulau Tiga in the south and the Mantanani islands in the north, to swarm over the sea walls, attack the Customs House and invade the main part of town. As they did so, Corporal Koram and his police friends, who were with a group designated as the 'Second Foot', went into action, setting fire to the main wharf and the warehouses, filled with highly inflammable rubber. It was hoped that the huge fires, which lasted for more than a week, would alert any Allied submarines that were in the area but, unfortunately, there was no response.

All Japanese attempting to flee to the safety of Government House or Victoria Barracks were shot dead and beheaded. Among those killed was the Japanese food controller, who was dragged from his car. Anyone who escaped was either extremely fleet of foot or jumped into the harbour and swam to Gaya Island, to hide among the mangroves or in the jungle.

The battle lasted just three hours. When the sun rose over Jesselton the next morning the inhabitants saw a wondrous sight: the flags of British North Borneo, Great Britain, the United States and China fluttering from every prominent building in town. It was the same elsewhere, especially in Mansiang, near Menggatal, where Kwok had his headquarters and where the victory celebrations were the most jubilant of all. Two days later, when Kota Belud fell to the guerrillas, they marked the occasion by executing every member of the Japanese police force.

However, it did not take long for the Japanese to regroup. Within four days they struck back, rushing reinforcements into Jesselton. Eight aircraft from Kuching bombed and strafed the villages along the Jesselton–Tuaran road, forcing the rebels holding Inanam to blow up the bridge and retreat to Tuaran. Reprisals were swift and merciless, with entire villages wiped out. However, in spite of this, many more rebels joined the cause. More than 2,400 men took part in the revolt over the next eight weeks, carrying out commando-like raids on Japanese stationed along the west coast and in the hinterland. The guerrillas lost 1,300 men. According to the number of severed heads, the Japanese dead totalled 1,900. However, without outside help, the attacks could not be sustained. Rewards of between $1000 and $5000 were being offered for the ringleaders, preferably alive. If dead, the head would be sufficient proof of capture. Ammunition and supplies were also running low, forcing Kwok to pull back to new positions – not to the safety of the mountainous interior, but in secluded valleys along the coast where they could watch for relief vessels sent from the Philippines.

Kwok was confident that help would come. Word had been received from Lim, now a Captain in the United States army, that not only were reinforcements on their way from the Philippines, but also that Australian soldiers were at Labian Point, about 140 kilometres south of Sandakan. It was not an invasion force, as he had hoped, but a small group infiltrated on 6 October to collect intelligence on enemy movements, particularly shipping in the Sibutu Channel. The six-man party was under the command of a man known to Lim, Albert Kwok and many other people in Sabah – Major Francis George Leach Chester. After meeting up with his old friend, Lim had sent an urgent message to Kwok and ex-police chief Charles Peter, pledging additional arms and assistance from Chester, and urging them to delay the planned uprising. However, although the message had been received, events had overtaken the guerrilla leader, forcing him to attack sooner than he had intended.

'Gort' Chester

Albert Kwok Fen Nam

Kwok's faith that his friend, Major Chester, would do everything he could to assist was not misplaced. Born in Johannesburg, South Africa, in 1899, to British parents who later settled in Kenya, Chester was educated in England – at Highfield Preparatory in Hampshire and The Kings School in Kent This historic college, situated in the precincts of Canterbury Cathedral, counted among its notable old boys writer Somerset Maugham and Field Marshall Viscount Montgomery. After graduating from Kings in 1916, Chester served with King Edward's Horse in the Great War, returning to Kenya at the cessation of hostilities. In 1923 he left Africa for British North Borneo where, after taking a job as assistant manager at the Lok Kawi Rubber Estate, just to the north of Kinarut, he moved to Lahad Datu, where he purchased a small rubber plantation and developed business interests with the large Japanese-owned consortium, Kuhara Rubber and Manila Hemp. When Germany began bombing Britain, Chester returned to England and in 1941 was commissioned into the King's African Rifles, a regiment that drew its men from the British colonies in East Africa and was commanded by officers seconded from the British Army. Commonly known as 'Gort' because of his uncanny resemblance to Field Marshal Viscount Gort, Chief of the British General Staff, Francis Chester, like his high-profile namesake, had a round head, a hairline receding to the point of baldness, bushy eyebrows and a lush moustache.

However, Chester was not simply a planter turned soldier. In May 1942, after seeing action against Italy in Abyssinia, he went to India where he was recruited by British Secret Intelligence and trained in internal sabotage and propaganda for a highly secret, very irregular, behind-the-lines unit known as Special Operations Executive, or SOE. As an undercover agent, specialising in silent assassination to espionage, sabotage and intelligence gathering, he undertook several covert missions against the Japanese along the Burmese border before being seconded in late September to Special Operations Australia (SOA).

General MacArthur

In order to extend covert operations into the Far East, this organisation had been established in mid-1942. Unlike its British equivalent, which carried out sabotage and espionage missions in occupied Europe, many of the operations planned by SOA were politically, rather than militarily, motivated. With the south-west Pacific under the control of America's General Douglas MacArthur, the British, with their close allies the Australians, realised that SOA missions could provide the opportunity to indulge in a little flag-waving in the Empire's former territories, to let the local people know that the British would be back. With American submarines already operating a shuttle service from Australia to supply Suarez's army in Tawi Tawi, British Borneo was seen as an excellent starting point. In late 1942 Gort, who spoke fluent Malay as well as Dusun, flew from India to Australia, via Egypt and America. The following year he was appointed to lead a covert mission in Borneo, known as Operation Python, whose tasks were to set up a local intelligence-gathering network and to prepare the way for a campaign of sabotage and underground resistance. The area of operation was Labian Point, south of Sandakan.

Mr Bede S 'Sandshoe' Willie

After a short training period in Brisbane, Gort and his five-man team left Western Australia on 24 September 1943 on board the United States submarine *Kingfish*. They took with them 97 bundles of stores and equipment weighing more than three tonnes – enough to last for four months. Twelve days later Gort Chester was looking at Labian Point through the submarine's periscope.

After setting up camp on a hill about three kilometres up the Tengian Kecil River, they established contact with the Americans and Suarez, who agreed that Lieutenant Valera, who had lived in Sabah for a number of years and had worked in Harry Keith's Forestry Department, should become Python's liaison officer. Using his pre-war contacts, Gort located two old friends: Sin Yen, a Chinese from Sandakan, and Mr Bede Soemole Willie, District Officer for the Beluran area from 1929–1935. Willie, who was of Dusun and European parentage, also had connections to the Philippines. His daughter, Margaret, had married Winfield Sherman, brother of Dora Stookes. Like Dora, Winfield was Japanese-American and had been born in Jolo, where their father owned a sawmill. Also like Dora, he had not been interned and was an active member of the resistance organisation. As Bede Willie was fond of wearing rubber-soled sandshoes when moving about the jungle, he was known to Gort Chester as 'Sandshoe Willie'. Using Willie's and Sin's valuable contacts, an intelligence network, stretching from Tarakan in the south to Sandakan in the north, was soon up and running.

Python's own observation point was high in a tree near the mouth of Sungei Nyamok, south of Labian Point. It overlooked the Sibutu Channel and had a clear view of every vessel moving to and from Tarakan and Balikpapan. Before long, Python's reports, along with information collected by special agents from local coast watchers, were being transmitted in a steady stream back to Australia.

On returning from a visit to Tawi Tawi in early December, Gort Chester received information that Kwok and his force of at least 2,000 Chinese guerrillas had already mobilised and that Lim Keng Fatt was looking for him. On meeting up with Lim, Gort promised to urgently request weapons, ammunition and medicine from Australia, as well as personnel to help Kwok set up an intelligence network in the west.

However, before either of these promises could be fulfilled, shattering news was received from Jesselton. Kwok was in enemy hands. With no sign of any assistance from the Philippines, resistance had faltered, forcing the rebels to scatter in smaller bands. In order to save the inhabitants of the valley near Penampang where his guerrilla group was sheltering, Kwok surrendered on 19 December. With the collapse of the Jesselton resistance, Gort Chester realised that any hope of revitalising the revolt, or of rescuing Kwok and his men, rested entirely with the urgent arms shipment promised from Australia, due to arrive with the next stores delivery.

The Jesselton uprising had serious repercussions at Sandakan, where most of the remaining members of the Constabulary were arrested and executed. By war's end only one-quarter of those serving in 1941 would still be alive. The rebellion also impacted on the Sandakan camp, where the collapse of the underground had already led to a decrease in the rice ration and an increase in the punishments handed out. The Australian officers were also confined to the camp, leaving the rank and file without any senior personnel to liaise with the guards at the airstrip. Then, without any warning, a new directive was issued. In order to prevent any further subversive activities among the Australians, all but eight of the officers were to be transferred to Kuching. At 1.30 pm on 16 October, the day after those involved in the Sandakan Incident were moved to the Sandakan Gaol, the officers were given thirty minutes to pack their belongings and report to the main gate for transfer by lorry to the government wharf, where a small coastal vessel, *Tiensin*, was waiting. The next day E Force was amalgamated with B Force. To accommodate them, some of the huts from the E Force camp were dismantled and re-erected in the main compound. This re-arrangement not only isolated the troublesome Australians from the British, it also confined them to the same area, allowing for tighter security.

Nine days later, all members of the underground were transferred to the wharf, with the exception of Celia Taylor and Mrs Mavor, who had departed earlier with two medical officers – Australian Marcus Clark and Canadian George Graham – and one or two other internees rounded up belatedly from the interior. As word circulated that the prisoners were to be moved, the families of the local people hurried to the road leading from the gaol to the dockside, hoping for a final glimpse before they were herded onto *Subuk*, a small coastal vessel. Mrs Khoo, who was seven months pregnant, jostled through the crowds hoping to catch sight of her husband, Khoo Siak Chiew, as he passed by. To her distress, she was unable to pick him out: the Japanese had shaved the heads of every prisoner in the trucks.

On ascertaining from the Japanese which of two routes the vehicle transferring those held at the interrogation centre would take, the heavily pregnant wife of Ojagar Singh waited by the roadside with Anup and her other children. The lorry appeared in the distance, but their vigil was for nought. The canvas blinds of the vehicle were rolled down tightly and it took the other road.

Covered by machine-guns mounted on the vehicles, the prisoners were loaded onto *Subuk*'s deck and handcuffed to the railings. The ship had scarcely left the harbour when it ran into a violent storm, sending such a mass of water swirling over the deck that the prisoners thought they would surely drown. After a 36-hour delay in Kudat they proceeded to Miri, by-passing Jesselton, which was in the midst of the guerrilla uprising. At Miri, where the prisoners baked on the open deck in the broiling sun, the Australians discussed the possibility of freeing Matthews so he could jump overboard and try to escape. He rejected the idea: repercussions would be too great and, in any case, there was nowhere a European could hide for long.

After a miserable and very trying eight-day voyage, *Subuk* arrived in Kuching, where the prisoners were transferred to the Batu Lintang Camp. Those not undergoing trial were sent to the relevant POW compounds. The Funk brothers and the other non-Europeans were confined, twenty-five at a time, in wire cages situated alongside the guard house. Taylor, Matthews and the others were sent to kempeitai headquarters, in a magnificent two-storey colonial building on Jalan Jawa. Part of the first floor, reserved for the kempeitai, had been divided into eight cells, with wooden floors and ceilings and expanded-metal walls – twenty prisoners in the larger cells and between five and seven in the remainder. A bucket in the corner, emptied twice a day, served as a latrine. The day at both detention centres began at 7 am, when the prisoners sat cross-legged, facing the wall. Apart from two short exercise periods they remained that way until 10.30 pm, looking neither to the left nor right. Any attempt to relax muscles suffering from the strain resulted in a beating with a rattan cane, sword sticks or even fists. Night and day the guards crept about, on the lookout for the slightest transgression. When Dr Laband was observed listening to a remark made by a fellow prisoner, he was ordered to beat him up. When he refused, the Japanese beat him instead.

The daily rations consisted of roughly 200 grams of rice and a tablespoon of vegetable matter, split into two meals at 2 pm and 8 pm, with a small piece of evil-smelling fish once a week, and two cups of water to be shared between five men, per day. Occasionally they were given a spoonful of rice polishings in order to stave off beriberi, but the effect was minimal, with many prisoners already suffering from advanced oedema. Dysentery was rife, as were skin diseases, and the cells were infested with lice, bedbugs and scabies. Prisoners were allowed only the clothing they were wearing, and no blankets or bedding were permitted. A wash with a sliver of soap was granted once a month; otherwise it was just a quick sluice with plain water, the time allotted for these ablutions being just 15 minutes for 100 prisoners.

Medical attention was denied to Ted Keating, who was very ill, but Gerald Mavor was admitted to hospital with a double hernia, caused by his interrogations in Sandakan. Five days after the operation, he was discharged and forced to walk 1.5 kilometres back to the prison, where his wound broke open. Had it not been for Dr Taylor's ministrations, he would have bled to death.

In mid-November all the accused were subjected to further rounds of brutal interrogation, which would continue, spasmodically, until February, or until the required answers to questions were obtained and recorded. The bashings were so severe that some of the cringing, frightened victims, beaten into insensibility, were bordering on insanity. Towards the end of the interrogation period there was some relief when a far less brutal captain took over the questioning.

Some prisoners, like Sergeant Colin Lander, were sent to the Kuching Camp or back home to Sandakan, owing to lack of evidence; others found themselves even more enmeshed in a web of facts, half-truths and outright lies. Sini's involvement in helping organise the arms shipments was fortunately not discovered. When asked about the letters he had carried to Tawi Tawi, he told the kempeitai he had done it purely for the money, as he was alone in the world and needed to buy food. Although the interrogator tormented him by placing a sword across his neck, his explanation was accepted, due in no large part to the efforts of interpreter Miura, who had been transferred with the prisoners to Kuching.

The situation, meanwhile, had become increasingly perilous for the captured Kinabalu Guerrillas. As Christmas approached, they were marched to the Hotel Jesselton before being handed over to the kempeitai, who had converted their headquarters at the Jesselton Sports Club into a house of torture. Although Albert Kwok was subjected to horrendous interrogation, he flatly refused to answer a single question, insisting that he, alone, was responsible for the rebellion. His courage and stoicism did not spare his men, or anyone even thought to be connected to the uprising.

On 29 December, just ten days after Kwok's surrender, a boat containing Lim Keng Fatt, a body of hand-picked men, the latest American arms and $25,000 in cash finally arrived from the Philippines. It was all too late. On learning that Kwok was in enemy hands, the party returned to Tawi Tawi. In January, any guerrillas not tortured or beaten to death during the preliminary interrogations were sent to the former Victoria Police Barracks at Batu Tiga to await their fate, along with their women and children.

All hope of revitalising the rebellion and saving Kwok and his followers now rested on the submarine due from Australia any day and bringing not only the arms and ammunition but reinforcements for Python: two officers, three sergeants and Warrant Officer Alex Chew – an SOA operative of Chinese descent who had escaped from captivity on Ambon Island early in 1942. However, owing to a communications breakdown between SOA and the American navy, the submarine did not leave Australia until 10 January. When it arrived in Borneo eight days later, Gort Chester was enraged, and not simply because of the delay. To make room for stores that he did not want, and had not requested, SOA administration had left behind all the arms, ammunition and medicine for Albert Kwok and his guerrillas. As there was no point going without the weapons, the trip to the west was postponed until the next shipment. But the current shipment, let alone the next, was already far too late.

By this time more than 400 guerrillas and their supporters were crowded into the Batu Tiga Gaol. On 18 January, the Japanese closed off all roads near Petagas Bridge, about three kilometres to the south, where deep trenches were dug in the sandy soil. All prisoners were photographed and forced to sign a 'confession', written in Japanese. They were then divided into three groups: 176 for execution, 130 for transfer to Labuan and the remainder for imprisonment in Jesselton. Among those earmarked for detention in Batu Tiga gaol was Ethelbert Dominic, Pedro's youngest son. He would later die in prison from a combination of wounds inflicted during his torture, and starvation.

At 3 am on 21 January, those condemned to death were marched to the nearby railway station and forced into six covered goods-wagons. On arrival at Petagas, they were herded across the grass to the open pits. Many of the guerrillas were Chinese, but there was also a large number of Sulus. Albert Kwok, Charles Peter, Chan Chau Kong, Kong Tze Phui and Lee Tek Phui, their arms bound and their shirts stripped from their backs, were ordered to stand in a row. After photographs were taken, each was decapitated with a blow from a double-handed swordsman. According to one report, Charles Peter was only partially beheaded.

The remaining prisoners, including Helen Funk's brother, Jules, were machine-gunned. Some who were not killed outright were dragged to the trenches where they remained alive for up to three days. Although their groans and cries could be heard in the nearby village, the occupants were too terrified to leave their homes and give any assistance. As a further act of intimidation, the group of 130 sent to Labuan, now sick and starving, were paraded and punished before the local people. Unable to work, all but nine died of starvation. On the islands, entire populations were virtually wiped out and villages burned. Men, women and children were shot, beheaded and tortured to death. Many of those arrested were beaten so brutally that their heads were reduced to a pulp. Others were crucified or slung from roof beams by their hands and feet, like fish to dry out in the sun.

Over in the east, oblivious to the blood being spilled in the west, Python was having troubles of its own. One of the party, Sergeant Bill Brandis, had became separated from the others and disappeared. Despite this worrying development, the party continued with its task of gathering and transmitting intelligence, including an updated report on the situation at Sandakan. According to Gort Chester's agents, there were now only 150 B-class enemy troops, forty POW guards, eleven military police, the governor, and 150 native police in the town. Although the airfield under construction was not completed, it was in use. Chester completed his message by advising that he had a 'reliable man' going to Sandakan in a few days' time who would contact his 'old friends'. Eight days later the man had completed his mission, enabling SOA to confirm on 15 February that Berhala was no longer being used as a POW camp and that the aerodrome was not only operational but being extended.

Chester did not know what had happened to Brandis, but he realised that the Japanese had picked up Python's scent – a conclusion confirmed by Sandshoe Willie and Sin, who also reported that the kempeitai in Sandakan were aware that white men were in the area. Since there had been no response from SOA for a submarine to relocate Python to the west coast, Gort took the initiative. He immediately dispatched Lim Keng Fatt to the west with £2,400 in gold sovereigns. He was to make arrangements for their arrival with Kwok's successor and organise a boat to pick them up.

The following day, 16 February, the Japanese captured Bill Brandis. After wandering for three weeks along the coast to the north of Labian Point, he had been found, naked and more dead than alive, by Osman Panjang on a beach near Kampong Atiam, Tambisan Island. Indicating by sign language that he had been in the water for three days and needed food, Brandis was taken to the village where his rescuer fed and looked after him. However, when village chief Mandor Alam heard that an informant named Jariahad had betrayed the soldier's presence, he reported Brandis's whereabouts to avoid serious repercussions to his local community. A Japanese named Sawa Mura, with assistants Pallsing and Muntin, arrested Brandis and alerted the Sandakan kempeitai.

Although Brandis had a cover story, he was unable to stick to it. Under torture, he revealed to Sergeant-Major Masaji Nakao that he was a member of a party commanded by Major Chester, who had come by submarine to transmit information back to Australia. Although he could not remember the name of the landing place, he stated that there was a boat under construction nearby. On 16 February, he was forced to accompany the kempeitai and a party of 100 soldiers, lead by First-Lieutenant Okamura, to a spot about 1.5 kilometres from Python's camp at the Nyamok River. Early next morning, while Gort was cooking breakfast over an open fire, two of his men spotted a small tugboat towing several troop barges and heading their way. At the same time, a spotter plane flew along the beach. Hurriedly dousing the fire, the party moved to a new location, about 6.5 kilometres to the north.

Despite the obvious danger, that night three of the Python team, plus some visiting American and Filipino guerrillas, sailed to Tawi

Tawi, where arrangements had already been made for the submarine bringing the next load of stores to extract the three Australians. However, due to a breakdown in communications, the submarine did not know that the rendezvous point had been changed. Unable to locate the shore party, it returned to Australia.

Contact was finally made on 5 March. However, the stores were only partially unloaded when the threat of enemy destroyers forced the submarine to submerge and make a fast getaway. Valera, who was on board organising supplies for the remainder of the Python team, had an unexpected trip to Australia. Also on board were three of the Berhala escapees. Steele, Wallace and Kennedy, after fighting with the guerrillas for the past eight months, were being extracted – Steele, as senior officer, to deliver a report; the other two for medical treatment. Blow, McLaren and Gillon were still on the island of Mindanao, fighting with the guerrilla forces under the command of America's Lieutenant-Colonel Wendell Fertig, but Butler and Wagner had been killed in action. On his arrival home, Ray Steele provided a long and detailed report regarding the fall of Singapore and the condition of various POW camps. However, the situation regarding Sandakan was very out of date: many of the people to whom Steele and his companions owed their freedom were now either dead or serving long terms of imprisonment in Kuching.

After the second round of interrogations were completed, the prisoners had been moved to the Kuching Civil Gaol. Conditions

The Catholic Convent, Kuching, where the trials were held

were similar to those of military prison, except that the prisoners, their heads now completely shaven, were confined two to a cell, about 2.5 metres by 1.5 metres, with a concrete floor and concrete pillows. Food, still poor in quantity and quality, was pushed through a slot in the iron door. A few days before they were due to appear in court, all those implicated in a particular crime were photographed together, along with various articles collected as evidence.

The trial venue was the art room in the teaching block of Kuching's Roman Catholic Convent, a low brick building that formed an annex to the main structure and chosen because it had a raised platform, or dais. The accused were facing special and very severe forms of 'gunritsu kaigi', a military trial reserved for civilians in occupied zones. The Australian POWs were to be court martialled.

The legal proceedings, which began on 3 February, generally lasted less than sixty minutes. With an automatic presumption of guilt, charges dovetailed to suit the evidence, a prosecutor who could also act as a judge, no defence counsel, and penalties determined in advance, they were quite unlike trials conducted in any British-style courtroom.

The first to appear were Doctor Taylor and Gerald Mavor, along with Mrs Cohen and some of those facing lesser charges. Mrs Cohen was fined, but Taylor and Mavor, convicted because of the deliberate mistranslations of Ozawa, were sentenced to fifteen years' hard labour in the high security kempeitai punishment gaol at Outram Road, Singapore. Those accused of less serious crimes, including POWs Blain, James, Graham, Stan Davis and Martin, received sentences ranging from three months to three years. Ted Keating, who was to be tried for passing letters and plotting to escape, did not reach the courtroom. Apart from two or three vitamin tablets, he had not received any medical attention for his crippling leg ulcer or any of his life threatening illnesses. He died on 11 February from the combined effects of amoebic dysentery, beriberi and malnutrition.

As the hearings continued, the list of those found guilty grew. Sentences ranged from one year (in the case of the Goh brothers, Dr Laband and others) to five years for Jakariah, Sidek and Foo Seng Chow. [For a full list of sentences, see Heroes' Roll]. Hi Li Tsia, Khoo Siek Chiew, Lo Hoi Tshi, Wong Wee Man, Yan Sec Chan, Kwan Choo Ming and Kwan Ming Ming were fined amounts ranging from $50 to $2000 and then released. The men survived the war, but the wonderfully generous, indefatigable Mrs Cohen, who left on the same ship, did not. According to the Japanese, she was washed overboard near Kudat on the return trip and drowned. According to a local report, the Japanese placed her in a barrel when the ship reached Kudat and rolled her about until she died.

Gordon Weynton was tried with Rickards, Small, Mills and McDonough on 26 February. Found guilty of spreading rumours and violating POW regulations, he received ten years. McDonough, saved from a longer sentence by Wells and Weynton, who insisted the chemicals had nothing to do with the radio, was given six months, while Rickards, Mills and Small faced terms of six years, two years and eighteen months, respectively.

By 29 February only five Australians and the most prominent members of the underground were left. With the capture of Brandis, and his confession that he was spying, their position had become even more precarious; the Japanese were now convinced that the Sandakan underground was part of a much larger Allied network. The POWs were to be tried first. As Matthews and Wells were by far the most important of the Europeans brought to trial, a number of interested and high-ranking Japanese officers filled the gallery at the rear of the room.

Seated at the judicial bench were the three officers who had presided at the trials of Taylor and Weynton: Chief Judge Lieutenant-Colonel Egami Sobei, Major Nishihara Shuji and Captain Tsutsui Yoichi, all from Borneo Headquarters. Watanabe Haruo, a thirty-three-year-old lawyer, was not only prosecutor, but also the legal officer who had assessed the evidence, framed the charges, prepared the case for trial and obtained the signed 'confessions' which would form the basis of his prosecution. He had also advised 37 Army's Lieutenant-General Yamawaki Masataka of the charges and recommended appropriate punishments. The remaining officials were court secretary Ishikawa Takeo, who assisted Watanabe, and three Formosan civilians: interpreter Sugama and two guards named Ito and Kusata. Major Suga, being on the spot and Commandant of all the Borneos, was present as a spectator. One judge who would not need to concentrate closely on the proceedings was Major Nishihara, who had been briefed by the prosecutor and had already seen all the evidence. He had also selected his fellow judges.

At about 9 am, the five remaining Australians were marched into court. All were handcuffed. While McMillan and Roffey were accused of violating POW regulations, and Stevens faced an additional charge of spreading rumours, Matthews and Wells were on trial for their lives. Neither man had been informed of the actual offences: espionage, rebellion, violation of POW regulations and spreading rumours for Matthews, and violation of regulations and rumour spreading for Wells. They were, however, aware that they were facing capital charges and that the outlook was not good.

After dispensing with the preliminaries of name, age, rank, and place of birth, the prosecutor read out the charges in Japanese, tabled the evidence and demanded that the trial proceed. At this point Chief Judge Egami handed over to the well-briefed Nishihara, who was to ask all the questions. Matthews, on behalf of his co-defendants, then asked for legal representation, but his request was denied. Nishihara, through the services of the almost unintelligible interpreter, asked the accused if the charges were correct. Wells, for one, said that they were not, but Sugama translated his answer into the affirmative. According to the court record, all prisoners pleaded guilty. According to Wells, they did not.

The acting chief judge, Nishihara, assuming the role of prosecutor, now presented further evidence: the signed 'confessions', a pistol, ammunition, the maps, the notebook and, to Wells' horror, the transmitter, which the Japanese believed was the receiver. Realising that a wireless expert had been called to testify, Wells was sure he was doomed. However, his fears were groundless on that point. Despite the huge, highly specialised valves, which should have been a dead giveaway, the 'expert' had no idea that he was looking at a wireless transmitter.

Once Major Nishihara had presented the case for the prosecution, he reverted to his position of acting chief judge by asking Watanabe, now back in the role of prosecutor, for his opinion about the evidence submitted and whether the charges against the prisoners could be upheld. Watanabe knew the evidence backwards, having prepared it himself and, as the accused had allegedly pleaded guilty, he had no problem in voicing his opinion. All were guilty as charged.

Now that the charges had been proven, Watanabe announced that all would be punished according to Japanese law and, since the trial had been held under special wartime regulations, appeals were not permissible. Apparently concerned that the proceedings should stand up to international scrutiny, Major Suga unexpectedly rose from his seat and addressed the court. After appealing for leniency for both Matthews and Wells, the Commandant of all the Borneos advised the tribunal to abide by International Law which, since Japan had failed to ratify the 1927 Geneva Convention, was the Hague Convention of 1907.

The proceedings, which had lasted all of forty minutes, were now over. The Australians had scarcely understood a single word. However, as the tribunal wished to delay the handing down of sentences until after the remaining civilians had been tried, the five Australians were taken back to the gaol.

It was now the turn of the civilians. Unlike the POWs' court martial, which was the court's interpretation of Japanese law, this trial was concerned with the interpretation of regulations and orders made by General Tarauchi Juichi of the South Seas Expeditionary Army, based in Saigon. Apart from this distinction, and with a Malay interpreter, Hanad, replacing Sugama, the proceedings and the composition of the court were almost the same as the previous trial. However, because of the large number of accused, this trial lasted two hours.

The defendants were seated according to the seriousness of the charges. Jemadar Ojagar Singh, whose smashed elbow had still not been set, Sergeant Abin, Ernesto Lagan, Heng Joo Ming, Wong Mu Sing, Alex Funk, Felix Azcona Junior and Matusup bin Gungau were all in the front row. Mohamed Tahir was in the seventh and behind him was Major Rice-Oxley, whose name was added to the list when the Japanese discovered he had been involved in the underground prior to his transfer to Kuching. At the conclusion of the proceedings, all those sitting in the front row were remanded for sentencing.

The remainder received terms of imprisonment with hard labour, to be served at various centres in Borneo. Sergeant-Major Yusup was given fifteen years, the severity of this sentence probably due to the pencil drawings of the King, Queen, Churchill and Matthews found in his house. Sergeant-Major Yangsalang and Damudaran, the gaol official, also received fifteen years. Salleh and Peter Lai were sentenced to twelve, while Apostol and Ng Ho Kong received ten, Inspector Guriaman and Sini eight, Dick Majinal seven and Paddy Funk six. Four-year terms were handed out to Johnny Funk and Chan Ah Ping, while Mohamed Tahir was given three years, and Rice-Oxley twelve months.

That night, when Major Suga visited Matthews and Wells in gaol, bringing two bananas and a copy of *Tokyo Ichinichi*, Tokyo's daily newspaper, featuring their photographs on the front page, they realised that they would be severely punished. Two days later, as they walked from the gaol to the courtroom, handcuffed together, Matthews turned to Rod Wells and said, 'You'll get home. Give my love to Lorna and to my son.' Wells, who thought that they would both meet the same fate replied. 'I won't be going home. I'll be with you.'

As they entered the courtroom, they saw the eight men who had risked their lives to help their Australian brothers – Ojagar Singh, Abin, Lagan, Heng, Mu Sing, Alex Funk, Felix Azcona and Matusup.

All had just been sentenced to death. Some were weeping bitterly. Those who were not drew their fingers across their throats to indicate they were to be executed. Wells spotted Suga in the gallery. He turned to face him, but the Commandants of all the Borneos could not bring himself to look the young Australian in the eye.

Lieutenant-Colonel Egami, who had reinstated himself as Chief Judge, now took centre stage. Reading from a long screed, which was later translated into passable English, he listed the many sins of the accused, including 'having hostile feeling against Japan and dislike for being a prisoner'. When he finally finished, Wells steeled himself for the pronouncement.

> Captain Lionel John Matthews: Death by firing squad.
> Lieutenant Roderick Graham Wells: Twelve years solitary confinement with hard labour.
> Sergeant Alfred Stevens: Six years penal servitude
> Corporals McMillan and Roffey: Eighteen months penal servitude.

Wells was stunned. He had been expecting the death sentence.

Years later an American, who had been intercepting wartime enemy signals, would tell him the reason for his unexpected reprieve – a careless Japanese signaller. Mindful that the Commandants of all the Borneos, a veteran of the Great War, had warned the court that the trials should stand up to international scrutiny, General Yamawaki had taken the precaution of seeking written approval from his superiors in Saigon to execute 'two Australian officers and eight natives'. The request, a mere formality, had been granted, but when decoding the return message, the Japanese signaller had typed numeral 1, instead of 2. As no Japanese, not even a general, would ever query an instruction issued by a higher authority, it was decided that Matthews, being the more senior of the two Australians and found guilty of more serious charges, would be the one to die.

As he left the courtroom, Matthews gave Wells messages to deliver to his family. There was no time for more than a token farewell to the courageous local people who were to be executed with him, but as the guards herded the condemned men into the prison van, Wells managed to hold Ojagar Singh in one final embrace.

As a shocked Wells, Roffey and McMillan watched the vehicle draw away, Lionel Matthews showed that, despite months of imprisonment and torture, he had lost none of his defiance or courage. His last words, shouted through the grille of the van, were directed at his men. 'Keep your chins up boys. What the Japs do to me doesn't matter. They can't win.'

Disappearing from view, the small convoy headed down the road. Eric Davis, who was marching along towards the civilian cemetery with a grave-digging detail, was startled when three Japanese staff cars, a small van and a black prison vehicle, driven by a civilian named Doi, whizzed by. He had no idea what was happening, but the sight of deathly white knuckles, grimly clutching at the wire mesh of the prison van, sent shivers down his spine.

The convoy stopped at a small clearing in an isolated patch of jungle about five kilometres from the courtroom. In the centre of the cleared area was a long pit, with nine stout T-shaped posts placed at three-metre intervals along one side. While a nine-man firing squad readied itself, the prisoners were tied securely to the posts and a mark placed in the centre of their foreheads.

Standing to one side were Colonel Suga, Chief Judge Nishihara, prosecutor Watanabe and Lieutenant Nagita Toru, a doctor. Watanabe watched as Sigimata, the rifleman assigned to execute Matthews, took aim. Just as he was about to fire, Matthews, who had refused a blindfold, shouted 'My God and King forever. My God and King forever.' The first bullet hit him between the eyes, killing him instantly. The rest simply ensured that he was dead, a fact confirmed by the doctor, who signed a death certificate. The other eight men, shot dead in a similar manner, were buried in the common grave. The body of Matthews, whose last request after sentence had been pronounced was to be buried in a Protestant cemetery, was placed in a rough wooden coffin and taken in the back of the smaller van to the cemetery near St Catherine's Church for interment.

The Japanese had come mid-morning to the 'other ranks' POW compound, looking for a grave-digging detail. British prisoners usually undertook this job but when Eric Davis learned that the grave was to be for an Australian, he asked the guards to allow him and eight other Australian prisoners to carry out the task. They were escorted under guard to the cemetery where they were joined by six Australian officers from Sandakan, Padre Henthorne from St Michael's Church, and senior Japanese officers including Major Suga, all wearing military decorations. As the burial team lifted the coffin from the van they noticed that the planks on the underside were covered with congealing blood, leading to the erroneous conclusion that whoever it was had been beheaded: an assumption which was given additional credence when two Franciscan monks, neither of whom had been near the killing ground, circulated a story that the executions had been by the sword.

The Australians attending the burial, including the officers, were unaware that decapitation results in massive and instantaneous blood loss, with a racing heart pumping vast amounts from the body, via the severed carotid artery. On the other hand, a gunshot wound to the head creates a large pool of blood, which will continue to seep for some time. The Japanese would later state that Matthews and his eight companions had been shot through the head, a fact confirmed beyond all doubt by post-war exhumation of their remains. Unfortunately, sensational stories that they were beheaded continue to emerge from time to time, despite irrefutable evidence to the contrary.

On returning to the camp after the funeral, Major Suga, who was Christian, gave permission for a wooden cross to be made for Matthews, describing him as 'the bravest man I ever met'. A day or two later he drove the senior Australian officer to the cemetery to place it on the grave. The Sikh community in Kuching, aware that one of their members had been executed, petitioned the Japanese to allow Ojagar Singh's remains to be cremated according to Sikh rites, but the request was denied.

Colonel Walsh and the other Australian officers had been informed of Matthews' execution, but it was a long time before Davis and his fellow gravediggers knew the identity of the man they had buried. The families of the eight men executed with him would have to wait even longer for any information. With no official notification, it would not be until after the war that Ojagar Singh's wife would learn, by chance, that her husband had been executed. Katherine Lagan, unable to believe that Ernesto was dead, would become mentally affected by her obsession that he was still alive.

Unlike Matthews, there were no funeral rites, no prayers, no priest and no acts of remembrance for those buried in the mass grave in the lonely jungle clearing. But their selfless sacrifice was honoured in a very special way. In the evening, as the last rays of the setting sun brought that terrible day to a close, their Australian brothers in the Kuching camp stood in silence, as a lone piper played The Lament.

Chapter 9

From bad to worse

On 2 March 1944, the day members of the underground were executed, Gort's friend and Kwok's deputy, Lim Keng Fatt, arrived safely back on the west coast, confident of obtaining a boat for Python. He was also buoyed by the thought that, as soon as the arms arrived from Australia, the guerrillas would be able to take up the fight for, despite the horrific outcome of the Double Tenth rebellion, the Chinese freedom fighters had by no means been subdued. Even as the bloody reprisals for the revolt continued, or perhaps because of them, a group of very resilient and determined men, lead by Dr Liu Lai and Cheah Loong Ghee, were plotting another insurrection. Funds were being collected from all over Sabah and clandestine meetings held. With the assistance of the Kapitans Cina at Kudat, Sandakan and Tawau, $250,000 had been collected or pledged to finance the revolt, planned for 13 April.

On 28 March, unaware that Python was now on the run, Lim dispatched a message to the east, giving an up-to-date report on the situation in the west. He asked for pistols to replace those surrendered to the Japanese and reminded his Australian friends to bring plenty of side-arms, hand grenades and sub-machine guns, not only to re-arm the resistance fighters but to bring the tribespeople on side. With malaria rampant, he added an urgent request for quinine, now costing $30 an ounce. However, before he had a chance to do anything else, he, too, was on the run. The Japanese, aware of his involvement with Kwok, had put a price on $5000 on his head. He was forced to retreat to Bayau, near Tuaran, where he was murdered and robbed of his remaining funds by the village headman on 6 April. Six days later, the night before the new uprising was scheduled to take place, Liu and Cheah were also betrayed.

The Japanese had used the old ploy of hosting a dinner party that evening for prominent members of the Chinese and Indian communities at the Koa Club, to which the two rebel leaders were invited. At the conclusion of the dinner, they were arrested and taken away for interrogation. The kempeitai, who knew that both men were implicated in the planned revolt, wanted signed confessions. Hands tied behind his back, Liu was strung up by his thumbs and burned with glowing embers. When this failed to extract the required information, he was given the water treatment. After twelve days of continuous torture, he could no longer hold out and confessed everything. That same morning, he was hanged at Batu Tiga Gaol. However, the kempeitai could not break Cheah Loong Ghee. His refusal to utter a single word was absolute, not even when pieces of flesh were sliced from his body and dangled before his eyes. He died in gaol, taking his secrets with him.

His silence did not save those who had been implicated by the unfortunate Liu. On 5 May, twenty Japanese officers removed a large number of Chinese and Dusun suspects from the gaol, tortured them and, when they refused to speak, executed the lot.

Meanwhile, Gort Chester and his Python men, unaware of the disasters unfolding in the west, or of the additional torment their spying activities had caused, were only just managing to keep one jump ahead of the enemy. With the discovery of a rubber dinghy and empty storage containers south of Labian Point, the Japanese had stepped up the search. Twelve patrols which landed between 22 and 24 March in the vicinity of the Mera and Tenagian Kecil Rivers found the food dumps and also the site of Python's wireless station, less than one hour after it had been abandoned. The Australians set up the wireless at a new location but, while Lieutenant Jack Rudwick and Sergeant Doug McKenzie were guarding the track leading to it, they disappeared.

By 29 March the situation was critical for the remaining Python men. Forced to keep constantly on the move and unable to access their supply dumps, Gort transmitted an urgent request for evacuation. The US Submarine Fleet Headquarters, operating out of Fremantle, Western Australia, arranged a pick-up, but due to a lack of co-ordination between the submarine and the shore party, it was not until 8 June, after four farcical attempts, that they were finally rescued. By this time the fugitives were in poor physical condition and suffering from malaria.

Unfortunately, Rudwick and McKenzie were now in enemy hands. They had moved from their posts in search of food and been spotted by a collaborator named Kokklo, who alerted the Japanese on Tambisan Island. Rudwick, shot in the leg, and McKenzie were taken to Sandakan, where they joined Brandis in a ground-floor cell at the Leila Road interrogation centre. All three were suffering from dysentery and fever. As they had no hope of resisting the finely-honed investigative skills of the interrogators, or of talking their way out of their predicament, it did not take long for the Japanese to find out the exact nature of their mission. However, although they were forced to repair radio equipment belonging to the Japanese, and to train the kempeitai how to use Python's set, recovered from Labian Point, they did not reveal the codes, despite intensive interrogation.

McKenzie had been found in possession of a notebook containing details of all shipping moving up and down the Sibutu Channel. Unaware that signals detailing the movements of these ships, many of which had been torpedoed by American submarines, were being intercepted and decoded by the Allies, the Japanese assumed that the three spies they had in custody were responsible – a conclusion that the SOA top brass, despite the capture of the Python men, viewed as a positive outcome as it protected the secret of the intercepts.

McKenzie's notebook also revealed that local people had been co-operating with the Australians, leading to the discovery of the identities of some of Gort's agents. Captured and imprisoned in Lahad Datu, Chin En Sung, also known as Michael Chan, took his own life on 20 April. His brother, En Fu, was beaten to death ten days later. That same month, police boy Samudi, who, like many of those forced to work for the Japanese had steadfastly maintained his loyalty to the British, was shot dead on Bukit Tungku near the old pirate haunt. Samudi's colleague, Abok, after a lengthy period in custody, was executed at Lahad Datu. Fortunately, other key agents, including Yan Cheong, Chong Fatt, Florianza Fernandez, Ismail bin Andan and the headman of Tungku village, Panglima Buaya, managed to avoid detection.

Although the prisoners at Sandakan knew nothing about the Kuching trials, the executions, the failure of the rebellions in Jesselton or the capture of the Python men, they had certainly felt the consequences – ration cuts every time there was an 'incident'. With the interrogation of Brandis, McKenzie and Rudwick now complete, the kempeitai were absolutely convinced that the Sandakan underground, and all those involved in the Sandakan Incident, were part of a highly organised spy-ring, so well advanced that it even involved the infiltration of special agents from Australia. Certain that, if plans were underway to invade the east coast, the prisoners at the airfield would be involved, the Japanese High Command took immediate action. To ensure that the POWs would not be fit enough to take part in any invasion, they permanently cut back the rice ration. In June a further rice cut was ordered, not as punishment, but because the Japanese knew that American domination of the sea-lanes would soon result in the cessation of rice deliveries from Kuching. Tapioca was substituted, and while the vegetable ration was still reasonable, meat and fish were now a rarity.

This diminishing food supply may have encouraged another escape. Sometime in the first half of 1944, two more Australians went under the wire. They managed to make their way to Pulau Nunuyan, a small island between Pulau Nunuyan Laut and the mouth of the Sibuga, and one of the places investigated by Sini for a possible arms cache. The men were helped by Haji Manso but were seen by an informant, Ali bin Omar, who reported to the kempeitai that Manso was harbouring escaped POWs. The Australians were able to flee, but their benefactor was taken into custody and has not been seen since.

Conditions had also deteriorated throughout Sabah. The Japanese had not only failed to look after the country's commercial needs, they also plundered and stripped it of anything of value, including tools, machinery, scrap iron and base metals, precious metals, leather and rubber. Fuel, clothes, and even matches were no longer obtainable, along with simple medicines and drugs. Many of the local people, unable to obtain any cloth, were reduced to wearing bark and using jungle remedies. Machinery fell into disuse and corroded as there were few spare parts and those that were available were recycled for use elsewhere. There was no local produce for sale and often no means to cultivate additional crops other than with bare hands as there were no tools: with blacksmiths' businesses strictly controlled, it was no longer possible to have knives, parangs or farm implements made without a written letter of authorisation.

Any cattle found were confiscated and exported. With farms burnt, and farmers planting only enough for themselves, food in general was in very short supply and, although village shops remained open, goods of any description were extremely scarce. Valuables that the Japanese had not already taken had been buried for safe-keeping, along with expensive clothing and textiles, placed in huge earthenware jars and sealed with wax. Staff remained on duty at the hospitals but, because of a lack of bedding, linen, bandages, disinfectant, soap, medicine, drugs and surgical instruments, there was little work for them. Patients with dietary problems, unable to eat the limited food available, died of starvation.

People living in the interior had been left alone for some time, but with supplies on the coast running low, Japanese garrisons were established in key agricultural areas, such as Ranau, Keningau, Tenom, Beaufort and Pensiangan, where what food there was could be plundered, or cultivated by forced labour. With the Japanese requiring airstrips and improved roads at many of these centres, the unpleasant task of finding conscripts to fill the quotas was delegated to village headmen. In Jesselton, all government servants, with the exception of the Japanese, had to work on the airfield twice a week, while at Keningau they were forced to provide labour for the airstrips and other projects for one hour in the morning and another in the afternoon. To speed up the work, 400 Indonesians, mostly Javanese, were brought in. Like so many of their countrymen, most would die of malnutrition or from malaria, dysentery, beriberi and other preventable diseases.

The majority of Muruts were no longer able to hunt as the Japanese had taken away all their firearms. This led to an increase in the number of wild animals which, in turn, resulted in a great deal of damage to what crops remained. With all fishing boats hidden, the local fishing industry had come to a complete standstill along every coastline, forcing people in urban areas to subsist on yams, tapioca and sweet potatoes. In an attempt to improve their deteriorating relationship with the local community, the Japanese claimed that they were suffering equally and, if they lost the war, the people of Sabah would be far worse off.

With spies and informants everywhere, no one dared say anything that could be misconstrued in the slightest; a new police force had been established as most members of the Constabulary had quit their posts, were dead or in prison. The small number who remained and had switched their allegiance to the Japanese were now supplemented by local people, enticed by promises of good pay or forced to work under duress. The Hoko spy system, where individual villagers were given the task of being responsible for the behaviour of others, was also introduced. In order to keep an eye on everyone, a watch was kept at strategic points day and night, with small huts provided for those on duty and a communications system introduced.

The increased surveillance and the collapse of the underground movement had not, however, stopped others from continuing to provide assistance to the POWs. With her husband and so many others arrested, Lillian Funk had come to the fore. A vital link in the chain to Tawi Tawi, she was fluent in English, Malay, Hakka Chinese and Tagalog, the Filipino dialect. As she could also read and write all these languages, she was able to communicate with a wide range of nationalities, including Filipino agents and the surviving members of the underground movement.

However, any plans of re-establishing the network from her base at Mile 7 came to an abrupt end towards the end of 1943. A few weeks after the three Funk brothers were sent to Kuching, the Japanese, in an act of pure vengeance, evicted John Simon and his family, which now included Dimit and her two children. With the soldiers ordered to shoot anyone who harboured them, John Simon, his wife, their three daughters-in-law, five grandchildren (two of whom were babies), as well as Ernie and his sister Lisa, headed for the family-owned estate at Mile 14, carrying whatever they could manage by way of cooking utensils and bedding.

The Funks spent their first night in a house on their estate. The Chinese occupying it were very hesitant to harbour the refugees but, as food was short, they finally agreed to risk their lives in exchange for Melvyn's pet hunting dog, which they immediately beat to death in a hessian bag. Heartbroken, the lad refused to eat his dinner that night, not even when his grandfather explained that the dog could not go with them in case it barked and gave away their position. As it was, the Japanese were on the rampage about something: the sound of rifle and automatic fire could be heard, close by. No one, especially the hosts, slept that evening.

The following morning the family headed into the jungle. Apart from Lillian, all were ill-equipped and untrained for jungle survival. Fortunately, the Filipinos working on her parents' estate had taught her how to recognise and understand the uses of various rainforest plants. Using this knowledge, she was able to differentiate between edible roots and ferns and those liable to cause illness or death. Foraging for twelve people was literally a hand-to-mouth existence and those depending on her, especially the children, soon learned that a regular supply of food was by no means assured. Fortunately, after a couple of weeks Dimit and her children Gabriel and Olga left the group to live with Dimit's parents at their farm at Mile 11.

Although their property at Sungei Manila was a considerable distance from the Labuk Road junction, life was far from peaceful. Just after Dimit arrived, the Japanese took her father, Puloro Mananai, away for questioning. It was not because of his relationship to the Funks, which they evidently did not suspect. Apparently, as a result of the second round of interrogations in Kuching, they learned that he had harboured the six escapees before they made their abortive attempt to sail to Australia. Although tortured, he was determined to remain silent to protect his wife and daughters. After two weeks of torment, the 72-year-old grandfather was released due to lack of evidence. He died three weeks later.

After his death, the Japanese came repeatedly to the farm. Claiming that were on the look-out for run-away prisoners, they set up a temporary camp each morning, killing and eating the chickens, ducks and goats, and helping themselves to the fruit trees. With scarcely anything left to eat, Dimit and her mother collected the leftovers, rinsed the rice and recooked it. Finally, when the intimidation became too much, they moved into a small atap hut which they built on the far side of Sungei Manila. Later they moved to another, more comfortable hut built by Paulo as his private refuge and where they planted vegetables. The access to both huts was via a large tree, which had fallen part-way across the river and been extended with planks. Fortunately, as the waterway was infested with crocodiles, the Japanese did not show an inclination to follow them. Once they had vacated the house, there was no further harassment and they were able to live in peace until the end of the war. Their neighbours, Thomas Fong Tham Soong and his family, adopted a similar lifestyle. When the soldiers raided the farm to take their pigs and chickens, they beat up Mrs Fong, who tried to stop them. With daughters Anna and her sisters also vulnerable to sexual assault by marauding troops, the family abandoned the house and erected a hut deep in the jungle, where they cleared a small patch of land and raised rice, sweet corn and sweet potatoes, supplemented by whatever they could gather locally.

Unable to show their faces, Lillian and the remainder of the Funks were condemned to lead the life of a nomadic jungle tribe, always on the move in search of food. Little fruit grew in the wild, but they learned to watch out for orang utans raiding banana plants and durian trees growing on the fringes of small farms. On spotting humans approaching, the great apes would scream and thrash about, shaking the trees violently in an effort to scare the intruders away. After quickly gathering up the fruit that fell to the ground, Lillian and the children scurried back into the jungle, leaving the orang utans in peace. Unfortunately, the Japanese patrolling the areas were encouraged to use the animals as target practice, especially the huge males with their magnificent red coats. While the Japanese killed the orang utans for 'sport', they made a good meal for any locals fortunate enough to come across a freshly killed carcass.

Lillian taught the children to be on the lookout for anything edible, especially the wild chilli that grew in profusion, and small creatures such as large freshwater snails, lizards and non-venomous snakes. When the group came across as small vegetable farm, Lillian would plead for some of the produce, generally without success, as the owners were terrified of being shot. Taking careful note of the farm's layout, she would then return after dusk with Melvyn to gather what they needed, taking care to select the vegetables at random to disguise the loss. One night, attracted to the smell of cooking meat, she hid Melvyn among the vegetables and crept to the kitchen to

Melvyn Funk (far right) with his parents and sister, Doreen

investigate. To her horror, she saw the human-like head and hands of a small orang utan, simmering away in the pot.

Despite living in the jungle throughout the latter part of 1943 and all of 1944, Lillian managed to maintain contact with the Philippines and continued to supply medicine, and whatever food she could buy, to the Australians. She funded the entire enterprise, which was considerable. Before the war, she had also run a profitable dressmaking business. On the advice of her mother, who owned pearl farms in the Philippines, she had converted all surplus cash into pearls, gemstones, jewellery and gold sovereigns. Before the Japanese arrived, she sewed the bulk of it – along with currency notes, her American citizenship papers and other important documents – into a long pouch, which she wound around her waist. The remaining valuables were stitched into the hems of her clothing. One by one, the jewels and sovereigns from her secret hoard were handed over to buy medicines and food, and as payment for those willing to take the risk of smuggling them into the POW camp, or under the wire. A slender woman, Lillian deduced, quite rightly, that if anyone noticed that she had put on weight around the middle they would assume she was pregnant again – a 'condition' which, in those days, was not commented upon.

Her loyalty to Johnny was absolute. Although her father, Guy Strattan, arranged on three separate occasions to evacuate her and the two children to Tawi Tawi by submarine, Lillian refused to go. As long as Johnny was a prisoner she would remain in Sandakan and carry on the work, even if it meant sacrificing her life. She had a fair distance to cover, so the excursions to keep the appointments in town with the resistance workers, and to the pre-arranged rendezvous points to meet Filipino agents, were spread over several days. She took Melvyn with her to these meetings, believing that a woman with a small child would not attract as much attention as one on her own. Although still very young, Melvyn understood that he must obey his mother implicitly, and say nothing about where they had been. It was a testing time for a little boy and often a long wait until it was dark enough for Lillian to emerge from their hiding place and meet her Filipino contacts, who had paddled in from a submarine. Whispering in Tagalog, which Melvyn could not understand, they exchanged messages and urgently needed drugs, and made arrangements for the next meeting. With the business successfully transacted, Lillian calmly began her long walk back to the jungle hideout, and the Filipinos paddled back to the submarine.

In September 1944, she decided to venture into Sandakan in broad daylight. She had told Melvyn that she wanted to buy some blachan (shrimp paste) to make their meals more palatable, but her real intention was to make contact with the underground. As a precaution, she donned coolie clothes – baggy pants and shirt, and a large, conical, straw hat.

Since his father's arrest, Melvyn, who had fair curly hair, was always in disguise. While they were living at Mile 7, friends had told Lillian that the Japanese, who had noticed her son's blonde locks, were curious about his background: European boys were to be sent to Kuching. Knowing that they would eventually come looking for him, Lillian had immediately shorn off all his hair and rubbed powdered charcoal into his scalp and onto his skin. When the day finally arrived, Lillian hid him in a dummy bamboo wall behind the huge wood stove in the detached kitchen, with strict instructions not to move or make a sound. As he crouched in terror in the confined space, Melvyn could hear the Japanese screaming and slapping his mother, who gone outside to meet them. She said that her son was not in the house, but they did not believe her and began a systematic search. One soldier entered the kitchen and started rummaging through the cupboards, throwing pots and pans about. Peeking through the slats of the bamboo, Melvyn saw that he was also thrusting his bayonet into the walls but, to his relief, the soldier did not bother with the one behind the stove. Although frightened, Lillian remained calm until, with much angry shouting, the Japanese called off the search and left. From that day on, she made sure that Melvyn's head and skin were kept permanently black. The mothers of other boys employed different techniques. Dimit's son Gabriel was trained to dive under the bed if danger threatened, while his aunt dressed his cousin Victor, aged just two, in girl's clothing.

Gabriela Lai's son Bryan, who had brown curly hair, had actually been snatched from the arms of his amah, Mama Kehow, who cared for him while his mother made camouflage nets for the Japanese. However, it was a case of mistaken identity. With Corporal Abin seriously implicated in the Sandakan incident, the Japanese had been on the lookout for his small son, who had 'disappeared'. As Mama Kehow's previous post had been with the Abin family, the Japanese immediately assumed that Bryan was the 'missing' child. Fortunately the interpreter Simuda was able to convince them that this was not the case, allowing the child to be returned to the arms of his hysterical mother.

Confident that Melvyn's disguise would continue to fool the Japanese, Lillian took him with her on her trip into Sandakan. On reaching Bukit Merah, where The Hundred Steps led down to the town, she paused to point out the Japanese fleet anchored in the harbour. Melvyn who, in his short four years of life had never seen anything remotely like it, begged his mother to take him down to the wharf for a closer look. As she considered it would be safe enough to mingle with the crowds already milling about, she agreed and, after making the necessary number of bows to the many Japanese soldiers who had come to see the ships, they were allowed to approach the dockside. At that moment, two squadrons of American planes, launched from aircraft carriers off the east coast of the Philippines, roared overhead. One group targeted the ships. The other bombed the wharf area. As vessels exploded into balls of flame, and bullets sprayed across the dock area, the sightseers turned tail and fled. Grabbing Melvyn's hand tightly, Lillian ran towards the monsoon drain leading to the base of The Hundred Steps. As she ran for her life, panic-stricken civilians were trampled in the crush, blasted to pieces by falling bombs or stopped mid-stride as the machine-gun bullets cut a swathe through the crowds, killing Japanese and local people alike. The sonic boom from one bullet, which almost grazed Lillian's left ear, left her with permanent hearing loss.

Relying on her survival instinct, she followed a zigzagging path, using what cover she could find, but at the same time moving closer to the drain. As they neared a group of Japanese soldiers, who were firing ineffectually at the aircraft, one shouted angrily at Lillian, pointing towards her hat, which, in his panic-stricken state, he believed was creating a target for enemy guns. When Lillian ignored him, he leapt over the drain and hit her with such force that she pitched into it, with

Melvyn still clinging grimly to her hand. As she hit the concrete, she shrieked in pain as her ankle buckled beneath her. Urging Melvyn not to cry, she led him along the base of the drain, crawling on all fours.

After what seemed to be an eternity, the bombing and strafing stopped. They had reached The Hundred Steps but there was no way that Lillian could climb them. Suddenly, a strong arm shot out, hauled her to her feet and dragged her up the steps, surrounded all the way by screaming, terrified civilians, and with Melvyn clinging on for dear life. On reaching the top, they turned and looked back at the chaos below. The warships, so proud in their camouflage paint such a short time before, were ablaze; their decks and guns a mass of twisted metal. The town had also suffered terribly, with buildings on fire, mangled bodies of Japanese and civilians littering the streets, and wreckage everywhere. As they turned their back on the devastation and the wailing sirens, Lillian vowed she would not return to Sandakan until the war was over.

This attack was just the first of many. The Americans were on a roll. On 10 October, the first anniversary of the disastrous Double Tenth rebellion, planes from seventeen aircraft carriers attacked the Japanese island of Okinawa. Four days later US naval aircraft completed a three-day sweep of Formosa, destroying 280 Japanese planes. And on 20 October, General Douglas MacArthur waded ashore near Tacloban in the Philippines to cover himself in glory and broadcast to the world, 'I have returned'. By nightfall, more than 130,00 American troops and 200,000 tonnes of stores and equipment were ashore. Three days later, in the greatest battle in the history of naval warfare, Allied naval ships and aircraft inflicted staggering losses on the Japanese in the battle of Leyte Gulf. Their Imperial Navy lost 34 ships, including three battleships, four aircraft carriers, ten cruisers, thirteen destroyers and five submarines.

The loss of the super battleship *Musashi* was a terrible blow to the enemy. This supposedly indestructible dreadnought was hit by twenty torpedoes and seventeen bombs before it rolled over and sank, taking half of the 2,200-man crew to the bottom. A week later the Japanese, in desperation, came up with a new form of attack – the Kamikaze or suicide plane – and on 11 November the giant aircraft carrier *Shinano* joined the Imperial fleet. With its 30-centimetre-thick steel deck covering a layer of concrete, claimed to be capable of withstanding any kind of attack, the 'unsinkable' vessel carried seventy planes and was considered a major boost to Japan's fading naval strength. Seventeen days later, *Shinano* was torpedoed by the US submarine *Archerfish*. The indestructible carrier sank in the Kumano Sea on 29

November, giving it the dubious distinction of having the shortest lifespan of any major warship in World War II.

The Japanese, angry at the way in which the war was going, became increasingly short tempered. Anyone at all who incurred their wrath for the slightest rule infringement was subjected to brutal treatment. At the end of 1944, Pedro Dominic's eldest son, Cornelius, better known as Cory and brother of Double Tenth freedom fighter Ethelbert, ran foul of the Japanese in Tawau and was beheaded. Because of the increased brutality and the bombing, many of the locals in Sandakan quit town to find refuge on farms and rubber estates owned by relatives or friends. Dominic abandoned Rose Cottage and moved his family to an orchard at Mile 13 owned by his son-in-law Andrew Pereira – the government printer who had gone out of his way to give cigarettes to POWs working round the town. With no work at the printery, the Pereiras had left their Leila Road house in May that year.

Shortly after Andrew arrived at the orchard, the Japanese had issued orders that every family member who was old enough must plant 2,000 tapioca bushes. Inspections were carried out regularly but, to the surprise of his son Alfred, no one ever bothered to actually count them. Once the crop was harvested, the Japanese confiscated the lot so, in order to get enough to eat, the family removed the roots and replaced the leafy stalks in the soil, giving the impression that the plants were still growing. When the leaves withered and died, it was put down to a fungal disease. The Australians, who crept under the wire at night in search of food, had been employing a version of this ruse for some time, by digging up the roots from below soil level. They referred to the practice as 'bandicooting' – named for a small furry marsupial which burrowed around in gardens at night for food.

Once the Americans gained a firm foothold in the Philippines, air raids on the Sandakan area were stepped up. Just before one of the raids, the entire Funk family, evidently in order to seek some respite from the harsh jungle conditions for the older members, returned to a house at Mile 14. While they were there, there was an air raid, forcing them to take cover in a shelter, along with wounded Japanese soldiers who were billeted nearby. The noise was deafening as the planes roared by, their pilots barely skimming the tops of the coconut palms as they strafed troops stationed all along the Labuk Road. Huddled in the shelter with her brother and Sonny Pereira, who had come from the adjoining orchard, Olga watched in terror as a plane, flying much lower than usual, screamed overhead. It crashed a short distance away, to the delight of the Japanese, who dragged part of the wreckage to Labuk Road where it was placed on display.

Once the raid was over, the family did not dally, but fled to the relative safety of their jungle hideouts once more. The children had long ago learned that the sound of aircraft engines could mean death, and were trained to dive for cover if out in the open, lest they be mistaken for Japanese. At Mile 11, Dimit and her family sought protection in the hollowed-out base of the tree-trunk 'bridge'. It was a very tight squeeze, and her mother's bottom stuck out, but it was better than nothing. At the POW Camp, which, like the airfield, came under increasing attack, prisoners dug a series of slit trenches or sheltered under the huts. Sometimes, however, they were either too slow or too far away to take cover, and there were a number of deaths as bombs falling short of the airstrip blew buildings apart, and huts in which the sick lay were strafed. In Sandakan itself, where places of refuge were diminishing with each air raid, civilians still living in the vicinity of Leila Road and near the padang sheltered in nearby caves.

Some of those whose relatives were involved in the Sandakan Incident had left town a lot earlier than the Pereira family. Although her family had not been harassed in the same way as Katherine Lagan, it nevertheless seemed foolish to Ojagar Singh's wife to remain in Sandakan, especially as there were many members of the Sikh community willing to help. With their assistance, the Singhs had moved into an empty house at Mile 1.5, where fourteen-year-old Hercharan assumed responsibility for the family, including his baby sister, born two months after Ojagar left Sandakan. As Hercharan had a working knowledge of Japanese, he was employed for a while as a translator, and also became a small-time fishmonger, selling fish and shrimps caught in a nearby stream. The family grew their own vegetables and, to earn some cash, sold oil extracted from coconuts.

In late 1943, Mrs Singh's brother, Dial Singh, a sergeant in the Lahad Datu Constabulary, arrived with his wife and two children. It was his intention to take the entire family back to his property outside Lahad Datu but, after all their belongings were loaded aboard the ship, the Japanese refused to allow anyone apart from Dial to leave. When he returned to Mile 1.5 seven months later, he brought with him eight porters: the family was going to escape overland to Lahad Datu, through the jungle.

Crossing the bay in a sampan under cover of darkness, they made their way along the coast to the Segama River, where Dial's friends were waiting with two larger boats. After spending a few days with the headman at Kampong Bikang, they continued upstream in pouring rain, frightening away crocodiles that approached the boats with pieces of burning wood. Forced to camp on an island due to rising floodwaters, and finding themselves surrounded by wild animals and snakes also seeking refuge from the inundation, the adults kept an all-night vigil beside a fire. About sixteen kilometres from Lahad Datu they left the vastly swollen river and all its perils behind and continued on foot along a road, wading through knee-deep floodwater for the first three kilometres. After living with relatives for about a month on Tengah Nipa Plantation, where the baby died of malnutrition and illness, they moved deep into the jungle, to a hut Dial had built on his eight-hectare property. Here they remained in hiding, subsisting on vegetables and tapioca that they planted, small fish and crabs caught in nearby streams, and salt extracted from seawater.

For some time, Dial Singh had been meeting Americans who came to Lahad Datu by submarine from Tawi Tawi to gather intelligence. A police sergeant who learned about his activities decided to report him – not directly, but by way of a letter written to the kempeitai chief, which he gave to Dial to deliver. Fortunately, Dial had doubts about the sergeant's loyalties and opened the letter. That night he escaped into the jungle, where he remained, alone, until the war was over. His family, meantime, only just managed to stay alive. Hercharan, who had been a tower of strength, fell ill, and the two surviving younger girls, weakened by malnutrition and beriberi, died after eating poisonous mushrooms. The others, apart from Anup, who did not like mushrooms, were extremely ill, but recovered and managed to remain hidden from the Japanese until the end of the war.

The POWs, who had no hope of escape, had no option but to put up with the increased brutality throughout 1944; this when combined with further ration cuts and malaria, saw the death rate climb dramatically in December. That month the Japanese also executed the three Python men, Brandis, McKenzie and Rudwick. After being taken to 37 Army Headquarters in Jesselton in June, all three were put on trial and sentenced to death for spying. On the afternoon of 30 December, blindfolded and bound, they were led up the wooden steps to the gaol's gallows, a legacy of the previous administration. Shortly after 3.30 pm, with Chief judge Colonel Maeda, Major Nishihara, Lieutenant Nagita, four members of the judiciary and four kempeitai as witnesses, all three were hanged. While the Japanese were keen to employ what was still, to them, a novel method of execution, the hangman had not yet mastered the art of ensuring instantaneous death. McKenzie and at least one other were finished off with a blow to the head from a heavy iron bar. According to Ahong, one of their escorts, who later gave details of the execution to Australian investigating officers, the condemned men had faced the inevitable bravely, standing firm and erect upon the gallows.

Back at the POW camp in Sandakan, the bombing of the airstrip had increased to such an extent over Christmas that the Japanese abandoned it. With the labour force now redundant, conditions deteriorated dramatically. On 10 January, on Hoshijima's orders, the rice ration to the Australian compound was cut out completely. Their emergency stockpile of 105 bags, which they had carefully hoarded over a period of months, was removed to the basement of Pop Wong's house, where Hoshijima had taken up residence, as Harry Keith's house was under constant attack from air raids. According to Hoshijima's calculations, the 105 bags, if consumed at the current rate of 130 grams of rice a day, would last the Australians two months.

On the assumption that the prisoners, no longer performing harbour manual labour, would be able to subsist on less food and, having no idea of how long the war would last, the camp's quartermaster Lieutenant Good set the ration at 70 grams – less than one tenth of the 1942 allowance. What the prisoners did not know was that under Hoshijima's house were another ninety tonnes of rice, with an additional 54 tonnes stacked in the barber's shop and a bomb-proof store at the nearby barracks. The official rice ration, which Hoshijima was still receiving for the Australians, was appropriated for the use of his troops.

Later that month Dr Yamamoto visited the camp, bringing with him five jars of Atebrin tablets, three jars of quinine (enough to give each prisoner one tablet) and a small box of bandages. Despite the paucity of his allocation, there were more than enough drugs in Sandakan to treat not only the POWs but also the entire civilian population. Along with the huge stock of rice in his basement, Hoshijima also had 160,000 quinine tablets and hundreds of Red Cross parcels filled with tinned meat and vegetables, canned fruit, condensed milk, tea, jars of Marmite (rich in vitamin B), and many other commodities which would have meant the difference between life and death, along with comforts such as clothing, soap, combs and razor blades. Also at hand were another 786,000 quinine tablets, 19,600 vitamin A and D tablets, large numbers of vitamin B and C tablets and an enormous amount of medical supplies and surgical equipment. Despite this massive stockpile of food and drugs, not a single tablet, grain of rice or teaspoon of Marmite was given to the prisoners. Like the local people, while under Japanese 'protection' they would die like flies from malnutrition, beriberi, malaria and easily treatable infections.

After observing the poor physical condition of many of the prisoners, Dr Yamamoto advised Australian medical officer Dr Picone that the best way to overcome beriberi was with more exercise and hard work. Ironically, in spite of the closure of the airstrip, the POWs were still receiving plenty of both. All those not confined to bed were sent out each day to spread sullage on the vegetable patch, collect wood, or forage for tapioca, sometimes as far away as sixteen kilometres. Towards the end of January, Dick Braithwaite, an Australian prisoner, was assigned to a party sent to gather tapioca about eleven kilometres from the camp. After spending an exhausting morning pulling up the roots by hand, the prisoners were ordered to carry them back to the main road, three kilometres away. Many of the men were ill and one was so weak that, once the guard was out of sight, Braithwaite began a shuttle service to help him with his load. As he moved back and forth along the track he noticed a young Chinese farmer sawing wood near his hut but, with a guard lurking nearby, the man kept his head down. As Braithwaite trudged past to collect his final load, the farmer handed him some native tobacco, indicating that he would like some tapioca roots in return. Unfortunately, a guard saw this attempted transaction and chased the farmer down the road, where he was caught and savagely beaten with a rifle butt. When Braithwaite returned with his load, three guards belted and kicked him. They were about to tie him, and the unfortunate farmer, to the back of the truck and drag them the eight kilometres back to camp when Warrant Officer Murozumi rode up on his bicycle.

Morozumi, who had been drinking saki and was the worse for wear, forced the farmer to his knees. Unsheathing his sword, he took a few practice swipes before placing the blade across the back of the farmer's neck. Raising the sword high in the air he brought it down with a mighty swipe, only to stop short. Cackling with laughter, he repeated this action several times, spurred on by the sight of a tiny Chinese woman, evidently the young man's mother, on her knees begging for mercy and with tears cascading down her face. Eventually tiring of the game, Morozumi cycled off to the camp and let the terrified farmer go. When the tapioca party finally returned to the camp at ten o'clock that night, they discovered that in their absence there had been an announcement. Five hundred of the fittest prisoners were to be moved from Sandakan to another destination.

Chapter 10

To Ranau

The order to transfer the prisoners had been issued a fortnight previously, when Lieutenant Yamamoto Shoichi, commanding officer of an infantry unit currently based in Sandakan, was instructed to move 360 troops and a machine-gun company to Tuaran, on the west coast. For the past three months, Yamamoto's men had been building fortifications in and around Sandakan, especially near the airfield. However, with the airstrip no longer in operation, except for light aircraft, and with Japanese military bases in the west now vulnerable to attack following the invasion of the Philippines, his regiment had been given their marching orders. He was also instructed to take with him about 500 POWs, whose labour could be put to use in the Tuaran–Jesselton area, where the Japanese garrison was being strengthened. The Allies had control of the air and seas, so the troops and POWs would have to make the journey on foot.

Although various river systems, linked by foot tracks, formed well-established routes to the west and north, Yamamoto was ordered to take a new, more southerly route. Normally, to travel overland to the west, people either went by boat up the Labuk River from Beluran to Tampias, where there was a native path leading to the coast, or followed a more northerly route along rivers and foot tracks through Meridi. This new, entirely overland route that Yamamoto was to use had been established in late 1944 by cutting a path from the Kolapis River at Mile 42 on the existing Sandakan–Beluran track, to Tampias. From here the native path led to the eastern flank of Mt Kinabalu and the village of Ranau, where other foot tracks from the north, south, east and west converged. The distance from Mile 8 to Ranau, at Mile 164, was almost 250 kilometres.

The 55-kilometre lower section of the new track, from Mile 42 to the Celo River (a tributary of the Sapi) at Mile 76, was surveyed and blazed by Orang Tua Kulang, headman of Kampong Muanad (Moyned), on the river of the same name. Kulang, acknowledged as local chief of the Dusuns, was an outstanding hunter, deadly with a blowpipe and rifle, and an expert in the use of a parang. His able assistant was Bede 'Sandshoe' Willie, Gort Chester's friend who had helped establish Python's spy network at Labian Point. He was now living at Kuala Sapi, a village north of the track where the Sapi-

Pandan Pandan Rivers met the Trusan Sapi River, before flowing into the estuary known to British cartographers as Kuala Labuk.

The track's mid-section, a distance of about 90 kilometres, stretching from Celo at Mile 76 to the river crossing near Tampias at Mile 133, had been assigned to Kanak, chief of the Orang Sungei (river people) and headman of Tandu Batu, a village on the Labuk, west of the Kemansi Estate. The headman of Tampias was responsible for the last sector, which followed the existing native path along a river known at that time as the Kuanan (now called the Liwagu). At the time the track was cut, the river system, known today as the Liwagu-Labuk, was called the Liwagu from its source on the slopes of Mt Kinabalu to the village of Nabutan, and then the Kuanan from Nabutan to its junction with the Kegibangan, near Tampias. Downstream from Tampias it was known as the Labuk as far as the junction with the Tungud, where it became the Lidong, which, in turn, emptied into Kuala Labuk, near Kampong Dawang. Modern-day maps give only two names to this complex river system: the Liwagu as far as Telupid, and then the Labuk.

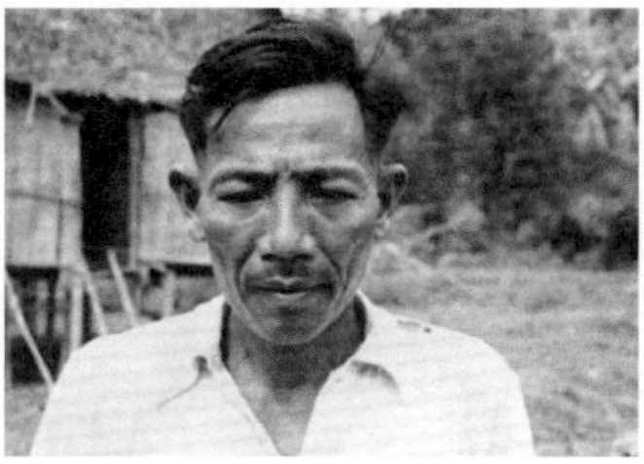
Orang Tua Kulang, who cut the track

Once the new sections of the route were defined by Kulang, Willie and Kanak, the entire track had been widened by Javanese and local coolies. Logs spanned the Samawang, Kolapis, Muanad, Mandoring, Sapipayu and Telupid Rivers and, as it was the rainy season, a split bamboo boardwalk had been erected along some sections of the existing 'dry weather' track from Sandakan to Mile 42, then a swamp due to continuous heavy rain.

Assuming the new track was to be used for enemy troops retreating from the Philippines, the fiercely anti-Japanese Willie, Kulang and Kanak had devised a most tortuous and difficult path between mile stones 42 and 133. To make life even more difficult for the Japanese, and to prevent them from harassing the people who lived in small kampongs near or along the Labuk, they had deliberately skirted Muanad, Sapi and Mandoring villages and had avoided going near any habitation at all between Mile 63 and Tampias. After leaving the Beluran track at Mile 42, the new path passed through low-lying, swampy ground to well beyond Sungei Muanad at Mile 49.5. Once out of the swamps, it then ran through undulating country, covered with rain forest so thick and dense that no sunlight penetrated. Cutting through this area were three sizeable rivers, all of which joined the Sapi: Pandan Pandan at Mile 58, Mandoring at Mile 60, and Sapipayu at 63. Once the track crossed the Sapipayu, it ran more or less parallel to, but south of, the headwaters of the Sapi River.

The new path had taken a longer time to cut than was necessary, not simply because it passed through the most difficult terrain, but because, in order to hold up proceedings, Kulang and Kanak had deliberately blazed the preliminary trail up the side of an impassable mountain, or along a blind valley. These tactics were responsible for a delay of at least four weeks. The track that Kanak finally cut was still extremely difficult. After leaving Celo and crossing the Bonkud River, he had struck out to the south, away from the wide-flowing Labuk, and routed the path over two mountains. From the Maliau River he had then followed an established native footpath leading to Kaling, before diverting even further from the Labuk and into the unexplored, uncharted territory of the Taviu valley: an area so remote that none of the rivers there were marked on any map and the positions of villages at Telupid and Tampias were wildly inaccurate in terms of latitude and longitude. The rivers along this sector came in quick succession – the Tapaang (Papan), Baba, Tara Rangang, Tundom and Lolosling. After a very difficult climb up and over Taviu Hill to the Monkilau River, the track began a long descent to the Liwagu valley, and Tampias. From the river crossing near Tampias, the old native track snaked to Mile 138.5 at Paginatan before beginning a final steep ascent across the Crocker Range to the Ranau plain, forty-two kilometres to the west.

Track near Bauto

Food dumps were to be set up Miles 49.5, 60, 84.5 and 120, where produce could be brought in from the Labuk River or along its tributaries. However, as the track beyond Bauto passed through wild, uninhabited country, at this stage there were no food stocks from Mile 84.5 until the village of Paginatan at Mile 138. To allow time for the dumps that had been established to be replenished, the 455 POWs deemed fit enough to undertake this gruelling journey were to leave Sandakan in batches of fifty, one day apart.

It was raining heavily and still dark when the first group set off early on the morning of 28 January. As Hoshijima had assured them that they were being transferred to a camp somewhere in Borneo where there was plenty of food, all were in good spirits. As it was obvious that the war was nearing its end, the prisoners, after some discussion, had taken his assurance at face value, figuring that when the Allies arrived it would be in the best interests of the Japanese to hand over as many fit POWs as possible. On reaching the bitumen road at the Mile 8 police post, they were therefore startled, and then dismayed, when they did not turn left towards Sandakan, but right, towards the jungle-clad, mountainous interior.

Waiting for them at Mile 9 were Yamamoto and fifty of his men, along with a mountain of hessian bags containing ammunition, rice and other supplies. After a delay of twenty-four hours, owing to torrential rain, the prisoners were loaded up with various bundles, which in some cases amounted to a weight of twenty-five kilograms. The groups that followed were equally, if not more, burdened. In addition to the standard load, one group was forced to carry the accompanying troops' mosquito nets, plus a dismantled mountain gun and ammunition. Another, under the command of a World War I veteran who did not believe in travelling light, had the unenviable task of transporting all his boxes and trunks, slung on three bamboo poles, coolie style.

As the prisoners neared the first of the marshy areas, they were relieved to see the boardwalk, perched on poles about a metre above the slush. However, their relief was short lived. The combination of split bamboo slats, rain and mud was far more deadly than any crocodile lurking in the swamps. The Japanese had made it quite clear that, as there were no medical facilities available, any prisoner, or soldier, who slipped and broke his leg would be shot. While the prisoners' reaction to this was one of dumbfounded horror, to the Japanese it was nothing new. Japanese army regulations stated that any troops unable to keep up in a retreat were to be 'disposed of'.

Aware that such an eventuality was inevitable, the Japanese command had attached a killing squad to each group.

The next two days were horrendous, so much so that many reasonably fit prisoners thought they would surely die. The heavy monsoonal rain, coupled with the increasingly swampy terrain, saw soldiers and prisoners alike struggling through knee-deep mud, trying to maintain a precarious footing on the short, sharp rises between the boardwalks. They were only halfway through the swamps when darkness fell and, with nowhere else to sleep, had no choice but to collapse on the bamboo slats, eaten alive by swarms of mosquitoes and attacked by leeches, some as thick as pencils.

The Muanad River crossing at Mile 49.5 was a designated stopping place. It wasn't much, just an open-sided hut which Kulang was building. The Japanese appropriated most of the available space, forcing the prisoners, as usual, to search for whatever shelter they could find. Kulang was still working on the roof of the rest house when group 5 arrived on 7 February. Striking up a conversation with an Australian POW who appeared to be their leader, Kulang learned that one of the party, who was too ill to walk, was in a smaller hut across the river. The headman's offer to care for the prisoner was rejected by the group's Lieutenant Sato, who was worried a more senior officer attached to the military post nearby might come along and report him. The following morning, when the group moved off, the sick prisoner and a less-ill companion were left behind. A short time later, as the able-bodied man was boiling some water over an open fire, two Japanese soldiers arrived and sent him on his way. Before leaving, the Australian handed Kulang a photo of his family, on the back of which was an inscription, his name and the name of his sick friend. Two soldiers from the military post then placed the ill man on a stretcher and carried him to a spot about 100 metres away, where he was shot dead.

While Kulang was doing his best to protect POWs at the Muanad River, collaborator Cheong Yu Kaw, aged thirty-three, who worked on a Japanese-owned estate, was doing his best to strip them of whatever valuables they still possessed. On 12 February, while a party of prisoners rested, he cheated and extorted them of clothing and valuables, including an inscribed wristwatch and gold ring – both of which, along with Kulang's testimony, would later see him arrested and brought to trial.

On 14 February, Australians Ken Molde and Eric Fuller, and British prisoners Bois Roberts and Herbert Beardshaw, had completed the difficult climb from Bauto. They were in the jungle beyond the Tapaang River, heading towards Taviu Hill, when ten prisoners who could not keep up were shot. All four men were suffering from dysentery so, rather than wait for the killing squad to finish them off, they decided to try and escape. As the Australians moved off, a guard spotted them and opened fire, hitting Molde in the elbow, but the pair kept going and managed to shake off their pursuers.

Hussin bin Ulan, described as a tall 'Dyak' with greying hair and moustache, lived at Telupid village, on the far side of the Labuk. Although the local people had been warned, on pain of death, to keep away from the track, three days after the prisoners escaped Hussin took his small son, Jamis, fishing. While looking for a good spot along the nearby Telupid River, they came across the two English prisoners. Japanese guards had been to the village searching for the escapees, so Hussin knew who they were. Thin and obviously ill, they indicated that they wished to know when it was safe to move. At about 4 pm he took them to his house and, a short time later, brought in Molde and Fuller, whom he had found earlier in the day.

At about 10 pm, after the fugitives had enjoyed their first warm wash in years, eaten a little chicken and rice and attended to Molde's wounded elbow, they set out for Kampong Kemansi (not to be confused with Kemansi Estate), a kilometre or two away, where they were handed into the care of Onsi (Unshi), the village headman and also an SOA agent. As the Japanese visited the village from time to time, the twenty families who lived in Kemansi built them a sulap (lean-to shelter) in the jungle. Onsi and his villagers did everything possible with their limited resources, but as the only food available was tapioca and a very small amount of rice, the prisoners gradually weakened, and died.

Japanese Army Headquarters was supposed to have organised food dumps, but the further the column moved into the interior, the more hit and miss the supplies became. On reaching the staging post near Bauto, one group of forty-nine Australians had discovered that their only sustenance for the next four days, until they reached Paginatan, almost ninety kilometres away, was six cucumbers. The lack of food and steep terrain beyond Bauto took a terrible toll. On the third day of their 'six cucumber walk', five prisoners died from exhaustion on Taviu Hill. The others, in a trance-like state from hunger, took an entire day to reach the top, crawling on their hands and knees. The path was narrow and the valley deep, so the Japanese simply rolled the bodies of anyone who died over the side and into the jungle.

Had a group of Dusuns out hunting in the forest not come across the starving prisoners and given them some tapioca in exchange for an enamelled army plate, more in this group would have died before reaching Tampias where, fortunately, they had an enforced rest. As the river was in flood, people from the village some distance away had been hired to row the prisoners and soldiers across, two at a time.

By this time Captain Yamamoto knew that the surviving prisoners were not going all the way to the west coast. As had been expected, there had been air raids on Jesselton and new orders had been issued; the POWs were not to proceed past Ranau. However, as the only accommodation at the village was an open-sided bamboo hut, for the time being the last four groups coming through were to remain at Paginatan, forty kilometres from Ranau.

Although heavily laden, half-starved, barefoot and clad in ragged bits of clothing, an amazing seventy-five per cent of the prisoners survived the march from Sandakan, a feat that had taken between fourteen and twenty days. However, having reached their destinations by sheer willpower, they were to find no relief at either Ranau or Paginatan: food was scarce, dysentery broke out and, since Yamamoto's well-disciplined soldiers had gone on to Tuaran, the prisoners were now at the mercy of their brutal camp guards.

On 22 February, twenty POWs from Ranau and some local people, escorted by two guards, left for Paginatan with supplies for Japanese troops passing through, and the POWs still held there. Each person in the party carried a twenty-kilogram bag of rice, brought up from Jesselton by coolie labour. Any POW who failed to keep up was a dead man. After climbing up and over Marakau Hill, they were about sixteen kilometres from Ranau when two local carriers who were well ahead of the main pack – Kangas and Batingi of Kampong Gana Gana, south of Ranau – stopped to rest. As the others came into sight they were horrified to see that the two guards had strangled one of the prisoners, by twisting a length of rope around his neck. Stripping him of what little clothing and possessions he had, they dragged his body into the jungle, where Kangas and Batingi were ordered to cover it with a ground sheet before rejoining the column. Just over a kilometre further on the guards shot another prisoner, leaving the body beside a stream.

The forty-kilometre journey to Paginatan took three days, with overnight stops along the way at Muruk, where there was a large Japanese staging camp, and near Segindai, about sixteen kilometres away. The return journey took two days, with only one stop, at Nalapak. The first eight kilometres from Paginatan, which roller-coastered along the side of the mountains, were generally manageable, but the gruelling climb 6.5-kilometre from the Liwagu River near Segindai sapped the energy of many prisoners, some to the point of death. However, while there was always a risk that the rice carrying might be a one-way trip, POWs who were still fit enough volunteered repeatedly for this task. Not only did it get them away from Ranau, where dysentery was rife and bashings frequent, it also gave them a chance to siphon rice from the bags through a piece of hollow bamboo; to steal food from native gardens along the way; and to trade their curry ration with local people. Local people such as Ikul and Saidin also slipped food to them as they passed by, and village dogs, if they could be caught, were a welcome addition to the communal pot. At Paginatan, a woman named Bureh, who had little enough to spare for her husband and child, gave what food she could to the prisoners, who called her 'Mumma'.

With rice supplies arriving each week, the Japanese guards at Paginatan had sufficient carbohydrate, but no meat. However, they had plenty of prisoners of war, all of whom were expendable. In acts of cannibalism, which would be repeated at the Muanad River crossing, and elsewhere along the track, the Japanese killed some of the POWs and ate their internal organs and flesh. They also did the same to local people employed as carriers along the track. While cannibalism, outlawed in most civilised societies, was repugnant to the Western mind, Japanese soldiers were permitted to eat the flesh of the enemy dead. Indeed, in November 1944 one Japanese general had publicly stated, 'Troops must fight the Allies, even to the extent of eating them.' However, to eat another Japanese was a capital crime.

In all, the Ranau rice carriers made six trips to and from Paginatan. Although about twenty overall died while carrying out this task, the death toll was infinitely worse at both Ranau and Paginatan, where dysentery and brutal treatment reduced numbers to such an extent that at the end of March, just five weeks after arriving at their destinations, the two groups were amalgamated. People from Ranau village and those attending the weekly tamu (market) a short distance from the POW compound often saw small groups of prisoners sent out on working parties to gather firewood or collect vegetables for Japanese troops. Moved by their pitiful state, the villagers made up small bundles of food, which they carried with them in the hope that they might be able to give them to the prisoners. Eight-year-old Yee Sing See, son of one of the local shopkeepers, passed on bananas and

Bureh, known as 'Mumma' to the POWs she helped

Track near Paginatan

Track on Marakau Hill

other food, supplied by his parents. Among those who also risked their lives were Singki, Gangung, Gopokau, Amit, Rijan, Janan, Hikandoa, Balinti, Galitang, Ingurru, Kalindai, Geronsi, Mansia, Jamin and Segindai, along with the entire population of Marakau, a small kampong on the eastern side of the Ranau plain. Distressed by the sight of prisoners being beaten as they passed through the village, Patuk binte Gijiran left cooked rice for them, hidden under banana leaves beside the track.

Despite the risks taken by the people of Ranau and Marakau, the POWs' overall physical condition continued to decline. Pooling food resources was now a thing of the past. Those able to obtain food now kept it to themselves, carefully watching every grain of rice distributed at mealtimes, lest one person receive more than another. Believing that escape was a viable option to a slow death from starvation, Australians Wally Crease and Neil Cleary had attempted to flee in March. Betrayed in return for a bag of rice, they had been brought back to the camp at Ranau, where they were subjected to terrible punishment. Crease managed to escape a second time, but was shot on the run to the west of the camp. Cleary, wearing only a loincloth, was tied to a tree where he was tortured and beaten for days until death came as a merciful release. By the end of April, when air raids on the neighbouring airstrip forced the remaining prisoners to move to a new camp in the jungle nearby, only 56 of the 455 who had set out from Sandakan were still alive. On 9 June there were twenty, and the following day, ten. The other ten, who were ill, were shot or bayoneted and buried in swampy ground near their wooden hut. It appears that a local girl, Laniam binte Baranting, was the sole witness to these murders, which she glimpsed through the wooden slats of the hut as she passed by on her way to Ranau. Post-war, confronted with irrefutable evidence of the prisoners' remains, the Japanese involved made a full confession.

The ten surviving prisoners were moved from Ranau, the place they called 'death valley', to a second jungle camp, tucked away in a deep river valley eight kilometres south along the Tambunan track. It was no better here. Four died between 13 and 19 June. A week later the surviving six were collecting sticks to cook their meagre rations when they looked up to see a straggling line of 183 emaciated creatures, hardly recognisable as human, enter the valley: all that was left of a force of 536 POWs who had set out from Sandakan, four weeks before. Their removal was not to make use of their labour, but to get them away from Sandakan, where Allied attacks had increased to such an intensity that the Japanese feared an invasion was imminent.

By this time, the 830 prisoners still alive at the Mile 8 Camp should have been rescued. The fact that they had not was due to a series of inexcusable delays and bungles.

* * * * *

A plan to rescue Sandakan's POWs, using paratrooper assault troops, had been proposed in July 1944 following Gort Chester's return to Australia after the aborted Python mission. Known as Operation Kingfisher, it was to be carried out in conjunction with a series of undercover and intelligence missions in Sabah, code-named Operation Agas. To pave the way for the various sub-parties, Gort was keen to establish a base on the west coast well before the onset of the monsoon. However, despite his urging, the head of the Allied Intelligence Bureau and SOA chiefs had moved too slowly. In October, with the monsoon already set in, the mission was postponed until January 1945.

On the appointed date Gort and his team, known as Agas 1, travelled to Western Australia, expecting to board an American submarine to take them to Borneo, only to discover that no one at SOA HQ had informed the Americans that transport was required. After some intensive liaison, the Agas men, with all their equipment and stores, were airlifted to Darwin where another US submarine, about to leave on a routine patrol, was assigned to drop them off. It was only now that Gort discovered that aerial reconnaissance photographs of the intended insertion point, ordered months before, had not materialised. Someone in SOA had sat on the request for weeks before finally dispatching it to the wrong agency. Gort and his team would have to go in blind.

On reaching the proposed entry point at Pulau Sisa, north of Kota Belud, a periscope reconnaissance of the coastline between the island and Sikuati revealed what appeared to be buildings and a radio mast, as well as a great deal of smoke. Unable to find a secure point of entry, the Agas team had no option but to abort the mission: a problem in itself as the submarine was on patrol and not returning to base for some time. However, the ever-accommodating Americans diverted another submarine to pick them up.

With the west coast appearing to be insecure, it was now decided to move Agas's general area of operations to the north-east coast. A specialised party would infiltrate the Sandakan area via the Gum Gum River, only a few kilometres from the POW camp, to obtain the vital intelligence needed to allow the 600 paratroops on standby to make a surprise raid. With an Allied invasion of Tarakan scheduled for 1 May and, with it, the possibility that the POWs at Sandakan could be killed, time was now getting short.

Despite the tight time frame, there was no reason to doubt that a rescue mission, as outlined in the plans for Operation Kingfisher, would not succeed. In February, the Americans had used this very plan as a blueprint. Deploying only one-third of the number of paratroops assigned to Kingfisher, they had pulled off a stunning rescue of more than 2,000 POWs and internees, many of them frail and ill, held at Los Banos in the Philippines. Although this camp was guarded by 250 well-trained enemy soldiers, with a company of troops armed with a howitzer and four machine-guns stationed less than three kilometres away, plus another 6,000 soldiers within easy reach, the paratroopers had rescued every single prisoner with the loss of only two men. Provided the special SOA party could obtain ground intelligence of the same calibre as that collected by the Americans, it was expected that the POWs at Sandakan should be back in Allied hands by 30 April.

However, at the last minute, despite the brilliance of the Los Banos rescue, the well thought-out and now thoroughly tested Kingfisher plan was revised. The plan to insert the specialised reconnaissance team for Operation Kingfisher had been scrapped. Locals were now to collect the necessary intelligence and bring it to the main Agas base, located many kilometres from Sandakan on the far side of Labuk Bay. Agas was also expected to organise a resistance movement, train a guerrilla army and gather general information to facilitate the evacuation from Kudat of a Mr Chong, described as a 'high priority target'. With hundreds of kilometres of mountainous jungle separating Kudat from the east coast, Gort knew that these tasks alone required the full attention of separate, fully briefed teams. He ranted and raved about the idiocy of the proposal, but it did him no good. He could agree to carry out the amalgamated tasks, or resign.

After an aerial reconnaissance of the area conduced by Chester and SOA's Major Nick Combe, the Agas men finally left Australia by submarine on 24 February. Seven days later, on the night of 3 March, they were paddling ashore at the revised insertion point about nine kilometres from the Tagahan River, on the far side of Labuk Bay. As a diversionary tactic, Sandakan was bombed. After selecting a site, three or four kilometres upstream, for a base camp and wireless station, Gort and three others departed on the first of a series of reconnaissance missions. A few days later the four men were lying in their hammocks in thick jungle near the Sugut River when a stranger suddenly appeared. Their unexpected visitor was Samak, a former Sandakan Customs' House boatman who now lived in Kampong Menanghutan, a village on Sungei Terusan, a tributary of the Sugut. On discovering that Gort spoke fluent Malay, he pledged his assistance, reporting that there had been a movement of POWs from Sandakan to Jesselton and that, although Sandshoe Willie had been in custody, he was alive and well.

Bede Willie had been arrested earlier in the year when a rumour, evidently sparked by the intensified bombing of the Sandakan area, was circulated, linking his name to an alleged native uprising. Willie, with his Japanese-American son-in-law Winfield Sherman, Doris Stookes' brother, was interned at Beluran for a month. As a prominent member of the community, Willie had been a person of interest to the Japanese for some time, along with Sherman, who had been raised in the Philippines. On their first visit to Beluran, the Japanese had singled out several young men, including Willie's son, John, to learn Japanese. The speed with which John had become fluent was evidently a worry, for he was sent to Kuching on the pretext that it was for further study. However, his father was sure that he had been taken as a de facto hostage to make sure the family did not step out of line.

Within days Samak had located Willie and spread the word that anyone who wished to join in the fight against the Japanese should report to Menanghutan. Although the Japanese were keeping a close

Gort Chester (centre) with members of his Agas 1 team

James, Thomas and Francis Willie, members of 'behind the lines' teams

watch on him, Willie turned up at the Agas camp on the Sugut River a few days later. When he offered to collect the intelligence needed for the rescue and bring it to the signallers, Gort gratefully accepted. He then continued with his reconnaissance, confident that Willie understood that the matter was urgent. In preparation for the invasion of Tarakan, thousands of Australian troops were about to converge on Morotai, the new forward Allied base in the Molucca Islands. There was less than six weeks to gather the intelligence, deliver it to the base camp, transmit it to Australia, and, if the 'green light' were given, pull off the rescue by 30 April.

Three weeks passed. SOA chiefs in Australia were confident that all would be well. The paratroops were on standby and the first of the C-47 transport planes were ready to move to Morotai. In the waters off New Guinea, British ships and the landing craft needed to evacuate the prisoners were waiting for the order to sail to Leyte Gulf, their crack Royal Marines itching to get back into action. They were part of a large British fleet dispatched to the south-west Pacific area after the D-day landings in Normandy and released for this special mission on the direct orders of General Douglas MacArthur, who felt that, being British, it was fitting that they should be involved. However, apart from the most senior officers, none of the paratroopers, sailors, marines or airmen knew the nature of their highly secret mission. The Royal Marines, who had been practising evacuation procedures on a beach in north Queensland, were told only that they were to evacuate Allied personnel from somewhere in Borneo. Having scant knowledge of the war situation in Asia, they assumed that the evacuees were Australian or British troops who had been cut off in battle.

On 3 April, the results of Sandshoe Willie's intelligence gathering arrived: the prisoners were no longer at Sandakan. The reaction at SOA HQ to this unexpected news was mixed. On the one hand, there was no longer any danger of a massacre when Tarakan was attacked. On the other, the weeks of delay meant that they had moved too slowly, and any chance of rescue was now lost. According to a native chief, the prisoners had been moved overland in groups to Jesselton, the incidence of beriberi was high, and those unable to keep up were shot. Although this information had yet to be confirmed, Agas signalled Australia that 'all signs indicate an enemy evacuation of Sandakan'. A week later, while awaiting further news, Agas moved camp to Jambongan Island. However, as the new site was a good sixty kilometres to the north, the signallers remained behind at the old base until 13 April, when they received information confirming that the previous information was correct, and that some POWs were being held at Ranau.

While those already at Ranau had virtually no chance of being rescued, the receipt of this faulty intelligence condemned the 1,000 or so Sandakan prisoners still alive at the end of April to almost certain death. Had SOA stuck to its original plan and inserted specialised intelligence agents to infiltrate the camp and gather the vital information, the outcome would have been very different. With SOA believing that no one was left at Sandakan, all rescue plans came to an abrupt halt on 16 April: the paratroopers were stood down and then sent on leave; the British ships, after waiting at Leyte for a fortnight, were redeployed on 6 May; and the airmen, after an enjoyable eight days camped under coconut palms and paddling about in the tropical waters at Morotai, returned to duty in Australia on 26 April, where they were sworn to secrecy. Officially, the flights to Morotai had never taken place.

It was not the fault of Mr Willie or his network. Although using local people to collect intelligence had worked well for Python in 1943, the situation was now vastly different: spies were everywhere, locals were prohibited from coming to within 400 metres of any prisoner of war, and punishment for aiding prisoners was decapitation, preceded by a new and terrible torture involving castration. Too frightened to approach the actual camp, the agents had relied on information from people living along the Labuk Road. All were in agreement – countless numbers of POWs had passed by. In fact, there were so many that the procession had lasted for more than a week.

The faulty intelligence was disastrous enough, but there was more to come. With reports coming in from Agas that 1500–2000 enemy troops were retreating from the southern Philippines through Lahad Datu, another 800–900 were camped in the rubber estates along the road leading to the Sandakan airfield, and 200–300 more were near the old Chinese school on the Sibuga Road, SOA now recommended that Kebun Cina Road (Labuk Road) between Mile 2 and Mile 9, an area which included the 'abandoned' POW camp, should be bombed as soon as possible. As the air raids began, many of the local people left town for the interior to seek refuge with relatives.

On 1 May, the day after this signal was received, Australian troops invaded Tarakan. On 8 May Agas signalled that everything was pointing to Ranau as a final Japanese stronghold. A week later the Sandakan area was bombed with such intensity that 600 Japanese troops stationed along Kebun Cina Road, mainly in the Gum Gum River area, were killed. There were heavy casualties also at Sandala Estate, and two steam launches were sunk – one on the Gum Gum River and the other at Beluran. Four British warships from the South-west Pacific Fleet shelled Berhala.

On 21 May, Gort Chester, who had been extracted by flying boat to Morotai for a debriefing, reported that, although a number of POWs had died en route, all were now safely at Ranau. He added that as first class, front-line enemy troops were now retreating along the jungle track, that low-level strafing would be in order. The next day, when SOA issued an updated intelligence report that 'ALL POW have been removed from Sandakan to Ranau, where they now are', it was the signal for American PT boats and Allied aircraft to shell, strafe and bomb Sandakan and the surrounding areas. The recent removal of a large POW sign at the Mile 8 Camp, on the orders of Japanese headquarters, simply reinforced the Allied perception that the camp had been abandoned.

From a strategic point of view, the news that the camp had been evacuated was regarded as fortuitous. As a massive Allied invasion of Labuan and Brunei Bay was due to take place on 10 June, a concentrated attack on Sandakan could help create the impression that any invasion would come from the east. With the POW Camp no longer a consideration, between 23 and 26 May the entire area was bombed and strafed, killing civilians and a number of prisoners. But this was merely a foretaste of what was to come. On 27 May, the Allies launched a massive combined aerial and naval attack on Sandakan.

Chapter 11

Leave no trace

It began at 7 am. As aircraft screamed in overhead, bombing and strafing everything in sight, six PT boats shot up the foreshores, drawing enemy fire as they launched torpedoes which exploded under the wooden dockside, wrecking the harbour facilities. When the raid, which lasted just on three hours, was over, almost every building in Sandakan was either damaged or destroyed. The Americans met no opposition – the few troops in town had retreated up the escarpment. Naval personnel from one PT boat not only entered the Sibuga River unchallenged, they also spoke to villagers. Others ran their craft onto the beaches along the harbour and came ashore, where some of the local people, keen to exchange news, also spoke to them.

Such a loss of face could not be ignored. As soon as the raiders had departed, a party of Japanese marines from Captain Aida Hideo's Special Attack Unit stormed into Sandakan. On the assumption that the Chinese community was assisting the Allies, they rampaged through the town, entering a number of houses and bayoneting men, women and children. Meanwhile, Colonel Otsuka, Military Commander of the Sandakan area, issued orders to arrest any civilian who spoke English, using a list supplied by a key collaborator.

Pedro Dominic was living in a hut in the jungle on his Sunny Rubber Estate at Mile 1.5 when the soldiers came for him. Aware that the Japanese had begun to round up prominent citizens earlier that month, he had moved from Andrew Pereira's orchard at Mile 13, thinking that the hut, which belonged to one of his estate's overseers, would provide a safer refuge. It didn't. As he was led away to the cells in the nearby kempeitai barracks near the old wireless station, his last words were for his daughters: 'Be good girls.'

Among those also under arrest were Kwan Yun Hin, a partner of the prestigious local firm Man Woo Long and Company and a member of the State Legislative Council; Mr Patel, the pharmacist at the Sandakan Dispensary who had provided Dr Mills with the massive dose of morphine for the POWs; flaxen-haired Mrs Linck, wife of the German doctor; Kong Su Leong, brother of Lieutenant Kong, both of whom had been in custody for some time, and Chan Chi Tau, a local doctor and family friend. Many members of the China

Mrs Kong, wife of Lieutenant Kong Su En

Relief Fund were on the list, including the Chairman Khoo Kim Cheng (also known as Yau Kam Chung).

The day before the final arrests, Lieutenant Kong's wife and son, Chong Yin, went to the barracks, hoping to deliver some food to Su En and Su Leong. The guards at the gate took the food but refused to allow them in. They were also told not to come again as all prisoners were to be sent to Kuching. Before they left, they spotted Su En inside the barracks' perimeter. Like the other detainees, his head had been shaved.

With the Japanese convinced that the locals had been in contact with the American forces in the Philippines, the Chartered Company's wireless operators Mr Tam and Kong Su Leong were marked men, as were schoolteachers Voon Thau Yin from St Michael's, Chong Wai Cho from the Basel Church School and Stella Teo, who came from Shanghai and taught at the Chinese School. Kong Su Leong was subjected to severe torture, including the severing, one by one, of each of his fingers. The remaining prisoners were from various other walks of life – building contractors, traders, chief clerks and ordinary clerks, merchants and senior civil servants. Apart from Mr Patel and a man described only as 'an Indian doctor', almost all were Chinese.

The one thing they had in common was an abiding hatred for the Japanese, a great loyalty to the British and the fact that they all spoke English. These attributes were more than enough for the Japanese. After appearing in court, over which no judge presided, the 26 men and 2 women were taken back to the military barracks at Mile 1.5, where ten graves had been prepared on the nearby hillside. After being split into three groups, all twenty-eight prisoners were either shot or beheaded. When the families of the victims, having heard no news from the court, went to the barracks, they discovered that the building had been damaged by fire. Sticking to the previous lie, a Japanese soldier told them that everyone had been transferred to Jesselton.

The Japanese did not stop with the slaughter at Mile 1.5. That same day, Dominic's son-in-law, Andrew Pereira, who was just recovering from a bout of malaria, was summoned at bayonet point to attend a 'meeting' on the Sandala Estate at Mile 15. The next morning he and his friends Richard Watson, Dr Taylor's clerk, and Foo Chi Ming, a

Mark Pang Ka Miew

coffee shop proprietor, were joined by two others. The fourth man was Mark Pang Ka Miew, aged thirty-four and father of four children, who lived at Mile 9 and taught English at St Mary's School. A member of the Scouting Movement, he also knew Morse code. The fifth was collaborator Jackie Lo Ah Fuh.

They were all taken to an isolated spot on the northern side of Labuk Road, not far from the Gum Gum River at Mile 17. The first two businessmen met their bloody fate with one swipe of the sword, but the decapitation of the third, Foo Chi Ming, was botched. Mark Pang was to be next. According to Lo Ah Fuh, he was praying out loud when the proceedings were unexpectedly halted. The senior Japanese officer, allegedly annoyed by the ineptitude of the swordsman and the subsequent loss of face, had decided to defer the two final executions until the following day. However, the next morning, both men were released. Why they were allowed to live remains a mystery. Despite Lo's story that the Japanese, moved by his prayers, had reprieved them both as an act of compassion, it seems very odd that the Japanese had earmarked one of their best spies for execution.

Whatever the reason for his narrow escape, Pang certainly had no intention of having anything more to do with the kempeitai. As soon as he was able, he collected some salt, rice and a parang from his home and fled into jungle behind a nearby six-hectare farm belonging to Hiew Ngee Fatt, one of his wife's relatives. When the Japanese realised he had disappeared, they imprisoned Mrs Pang and her youngest son, John, leaving the older children, Ambrose, Vincent and James, to fend for themselves until taken in by other relatives. Although Mrs Pang and the baby were kept in gaol for a month, Mark sensibly remained in hiding until the end of the war, communicating by way of notes left at the edge of the jungle.

Shortly after the execution, a very high-ranking Japanese army officer arrived at the Pereira's Mile 13 house and announced he would be moving in: the family members were to serve him and his troops. At first the unwelcome guests occupied only one or two rooms upstairs, but as more arrived they took over the entire upper floor, forcing the Pereiras to retreat downstairs, then to the coffee drying shed and finally the pigsty. With their food confiscated, they were compelled to live on watery porridge, made from whatever scraps the Japanese had left. The troops occupying the house, now a recognised garrison, left early each morning and returned later at night. They told young Alfred Pereira, aged thirteen, that they had been beheading people – a story he believed as they had not bothered to wipe the blood from their swords. Exactly how many civilians were executed on or around 27 May is not known, but three former members of the Constabulary extracted the following month by SOA for intelligence purposes reported that the total number murdered as a result of the air and sea raid was fifty. They added that every time PT boats were involved in an attack on Sandakan, civilians were seized and executed.

While his fellow members of the kempeitai had been arresting prominent citizens, Sergeant Hosotani Naoji had been busily rounding up five Chinese suspected of collaborating with a guerrilla group said to be operating among the islands in Sandakan Harbour. On 27 May he shot the first two, Sui Chong and Ten Pek, at the barracks at Mile 1.5. He executed the next one a week later and the last two a short time afterwards, in a rubber plantation at Mile 9. It was also reported that Chen Tien On and eleven other Chinese were forced at gunpoint dig a large grave at the Japanese camp at Mile 4 before being beheaded.

It was now far too dangerous for people to congregate anywhere, even in church. All services ceased at St Michael's, where the faithful had been gathering in the home of Reverend Sung Khi Fong, the church itself having been commandeered as a military store at the end of the previous September, when there had been a general clampdown following the Sandakan Incident. In any case, a week later there was nowhere left to hold a service. Apart from the stone church, which had lost its roof, and a small wooden house, all buildings on Elton Hill, including the Catholic Church and convent, were razed to the ground when the Japanese, in a fit of vengeance, rampaged through the town, murdering civilians and torching their homes and property. Fleeing for their lives, Lieutenant Kong's family headed out along the Labuk Road, diving into the bushes at the sound of approaching vehicles.

St Michael's Church minus the roof. The school (foreground) was completely destroyed

After an all-night trek, and a narrow escape from strafing aircraft, they reached the farm of a friend, where they were able to remain until war's end, surviving mainly on tapioca and sweet potatoes.

The only things saved from destruction on Elton Hill were the pews and baptismal font from St Michael's, which had been removed previously for safe-keeping, wrapped in tarpaulins and hidden in the jungle. Fortunately, Reverend Sung, who had smuggled food to internees on Berhala Island when he made pastoral visits to the Leper Colony, was not caught up in the 27 May purge although he had been under constant surveillance and interrogated several times. The kempeitai, after attending his services to ascertain if he had any political leanings, eventually decided he could not speak English and left him alone. Fellow priest Fu Yun Fatt, whose name was on the kempeitai's list, had moved with his family to a relative's farm at

Mile 11 in February 1942. On discovering in March 1945 that the search for him had been stepped up, he moved deep into the jungle, where he remained until the war ended.

On 28 May, in response to an intelligence report that one enemy division was expected to land at Kudat, and another at Sandakan, Colonel Otsuka ordered his garrison to withdraw immediately to Mile 11: a move that would leave the POW camp in front of the defending soldiers and a direct contravention of orders issued on 17 March by Japanese Minister for war, Shibayama Keneshiro, stating that:

> *Prisoners of war must be prevented by all means available from falling into enemy hands. They should either be relocated away from the front or collected at suitable points and times with an eye to enemy air raids, shore bombardments etc. They should be kept alive to the last wherever their labour is needed. In desperate circumstances, where there is no time to move them, they may, as a last resort, be set free.*

Before the threat of invasion arose, plans had actually been in train to take the prisoners to the timber camp near the Kemansi Estate, but on 20 May Takakuwa, who had taken over as commandant from Hoshijima in April, was ordered to move 600 of the fittest to Ranau. With Otsuka now convinced that invasion craft and enemy paratroops would soon appear, he ordered Takakuwa to leave the camp immediately, evacuate all Japanese patients from the hospital and destroy everything that could be of use to the enemy.

Munition dumps were still exploding the next day when Takakuwa arrived at the POW camp and ordered the huts in the old E Force camp to be torched. At about 10.30 am, the prisoners were given thirty minutes to clear the camp and reassemble in the vegetable garden area of Number 2 compound, abandoned when the British moved into the Australian camp a few weeks earlier. The evacuation included the seriously ill, but three died before they reached the main gate. With no time for proper burial, they were placed in a slit trench and hastily covered with earth. The last stretcher case had just cleared the compound when the Australian huts were enveloped by fire. The prisoners as well as their guards were certain that the Allies were on Sandakan's doorstep; the removal of the sick must mean that arrangements were already in train for their immediate evacuation, especially since an American flying-boat had just passed so low overhead that the faces of the crew standing in the doorway were clearly visible.

At 7 pm orders were issued for the 'able-bodied' to line up under The Big Tree, ready to leave on a 'short journey'. The sick would be transported in trucks later. Keen to walk to freedom under their own steam, all those who could get to their feet joined the throng. The ulcer cases were there, hobbling on sticks and crude, home-made crutches, their shinbones exposed from ankle to knee. So were those suffering from advanced beriberi, their limbs puffed up like over-inflated tyres. The dysentery patients and the severely malnourished were the exact opposite, so thin and wasted that their abdomens appeared to be fused to their backbones.

Even with these ill men, the quota fell far short of the 600 ordered. To make sure that no one was malingering, the guards moved about the stretcher cases with their rifle butts and bayonets, prodding as many as possible to their feet. Of the 536 finally assembled, only about 100 could be classified as being anywhere near fit, including a small group whose activities were such that they had been receiving preferential treatment from the Japanese.

Expectations among the prisoners were high, until they reached the 8 Mile police post. When those in the lead turned right, hopes plummeted. They all realised where they were headed – into the interior. In their eagerness to quit Sandakan, the Japanese marched the men all night and well into the next day. On May 31 they covered another four miles, but the prisoners were so exhausted that a 24-hour rest was ordered. Six died that day, bringing the total to eleven. They moved on the next morning, but progress was slow, especially for those carrying Japanese equipment. To step up the pace, the guards bashed and belted anyone who lagged behind. The Australians lost twenty-six men that day, far more than the first four days combined. The muddy areas also took a dreadful toll, so that strong-willed men who might otherwise have been able to go on dropped with exhaustion.

Each day the sound of rifle fire from the rear of the column became more frequent, along with the sight of the scattered skeletal remains of those who had died on the first march. Unless a POW died close to a rest house, there was no hope of burying him. Even then, few prisoners had the energy to scratch out a grave. Most bodies were simply left: alongside the track, propped up against a log, between the roots of giant rain forest trees, in swamps, and on the side of precipitous slopes. Those who dropped out faced death with dignity, giving messages for their loved ones to their friends, along with anything they valued, before shaking hands with them for the last time. However, when their time came they did not submit meekly, shouting curses and insults to their executioners and demanding that they hurry up and finish the job.

With food supplies for retreating Japanese troops a priority, 100 prisoners were siphoned from the column to carry supplies along the lower section of the track to Bauto. By 8 July three large huts at the Kolapis crossing were stacked with rice, sweet potatoes and tinned fish, three storehouses were filled with rice at Muanad River, with another 450 kilograms at Mandoring, and four more storehouses at Bauto. Supplies brought from Jesselton by coolies also filled six store-rooms at Tampias, where there were also 110 forty-four-gallon drums of fuel, a number of boats hidden up a small stream, and an ordinance depot.

These supplies came far too late for those already on the march. At Mile 55, thirty-five prisoners, tied together by their genitals, were massacred on 7 June. One Australian who pretended to be dead, escaped and made his way back down the track, dressed only in his singlet and slouch hat. A few days later he reached a house near Mile 15, where Choi Hee, his brother, sister-in-law and their three children lived. Although terrified of reprisals, the family gave him some Chinese clothing and found a hiding place in the jungle, where the two brothers delivered food at regular intervals. At great personal risk, they continued to care for the Australian, who was so badly beaten he was lame in one leg, carrying him into the jungle just before dawn each day and fetching him each evening. Unfortunately, they could do nothing to combat the effects of tetanus, for which there was no cure. In about mid-July the soldier, who spoke Malay, told the Choi family, 'Don't worry about me. I am going to die. When the Australians land here, tell them all about me and show them where you have buried me.' Before he became completely paralysed, he wrote a testimonial so that his hosts would be rewarded. Shortly afterwards his condition deteriorated rapidly. Choi Hee, terrified that the Japanese might search the house and find the incriminating paperwork, burnt the note, and in so doing, consigned the soldier for whom he had so bravely cared to eternal anonymity.

On 7 July, just beyond the massacre site at Mile 55, American planes strafed the column, sending the prisoners and guards scattering in all directions. Up until now, with one Japanese guard for every five prisoners, escape opportunities had been almost zero. Realising that it was now or never, Australian Owen Campbell and four of his friends took advantage of the confusion by diving into the jungle. The next day, possibly in order to search for them, the Japanese called a 24-hour halt at Mile 60, in a clearing on the far side of the log spanning the Mandoring River. Although there was a handrail of sorts, the log was slick with mud and two of the POWs lost their footing and were swept away. The next morning, several prisoners and Ozawa, the Japanese interpreter, who was walking round in circles, were unable to continue and were left behind. The others had not gone far when they heard the inevitable rifle shots. As they crossed a small gully partially blocked by a fallen tree, the line became strung out. Suddenly finding himself alone on the track, Dick Braithwaite ducked off into the jungle.

In the week following Braithwaite's escape, the prisoners began eating frogs, grasshoppers, snails, lizards, wood grubs and slugs: in fact, anything at all to supplement the daily rice ration of 70 grams. As they entered the area to the west of Bauto, the death toll escalated rapidly. The poor rations and tough terrain did not help, but the Japanese were now nominating which prisoners must remain behind each morning. As they moved through the thick jungle of the Taviu valley towards a staging camp at the foot of Taviu Hill, they were spotted by Zudin, a young Dusun warrior. He and a small band of young men, under the leadership of the Kemansi headman, had formed a group, 'Onsi's blowpipes'. They hunted for Japanese, with small isolated parties or tail-enders the preferred target. SOA would officially credit them with 85 kills between April and August 1945.

Although Zudin was aware that local people carrying supplies for the Japanese had been beaten for passing food to POWs, he traded tapioca with some prisoners for a metal plate. Keeping well hidden, he followed the track to the POWs' overnight stopping place at the foot of Taviu Hill. Alerted by agonised screams, he crept forward to see Japanese soldiers slicing slivers of flesh from the thighs and arms of several POWs spreadeagled against the trunks of large trees.

This was not an isolated case. Aki Lagan, a mandor supervising coolies working as forced labourers, had also seen POWs tortured in this way and their flesh consumed. It appears that instead of immediately dispatching those selected to die, the killing squad had decided to put what was left of their poor, wasted bodies to some use. They did not remove enough flesh to kill their captives, just enough to add some flavour to their rice. They then bound up the wounds, to keep the remaining 'meat' fresh for the next meal: if the prisoners lasted that long. If they did, or didn't, no one would be any the wiser – the prisoners selected were well behind the main pack. The use of humans to provide 'meat on the hoof' for hungry Japanese was not confined to Sabah. There were also instances reported in New Guinea, where local people were captured and kept alive for the same

Aki Lagan (2007)

Zudin (2006), a member of 'Onsi's Blowpipes'

The author interviewing Yumpil, 2009

reason. And it was not only POWs in Sabah who were killed for food. Jikidans working as guards were also targeted, along with local people sent out to hunt for game and who returned empty handed.

There was no boat this time for POWs who survived the climb up Taviu Hill to reach the river crossing at Tampias. This was the dry season, and the boat was reserved exclusively for the use of Japanese officers. All other travellers had to ford the river. The boatman, paid $2 a week in occupation money to ferry officers across the stream, was generally twelve-year-old Yumpil bin Yaron, whose father, a Dusun farmer, grew hill-rice at Kampong Teporoh. Although Yumpil was not allowed to take prisoners of war across the river, he did show them the safest place to cross. Those who did not have the energy were shot, and the bodies left on the bank, where the flesh was often eaten by wild boar. When not on boat duty, Yumpil, with his friends Yasar Kamai, Masian Liwas and Ongulung, were forced to carry supplies and equipment for the Japanese from Tampias to the top of Taviu Hill. From here, another coolie train transferred the goods to a large staging camp at Lolosling where, at its peak, up to 4,000 troops were accommodated in atap huts. Japanese camps were also at Tampias, upstream from the river crossing, and at Paginatan.

Yumpil and his friends saw many bodies scattered along the track. However, while some were POWs, the overwhelming majority were Japanese. At first, the remains were cremated and the ashes sent back to Japan. Later, due to a shortage of wood and an increasing number of bodies, the hands were removed with a parang, and cremated. Not all enemy troops died of illness or exhaustion. Some were killed when American aircraft attacked the camp at Tampias, which was on a rather exposed piece of ground by the river. The planes also strafed the track: an occupational hazard for Yumpil and his friends, who fled into the jungle at the first sound of the engines.

Yumpil's patch, between Miles 125 and 133, had been clearly defined with posts cast in Ranau from low grade cement and installed by a Mr Kuda. These posts, following a tradition long established by the British, had been placed at every mile, and sometimes half-mile. Used by the Japanese to record the place of death of many prisoners, and post-war by Australians teams recovering the skeletal remains, they would become integral decades later in identifying 'unknown soldiers' buried in the Labuan War cemetery, and in determining the route taken by the prisoners of war.

Somewhere in the vicinity of Paginatan, six prisoners escaped. Twelve-year-old Domima Akui, daughter of the village headman, was feeding the family's pigs when she thought someone was throwing small pieces of wood at her from the nearby jungle. As she could not see anyone, she took no notice. The next day, the same thing happened again, but this time she was showered with small pebbles. Looking up, she saw a 'white' hand waving at her from the jungle, near a spot where the prisoners of war had rested on their way to Ranau. Realising from the gestures that whoever it was wanted food and water, she ran inside to tell her father, who told her that the men in hiding were escaped prisoners of war. He instructed her to take them some rice and fish, warning her to take great care she was not seen by the Japanese, whose barracks building was on the far side of the stream. Three times a day for the next six days, at 6 am, noon, and 6 pm, the young girl left food and water on a piece of wood at the same spot. She only saw the prisoners once, but their thin, wasted bodies were a sight she would never forget. Her father offered to hide them in his house, but they refused, saying that if the Japanese found out it would be death for the family, and probably the entire village. On the seventh day, when Domima went to check on the food, it was untouched. However, as a token of their gratitude, they had left behind a small tobacco tin. Inside were six gold wedding rings, their most treasured and valuable possessions. Not long afterwards she heard the sound of gunfire. Who the white men were, she did not know, but she never saw any of them again.

On 24 June the column reached Muruk, where a large Japanese camp extended for some distance along the river. The prisoners were now thirteen kilometres from Ranau and twenty-one from their final destination. Moved by their plight, some of the villagers managed to give them a little rice and tapioca, which they gratefully hid in the pockets of their ragged shirts. The

The site of the last POW camp, near Ranau

number of marchers was now fewer than 200, and the climb up and over Marakau Hill took the lives of several more. When the final 183 stumbled into Number 2 Ranau Jungle Camp on 26 June to join the six survivors of the first march, most were more dead than alive.

The Japanese had provided no shelter, so the prisoners were relegated to a flat area on the side of the hill. Some, who had enough energy, built small shelters from sticks, leaves and remnants of ground sheets. Those who did not lay in the mud for the next three weeks until working parties brought sufficient atap from the old Ranau camp, eight kilometres away, to build a hut on a stretch of flat land beside the river.

On 1 July, an opportunity to take over the camp was lost when a Japanese soldier, who told the Australians he was planning to kill himself and his senior officers, bungled the job. He managed to shoot dead one of the lieutenants, wound Captain Takakuwa, and slightly wound two others but, unfortunately, in his panic he failed to pull the pin on the hand grenade he had tossed into the hut to dispatch the others. Realising his mistake, he shot himself through the head. Had his murder/suicide plot gone according to plan, the prisoners were prepared to attack the remaining guards at the compound, using vegetable knives and parangs evidently taken from the Japanese kitchen, where some of the POWs worked. These, and other useful odds and ends, had been hidden among the roots of a big tree beside the POW hut.

On the night of 7 July, six days after the failed murder/suicide and hoped-for coup, four Australians escaped. An enraged Captain Watanabe, the officer in charge of the camp, confiscated the day's vegetable ration and cancelled all future deliveries. From now on, the POWs would have to exist on 70 grams of rice a day. However, in spite of the reduced food intake, working parties were sent out as usual. A road, mending gang, made up of local coolies and Australian POWs, was working on the bridle track near the 111-mile peg from Tambunan when an air raid started. The guards scuttled into a nearby hole, while five Australians and Janan, a worker from Kampong Matang, dived for cover in the long grass. Now out of sight of the guards, Janan gave the prisoners some cooked rice, while Wally Read took the opportunity to hand him his wallet, which contained a photo of his five children. Wally, who spoke a little Malay said 'Hold these things for me until I collect them. If I don't collect them, you will know that the Japanese have killed me'. As soon as the raid was over, the Australians and the coolies went their separate ways. They did not meet again for, by 15 July, when the rice ration had been further reduced, the prisoners were so weak that heavy chores, such as carrying supplies and road mending, ceased. However, they were still required to continue with the construction of their hut, which was finally completed on 18 July.

By the time the next two prisoners escaped ten days later, there were about forty POWs left alive from the 189 who had lined up for roll call on the night of 26 June. The rest had died from starvation, disease, been beaten to death or perished from exhaustion, hauling water from the river to the Japanese officers' hut, high on the hillside. Dysentery was the major cause of death, due to the Japanese insisting that the POWs draw their water downstream from the Japanese latrine.

On 1 August, the number of prisoners in the camp was thirty-two. Seventeen, who were deemed too ill to last more than a day or so, were carried on stretchers or forced to crawl up the slope to the POW cemetery, where all were shot through the head. The remaining fifteen, possibly because there was now a little more food to go around, managed somehow to cling to life.

They had no idea where they were, only that it was somewhere in the heart of Borneo, a long way from Sandakan, and a very long way from home. At the rate everyone was dying, soon there would be no one left; no one to tell their families that their last days had been spent here, deep in the jungle, in this remote corner of the world. It appears that, following the murder of their sick companions, the others decided to try and leave a message. Not on paper, which was so easily destroyed, but something that would not corrode or rot away; something that would link this last camp to Australia. In what appears to be an inspired decision, they pooled everything they had that was made of brass: the adjustors from their army haversacks and pieces of assorted webbing; clips and buckles from their belts; the pieces riveted to the ends of haversack straps to stop the webbing unravelling; and, most important of all, one solitary, solid brass, tunic button. Emblazoned with a map of Australia and the words 'Australian Military Forces' it would prove beyond all doubt Australian soldiers had been there. Dividing the brass fittings into two separate piles, the prisoners buried them just inside the bamboo fence, close to the river crossing. They stacked the items neatly, placing the precious button on the very top.

The fifteen surviving prisoners were not aware that the camp and its occupants were being monitored by local agents who were reporting back to Gort Chester through Sergeant Stan Neil, who had been with the Python mission and was now working with Agas 1. He had moved along the track to Nalapak, where he saw two Australian bodies lying beside the track. He then crossed Marakau Hill to the edge of the Ranau plain, where he saw another. Agas agent Salunti visited the last camp site twice – once on 11 August and again two days later. Gaining entrance to the compound in the guise of a vegetable seller, he saw several prisoners moving about and another tied to a tree. During the next week Kambating of Kandowai-an, a village to the north-west of the camp, also brought vegetables. As he passed the 113-mile peg, four or five kilometres from the compound, he saw about ten prisoners, dressed in ragged shorts and wearing slouch hats, building a hut.

It must have been a huge relief when the five remaining officers and ten men realised that the war must be finally over. There had been two leaflet drops in the area from Allied aircraft to let the local people and Japanese know that hostilities had ceased. There is no doubt that the camp guards, who had copies of the leaflets, knew this, and that they must lay down their arms. On 27 August, twelve days after the war ended, and in what must have appeared to the prisoners to be in keeping with such an edict, they were given two sets of instructions: the officers were to walk to Ranau to hold discussions with the kempeitai, while the men, who were still working on the hut at Mile 113, were to collect vegetables from a village to the south.

The ten prisoners working at mile 113 were handed sacks and marched down the track with an escort of ten armed guards. Near mile 112, they were seen by a Ranau villager, Jaimi bin Gunsand (also known as Edmuno), who noticed that all were thin and dressed in rags. When the prisoners were about 500 metres south of the track branching off to the camp, the guard commander, Sergeant-Major Tsuji called a halt. He informed the prisoners that they were to be killed. According to the guards, they were then given food, water and cigarettes, which they smoked while Tsuji issued his instructions. The prisoners were then taken by a guard, one by one, about 200 metres down a path on the eastern side of the main track where, shielded from view by a small, jungle-clad hill, all were shot through the head.

At about 12.30 pm, the five officers set off in the opposite direction for Ranau. It was a hot day. In what seemed to be an act of uncharacteristic benevolence, the Japanese invited them to rest for a while in the shade, on a shortcut near the 111-mile peg. After discreetly placing lookouts at either end of the short, secondary path to make sure no one was coming, the guards shot every one of them dead. Two of the victims were Australian doctors. They had not escaped, although they had the chance, as they had refused to leave their men.

Gort Chester's agents were aware almost immediately that something was amiss. Jaimi bin Ginsund, chief clerk to the Japanese garrison commander at Ranau, had seen the prisoners on the track and knew that they had not arrived at their destination. Aware that some of the POWs were to be moved south from the compound on 27 August, another agent had hidden by the track to see if it would be possible to try and rescue them. He had waited all day. When no one appeared, he retraced his steps towards Ranau where, at mile 111, he found two fresh graves at the place where the officers had been murdered. Yet another agent, searching for clues to account for the prisoners' sudden disappearance, found a pile of hats and caps near the track at Mile 110, and what appeared to be a large grave. Shortly afterwards, Kabiaru, on his way home after delivering vegetables, came across the same pile of headwear, a length of rope and a vast amount of congealed blood. A few days later, while taking the short cut near Mile 111, he also stumbled across the officers' graves. Meanwhile, villagers reported that the camp was definitely empty. As Australian investigating officers would soon discover, apart from the escapees, there was now no one left alive, at all. The 288 prisoners left behind at Sandakan when the second march departed had also perished.

* * * * *

A few days after the departure of the second march on 29 May, the Japanese had constructed a barbed wire fence to confine the remaining prisoners to a small area in the corner of the old British compound. Unable to access the huts still standing on the far side of the small stream, their only shelter was a small grove of old rubber trees but, as they still expected to be rescued, it was of no importance. On 31 May, PT Boat 149 shelled Sandakan. Once again members of the crew came ashore, but there was no large-scale attack. As the days wore on with no sign of battalions of bronzed Australian troops, the prisoners organised a camp of sorts, protecting various records by placing them under logs and in ground sheets, and building small individual shelters from sticks, banana leaves and various odds and ends. The handful of guards who were left occasionally tossed a few vegetables over the wire to supplement the rice ration and, somewhat surprisingly, made a few Red Cross parcels available, which the prisoners used to set up a small 'aid post' among some banana trees.

With no sign of any invasion, in mid-June the guards were instructed to send about seventy of the 'fitter' prisoners to Ranau. None survived beyond Mile 42. Three who reached Mile 15.5 were murdered by the kempeitai's Sergeant Hosotani. After killing the last of the five Chinese suspected of working with the guerrillas, he had gone to his billet at Mile 15.5. He was still there recuperating from an attack of malaria when the third march passed by. Seven of the prisoners, who were crippled and unable to walk without the aid of a stick, could not continue. Beating the men with their own walking sticks, Corporal Katayama and another guard succeeded in moving them another twenty metres or so down the road, where they forced them off the track and shot them.

Hearing the sound of rifle fire coming from somewhere behind his house, market gardener Chin Kin, his brother and a neighbour went out to investigate. They found six of the men shot in the back – four dead and the other two seriously wounded. The seventh had escaped into the jungle. While the three Chinese were burying the dead, the Japanese cornered the escapee and shot him twice in the stomach. They then returned and shot the two wounded men in the head. Before Katayama moved off with his fellow guard to join the rest of the party, he asked Hosotani to dispose of any stragglers. Shortly afterwards two prisoners wearing battered slouch hats stopped to rest on the side of the track near Chin's house. Borrowing a gun from a Malay police boy who was billeted with him, Hosotani shot them both in the head. At about the same time another member of the kempeitai shot a prisoner dead at Mile 17. By the time the column reached Mile 42, there was not a single prisoner left alive.

Instructions had been issued to the handful of guards still at the Mile 8 Camp to move to Ranau as soon as the remaining prisoners had died. However, contrary to expectations, they were not dying fast enough. On 13 July, twenty-three who looked as if they had no intention of expiring in the immediately foreseeable future were marched off to the airstrip, where they were lined up either side of one of the anti-aircraft ditches, and shot. The camp's senior officer, who had stolen a pig from the Japanese sty and cooked it for his starving men, was also dead. As punishment, he had been nailed to a cross and his body cannibalised. The rest of the prisoners, who died in twos and threes, were buried by Javanese coolies in slit trenches near the British huts, arranged head to tail, like sardines in a tin.

On 1 August there were nine Australians and one British prisoner still alive. When Ali Asar was sent to deliver some kangkong four days later, another four had died, as no food had been sent in for the past week. Wong Hiong, a fifteen-year-old Chinese youth employed as a kitchen-hand in the Japanese barracks, had been sneaking food to them but his activities had come to an abrupt halt when he was seen exchanging salt with one of the POWs for a pair of shorts. He was beaten and warned that, if he did it again, Sergeant-Major Murozumi would cut off his head. The six surviving Australians asked Ali Asar to bring more food but, as he was a known collaborator, it is unlikely he would have done so. In any case, the penalty was now death. On discovering that Wong Hiong and local people had been pushing food under the wire, Murozumi had announced that any Malay or Chinese worker who went anywhere near the POW compound without authorisation would be shot.

Ten days later, when dawn broke over Sandakan on 15 August, Private John Skinner was the only prisoner left alive. He was lying beneath his crude shelter when, shortly before 7 am, Murozumi led a contingent of guards into the compound. Wong Hiong secretly followed them, in spite of explicit instructions to remain in the barracks. Climbing a nearby rubber tree, he watched as the guards strode to the shelter and dragged Skinner to his feet. Lashing out with fists and boots they forced him outside the wire and up the slope to the slit trenches near the British huts. While the others forced Skinner to his knees and tied a piece of black cloth around his eyes Murozumi positioned himself to the left of the trench. Gripping his sword in both hands, he brought the weapon down with one tremendous swipe to decapitate Sandakan's last prisoner of war. Five hours later, on domestic radio, the high-pitched voice of Emperor Hirohito announced Japan's unconditional surrender.

Chapter 12

Against all odds

Dick Braithwaite

Although a staggering 2,428 Australian and British prisoners of war had perished at Sandakan, Ranau or on the death marches, six Australians who had escaped were still alive. All owed their lives to Kadazandusun headmen and villagers who, apart from selflessly risking their lives, had ensured that every attempt made by the Japanese to obliterate all traces of their monstrous crimes would be in vain.

When Dick Braithwaite escaped from the second march after crossing the Mandoring River, he had no idea where he was. He did know, however, that if he followed the river downstream he would either hit the coast or a larger waterway. Whatever the outcome, he hoped it would not be long before he was safely in Allied hands. Unaware that the thirty-five POWs had been massacred at Mile 55, he assumed that the chatter of distant automatic fire heard a couple of days before he escaped, had come from American PT boats taking part in the much-awaited invasion.

After the remainder of the column passed his hiding place, Braithwaite was retracing his steps to the river when a lone Japanese appeared on the track. He was not armed. Before the soldier knew what had happened Braithwaite grabbed a heavy stick and felled him with one blow. The sight of one of the hated enemy, who had caused such unmitigated suffering and terror, on the ground and helpless, unleashed in the Australian an uncontrollable fury. Braithwaite, normally a quiet, gentle man, went berserk, venting his anger for the death of all his friends until the Japanese was well and truly dead. After dragging the body into a gully, he continued along the track to the river.

He made his way along the western bank without too much trouble, but the next day the going was far more difficult. The way was often blocked, forcing him to cross and recross the river so often that he gave up following it. However, he discovered that being away from the waterway was far worse. Paths that appeared man-made often led to dead-ends and, when he did find a proper track, he almost ran into a Japanese patrol. For the next three days he plodded on, losing all sense of direction, living on whatever he could forage and often finding himself in snake-infested swamps or impenetrable thickets. Finally, exhausted and weak with hunger, with his feet raw and bleeding from the bites of a swarm of army ants, he came to a river. It was the Pandan Pandan, which crossed the track at about Mile 58. As the thick jungle made it impossible to follow the bank, Braithwaite was contemplating using a makeshift raft when he spotted an elderly fisherman in a kolek and called softly to him in Malay. After a few anxious moments the old man paddled over, motioned for him to hop in, and made off downstream. Before long they came to a wide bend and a village built out over the river, about five kilometres upstream from the junction with the Labuk: Kampong Sapi, currently the home of Bede Willie, Gort's secret agent. He was also a friend of Braithwaite's rescuer, village headman Abing bin Luma, who had been on his way to examine his fish traps when the Australian hailed him.

Braithwaite was now so weak that he was unable to climb the ladder to Abing's house. As there was a large Japanese camp on the nearby Labuk, Abing's son-in-law, Amit, who was bathing one of his children in the river, wasted no time in helping Abing's son, Aliudin, get the exhausted fugitive indoors and out of sight. After giving him a little food, Amit hid Braithwaite behind a false wall, where the family kept their precious rice supply. When the village elders arrived shortly afterwards, bearing gifts, sweets and other delicacies, they were accompanied by Abdul Raschid, a Filipino who spoke fluent English. Raschid, whose real name was Loreto Padua, had worked for one of the large timber companies and was keen to become involved: the Japanese had murdered his wife and child, and he was wanted by the kempeitai for his high profile, pro-guerrilla activities. Being well acquainted with Willie, whose sons Francis, James and Thomas, and son-in-law Winfield Sherman, were all working for SOA, Raschid knew that Gort Chester, described as 'the man who came back to Borneo' was now operating in the north of Sabah.

The villagers also knew that they were taking an enormous risk. Amat and Panjam, who were Agas agents and came from Sapi, knew exactly what the Japanese were capable of doing. They had reported an atrocity they had witnessed at Kolapis, when villagers, called onto the jetty by the Japanese, had been shot, and babies thrown into the air, caught on bayonets and tossed into the water. The agents also reported to SOA that pregnant women were shot outright.

Raschid explained to Braithwaite that the people of Sapi were extremely keen to contact Allied forces, not simply to help him escape but because they wanted him to ask the Americans to stop strafing their village from the air. Before Braithwaite knew it, he was off. Abing and Amit supplied the boat, an escort (Abing, Raschid and Sapan), and a crew of five – Omar, Sagan, Buang, Salim and Mangulong. Braithwaite had no money to pay Amit, who was remaining behind to care for his sick wife, so he gave him two fountain pens as a token of his appreciation. They left Sapi at about 10 pm with a decoy boat, which went ahead with a crew of two in case of trouble. From time to time, in order to avoid other river traffic, the two boats pulled into the shadows and drifted along by the shore, but neither attracted any interest from other craft or from the Japanese in the camp. It was so peaceful that Braithwaite, hidden beneath a blanket of banana leaves, fell asleep. The next morning when he awoke they were out at sea, on their way to Pulau Libaran, the island guarding the southern entrance of Labuk Bay. A local guerrilla HQ, it was a collection point for arms and ammunition to supply Agas's guerrilla army and was serving as a temporary safe haven for Sandshoe Willie and Sherman.

Willie, who had narrowly escaped being beheaded at Beluran on 27 May when an air raid interrupted proceedings, was high on the kempeitai's list of 'most wanted'. As his involvement with the Australians had become well known to the Japanese, they had begun an intensive search for him, and for Gort Chester. Gort's photograph, evidently obtained from files held at the Sandakan Passport Office, had been circulated by the kempeitai, who had a price of $5000 on his head. However, neither man was betrayed. When the Japanese reached Kolapis in search of Willie, Samuel Dumpangol Ambrose sent them to Sapi on a wild-goose chase. A SOA agent and guerrilla fighter, Ambrose knew that by this time Willie had been rescued by Kulang from Bukit Uting, in the jungle to the west of Sapi, and was safely on Libaran Island with Winfield Sherman and Thomas Willie, an Agas guerrilla section leader. In July, all three men would move on to Tawi Tawi to help Gort establish a food depot to drop supplies to the Australian troops fighting at Labuan and Papar.

Any boats moving into Labuk Bay from the south-east had to pass by Libaran, and it was not long before Braithwaite's rescuers spotted US PT boat 112 on its way to shoot up Japanese camps along the

Labuk River. On seeing the native craft approaching with a white flag, the PT boat stopped. As Braithwaite looked up, a huge American looked over the side and exclaimed, 'It's an Aussie.' Deciding that Libaran was a safe enough refuge for the time being, the Americans left Braithwaite with some food, promising to collect him on the way back. Knowing that Abdul Raschid was itching to see some action, the Australian recommended him to the PT's commander, Lieutenant James of USS *Oyster Bay*, who took him along. When the boat returned, Braithwaite asked James if the crew could spare some cigarettes for the men who had saved his life. The Australian meant a packet or two. The American, to the joy of the villagers, handed over six cartons. The next day, June 15 and his twenty-eighth birthday, Braithwaite was safe in Tawi Tawi, pouring out his incredible tale.

Meanwhile, life for the villagers along the Labuk was becoming even more precarious. By mid-June, with the repeated air and land strikes, Japanese tempers began to fray. On 23 June, two PT boats shelled Beluran, where an estimated fifty enemy troops were dug into the south side of the hill. At midnight, six Japanese soldiers arrived at Kolapis village and banged on the doors of three Chinese shopkeepers. Whoever opened the door was shot dead – two women, a child and a man. By the time the killers returned to Beluran, many of the locals had fled – to the safety of Gort's SOA base on Jambongan.

It was not only villagers who were relocating. By the end of June, nervous Japanese senior officers in Sandakan had moved their headquarters to trenches dug into the side of Elton Hill, protected by three three-inch guns. Nearby was a stockpile of a new 'secret' weapon – 30 one-man, suicide torpedo boats. About 300 marines also relocated to Sandala Estate, where they took over seven large plantation houses, while another 200 troops took up residence in Chinese homes between Miles 16 and 18.

Owen Campbell, who had escaped two days before Braithwaite, was still a long way from Allied lines. When the three planes had fired at the column (their pilots assuming that anyone now using the track must be Japanese), the five men had stopped only long enough to ransack the packs abandoned by the Japanese as they took cover. Loaded up with five or six kilograms of rice, a dozen tins of meat and vegetables, six tins of salmon, and some protein-rich, dried soya-bean powder, the prisoners plunged into the jungle. Believing that the Japanese, on the assumption that the escapees would make for the coast, would concentrate their search on the northern side of the track, they headed south for a kilometre or two, before stopping for the night.

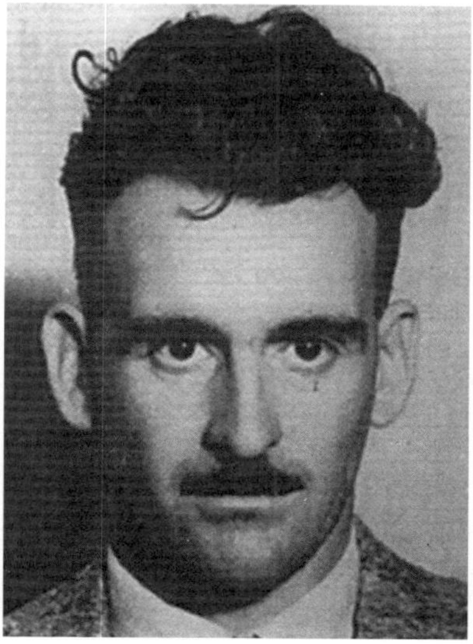

Owen Campbell

The next day, confident that when the column moved on the guards would give up the search, they turned north, using a compass which one of the party had somehow managed to keep hidden throughout his captivity. Forced to stop for a day when Campbell came down with malaria, they continued towards the coast, only to have Ted Skinner, brother of John, fall ill with dysentery. It became obvious after three or four days that he was too sick to go any further, so Campbell, who was suffering with beriberi, volunteered to remain behind. The others kept going in a north-easterly direction, marking their trail as they went. Ignoring Skinner's pleas to leave him and go after the others, Campbell stayed by his side for four days, until hunger forced him to go to a nearby creek in search of food. When he returned, Skinner was dead. He had cut his own throat with a lid from one of the empty salmon tins.

Sustained only by freshwater crabs and an unidentified animal, which he caught and ate raw, Campbell caught up with the others at what appears to have been the Saraun River, a tributary of the Labuk. They had been forced to stop as another member of the party, Keith Costin, was very ill with dysentery and malaria. All four now agreed that their only hope was to appeal for help from local people. Late that afternoon, when they heard the sound of a boat, Ted Emmett and Sid Webber ran to the bank. Two fishermen paddled over but, as they drew nearer, a Japanese soldier, hidden from view at the bottom of the boat, opened fire. The Australians, shot in the head and chest, fell into the river and disappeared.

Campbell, who was some distance behind the others, had not been seen. Living on soya-bean powder, he remained with Costin, who died three days later. Moving on, Campbell had a narrow escape when a Japanese sentry shot at him as he crossed the river clinging to a log. However, it was only a flesh wound. He pushed on for another nine days, often in a state of delirium, eating whatever he could find: fungus, raw fish, crabs. On about 5 July, after covering only possibly eight or ten kilometres as the crow flies, he followed a wild boar track to a tidal river – Sungei Muanad. Campbell hid among the mangroves, hoping to raid a fish trap, when he saw a man in a fishing kolek. In response to his call ('Abang', or elder brother), the man, whose name was Galunting, paddled over. Instructing Campbell to stay where he was, Galunting disappeared down river, returning forty-five minutes later with another villager, Laip. As Galunting helped Campbell down from the bank, he told the fugitive to dunk himself in the river so that, if stopped by a patrol from a Japanese camp, only 300 metres away, they could claim they had fished him out of the water.

Campbell's saviours were from Kampong Muanad, home of Kulang – Dusun chief, friend of Bede Willie, principal surveyor of the Sandakan-Ranau track and SOA secret agent. He was also one of the fiercest enemies of the Japanese, with 96 kills to his credit, either shot with poison darts delivered with deadly accuracy from his blowpipe, bullets from his equally deadly rifle, or beheaded with his jungle parang. Most of the Japanese had been killed on the Sandakan-Beluran track, where the headman waited in ambush. Although Kulang was away, cutting a track for an Agas party on the Bongaya River, his brother Laip and loyal villagers soon had Campbell across the river and into the safety of a house. As soon as it was dark, Saliam, Kulang's deputy, arranged for Galunting and Laip to take their visitor deeper into the jungle to a new kampong which the villagers had built to avoid harassment by the Japanese. Here, in Saliam's house, Campbell was given a bath, clean clothes and fed broth for the first two days until his stomach was able to cope with more solid food, cooked by Saliam's wife, Ambiau. A Japanese agent visited the village twice during this five-day period, but Ambiau hid him in a back room of the house. By the time Kulang arrived from Bongaya on 16 July to check on the village, Campbell had progressed to eating rice and was beginning to regain his strength. At first, he was very wary of Kulang, but relaxed when the headman produced a letter, stating that he was in the employ of SOA.

After further tender ministrations over the next few days from Kulang, who cut Campbell's hair and shaved him with a cut-throat razor, the headman decided it was time to move. Accompanied by a number of villagers, he led Campbell in easy stages to the Kolapis River, roughly five kilometres away, where about fifty people boarded four large perahus. The first three boats were decoys. The fourth held Campbell, lying on the bottom and clutching an Owen gun, part of the weaponry Kulang and five of his followers had brought back from Bongaya. Kulang was toting an Austen sub-machine gun, while four others were armed with .303 rifles. Some hard paddling brought them to the mouth of the Bongaya and, seven hours later on 20 July, Campbell was handed over to Lieutenant Jock Hollingworth, one of Gort Chester's men. Four days later, after being picked up by a Mariner flying boat near Kandawan Island, Campbell was tucked up in a hospital bed on board US *Pokomoke*. On 28 July he was debriefed by SOA's Dick Noone. Nothing Campbell had to say gave Noone much hope for the fate of those who had continued on the march to Ranau. Campbell's information, already relayed to SOA by Braithwaite over five weeks before, simply confirmed that the entire rescue mission was an unmitigated disaster, something which had come as a huge shock to SOA.

It was not until Braithwaite had been debriefed that SOA realised the intelligence sent by Agas had been incorrect. The Sandakan camp had not been evacuated: more than 500 prisoners had only just been marched into the interior, and almost 300 had been left behind. In order to salvage what they could from the calamity, SOA ordered Flight-Lieutenant Ripley to take a sub-party, known as Agas 3, to Ranau, via the Sugut River-Meridi route. His task was to ascertain if a rescue were feasible and, if so, to possibly carry it out. Meanwhile, Rex Blow, who had been evacuated from the Philippines and posted to SOA, was ordered to infiltrate the camp at Sandakan and check on the situation there.

Neither of these missions would result in a single prisoner at either the Ranau or Sandakan camp being saved. On 21 June, when Ripley arrived at an Agas base at Lokopas, on Sabah's north-east coast, he discovered that all the signallers, including the one assigned to him, were no longer there. They were at Pitas, on Marudu Bay, with Agas 2, under the command of Major R G 'Nick' Combe, a former District Officer and Magistrate at Kudat. A signaller was integral to the mission, so Ripley had no alternative but to chase after them. It was not an easy journey. As a local boat could take him only as far as Melobong, he had to walk the rest of the way. When he eventually arrived at Pitas, he discovered that none of the signallers was available. By the time a replacement, Amos Hywood, arrived from Morotai it was 8 July. With Pitas so far away from the Sugut, Ripley decided to change the operational plan. Instead of proceeding along the well-established original route, he would approach Ranau from the north, via the Bengkoka River, and then strike out across the Crocker Range to Meridi.

Nick Combe, who had lived in the area for years, knew that the vast region beyond Bombong Bombong was uncharted territory. Why he allowed Agas 3 to use this untested route is a mystery. Ripley and Hywood could have been picked up easily by flying boat and flown to the Sugut, where a journey of ten days would have brought them directly to Ranau. However, as time was of the essence, a far better option would have been to parachute directly into the Ranau area by one of the B24 aircraft that SOA's new air wing had at its disposal. By this time airdrops were well established: Combe and his team had parachuted into Lokopas on 5 May and supplies to various SOA teams were delivered this way, in special tubular-metal canisters called 'storpedoes'. The next morning, Ripley and Hywood, accompanied by Police Constables Sampura, Ampun and Jalil, left Pitas for Ranau, unaware that between them and the dying POWs lay some of the most difficult terrain on earth.

Discovering that they had gone, Pitas headman Andong Ajak, a wiry old fellow of indeterminate age, went after them. After travelling down the Bengkoka River, they struck out for Melinsau, which they reached on 16 July after a most arduous journey. The party was now in urgent need of food but as no suitable drop zone could be located, they went on to Kiayap, arriving on 22 July. Three days later, when ten storpedoes were dropped, all missed the target, forcing the team to waste three days looking for them. Even worse, instead of sending the six tins of 'compo' rations that Ripley had ordered, SOA had sent a massive 1.5 tonnes of stores. In a master understatement, Ripley later reported that this enormous over-catering 'was a source of trouble from beginning to end'.

Meanwhile, Blow, who had spent many months chasing and killing Japanese in the Philippines, had arrived in Morotai. He was anxious to get back into action but was assigned instead to a reconnaissance mission, with orders to infiltrate the Sandakan area and see if there were still POWs at the Mile 8 Camp. Towards the end of June, Blow flew from Morotai to Zamboanga in the Philippines where he and several others boarded a PT boat. The next stop was Pulau Nunuyan Laut, the small strategic island five kilometres from the mouth of the Sibuga River: the river that led directly to the POW Camp; the river that was to have been used to evacuate the POWs, had the rescue

Rex Blow

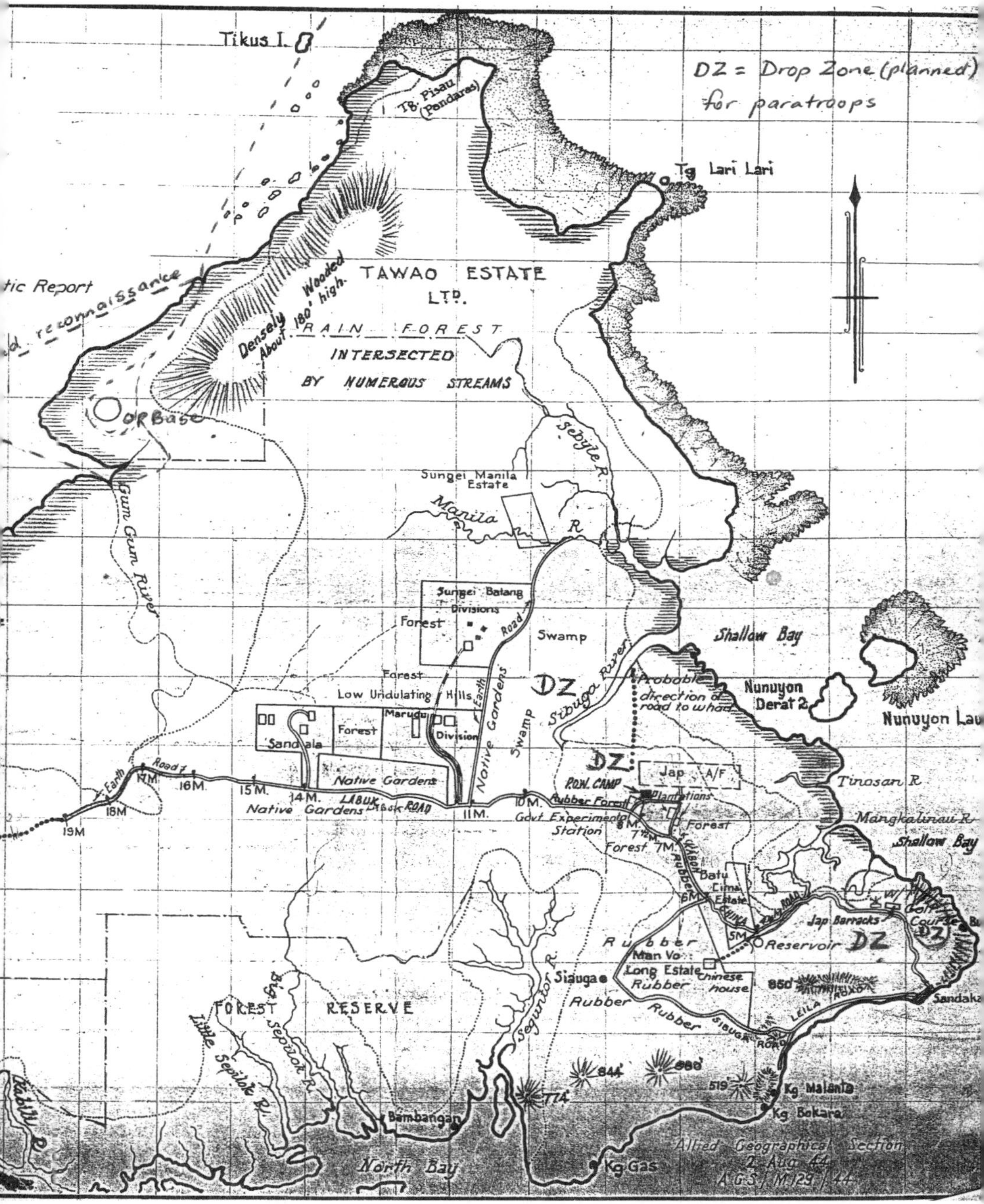

Map showing planned drop zones for the aborted rescue mission, and Pulau Nunuyan Laut

mission not been abandoned; the river so clearly marked on the map prepared for the paratroopers, even to the extent of showing the line of the track leading from the Sibuga jetty to the camp.

Yet, despite this wealth of information and intelligence gathered by SOA, which had then been transferred so carefully and with such detail onto large-scale maps, no move was made to conduct the reconnaissance from Nunuyan Laut Island or from Nunuyan Derat 2, which was even closer to the coast. Instead, after feasting on turtle eggs, the reconnaissance party went to Libaran Island where Sandshoe Willie arranged for Blow and an Australian corporal to be transferred by perahu to the mouth of the Labuk. From here they went by native canoe up a river: not the Gum Gum, Kingfisher's original insertion point that cut the track at Mile 17, but the Samawang which, as the Dusun, crossed the POW route at Mile 33 – a further twenty-six kilometres inland.

There is no explanation why this route was taken, or whose decision it was. In the absence of any further information it is not unreasonable to assume that whoever decided on this ludicrous insertion point not only had a scant knowledge of Sandakan and its environs but also did not bother to consult a map. Perhaps it was Blow, who had never set foot on the mainland, or perhaps it was the same SOA officer who, in March that year, had broken strict radio silence to ask Gort Chester, surrounded by mangroves and thick jungle, many miles from civilisation and with a labour force of just seven men, if he could build an aerodrome suitable for dive bombers.

After paddling as far as possible up the Samawang, Blow and the corporal proceeded south on foot until they found the track. From the number of footprints, it appeared to have been subjected to heavy traffic only recently: an assumption confirmed by a coolie labourer employed to carry supplies between Mile 17 and Mile 42. He told Blow that he had seen prisoners moving in the direction of Ranau, and had heard that the POW camp had been burnt to the ground. Following the track a short distance to the west, Blow came across several corpses. However, despite the fact that the previous intelligence about the Sandakan prisoners was now known beyond all doubt to be faulty, he did not turn east to check the camp and the accuracy of the information for himself, although it was just a relatively short journey, and the sole purpose of his mission. Assuming the information to be correct, Blow returned to Libaran Island, and his next assignment. As he paddled down the Semawang River, the last chance to save the lives of almost 100 POWs, still alive at the Mile 8 Camp, was irretrievably lost.

In mid-July, while Blow was in the southern part of Sabah, organising the successful evacuation to Tawi Tawi of a Eurasian woman and her three children from Mas, near Lahad Datu, the four Australians who had escaped from the last camp on 7 July were in the jungle, fending for themselves.

On 6 July, four days after the Japanese guard's murder/suicide, the six survivors from the first march, who were being held in a separate compound across the river, were ordered to join a cane-cutting detail. They had only gone about ten metres when Arthur Bird, who was suffering from malaria and beriberi as well as a large leg ulcer, collapsed. Refusing to accept explanations from fellow prisoners Keith Botterill and Bill Moxham that Bird was ill, one of the guards beat and kicked him savagely; so savagely that he sustained fatal injuries and lapsed into a coma. The next morning, Moxham, Botterill and the three other first-march survivors were ordered to join the other prisoners on the eastern side of the river.

There were now only about 100 men left alive in a camp that Botterill believed would soon be inhabited only by the dead. His opinion was shared by Moxham, who had been told by a Christian guard that orders to this effect had been issued. The brutal attack on Arthur Bird helped make up their minds. They would escape that night. Believing that, if they ran into trouble, four men would be better than two, they canvassed some of the others, none of whom they knew well. Some, who had heard what had happened to Crease and Cleary after their escape attempt, were too scared. Others were too ill. However, Nelson Short and Frank 'Andy' Anderson were willing to give it a go. As the would-be escapees did not trust the senior Australian officer, who had a close relationship with the Japanese, they confided only in Captains Oakeshott and Picone, the two Australian doctors. Neither officer would leave his patients, but they did wish the three men well and gave them a large wad of occupation money in the hope that they might be able to bribe people to help them.

They left at nine that night. The rain, which was coming down in torrents, was a mixed blessing. In hindered their progress, but it had also driven all but one of the Japanese guards into a lean-to shelter. Fortunately, the sentry still braving the elements was sitting on a log, and looking the other way. After breaking into a Japanese rice store about five kilometres along the track, the three men, loaded up with about four or five kilograms of rice each, sneaked past Ranau. Once clear of the village, they followed a path that wound around the slopes of Mt Kinabalu to Jesselton, over 100 kilometres to the west. Realising that they must put as much distance as possible between

Barigah Katus

themselves and the camp, they kept going all night. As dawn broke, they made their way down the hillside to a small valley and sought refuge in a cave, which they camouflaged with leafy branches. They remained there for the next six days, cooking over a shaved-bamboo fire, which they lit by concentrating the sun's rays through a single spectacle lens. There were no freshwater shrimps in the nearby creek, but there were plenty of green bananas, which they chopped and cooked with their rice. However, on the night of 14 July, realising that they were becoming progressively weaker, and with their food stocks running low, they climbed back up the hill to the track and sent off once more in the direction of Jesselton.

The next day, after a cold and miserable night, they found shelter in an abandoned hut. Some tapioca and sweet potatoes, dug up from the remnants of a nearby vegetable patch, provided a welcome meal. However, while Short was keeping guard and the others rested, a lone Japanese came by and asked for a light from their fire for his cigarette. Certain they would be reported, the four men moved further down the mountainside, where they found another hut. They had just made Andy Anderson, who was ill with dysentery, comfortable when the owner of the land, Barigah (Beriga, Baregah) Katus, passed by on his way to market, carrying a large bunch of bananas. The fifty-year-old Kadazandusun farmer, and a headman of Batu Lima village, was extremely anti-Japanese. Assuring the Australians that he was 'kawan' (friend), he gave them 40 large bananas, told them not to move as there were many enemy troops about, and promised to return with more food.

He had been gone only a short time when another Japanese soldier suddenly appeared. After poking his head through the door to ask if they had a watch, he asked if they were the prisoners of war who had escaped. Feigning surprise, the Australians claimed it couldn't be them: they were only resting in the hut while the guard in charge of their working party went to fetch some medicine for one of their group, who had suddenly become ill. Andy certainly looked sick, but the men did not have the chance to discover if the soldier believed them. Hearing the sound of approaching aircraft, he scurried off to seek shelter. As soon as he had gone, the others picked up Anderson by his arms and legs and headed into the jungle.

Barigah found them at noon the following day – he had smelled the smoke from their fire as they boiled up the last of their rice. Dousing the flames, he told them that the alarm had been raised. The kempeitai, who were offering bags of rice and salt, plus $1000 in occupation money, for every prisoner turned over to them, were not far off. Instructing the Australians to remain hidden, Barigah gave them a parcel containing his own mid-day meal, reassuring them he would be back. When he returned a few hours later he took them further into the jungle, where he built a small sulap beside a creek. However, a week later, worried that the stream of visitors from the village would alert the Japanese, he moved them to a new site, 200 metres west of the 5-mile peg on the Ranau–Tuaran track. On a steep mountainside, 200 metres below, he and his brother Orang Tua Gunting, the village elder, built a more substantial hut in a small clearing on a steam known as Sungei Kihunot, an upper tributary of the Kinumut.

It was here that Barigah's cousin, seventeen-year-old Suamin bin Gadalip, also known as Kaingal, heard their voices while looking for a spot to fish. As both of his parents had died, Kaingal, a Kadazandusun farmer, lived with his maternal uncle, Guak, in nearby Kampong Kaparingan. 'I saw four orang puteh in a clearing in the jungle', he said. 'As I neared them they called out "Tolong! Tolong! (Help! Help!). At first, I wasn't sure what sort of help they needed. It could mean they were in trouble or danger and wanted to be saved. In fact, I was very scared, thinking that the Japanese might be after the men. We talked for a while. I had difficulty in understanding their language. We were like a chicken and a duck. I then realised they were asking me for food and drink. They used sign language, pointing to their mouth and stomach.'

After returning home to report the incident to his uncle, Kaingal returned with food and water. Despite the obvious danger, Guak and his family, as well as Barigah's villagers, continued to supply whatever rice, tapioca, eggs and meat they could spare. However, there was nothing anyone could do to save Andy Anderson. Stricken with dysentery, he died on 29 July, a few days after moving to the new hiding place. His friends, lacking the energy to dig a grave, took him to a spot on the far side of the creek, where they covered his body with dirt and stones. The next day they helped Barigah bury him properly, as scavenging animals had found the site.

A couple of weeks later, when Barigah reported that fewer than twenty of the POWs at the last camp were still alive, the three men took little interest. The close confines of the hut, coupled with the stress of not knowing what the next hour, let alone the next day, would bring, had taken its toll. The co-operation and mutual goodwill that had been so necessary to their escape had vanished, replaced by wariness and distrust. It was now a case of every man for himself. Each watched every move the others made, lest someone take more than his fair share of the food. They were beginning to hate the sight of each other when Kaingal rushed into the hut on 15 August with the news that his friend's cousin had seen white soldiers at a camp in the jungle at Lansat, north-east of Ranau. After four long and gruelling weeks, Flight-Lieutenant Ripley and his Agas 3 team had finally made it!

After receiving their 1.5 tonnes of mostly unnecessary stores, Ripley had learned from locals that Japanese based at Meridi and Merungin, who were raiding nearby communities for food, could create problems. In an effort to counteract this, Ripley made repeated requests to SOA, while at Kiayap, for both villages to be bombed. Meridi was never attacked but, on 2 August, American Kittyhawks made a strike near Merungin. Neither the village nor its Japanese occupants were harmed – the sole casualties were a cow and pig belonging to the pro-British headman, Dampulok. Slowed by the necessity to by-pass Merungin, which was still full of Japanese, the mountainous terrain and the difficulty of finding porters to carry the mountain of supplies, it was not for another five days that the party reached Lansat, north-east of Ranau.

News of their arrival travelled fast. The following day, 8 August, they had a visitor – Zimban bin Dittuan, a member of the Constabulary, who had come from Kampong Samaang, where two POWs were living in the jungle, a few kilometres south-west of Ranau. He had brought a note from one of them, dated 5 August and addressed to the Commander-in-Chief, Allied Forces, Jesselton. It was from William Sticpewich, one of two men who had escaped from the last camp on 28 July.

When Sticpewich escaped, more than three weeks after Botterill and the others left, there were only 42 prisoners still alive. He had decided to leave when a guard had bragged that he had seen an order from the Japanese High Command to eliminate all POWs. Sticpewich believed him. The same guard had tried to obtain a hypodermic syringe a few days before to inject ill prisoners with petrol. That evening the camp guard, already strengthened after the previous escape, was doubled. At 9 o'clock the next night, 27 July, Sticpewich was pulled aside by a Christian Japanese soldier who whispered, 'you go now. Go jungle. You stay here you will be mati (dead). I see papers. Papers say all men soon be mati mati here.'

The next day Sticpewich approached a member of his technical party, Herman Reither, who, although ill, was willing to join him. At about 9.30 that night, they slipped out of the camp. They didn't go far – just up the track a short distance, where they remained hidden for twenty-four hours, observing the camp and the Japanese guards out looking for them. At dusk, after watching the unsuccessful search parties line up for a brisk round of face slapping delivered by their senior officer, the two men crept towards Ranau. They reached Kampong Samaang, where Ginssas bin Gangass sheltered them in his hut for the night, hiding them under grass matting when a lone Japanese dropped by. What happened next is not clear, but by the time they were taken into the care of farmer Adihil bin Ambilid, the village headman, Reither, who was now suffering with dysentery, had sustained injuries to his stomach, arms and legs. Adihil, who had heard shots on the night of 29 July, thought the wounds were caused by either a bayonet or bullet but, as neither fugitive enlightened him, he had no idea what had happened or who was responsible. The cause of these injuries, how serious they were, and what impact they had on two men who had to remain in hiding, is not known.

Godohil in 1985

Adihil, also known as Godohil, was a Kadazan Christian. He refused to betray the escapees, in spite of the $2000 reward, the equivalent of two years' pay for a high-ranking civil servant. He and villagers such as Salunda bin Gambuai harboured them for over a week, hiding them beneath grass matting or in the jungle. Zimban, his brother-in-law (also known as Limbaan bin Kumporo), had agreed to walk to Jesselton with Sticpewich's note but, when he learned that white soldiers had arrived at Lansat, he went straight to Ripley. On receiving the message, Ripley immediately organised medicine and food, which he sent to Samaang with the headman of Lansat village,

Gilenki. The two men did not arrive in time to save Reither, who died that same day.

The next morning Ripley established a new base at Narawang, south of Lansat. Twenty-four hours later Gilenki and Zimban arrived with Sticpewich, who was on horseback. He told Ripley that four others had escaped earlier and that when he had left the camp 42 were alive. When the local agents observing the camp reported to Ripley that up to twenty of these men were still there, Zimban agreed to try and smuggle food and medicine to them, while other agents tried to locate the other escapees. Ripley, whose task was to try and rescue the surviving POWs, was therefore unprepared for a signal he received on 12 August. It was from Gort Chester. With the massive build-up of enemy troops in the Ranau area and Agas 3 not having the resources to effect a simultaneous rescue of all the remaining POWs, he ordered Ripley to 'Stop all further activities. Do not want to aggravate danger of POWs being killed.' While Ripley understood the reasoning – that to try and evacuate the fitter POWs would surely result in the death of the rest – he nevertheless arranged for a white arrow to be placed on a hillside clearing opposite the camp, in the vain hope that paratroopers might be able to pull off a rescue.

By this time the news of Agas 3's arrival had reached Kaingal's friend's cousin, and was on its way to Kaingal. However, when he rushed into the hut near Mile 5 with his third-hand news, the Australians did not believe him. It was not until Barigah and Gunting arrived, confirming Kaingal's information and asking Moxham to write a note for Barigah to deliver to the white men, that hopes, and spirits, skyrocketed. Addressing his message to the Officer-in-Charge of English or American Forces Moxham wrote:

> *We are three Australian prisoners of war. We escaped from camp early in July as Nippon was starving all men. They were dying six and seven a day. After a few days out this Dusun O.T.* [Orang Tua] *found us and has looked after us ever since, building a little hut in the jungle. We are still in very weak condition but quite OK. O.T. Baragah is a Tuan Besar* [big chief] *around here and you will find all the Dusuns very friendly and sincere.*

Twenty-four hours later Barigah was back, asking Moxham to write another note, as heavy rain had prevented him from delivering the first. On 17 August, Barigah, who was met partway by Andong Ajak and other Agas agents, delivered it to Ripley. The next day he and Andong arrived at the hut, loaded with medicines, vitamin tablets, matches, powdered milk and packets of sweets, ironically known as 'Lifesavers'. A note enclosed in the parcel informed them that the war was over but, as the Japanese were hostile, the escapees must remain where they were. However, a day or two later, the waiting was over when Barigah, who had taken some sweet potatoes to the Agas 3 base, returned with a most welcome instruction, 'Come to us'.

On hearing that some POWs had escaped, SOA had immediately dispatched a doctor, medic, signaller and four more operatives to reinforce Agas 3. Fortunately, unlike Ripley, they had parachuted in. Apart from one soldier who remained at Narawang to look after Sticpewich, on 20 August the entire Agas 3 party relocated to Silad, about fifteen kilometres from Ranau. Four days later, a runner arrived with the news that the escapees were on their way. Using little-known back trails, they had been walking for three days and one night.

It had been a slow and painful process. Barigah and Andong Ajak had organised about thirty villagers to act as stretcher-bearers but the makeshift rattan-and-bamboo litters were too hard for the Australians' wasted bodies to bear. They were forced to shuffle along the remote, barely discernable jungle trail, leaning heavily on sticks and so weak they could scarcely lift their feet a centimetre or two above the ground. On day two, they heard the sound of rifle fire. Worried that they might still be recaptured, they pushed on throughout the night, often on hands and knees, their way lit by flaming bamboo torches. Botterill

Kaingal and Sumping, Barigah's cousins

John 'Lofty' Hodges

and Short, at the head of the line, were slumped over the track next afternoon, sure they could not go any further, when they heard the tramp of heavy footsteps. They were expecting the worst when an undeniably Australian voice boomed, 'How ya going, boys?'.

The two exhausted men looked up to see a sight they would never, ever forget: handsome, sun-bronzed Lofty Hodges. Tall and strapping, clad in jungle greens and cradling his pistol like a toy, he was everything they had dreamed about during their long and terrible captivity. Hodges, in turn, could hardly believe that the bearded, ravaged, stick-like figures staring at him with looks of profound wonder could have once been fit, well-fed Australian soldiers. Botterill wept, and so did Hodges.

Botterill was extremely ill, so ill that the doctor warned Hodges he would not last through the night. But Botterill, having been to hell and back, was not going to give up now, and Hodges was equally

Short, Botterill and Moxham with some of their rescuers

determined not to let him. For the next three weeks he looked after Botterill like a baby – attending to his every need and slowly rebuilding his strength with small and frequent amounts of nourishing food.

Throughout this convalescent period, the villagers continued to visit the Australians, bringing parcels of food and other small gifts to help maintain their spirits until evacuation by air could be arranged. This took some time: Japanese who refused to lay down their arms had to be subdued and a landing field prepared. Forty local people created a rudimentary strip in a clearing two kilometres away and fuel

The author interviewing Gapang Durapong at Muruk, 2005

was dropped in, but the pilots were unable to land as the mountains and the surrounding jungle were too close to take off again. On 14 September everyone, apart from the evacuees and a soldier to watch over them, moved from Silad to Tudangan village to repair the badly damaged Ranau airstrip.

Since there was still a large number of hostile Japanese either in the area or passing through, the positions of larger bomb craters were observed visually from a safe distance, but the smaller bumps and hollows had to be surveyed at night. Forming a long line, the Agas men and their agents moved slowly down the runway, carefully counting their paces and using their feet to feel for any irregularities, which were then noted and plotted on a grid. Once the entire surface had been covered, a local labour force of men and women filled in the craters after dark, tamping down the soil, which they had heaped at the side of the strip, with their bare feet. One labourer engaged for this work was Gapang Durapong, who had also helped widen sections of the Tampias–Muruk track. During the day, the Australians occupied their spare time by disarming enemy troops trying to retreat along the Sandakan–Ranau track, which cut across the airfield at the southern end.

Once the airstrip was ready, a signal fire was prepared by a group of villagers, the smoke providing a guide and a wind-direction indicator for the four evacuation aircraft. Finally, on 20 September, due to the combined efforts of the Agas team and the selfless courage of so many local people, the four escapees were airlifted to Labuan on the first leg of their long journey home.

For a few short days in August, SOA had held out hope that there might be more survivors, following the successful escape to the Philippines of Dr Chan Chi Tau, a Chinese doctor from Gas, a small bayside village to the west of Sandakan town. Allowed to continue with his medical practice after the Japanese occupation, Chan had kept out of harm's way by moving from his house in town in August 1942 to Sandy Plain, near Bokara. Two years later, when the Japanese moved into the neighbourhood, he was off again, this time even further around the bay to Lopak Maluas, near Gas.

However, at some stage the kempeitai had caught up with him and he had been held for interrogation in Sandakan in a cell alongside Lieutenant Kong, who was in and out of custody. However, unlike the unfortunate Kong, Chan's chance to escape the clutches of the kempeitai came when he received a message that his Spanish-born wife, Carlotta, was ill. He was released from detention to treat her, and never came back.

At 2 am on 6 August 1945, Chan, Carlotta, their son Carlos aged eight and his amah, their sixteen-year-old adopted daughter Elizabeth Lee, and two family friends, Mr Chong Ming Huin and Mr Koh Huen Ting, escaped from Gas in a sampan. Eleven hours later they were safely on the small Philippine island of Taganak, north-east of Sandakan, where PT boat 142 picked them up and took them to Sanga Sanga. From here they were evacuated to the forward Allied base at Morotai, and finally to Australia.

On his arrival at Australian headquarters in Morotai, Chan was able to give intelligence officers an up-to-date appraisal of the situation in Sandakan. It was not until SOA read the last line of his report, compiled on 11 August, that anyone realised that Rex Blow's intelligence was incorrect. The Mile 8 Camp had not been abandoned in June. According to Chan, in July there were at least 100 POWs still alive. Although all were weak and suffering from beriberi, they were being helped by local Chinese, who slipped food under the wire.

A plan was immediately implemented by the Australian army to mount a rescue from Tarakan, now firmly in Australian hands. Crack commando troops were put on standby, along with relief equipment and stores, a hospital ship was prepared and medical staff assembled but on 20 August, a few hours before the rescue fleet was due to sail, an advance party reported the worst possible news. The hoped-for rescue was a lost cause. The was no longer anyone left alive at the Mile 8 Camp.

Chapter 13

Picking up the pieces

The members of the underground who survived their terms of imprisonment in Singapore and Sarawak were now also finally free. Jim Taylor, released from the purgatory of Singapore's Outram Road Gaol on 19 August, was transferred to the Sime Road Civilian Internment Camp, where he was kept in hospital for a month. Given his age and the terrible deprivation he had endured, he was fortunate to be alive. His cellmate and good friend Gerald Mavor had not survived. He had died in gaol on 5 May 1945, from neglect, malnutrition and beriberi. Six of the twenty-eight Australians soldiers sent to Outram Road Gaol, including the various escapees, died during 1944: Allen, Davis, Marshall and Small in gaol, and Fairey and Shelley in the POW hospital at Changi. Rod Wells, Gordon Weynton, and the surviving twenty-two other ranks were also sent immediately upon release to Changi hospital. Taylor, a strong, sturdy man when he had been imprisoned, weighed just 44 kilograms. Once he had regained some of his strength, he was flown to Labuan to be reunited with his wife Celia, recently released from the Kuching Camp.

Outram Road Gaol, Singapore

Unlike the camp in Sandakan, Kuching's Batu Lintang Camp was large and, by comparison, had reasonable facilities. Those imprisoned there suffered varying degrees of hardship, and food became much scarcer in 1945 but, for those who were not required to work, it was much better than most other large camps. The Australian officers, being among those exempted from manual labour, alleviated the inevitable boredom of camp life by debating, playing cards and chess and attending meetings of the POW Masonic Club, Toc H and other associations. They also produced high-quality plays and musicals, which they advertised with professional-looking handbills and posters, read books borrowed from the 2,000 volumes held in the camp library, and attended courses run by highly qualified officers as part of a 'university' programme. These courses were of such a high standard that prisoners, who sat for exams marked by their lecturers, received signed certificates, enabling them to enter the next year of university tuition when they returned home.

Although rations were progressively cut, Major Rayson, the senior Australian medical officer, recorded that calorie count per prisoner in mid-1945 was 2,600 per day, well above starvation level. The rice ration was about 170 grams: 2.5 times the amount that POWs at Sandakan had been receiving since January that year. Although reduced rations and lack of a balanced diet resulted in some weight loss and debility as time wore on, the difficulties encountered by the Australians could not compare to the hardship of the British 'other ranks' forced to undertake hard manual labour, 600 of whom died between April and August 1945. The twenty-six Australian other ranks who were put to work all survived, along with all but five of the 149 Australian officers: a death rate of less than three per cent, compared with Sandakan's massive 99.75 per cent. The first Australian death in the officers' camp, from beriberi, did not occur until early July 1945. The last, from the combined effects of a heart attack and malaria, was on 2 September. A third died from tuberculosis, and the fourth from dysentery. The fifth, who died at the end of July, lost the will to live. Caught receiving extra food from the kitchen, he had been ostracised by his fellow officers. The shame was so great that he refused to eat, turned his face to the wall, and died. He was 27 years old. Officially, the cause of death was malaria.

The death rate in the civilian men's camp, where the average age of the 260 inmates was higher, was 15 deaths, or just under six per cent. While there had also been deaths in the women's camp, Mrs Mavor and almost all the other Sandakan women internees had survived. So had Agnes and Harry Keith and their son George, along with Bert

Newly liberated Australian officers at Kuching POW Camp

Rus Ewin, second from right, being interviewed for a radio broadcast following the liberation.

Civilian internees raising the flag at Kuching Camp following their liberation

The newly liberated Sandy Young and Bert Walker

Walker, the Governor, Major Rice-Oxley, Residents Owen Smith and Richard Evans, Doctors Laband, Laidlaw, Wands and Sternfeld, and Reverend Henthorne and his staff. As the camp had a radio, the internees, who had followed the course of the war throughout their captivity, knew on 15 August that the Japanese had surrendered – a fact which was not publicly admitted by Suga for another nine days. Always referred to as Granny, Mrs Harrison, Ice Cream, or the Old Lady, the wireless had functioned throughout the entire war apart from a four-month period in early 1945 when, after electricity to the huts was cut off, it had taken four months to construct a hand-generator.

Like the Sandakan radio, the Kuching receiver had been constructed from scratch but, unlike Sandakan, making it had been a lot easier. With 4,000 prisoners and internees in the camp, the pool of material to create components was far greater than at the Mile 8 Camp, as were opportunities for the many working parties to steal vital parts. Furthermore, the British officers, who were permitted to form a Science Committee to investigate the production of alternative forms of medicine and vitamins, had a small forge with which larger tools and parts for the generator were made from soft steel. The forge and vital components were supplied by the Japanese, who watched the 'scientific experiments' with great interest. Smaller tools needed to construct the radio were provided by the 'watchmaker's workshop', where Japanese soldiers and guards who had acquired watches from prisoners and internees brought them to be repaired. However, although tonnes of stores, medical supplies and food were dropped into the camp shortly after Suga made his surrender announcement, the inmates were not actually free until 11 September, when they were liberated by troops from the Australian 9th Division, which formed part of a huge invasion force that had landed at Labuan and Brunei Bay in June.

Tragically, Dr Val Stookes had not survived the war. After being interned in the Kuching Camp he had once again involved himself in subversive activities, this time with dire consequences. In July 1943, shortly after Stookes arrived, the Japanese found a diary belonging to Ernest Morris of the Royal Engineers, the result of a search evidently sparked by the 'Sandakan Incident'. Nothing untoward occurred at that time, but in June 1944, after the diary had been translated in Tokyo, a number of prisoners whose names were linked to the Kuching underground were taken to the guardhouse.

Their case was not helped by the discovery that they had been receiving copies of a local newspaper, *Harian Kuching*, banned since August 1943, and smuggled into the camp by Harry Webber (the American engineer who had tried to escape from Manila) and Sergeant Percival Bent, a British POW who had served with the Gordon Highlanders. After a fortnight, the main suspects were moved to the Kuching Gaol, where they were interrogated by the kempeitai. Included in this group were Webber, Bent, and another British POW, George Goldsbrough, known as The Duke; Val Stookes; the Consul General for China (Cho Huan Lai, also known as Henry Cho, who had been based at Sandakan); Sarawak's Chief Secretary, Cyril Le Gros Clark, who was in charge of the civilian internees; Englishmen Stanley Hill, Richard Abbott and Mr Humphrey; Ronald MacDonald, a planter from Kuching; and three Dutchmen, D F Bunte (Boende), Wilhelm A Knibbe and Hartsenck Marseles. Apart from Goldsbrough, Abbott and Hill, most were in their mid-to-late 40s, and early 50s. The oldest was Webber, aged 55.

On 3 August 1944, Morris, Cho, Le Gros Clark and Hill were sent back to the camp. Shortly afterwards, all but Morris were reimprisoned. Some weeks later, Stookes and Webber returned to the camp, only to learn that they, along with Hill and Cho, were being sent to an unknown destination. Before they left, the five men were allowed to see their wives – in Suga's office and under guard. They were then sent by boat to Jesselton, via Brunei, where they were confined in the police station from 7–9 September. The next day they were interrogated at kempeitai headquarters in Jesselton. Stookes realised he was in deep trouble. Besides being in direct contact with the underground movement, he had given medical advice and smuggled food and drugs to British POWs, whose camp adjoined the male civilian camp.

On 6 December, the prisoners were tried. Six days later all were sentenced to terms of imprisonment ranging from two to nine years, to be served in the Jesselton Gaol at Batu Tiga. Six died of illness: Bunte on 14 January, Knibbe on 4 February, Hill on the 12th, Abbott eleven days later, Goldsbrough on 11 March and Bent on 15 July. On 12 April 1945, Cho, Stookes, Le Gros Clark, Webber and MacDonald, who had been transferred temporarily to Beaufort in March, returned to Jesselton, where Le Gros Clark wrote a letter to Colonel Suga, asking him to recommend that the prisoners move to Kuching. He hoped that Dr Yamamoto, who was visiting Jesselton, would deliver the letter, but before he had a chance to see him again, the five men were moved to Keningau, where they were imprisoned in the local lock-up with some Chinese and local people. Henry Brand, an Australian-Filipino, found guilty of spreading rumours, saw them in custody shortly after their arrival. They were not being ill treated, and loyal police and villagers were smuggling extra food to them.

A track linked Keningau with Tenom and Japanese Headquarters at Sapong Estate in the south, and Tambunan and Ranau in the north. In early June, prior to the invasion of Brunei Bay, Keningau was bombed and strafed. On the orders of the Japanese, the warder left the door to the gaol unlocked during air raids, allowing the prisoners to take shelter in the nearby jungle. While waiting for the 'all clear' the Europeans were able to make contact with local people, who urged them to escape. When they refused on the basis that any escape attempt would imperil the life of anyone who hid them, a local man named Dower tried to change their minds by building a shelter in an inaccessible part of the jungle, which he then stocked with sufficient food to last a month. Although the likelihood of the hideout ever being found was extremely remote, the five Europeans still refused to flee.

While one of the air raids was taking place, Cyril le Gros Clark, obviously aware that they might not survive the war, managed to scratch a message into the trunk of a tree:

'I, together with the Consul General, Dr Stookes, MacDonald and Webber, have been taken from Jesselton to Keningau. Now every day Allied bombers are coming and I feel that landings will soon take place. But my life is soon to be taken and, when victory comes, only my words written here will remain.'

The kempeitai later eradicated all trace of this message, but not before it was spotted by a Formosan named Kiyama, who could read and write English and had the foresight to make a written copy. A leading member of the Formosan Independence League, an organisation committed to freeing his country from its long-term Japanese domination, Kiyama had suffered at the hands of the Japanese and was very pro-British.

During a concentrated bombing attack on 19 June, the police compound was destroyed. Before the police retreated with their prisoners to a house in Kampong Bulu Silou, about two kilometres away, the district civil administrator, Okabayashi Takasui, met with Lieutenant-Colonel Abe Keichi of 37 Area Army Command, Police Commissioner Kamura, and Lieutenant Akutagawa of the kempeitai. They were concerned that, as Australian invasion forces had already landed at Labuan Island and on the mainland, the five men would escape and give valuable information to the enemy. They agreed that the best solution was to dispose of the prisoners, a suggestion in keeping with a similar policy that had resulted in the massacre of forty-six British POWs at Miri on 10 June, the day of the Allied landings.

The prisoners remained in the house at Bulu Silou in the custody of policeman Number 480, Lance-Corporal Ladam. At about 4 o'clock on the morning of 6 July, Ladam was ordered by Kamura to wake the prisoners, who were informed that they were to be moved to Ranau. They were not permitted to have a meal or to take any baggage. Escorted by Kamura and Police Constable Kemagi, the five men, with Ladam in tow, were taken into the village, where they were handed over to Lieutenant Akutagawa, before being herded into a lorry, closely guarded by Warrant Officer Kuichi and ten Japanese troops. Ladam was not permitted to go with them but, before he left, Webber asked him to inform the Australians, when they arrived in Keningau, of their whereabouts.

At about 6.30 am, the truck came to a halt beside a large ditch on the far side of the Liawan River, about forty or fifty metres from the Keningau–Apin road junction and the airstrip. Constable Meraat, who was on his way from Kampong Taud to the police post at Bulu Silau, saw the prisoners and soldiers, but was ordered to move on. Some time later, he heard the sound of rifle and automatic fire and assumed they had been shot.

Bede Willie's son, John, sent to Kuching many months before, also reached Keningau. According to information passed to the family, he had made his way from Kuching to Miri and Brunei by boat. After passing through Beaufort he reached Keningau – a journey taken at about the same time and also remarkably similar to that taken by Val Stookes who, through his brother-in-law Winfield Sherman's marriage to Margaret Willie, was part of John's extended family. With the Willie family and Val Stookes closely involved in the underground movement, it is possible that John was with them, especially since local agents reported to Gort Chester that John had been 'helping POWs'. If he were part of this group, John Willie may have made good his escape during an air raid at Keningau – an option open to him as he was a local, not European. Although ill with dysentery, he reached Ranau and then Telupid, where he died on 25 July 1945 – nineteen days after Stookes and the others were murdered. His body, which was buried by Orang Tua Gundi, the village headman, was never found.

Six other members of the underground, besides Stookes, Moselle Cohen and the fourteen who were executed, did not survive the war. All had been sentenced to between two and six years gaol, and all died in custody in Kuching: Kassim bin Jumadi, who had brought food to the four escapees hiding near Sungei Manila; Police Constable Kassiu; Sastroh; Amigau bin Hassan from the Post and Telegraph Office; and Sini's friends Sidek bin Simoen and Soh Kim Seng, who had helped with the Berhala escapes. Surat Min bin Jumadi, brother of Kassim, managed to escape from gaol. As for the rest – some remained in gaol in Kuching, while others were sent further afield to make use of their labour.

Among those who were detained in Kuching were Dr Laband and Mr Phillips. On 3 March, they and the others serving prison terms were transferred from the kempeitai cells to the civil gaol, where conditions were even harsher. European prisoners who attempted to escape were executed. Asiatics were placed in irons: a six-kilogram contraption which consisted of a pair of ankle shackles to which two vertical iron bars, about one metre long, had been riveted. On top of each bar was an iron ring, through which a rope was passed and tied behind the prisoner's neck. Victims who had been 'ironed' invariably developed large and painful ulcers, some of which, when combined with malnutrition, were fatal. Food comprised about 100 grams of rice and 100 grams of kangkong a day, with a small portion of rotten fish every ten days. There was no salt ration. All efforts made by Phillips and Laband to improve conditions were useless, while anyone attempting to help the prisoners was severely punished.

Although the work was hard, those labouring outside the gaol were generally better off. After being transferred temporarily to the civil gaol, where they were put to work planting vegetables, fetching firewood and other menial tasks, Paddy Funk and Lamberto Apostol were taken by motorboat to Bau. After carrying rice at Seria and planting it at Panchor, they worked on the aerodrome at Sibu and constructed roads in Kukong. While at Kukong, Paddy escaped. He remained at large until Apostol sent word to him that Japan had surrendered.

Peter Lai was not as fortunate. His hard labour included working in the blazing sun for days on end, building the Sibulau rail line for the Japanese Air Force. However, it was bombed so often it was never completed. While slaving on the line, and trudging to Sendungus for salt, the rations were so poor that he and his companions were reduced to catching lizards and rats, which they ate raw.

Johnny Funk, Mohamed Tahir and Henry Chang, sentenced to four, three and six years hard labour respectively, spent the first fifteen months of their sentences constructing roads, felling and cutting timber for the Japanese military, burying dead soldiers and prisoners of war (at any time of the day or night), planting vegetables, making salt and unloading cargo at the wharf. When Allied planes began to strafe and bomb the town, the workers were forced to continue, while their guards directed operations from the safety of nearby air raid shelters. Food was scarce, so the rations were poor – a bowl of watery rice gruel, with a couple of strips of vegetables and occasional tiny fish, normally fed to pigs. In mid-June, word arrived that a large Allied force was approaching Brunei Bay. As the Japanese intended to make their last stand at Sambas in Dutch Borneo, the prisoners were ordered to move supplies to the border on buffalo carts, with one prisoner between the shafts and another six pushing from the rear. Working from 5.30 am until 7 pm each day, the labour force made several trips. When they finally crossed the border and were ordered to find their own shelter, the three men escaped into the jungle. With the help of a local tribesman they made their way back to Kuching, where an Australian soldier told them that the war was over, and that they were free. They discovered later that the final trip was supposed to be literally their last journey: after shooting all the sick and poisoning the children, the Japanese had intended to march all prisoners and internees from Kuching to Sambas where, under the blanket orders that had been issued, anyone who survived the trek was to be 'disposed of'. Fortunately, the speed with which Japan surrendered, following the dropping of the atomic bombs on Hiroshima and Nagasaki, did not give Colonel Suga time to implement his orders.

The sudden end to hostilities also saved the life of Sini who, in early 1944, was sent to Sanggau, on the Kappaus River in Dutch Borneo, carrying supplies and foodstuffs from Kuching. The Formosan guards did not beat the prisoners, but food was poor, and they had no shoes and very little clothing. When Japan surrendered Sini was across the border. Finally liberated by Australian occupying forces in October, he made the long journey back to Kuching, where he was reunited with other civilian internees before being flown by Catalina flying boat to Labuan, where he boarded a ship to take him back to Sandakan.

There was nothing to come back to. With the intense Allied bombing, and the Japanese setting fire to what was left, the town had been reduced to piles of rubble and charred sticks. Only five buildings had withstood the onslaught. All were places of worship: St Michael's Church (minus its roof); the Chinese temple near the padang and another further up Happy Valley; the Sikh temple (which was damaged); and the mosque. Apart from one or two isolated houses tucked away among the hills, everything else had been damaged

Sandakan in ruins, September 1945

The mangled remains of the Jubilee Clock Tower

King's Theatre in ruins

Harrison and Crosfield's, September 1945

or destroyed. When Lamberto Apostol arrived in Sandakan, Harry Keith, who had remained in Borneo to help with the rebuilding, gave him his old job back. All the forestry houses, including Harry's, were in ruins, so Apostol searched for something suitable among those that were still standing. It took him some time before he found one that did not hold the remains of decapitated corpses.

Some of the other underground members, on returning from Kuching, learned that family members had died in their absence. Sergeant Yusup's wife, unable to obtain any medical help, had succumbed to her injuries sustained when the Japanese had discovered the pictures of the King, Queen and Winston Churchill in her house. Chan Ah Ping's wife was dead and so was Inspector Samuel Guriaman's twelve-year-old daughter, left alone after her mother died of a broken heart. Ng Ho Kong's unexpected reunion with his wife and daughter Alice, on the road as he headed home, was tinged with great sadness by the discovery that five of his family members living on the rubber plantation on Trig Hill had not survived: his brother; his parents, who had died of stress and worry; and two daughters, both dead from malnutrition. His eldest sister and her two daughters had died on another plantation at Mile 11. Alex Funk's widow Maggie mourned not only Alex, but their eldest daughter, scalded to death in an accident at Mile 7 in October 1945. Thirteen days later, the family learned that Alex had been executed.

When hostilities were finally over, those who had been living in the jungle left their hiding places with great caution. In returning to the house at Sungei Manila, Dimit Funk and her family discovered that Dimit's uncle, Mr Pascual, a surveyor, had been beheaded while working in the jungle. Shortly afterwards, his older daughter, aged 11, and her friend had disappeared while looking for edible shells among the mangroves. Mark Pang, finally reunited with his family after long months hiding out near Mile 9, returned to teaching for a short period. After working for the local council, he obtained a timber concession, which put him on the road to prosperity. Once life returned to a degree of normality, his sons, who had been too busy planting food to stay alive during the war years to attend school, were able to continue with their education.

Alone in his hideout near Lahad Datu, Anup Singh's Uncle Dial had realised from the crump of exploding bombs that the war was coming to an end. In their little house in the jungle, Anup and others cowered in terror as Allied planes swooped low over the rooftop, firing on Japanese positions in the town. Finally, after leaflets had been dropped and all sound of hostility had ceased, the family returned to Sandakan where, after selling her last remaining gold bangle, Mrs Singh set about creating a new life for herself and her surviving family.

Although the Funk family were on the kempeitai's 'most wanted' list, Lillian did not wait for the war to end, or for Allied occupation forces to arrive, before venturing closer to town. Throughout the long months of occupation, she had never considered that Johnny might be dead and, despite the obvious risks, she was determined to be at hand when he returned home. Taking Melvyn, now aged six, and three-year-old Doreen with her, she made her way cautiously to a rubber plantation near Sandakan owned by friends, ducking for cover whenever Allied planes roared overhead. Aware of the risks to her hosts, she and the children entered their house only at night, lying on the floor under the beds to sleep. There were still plenty of Japanese roaming about, but fortunately the family's two hounds were excellent watchdogs.

And then, one day in mid-September, a Japanese jeep and an army truck, packed with heavily armed soldiers, suddenly arrived. Alighting quickly, the troops took up defensive positions around the house, sending the children, who had been trained to hide at the first sight of the military, slithering under the beds. Frightened that Lillian's calls of reassurance to come out were made under duress, they stayed put until Melvyn heard the sound of joyous weeping. The soldiers were Australian, and they had brought his father home.

Johnny Funk was certainly not the father his small son remembered: the strong sturdy body now thin and wasted, his face drawn and haggard. But he was very much alive and, furthermore, he had a job. As the soldiers dug about in their rations and handed out bread, corned beef, chewing gum and chocolates, Johnny explained that he was now a guide with the Australian army. Also working with the Australians was his brother Eddie, who had successfully remained at large following his escape from the Jesselton POW Camp, and had joined the 9th Division Liberation Forces.

The top priority of the Australian occupation troops, who had arrived in Sandakan on 12 September, was to conduct a formal surrender, and distribute ration cards and food to the starving population. Six-year-old Daniel Chin, whose mother had died of malnutrition, watched wide-eyed as the soldiers used their bayonets to lever open truckloads of wooden boxes, packed with large, khaki-coloured tins holding all the goodies Daniel and his family had dreamed about during their many months of hunger and deprivation: biscuits, powdered milk, corned beef, tinned butter and cheese, peanut butter, Marmite and, best of all, chocolate.

When their friend James Abitory brought the news to the Pereira family at Mile 13 that the Australian liberation forces had landed, an excited Albert Pereira and his sister Mathilda climbed aboard an Australian army truck for the trip into Sandakan. They were hoping to stay in town, but Rose Cottage had been burned to the ground, and any houses still reasonably intact had human remains inside. However, the house at the water village on Leila Road was still standing and, after removing all the debris, they patched the roof and waited for the rest of the family. When their sister Gertrude and her husband arrived, they brought bad news. Their mother, Theresa, had reported to the food distribution point, carrying their little sister, Mary, aged 5, but the child was too weak to eat and died in her mother's arms.

As the war had entered its closing stages Winfield Sherman and his brother-in-law James Willie had flown to Sandakan from the Philippines to identify various military sites for the Americans. Seeing the plane pass low over the farm at Bilit, Dora Stookes realised that the end of the war was near and, fearful of retaliatory action from the Japanese, fled by boat up the Kinabatangan River with her seven children. When it was finally safe to come out of hiding, they made their way to Sandakan, where they discovered that the Japanese, who had used their house as an officers' mess, had burnt it to the ground. Fortunately the garage, which in peacetime had housed five or six cars, was still standing. Dora subdivided the space, which she shared with Winfield and his family. Although not formally trained, Dora was an experienced midwife and nurse, and soon found employment. She remained in Sandakan until 1949, when she moved to Singapore to obtain formal qualifications. She did not have sufficient funds to rebuild the house, but Harry Keith was able to construct a new home for Agnes and George, who returned to Sandakan in 1947.

However, before any rebuilding could begin, the whole of Sabah had to be secured and processes put in place to ensure that those responsible for the many atrocities were brought to justice.

At Ranau, with the four escaped POWs now well on their way home, Ripley turned his attention to gathering evidence for war crimes investigators and collecting what information was available on the fate of the POWs. On 21 September, accompanied by four Agas operatives and five local agents and guerrillas, he marched into Ranau. It was pouring with rain and Ripley was in no mood for niceties. Before the 200 enemy soldiers and guards stationed in and around the village knew what was happening, the Australians had confiscated and burnt all their weapons, and seized anything believed to have belonged to the prisoners. Although the Japanese had destroyed most of the incriminating articles, the Agas men still managed to find thirteen wristwatches (three of which were inscribed with the names of dead POWs), 28 fountain pens, six propelling pencils, four pocket watches, eight wallets, one pair of opera glasses and one pair of binoculars. After freeing about a dozen Javanese slaves, Ripley lined up what was left of the Japanese garrison and made them salute the British flag before sending them, on foot, across the mountains to Jesselton. Helped by his agents, including local police constables Sampura and Solum, he then focused on collecting as much intelligence as possible before he and his team marched to Keningau on 3 October, with another batch of prisoners.

Meanwhile, Gort Chester had dispatched three Agas 1 men, accompanied by four guerrillas, four police boys and five coolies, to all the villages along the Labuk between Beluran and Bauto. At Telupid, Orang Tua Gundi told them of John Willie's fate and showed them the graves of the four escapees the villagers had hidden. He also produced a keepsake autographed by several POWs and a signed statement from each of the four escaped prisoners, promising to pay him $400 if they reached Allied lines. Unfortunately, he had no further information to add as the escapees had used their diaries for toilet paper. The headman did, however, report that there had been acts of cannibalism, a claim later supported by Kulang's brother, Laip, who reported that two members of the kempeitai had shot two prisoners dead near Muanad, hacked off their scabies-infected limbs and packed the torsos into a boat, which had then headed downstream to the Japanese camp.

In mid-October a troopship, escorted by two Australian corvettes, sailed into the harbour. On board were Australian reinforcements for the occupation force and a detachment of a dozen Australian officers: a lieutenant-colonel, four majors, four captains, a lieutenant, a squadron leader and a flight-lieutenant. They were members of an interim government organisation, the British Borneo Civil Administration Unit (BBCAU, or, as it was known to the locals, 'B Cow'). Their task was to re-establish government administration, organise food and medical relief, restore community services, break up the black-market food supply, and clamp down on petty crime. In short – do whatever was necessary to get the town functioning again. They had brought everything they needed with them: vast quantities of food and medical supplies; fuel; tents; camp stretchers;

Australian officers with the Japanese Governor, September 1945

A dispirited Japanese soldier outside the public toilet block, September 1945

A food distribution centre

Japanese POWs constructing access to Sim Sim hospital

bedding; essential commodities such as candles, matches, hurricane lamps, kerosene and soap; footwear and clothing; cooking and eating utensils; tools, jeeps, trucks, bulldozers, graders and a tip truck. As the airstrip would not be useable for some time, flying boats based in Singapore would call with mail and urgent medical supplies once a week. With no telegraph service and, indeed no telegraph office, until the lines were restored all communication would be by field radio, operated from a small room in what was left of the Secretariat.

It was impossible to know where to begin. The local people were in poor health, most were starving, and all were dispirited. A call went out for anyone who wished to have paid employment to report to BBCAU at once. Not only were their labour and expertise essential but also, by paying them, a cash economy could be restarted. Paid jobs would also help restore the people's self esteem and prevent them from becoming 'welfare dependent'.

Hundreds of Sandakan's citizens answered the call: clerks, PWD staff, power house workers, water and sanitation inspectors, labourers, technicians, former policemen, mechanics, hospital dressers and nurses. With the help of the military, tonnes of supplies were unloaded from the ship and stacked in the old, open-sided fish market; the only structure in the town centre which still had any semblance of a roof. From here they were taken to distribution points established along the roads leading out of town. As the word went out, more people began to emerge from the jungle. However, like little Mary Pereira, for many the relief effort had come too late. Although they reached the food depots, some were so emaciated and weak that nothing could save them.

Richard Low

Food distribution was vital, but equally pressing was the need to establish a hospital where the sick and dying could be treated. As the mental hospital at Sim Sim was still intact (apart from the roof, which was riddled with jagged bullet holes), local people and Japanese prisoners were put to work building a bridge over a wrecked section of the road to restore access. Once the rubble was cleared from around the building and the roof repaired by the PWD, BBCAU's Dr Ian Byrne set up a series of aid stations near the food distribution centres. The aid posts were simply a tent fly rigged up over a folding table and some chairs. Each was manned by a soldier with first aid experience and a male or female dresser, whose task was to either treat minor ailments on the spot, or arrange for transportation to hospital by the jeep-and-trailer courier service, which delivered food and medical supplies to the depots throughout the day. Once at Sim Sim, the patients passed to the care of Dr Byrne and Matron Helen Luk, wife of prominent citizen Luk Shee Shin. Some of the local people employed at the hospital had connections with the underground: the head dresser, Richard Low; Rosalind Dominic, daughter of Pedro, who had been sitting for her exams the day the Japanese landed; Dora Stookes, Lillian Funk and Phoebe Lai; and also Helen Chin, Rosie Kong, Rosie Lo and Alice Watson. Now that hostilities were over, Dr Chan returned from Australia to lend a hand, while Nurse Rose Kong, widow of his friend Lieutenant Kong, was given the responsibility of distributing the food rations.

When a report came in that a group of Javanese labourers were camped near the now defunct airstrip, Major Fullford and Richard Soong, a local man working as his interpreter, went to investigate. Aware of the terrible deprivations experienced by the prisoners of war, the imported labourers and the local community, the Australian feared the worst, especially since SOA agents had reported that, of the 1,700 Javanese collies at Kudat in August 1944, only 300 were left alive. Leaving the vehicle at Mile 7, Fullford's guide, a Japanese officer, led them on foot for a kilometre or two beyond the road, through tapioca gardens and jungle to a camp of atap huts. There, to his surprise, the major found several hundred Javanese men and women, in good health. They had been living on rice from a nearby store (possibly from Pop Wong's house), and tapioca, which they were cultivating. Once they were relocated closer to the road, they were put to work in groups of about fifty, clearing rubble, filling in craters, mending roads, sorting anything that could be recycled and removing anything that could not.

By November, numerous teams were based at Sandakan and Ranau: to collect information on missing POWs, investigate war crimes, and locate the bodies or graves of the 2,428 POWs who had

Staff and patients, BBCAU hospital at Sim Sim

Hakka women at work, rebuilding Sandakan

The Post and Telegraph Office constructed in late 1945

died. Kulang and Bede Willie were integral to the search for bodies along the track, which was scoured no fewer than three times over an eighteen-month period, each time increasing the distance either side of the path. It was a soul-destroying task. On steep mountainsides where the Japanese had rolled bodies over the side, along fast-flowing streams, and in the swamps, they found nothing. There was little to find in some areas of the low-lying Labuk estuary, the haunt of many crocodiles, and parts of which had been inundated by monsoonal floods to a depth of almost three metres. Wild boars had accounted for the disappearance of some corpses, while other POWs had wandered so far from the track that no trace of their remains would ever be found. However, despite these difficulties, and the length of the track, which passed through some very rugged terrain, the searchers managed to locate 315 of the 500 POWs who had perished along the 250-kilometre track. The recoveries at the various camps was almost 100 per cent. This was an outstanding result as the burial sites (four at Sandakan, one at Paginatan and at least a dozen at the three Ranau camps) had been overrun with rampant jungle vines. Furthermore, only a fraction of the graves at Sandakan, and only one at Ranau, had been marked in any way.

Supporting the recovery teams in this long and unpleasant, but very necessary, task were scores of local people, who helped locate, wrap and transport the remains to either the west or east coast. All bodies found downstream from Tampias were placed on bamboo rafts built by villagers and floated down the Labuk River, all the way to Beluran, where a coolie train transferred them on foot to Sandakan. West of Tampias, every single body recovered was taken by foot up and over the mountains to Ranau, in preparation for a further overland journey, also on foot, across the Crocker Range to the jeep track at Tamparuli: a round trip from Ranau of nine days.

Apart from helping locate remains, policemen Kamon and Segulu were able to shed light on the fate of some of the marchers. In October 1944, both men had been sentenced to gaol in Sandakan for raiding the main Japanese storehouse during an air raid and dumping a large amount of rice into the harbour. In April 1945, when the gaol was bombed, they were sent to the track to work as coolies. In June, when Kamon had walked from Tindok to Muanad, he had counted 38 bodies between Mile 28 and 50. Segulu reported that he had been working at Mile 27 when a party of 100 POWs arrived. Many had looked reasonably fit, but some were suffering from beriberi and malnutrition. The next day he saw the bodies of two who had died during the night. Returning to Mile 28.5 a few days later, he observed two Japanese and two POWs, wearing Australian hats and looking quite fit. The following morning one of the guards, Kabautu, took the prisoners into the jungle. He was wearing his sword. When he emerged, thirty minutes later, he was alone.

Kamon escaped from the coolie train while carrying rice to Sandakan from the Muanad River crossing. Arriving at Mile 17, he was sheltered by Chong Kwey, who showed him the remains of an escaped POW who had been hiding in the undergrowth about 200 metres from the house. A Japanese soldier who spotted the smoke from his fire had shot him. Villagers living on the Labuk near Gumbaron also had information about a POW whom they found beside the track. He had not been killed, as the Japanese thought he would die within a few hours. His rescuers hid him in the jungle about 90 metres from the track and supplied him with food. He may have survived had the Japanese not ordered all able-bodied men in the village to take their boats upriver to Tampias. When they returned ten days later, they went immediately to the hiding place, but the prisoner had died in the meantime from dysentery and starvation. Kulang, who had already reported the murder of the prisoner at the Muanad Crossing rest house, and handed over the photo the victim's friend had given him, also reported that on 24 October he had found the remains of ten POWs near Tindok. As the bones were very weathered, he thought they were from the first march.

He also had information about the other group of POWs who had been diverted from the second march to carry stores to Bauto. It seems likely that these were the prisoners Kamon had seen at Mile 27. Reports of their movements to and fro in the area gave rise to the assumption that POWs were being sent to Ranau via the northern route, through Meridi. However, if they crossed the Labuk they did not go far, and it appears they operated mainly between Mile 42 and Bauto. Kulang reported that six had been shot at Muanad on 27 August, the same day as the Ranau massacres, while a Chinese named Ah Chang reported that another fifty-four had been shot to the west of the crossing the same day. Kulang was emphatic that these POWs were definitely rice carriers and had not, at any stage, ever proceeded past Bauto. It also seems highly likely that graves marked with crude wooden crosses, spotted in a clearing near Beluran by an Australian pilot, are most likely the graves of other members of this group. Unfortunately, although the pilot reported the sighting, there was no further investigation.

Information about the fate of Dr Stookes and his four companions was, however, followed up. On October 4, Richard Evans, the West

Coast Resident, accompanied by 9th Division's Major Irving and two Australian soldiers, went to Keningau to investigate the disappearance of Le Gros Clark and his companions. As the area was not yet secure, there were still many Japanese soldiers about. According to a senior Japanese officer, the five men had escaped. According to Sergeant-Major Sagunting of the local police, they had been killed near the airfield – a story later supported by the kempeitai chief who, under interrogation, claimed that Lieutenant-Colonel Abe had ordered him to execute the prisoners as they had been waving at aeroplanes. After locating and examining the contents of two suitcases, embossed with the initials of Clark and MacDonald, which had been safeguarded by a local Chinese, the party focused on the whereabouts of the bodies.

Ex-police Constable Kaliun reported that he had seen a dog eating a human leg bone near what appeared to be several graves at the spot where Meraat had seen the prisoners. On opening the graves, which were very shallow, they found only a grey sock, identified as belonging to Webber; a white canvas shoe; bits of bone and pieces of decayed flesh; and hanks of hair which, by their colour, were identified as those of MacDonald and Stookes. There was no sign of any skulls. According to the Japanese, the bodies had been removed. Where, they did not know.

At the end of October, just after Evans returned to Jesselton, Captain Collins, the commanding officer of an Australian War Graves Unit recovering bodies along the track, was asked by the Americans to investigate the disappearance of Webber and the whereabouts of the bodies of six American airmen who had died in a plane crash in the Sepalut area in November 1944. Five other aircrew who survived the crash had vanished. At about the same time, Collins received a letter from Dora Stookes in Sandakan, enquiring about the fate of her husband. Collins, who began an immediate investigation, was somewhat annoyed to discover that Evans had located the bodies of the six airmen on his visit to Keningau and had removed them without authorisation. He had also removed, without authorisation, the remains and personal items he had found in the graves of Dr Stookes and his companions, and had buried them in a common grave in the Jesselton Civil Cemetery.

The Americans managed to reclaim their airmen. However, as it was impossible to ascertain if any of the civilian remains found were Harry Webber's, his widow did not press to have the common grave in the cemetery opened. Shortly afterwards, headstones inscribed with the names of the four Europeans were erected in a row in the Jesselton cemetery. Since Dora Stookes and her family had no idea that the few remains found had been reburied, or that these headstones even existed, it appears that Evans had acted of his own volition. Collins' investigation also established that the remains at Keningau not taken away by dogs had been removed and destroyed by the Japanese in an effort to hide the identities of the victims.

In 1999, new information regarding the actual executions came to light when Bruce Blanche, a Scotsman who was researching Val Stookes' life, contacted a man named Tabrett who lived in Sabah and had been investigating local war history for some years. He stated that the five men had not been shot, as was generally believed. There was a witness to the executions: a Murut man, the father of Tabrett's 'wife'. He had been supervising Javanese slaves on the Keningau–Apin road in July 1945 when the truck carrying Stookes' party drew up. He and his terrified labour force had then watched as the prisoners, stripped and with hands tied behind their backs, were dragged from the vehicle, savagely beaten, and beheaded. The heads and torsos were then kicked into the shallow ditches. If this account is true, and there seems to be no reason why it is not, then the rifle fire heard by the policeman on 6 July may have been a firing squad executing the five other American airmen, whose bodies were also never found.

Not everyone who came forward had information about prisoners of war. The local people had suffered as hideously as the POWs and, now that the war was over, Sandakan's civilians were anxious to impart whatever information they had: the names of twenty-five known Japanese war criminals; the identity of local collaborators and black marketeers; and details of many war crimes perpetrated against local people, from persecution of individuals to the massacre of entire communities. SOA party leaders also passed on to civil administrators comprehensive lists of collaborators who had operated in their areas.

With the destruction of Sabah's infrastructure, which was far beyond the power of the Chartered Company to restore, the British were relying on BBCAU, headed by a former Chief Judge of British North Borneo, Brigadier Macaskie. While the soldiers of 9th Australian Division concentrated on military matters, BBCAU looked after the day-to-day administration, which included bringing to justice civilians accused of aiding the enemy. In Sandakan, the trials were conducted initially by Major Fullford, who incurred the disapproval of BBCAU's Chief Judge in Jesselton by handing down sentences that were far too light, particularly in the case of collaborators whom he had set free. These included a man who had travelled for several days from his village to alert the Japanese to the whereabouts of an escaped POW whom a fellow citizen had refused to betray. The escapee was beheaded. The informant, bound with strips of bark, had been brought to Sandakan, several days' paddling from the village. The Australian prosecutor, Captain Yorke, held that the collaborator was responsible for the murder of the POW. Major Fullford dismissed the charge. His justification was that the offence had occurred at a time outside the present law, and that the informant could have been in fear of his life. The Chief Justice did not agree, holding the view that there was indeed a case to answer and that Fullford should have remanded the case to a higher authority. It was an opinion shared by many local people, who expressed amazement at some of the Major's verdicts. The perceived failure of the immediate post-war judicial system to ensure that justice was not only done, but seen to be done, may have been the reason why the Mumiang Volunteers, a local organisation committed to the apprehension and punishment of people they regarded as traitors, extracted their own form of summary justice.

Although Jackie Lo Ah Fuh escaped the vigilante group's attention, his prominence in the community and his betrayal of the underground was too well known to save him from arrest. His name, along with his last known address at 179 Jalan Lima, was on the 'wanted' list. The case was cut and dried, but those expecting him to be severely punished were in for a shock. He was sentenced to just three years' gaol. It is not known if the leniency of his sentence was due to a lack of understanding of the Sandakan Incident by the judge, or because Lo may have stated he had acted under duress. If the judge accepted such a claim as a mitigating factor, Lo was extremely fortunate. This excuse, which Jewish collaborators in Nazi concentration camps used to try and justify their behaviour, was not accepted at European trials.

In what appears to be an attempt to start anew, Jackie Lo changed his European and Chinese given names. Irrespective of why he had agreed to collaborate with the Japanese, or what pressure they may have exerted, it was a past he would certainly want to forget: his actions had cost the lives of at least fourteen of his fellow citizens and the untold suffering of so many others. The flow-on effect from the collapse of the underground had put paid to any uprising, increased the level of general brutality for citizens and prisoners alike, left families destitute, and was directly responsible for the removal of almost all the POW officers to Kuching, leaving the prisoners without proper leadership or anyone of any substance to stand up to their captors.

Dominic Koh, who had been the catalyst for Lo's betrayal with his attempts to blackmail Heng Joo Ming over the 'singlet affair', was gaoled for eighteen months. Ironically, the crime which put him behind bars was not for assisting the Japanese, but theft. Unfortunately, accusations levelled by two Australians saw two leading members of the underground sent to prison, evidently by a far tougher judge than Fullford, who had handed over the administration of justice in early 1946 to former magistrates, including John Simon Funk, who came out of retirement to sort out complex land title issues. Appointed as First Class Magistrate Sandakan, he retained this position until his (final) retirement at the end of 1947.

Poor Mr Phillips, who had been arrested, tortured and then tried and gaoled by the Japanese, was released from Kuching at war's end, only to be arrested in Sandakan for betraying the four escapees who had sought refuge at his house in 1942. He was denounced by survivor William Sticpewich. Not only had Sticpewich no idea of the circumstances surrounding the apprehension of the escapees, but he also had no knowledge of the underground organisation other than the fact that he made the false drawer in which the radio was temporarily hidden. In reporting Phillips, he didn't even get his name right, referring to him as 'McKenzie'. However, investigators eventually located the 'traitor', whom Sticpewich stated was the manager of the North Borneo Trading Company's timber mill. Mr Phillips did not have any hope of acquittal. Sticpewich was a powerful personality, and with no one to speak up for the defendant, he was found guilty.

However, it was Sergeant-Major Yangsalang who suffered the greatest miscarriage of justice. It appears that, like Phillips, a far tougher local judge tried his case.

Not long after Yangsalang returned from Kuching, having spent the past two years in gaol, he unexpectedly found himself under arrest. Doctor Taylor, who alleged that Yangsalang had assisted the Japanese by telling them more than was necessary while under interrogation, had denounced him. Court martialled and found guilty, the sergeant-major was sentenced to three years' gaol – the same sentence as that handed down to that well-known collaborator, Lo Ah Fuh. Those who knew Yangsalang were appalled by the verdict. He had fed the eight Australians hiding on Berhala and been integral to their escape, had contributed a substantial amount of money to the POW and internee assistance funds, and had arranged for loyal members of the Constabulary to be posted to Berhala. When tortured during his initial interrogation regarding the Sandakan Incident, he had told his tormentors nothing. It was not until he had heard the confessions of others under torture and heard Lagan's denunciation that he realised that it was futile to hold out any longer and had made a statement.

Yangsalang was sentenced to fifteen years, the maximum gaol term handed out at the Kuching trials. Although this alone should have made it patently obvious to the judge presiding over the collaboration case that he was no friend of the Japanese, British justice, under the newly liberated Sabah, found him guilty and sent him to prison, in the very gaol he had once helped administer. His job prospects on release were virtually nil. After many loyal years of service, and terrible suffering at the hands of the Japanese, the best Yangsalang could hope for, if he survived the shame and bitterness of his imprisonment, would be to find employment somewhere as a coolie. Jackie Lo Ah Fuh, after changing his name, returned to, and enjoyed, a normal life.

Meanwhile, teams of Australian investigating officers, with the assistance of local people, were travelling all over Sabah to collect the evidence required by prosecutors at war crimes trials. The first of the high-profile war criminals to be tried were Captains Hoshijima and Takakuwa, Lieutenant Watanabe, and the soldiers and guards who had accompanied the first march. Hoshijima's greatest mistake had been to cut the rice ration to zero without authorisation and to withhold vital drugs and medicines. Found guilty of murder in January 1946 at Labuan, Hoshijima and Takakuwa were hanged at Rabaul on the island of New Britain on 6 April, there being no gallows at Labuan. Watanabe was executed by firing squad in March at Morotai.

Initially, Captain Yamamoto and nine others escorting the first march were all sentenced to death. However, since the prosecution had relied on very garbled depositions from Botterill and Moxham, neither of whom could appear in court as they were still too ill, the judicial reviewing panel in Australia decided, quite rightly, that the verdicts were unsafe. Nine of the accused were re-tried in Rabaul in May, the tenth having died in the meantime. At their second trial, six defendants received gaol terms. One of the accused, on Botterill's evidence, was acquitted; the prosecution had the wrong man. Yamamoto was sentenced to death for allowing POWs to be shot, and Lieutenant Abe for being in command of the killing squad. In hindsight, this appears to be a somewhat harsh sentence. Yamamoto had not allowed any of his regular soldiers to mistreat the prisoners and it was standard practice, under Japanese military law, to shoot anyone, including Japanese troops, who could not keep up while in retreat. However, this potentially mitigating factor was not raised at the trial, possibly because, being standard procedure, Yamamoto did not think to mention it to his Australian defence lawyer. By the same token, as the Allies did not kill their own men, that any nation might legally sanction such an act was evidently a consideration outside the defence lawyer's experience. At least six other Japanese, found guilty of murder, were executed. Among them was Hosotani, of the Sandakan kempeitai, who had killed POWs from the third march as well as the five Chinese civilians suspected of being in contact with the Filipino guerrillas.

Despite the diligence of the many investigating teams, who followed up every possible lead, there was one 'war crime', sparked by wild rumours and which, many years later, Sabahans assumed had gone undetected. While being interviewed by a reporter in September 1998, Mohamed Tahir claimed that, during the search for the radio (which took place in the officers' quarters and which no outsiders witnessed), some of the Australians had fought back. Three, said to have been beaten and stabbed with bayonets, allegedly seized the weapons and thrashed the guards severely, before disappearing into the crowd. Fearing that retaliations would follow, the senior officers had supposedly persuaded the offenders to give themselves up. Tahir stated that after torturing and beating them severely, the Japanese shaved their heads and cut strip of flesh five centimetres wide from their foreheads, which they then packed with salt and stitched up. The victims, he said, were then left in the sun to die a slow and agonising death as their comrades looked on helplessly.

Although, since 1998, this story has appeared in at least one book written on Sandakan POWs, it is a fabrication from beginning to end. Had it occurred, it would have been a major war crime, known to the many hundreds of prisoners, including the six escapees and the 144 officers sent to Kuching who survived the war. Nothing even remotely resembling this tale was ever reported, although survivors provided detailed accounts of every Japanese atrocity or act of brutality that had taken place, including the names of people who had their faces slapped.

Furthermore, logic dictates that, if this story were true, the officers would not need to persuade the offenders to give themselves up: in the confined space of the compound, the guards would have had no trouble finding three men who had been bashed and suffered multiple stab wounds. However, as rumours usually have a small scintilla of fact hidden somewhere among the fabrications, the incident may refer to a fairly common punishment in some places of making POWs stand in the sun with bags of salt on their heads. The weight of the bag was bad enough, but as the prisoners sweated, the salt would dissolve and run into any sores or open wounds, and also into their eyes.

The Japanese at Sandakan, who considered prisoners of war to be beyond contempt, and surrender a fate worse than death, had boasted repeatedly to the Australian POWs that they would commit hari kari rather than fall into enemy hands. Despite their bravado, the only person involved with the Sandakan POWs who had the courage to kill himself was Colonel Suga, and he only did it to cheat the hangman. Faced with the almost certainty that he would go to the gallows, he committed suicide by cutting his throat. It was not a quick death. The knife was blunt and the blood loss not great enough for a merciful end, so his faithful batman hurried up the process by hitting him over the head with a water bottle. He also tried to fulfil Suga's last request to place burning incense beside his body, but there was none available so the batman had to make do with a mosquito smoke-bomb. General Baba, Borneo's most senior officer, also tried to kill himself, but the attempt was foiled. The Australians patched him up and, as soon as he was well enough, hanged him.

Although Australia actively pursued war criminals until 1951, long after Britain and the other Allies had closed down their war crimes units, the execution at Rabaul in 1947 of General Baba brought an end to the Borneo trials. Of the 898 names on the Borneo 'wanted' list, 444 had been arrested. Of the remaining 454, thirty-six had died, sixteen had left Borneo and thirty-three could not be traced. Another 131 were not pursued as they had assumed another name, or there was insufficient evidence to bother. After simple interrogation, a further 238 suspects had been released. Overall, 5,725 Class A, B and C Japanese war criminals were brought to trial by the Allies for murder and crimes against humanity in South-East Asia. Only sixty per cent of those accused of war crimes against Sandakan POWs and civilians were tried. The remainder, including Sergeant-Major Ehara Kesao of the kempeitai, the man responsible for the tortures at the Leila Road interrogation centre, and a man described by Dr Taylor as 'fiend', were never punished.

However, while some of the sentences handed down by the Australian military tribunals were quite hefty, most Japanese served only a fraction of their sentences. In April 1952, a peace treaty between all the Allied powers and Japan came into effect. Under its terms, further prosecution of war criminals was prohibited and those still serving gaol terms in Allied prisons were transferred to Sugamo Prison in Tokyo. As a result for pleas for mitigation, all were set free by December 1958, and the prison demolished. The longest sentence ever served by any Japanese war criminal, convicted at any Allied trial, was less than thirteen years.

While the legal teams were chasing after war criminals, other Australians had been sorting out the chaos that was Sandakan. The local people, most of whom were hiding in the hills, had realised that the war must be over when the air raids stopped – a hunch that was confirmed when a plane flew overhead a few days later, dropping clouds of leaflets which floated to the ground like a giant ticker-tape parade. They had crept back to the town to find it a mass of charred and abandoned ruins, overrun by weeds and jungle vines. People had set up house in whatever they could find: under sheets of corrugated iron, in the concrete strongroom of the Secretariat, in the public toilet block, and in the bullet-shattered base of the derelict Jubilee Tower. There was no running water and no sanitation of any sort.

The kampong across the bay had also been wiped out. As the war drew to its close, the Japanese had razed the houses and killed all but one of the villagers. The sole survivor was a small Dusun girl whose head had been only partially severed by the rampaging enemy. Found alive the next day, she was brought back to Sandakan, and nursed back to health.

Every public utility and facility that had existed before the war was gone. The town square, where members of the Sandakan Club had played tennis on the immaculate grass courts, was just a piece of flat land among the ruins; a handy spot to store fuel drums and to park the ramshackle vehicles used by the Japanese. The padang, on which the Volunteers and members of the Constabulary had so proudly paraded, had disappeared beneath rampant weeds and head-high grass. An inspection of the experimental farm revealed that it no longer existed. The entire area was now covered in tapioca. Mr Phillips' timber mill was flattened, the wharves and logging pens disintegrated, the machinery rusted to the point of uselessness, and the entire plant in such disarray that it was completely unsalvageable. It was the same with the bark tanning factory, the boat building yards, the warehouses and the rubber plantations, where drying and treatment sheds and machinery were in a deplorable state due to years of neglect. The one bright spot was that the rubber trees, not having been tapped for more than two years, could be brought into immediate production.

There were no calls for compensation. No wringing of hands, no lawsuits, no demands for payouts or reparation. People simply got on with the job of rebuilding their lives, their homes and businesses. For some time the Pereira family lived near the Hundred Steps in tents provided by the Australians. However, with her husband and four other male members of the Dominic family executed by the

Typical market scene, Sandakan, 2005

Japanese, and several fatherless children to care for, Theresa Pereira could depend on no one – except herself. With proceeds from the sale of the Mile 13 orchard, the property on Leila Road and in town, and other real estate in Jesselton, she built a new house where Rose Cottage had stood, surviving on rations supplied by the Australians. With bricks, cement, corrugated iron, roofing tiles and window glass impossible to obtain, the house was constructed from whatever was at hand; what had always been at hand – bamboo and atap. Before long, Sandakan began to resemble the town that William Pryer had founded, sixty-six years earlier.

It would take years to recover, but over the next few months, slowly but surely, Sandakan's citizens breathed life back into their shattered town. It would never again be the beautiful tropical paradise that had existed pre-war, but it would rise from the ashes to become, in time, a vibrant, multi-cultural community; a tribute to the strength of the human spirit, to the resilience of those who had lost and sacrificed so much, and to those who could still hold out hope for the future.

Chapter 14

Preserving the memories

The immediate post-war period brought a flurry of acknowledgement, with the presentation of war service and campaign medals by the British government to Sabahans who had served with the Volunteers or worked with Australian SOA teams behind enemy lines. Too many of the medals were awarded posthumously. The Kong family were the sad recipients of service medals for Lieutenant Kong Su En, who was also awarded an Honour Scroll in recognition of his sacrifice to King and Country.

Mohamed Tahir, Sini and Peter Lai were among those who received the King's Medal for Courage in the Cause of Freedom. This prestigious award was given to civilians, in recognition of their courage and for risking torture or death to help British service personnel to escape, or for other dangerous activities requiring exceptional bravery. A King's Scout, Sini also received the Scouting Association's highest award for bravery. Others, including Foo Seng Chow, received a King's Commendation for Brave Conduct, a citation with a silver oak-leaf badge, to recognise acts of courage in a non-battle situation. In 1946, Mr Bede Willie and Paddy Funk were among those proudly representing British North Borneo at the Victory Day Parade in London.

MacAlister Blain showed his personal appreciation for Sini's efforts by arranging for him to go to Australia, where he was employed in a bar in Darwin, part of Blain's Northern Territory electorate. However, the experience was not a happy one. A belligerent hotel patron, who had never been a member of the armed services, objected to being served by an Asian and demanded to know why Sini's job had not been given to an unemployed white Australian. Homesick, as well as humiliated, Sini begged to be sent home.

Meanwhile, 1,787 registered parcels, containing war medals of the Australian POWs who had died, were delivered to grieving relatives. Another 641 similar packages were sent out to the families of the British prisoners. It was also announced by the Australian government that the King had conferred a posthumous George Cross for Gallantry on Captain Lionel Matthews.

The pledges made by prisoners to local people who had helped them were also followed up and honoured by the Australian

Sini receiving his King's Medal for Courage

By the KING'S Order the name of
Wo Sing Chow,
Clerk Sandakan,
was placed on record on
18 June, 1947,
as commended for brave conduct.
I am charged to express His Majesty's
high appreciation of the service rendered.

C. R. Attlee

Prime Minister and First Lord
of the Treasury

King's Commendation for Brave Conduct to Wo Sing Chow (Foo Seng Chow)

GVI RI

DIEU ET MON DROIT

This scroll commemorates
Lieutenant Kong Su En
North Borneo Volunteer Force
held in honour as one who
served King and Country in
the world war of 1939-1945
and gave his life to save
mankind from tyranny. May
his sacrifice help to bring
the peace and freedom for
which he died.

Scroll presented by King George VI to the family of Lieutenant Kong Su En

Sini, in his later years, with his medal

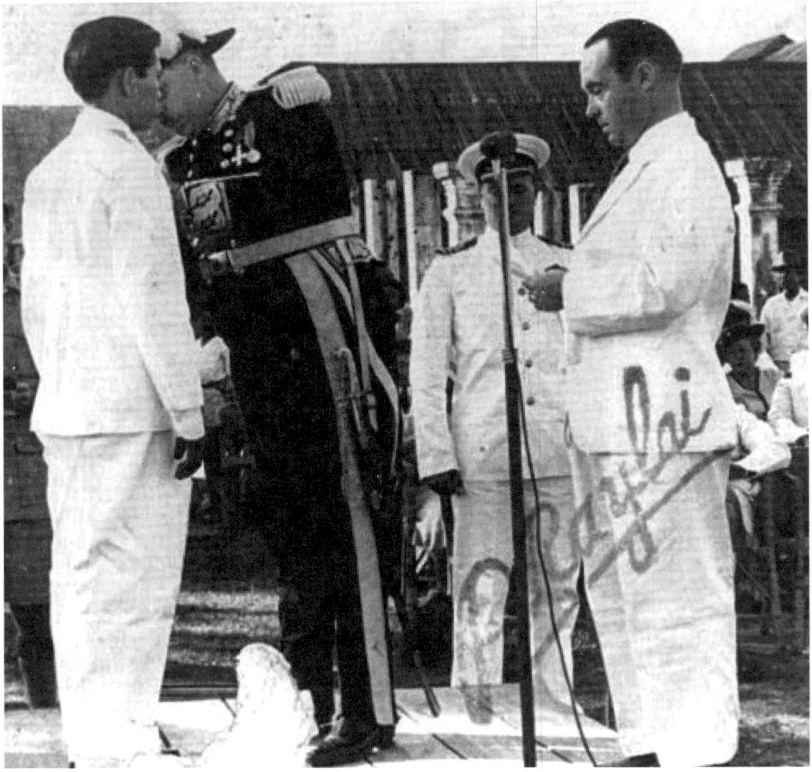

Peter Lai receiving his King's Medal from the Governor

Colonel Harry Jackson

Paddy Funk, who represented Sabah at the Victory Parade, London

government. That many civilians had placed their lives in jeopardy first came to light in early 1946 when villagers, bearing chits and testimonials signed by Australian soldiers, approached members of an Australian war graves recovery team. Following petitions by senior army staff, the Minister for the Army, Frank Forde, agreed to send an experienced officer to investigate the claims.

Towards the end of November that year, Colonel Harry Jackson arrived at a War Graves Unit headquarters at the Menggatal Estate, where he was joined by three other Australians: writer Colin Simpson; Bill MacFarlane, a sound recordist from the Australian Broadcasting Commission; and Major Dyce, currently serving with the British Army. Jackson's first claimant was Andu bin Patrick, formerly a forest scaler at the Experimental Farm, who produced a note from Lieutenant Rus Ewin, stating that he had given food to prisoners. He received $281 in Straits dollars.

On 4 December the four-man team, accompanied by Captain Collins (the war graves officer who had investigated the disappearance of Val Stookes), set off by jeep for Tamparuli, where thirty-five Dusun villagers, hired to carry the supplies, were waiting. It was a slow journey. Two of the party were approaching middle age and all were encumbered with what Collins considered to be an overabundance of gear. After a three-day climb along a narrow and overgrown foot track, passing through Kelawat and Kuang, they reached Denompok, where the footpath joined the main bridle trail leading to Kota Belud. From here it was mainly down hill to Kundasang and a wide, well-worn gravel track leading out of the jungle and into Ranau, where the army officers set up headquarters at the end of the main street, in what had been the District Office. While Collins and Sergeant Roberts, another member of his unit, searched for bodies that might have been previously overlooked, Jackson began interviewing claimants.

News of the reason for his visit had spread quickly. The first to arrive, at 8 am the next day, were Orang Tua Gunting, Barigah, and Barigah's cousin Sumping, all of whom were involved in the rescue of Botterill, Moxham and Short. After MacFarlane recorded their story, Jackson gave them money, medicine and clothing, assuring them that further cash rewards could be collected through the District Office once their claims had been properly processed. On top of the immediate compensation which Jackson was authorised to distribute, Barigah would receive an additional $168 and Gunting $267. With an unskilled labourer earning 60 cents a day, these payouts represented more than a year's wages. The next visitor was Ginssas bin Gangass, who was so badly affected by beriberi that he could hardly walk.

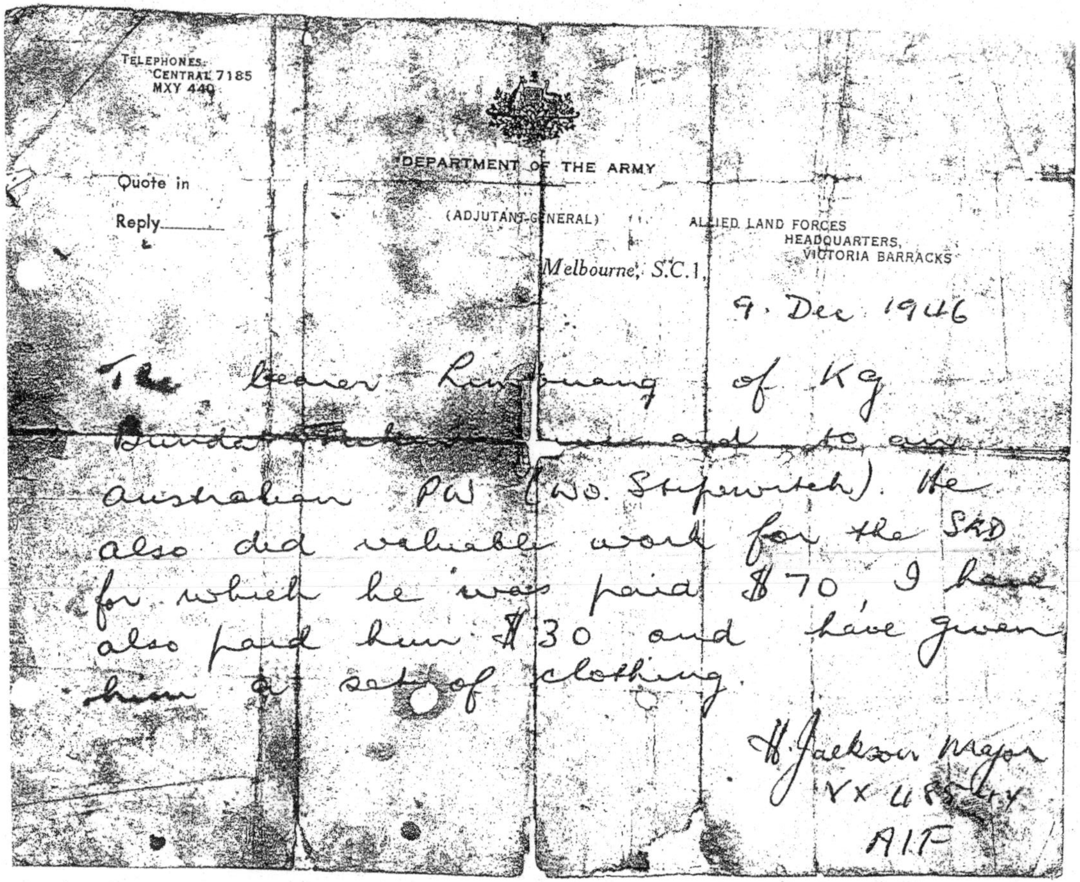
TELEPHONES:
CENTRAL 7185
MXY 440

Quote in
Reply______

DEPARTMENT OF THE ARMY

(ADJUTANT-GENERAL)

ALLIED LAND FORCES
HEADQUARTERS,
VICTORIA BARRACKS

Melbourne, S.C.1,

9. Dec 1946

The bearer Lansuang of Kg
Bundu [illegible] and to an
Australian PW (WO. Stipewitch). He
also did valuable work for the SRD
for which he was paid $70. I have
also paid him $30 and have given
him a set of clothing.

H. Jackson Major
VX 48544
AIF

One of the chit's issued by Jackson to a local helper

He had made the journey from his village on a water buffalo led by his son, who was almost crippled by the large tropical ulcers on his feet. After receiving medical attention and drugs to take home for on-going treatment, the pair made their way painfully back to their village, clutching clothing and a wad of cash as partial compensation to for sheltering Sticpewich and Reither.

Adihil bin Ambilid (Godohil), who had also harboured Sticpewich and Reither, and many others came forward – men, women, and children. Some had walked almost thirty kilometres, scarcely able to believe that the Australians had come so far to honour the promises of dead men. The youngest recipient was eight-year-old Balabiu, and the oldest was Rijan, a very elderly citizen whose exact age was not known. Their stories varied from passing food or money to the prisoners, to hiding them from the Japanese. Jahan, who had Wally Read's wallet, was able to identify the owner from photographs that Jackson showed him, while Pelula, of Kampong Paka, handed over a gold locket with a photograph of a woman inside, given to her in return for five cakes. Pelula did not remember the name of the soldier, aged about thirty, but recalled that he had few upper teeth, grey eyes, and dark brown hair that was inclined to curl. While the villagers were pleased with the gifts and pledges for further compensation, the most exciting news was that they, and anyone else who had helped prisoners of war, were to receive Certificates of Appreciation, which they called 'Letters of Good Name'.

The story told by Tima, who had seen the working parties sent out from the last Ranau camp, was typical of many. Sucking her teeth and shaking her head at the memory, she described the prisoners as 'very thin, weak and sick looking . . . without boots, some without shirts. All had long beards, long hair and walked with bowed heads that swayed from side to side. Whenever they passed, they made signs with their fingers and mouths that they were hungry, and wanted food.'

Not everyone who called came to tell a story or claim compensation. Some simply wanted to say 'hello' and hand over small gifts of food. From Ranau, the team crossed the Liwagu River, spanned by a small bamboo footbridge, to the Number 1 Camp. There was no sign of any previous habitation, but Jackson easily identified the site by the piles of disturbed earth marking recently exhumed graves. Crossing the airstrip the villagers had repaired, now completely overgrown with metre-high grass, they edged carefully along a log bridge spanning the river on the far side of the plain, to begin the steep ascent up and over Marakau Hill. On reaching Muruk, they rested beneath a large shady tree on the banks of the Kenanapan River, near the place where

Jackson with Mrs Abin and her daughter

Jackson and MacFarlane with 9-year-old Balabiu

Domima binte OKK Akui, 2008

Halima binte Binting, widow of Matusup bin Gungau, and her baby

Halima binte Amat, widow of Wong Mu Sing

the prisoners had stopped overnight. About ten metres away, on the far side of the stream, were the remains of one of the 'comfort women' who had accompanied the Japanese troops from Sandakan. Plagued by battalions of leeches, the group pushed on towards Segindai, at the junction of the Bulantu and Kuanan (Liwagu) Rivers.

It was relatively easy going to Paginatan, where they met Bureh, called 'Mumma' by the hungry prisoners she had fed. Her husband had died of malnutrition shortly after the column had passed by, leaving her and their small daughter to fend for themselves. She and the village headman were rewarded, but the role played by his young daughter Domima would not emerge until 2005, when she told her story to historian Lynette Silver. While at Paginatan, Jackson also interviewed Hussin and Onsi, who had been fetched from Telupid, over sixty kilometres away, by a police boy. The pair confirmed it was impossible to move east along the track beyond Telupid owing to monsoonal flooding so, with no villages between Paginatan and Telupid, the team returned to Jesselton, where a boat would take them to Sandakan. On their way through Ranau, Jackson spent a further two days interviewing many more people, bringing the total number rewarded to forty-eight.

After delivering a report to Richard Evans in Jesselton, Jackson interviewed the widows of Matusup and Wong Mu Sing, executed at Kuching. Twenty-three year old Halima binte Binting, Matusup's widow, was now living in a kampong near Batu Tiga Gaol, where her brother, a rubber tapper, provided for her and their elderly mother from a wage of 80 cents a day. Their baby, just ten days old when Matusup was arrested, had died at the age of two. Halima binte Amat, Mu Sing's widow, was supporting herself by working at the Jesselton home of a Chinese family in return for her keep.

That night, another survivor from the Sandakan Incident, wearing highly polished boots, a dashing scarlet sash and a grey serge forage-cap, all of which proclaimed him to be a member of the North Borneo Armed Constabulary, arrived on Jackson's doorstep. He was Sergeant Koram bin Andaur, the former conspirator, escapee, saboteur, Japanese census taker, guerrilla fighter and SOA operative, who had more lives than a cat.

* * * * * * *

Following the Double Tenth rebellion, Koram had become ill and returned to his father's house in Pensiangan, just before the purge that had wiped out most of the Kinabalu Guerrillas. As soon as he recovered, he reported to the nearest Japanese HQ to 'confess' that he had helped eight POWs escape from Berhala Island and, by way of apology, offered himself as a spy. Within days he was on a plane to Sandakan. After fifteen days' leave, granted by his new employers, he began the task of tracking the fugitives who, he assured the kempeitai, had not left the country. Six months later he was back in Sandakan, after completing a round trip from one side of Borneo to the other, including the major Japanese troop centres at Ranau, Keningau, Beaufort and Jesselton. Reporting that he had found no trace of the missing men, he offered to continue the search, this time to the south. Unaware that Koram was busily sketching enemy installations and collecting information on the movement of troops, the kempeitai agreed. However, Koram had no hope of getting away with this trickery indefinitely. On 1 May 1945 he was betrayed to the kempeitai at the Segama Estate, near Lahad Datu, and arrested.

Five days later he escaped, fleeing across the Sibutu Channel to Tawi Tawi and taking his precious sketches, dossiers and reports with him. After being interviewed by Suarez, he was sent to Morotai, where he formally joined the ranks of SOA as a sergeant, was given a secret number (AK 470) and assigned to Agas 4. From mid-July until 13 October 1945, he worked with Rex Blow, gathering intelligence, extracting civilians from Mostyn and Mas, and searching for an Australian airman who had parachuted into the Semporna area. He also participated in the evacuation of Dr Blaauw, the Chinese medical practitioner from Kudat, whom local agents reported was being harassed by the Japanese in Mostyn. And now, here Koram was again, proudly wearing his sergeant's stripes, to which would be added several war and bravery medals, and an MBE from His Majesty King George VI, in recognition of Koram's loyalty and service to the Empire.

* * * * * *

On the night of 25 December, Christmas Day, Jackson and the team sailed on SS *Darval* for Sandakan. They stopped off at Kudat, where Johnny Funk, now working for the local PWD, was waiting on the wharf to meet them. Although still having trouble with his broken jaw, and with eyesight not completely restored, he had prepared a lengthy statement with details of the various roles played by members of the underground. As his health was not good, he decided to take out his reward in the form of hospital treatment in Singapore, plus travelling and accommodation expenses.

Back on board ship, Jackson interviewed three passengers, all of whom were connected to the assistance group: Chan Tian Joo, Lau Bui Ching and Francis Heng, brother of Heng Joo Ming. Arriving at Sandakan three days later, Jackson went immediately to War Graves Unit HQ at the Experimental Farm, where he discovered that his arrival had been well publicised, with posters in English, Malay and Chinese displayed all round the district. The first claimants were sisters Maggie Funk and Katherine Lagan, widows of Alex and Ernesto, followed by Heng's girlfriend Siti binte Jakariah, and Sini. Jackson was distressed to find that Katherine had suffered a nervous breakdown. Turned loose in the jungle to cope as best she could after Ernesto was taken away, she had lost her reason completely when he did not return and was now living in a tumble-down hut with her four children, her widowed mother, four younger sisters and a brother. She spent her days cowering in a darkened corner, her clothes filthy and her feet bare. Her only response to Jackson's compassionate questions was a sigh or a giggle.

From Sandakan the team went by boat to Beluran to meet Kulang, and to then to Muanad and Sapi, where they located the villagers who had helped Braithwaite and Campbell. An outraged Jackson also visited Sergeant-Major Yangsalang, languishing miserably in gaol, noting in his official report the miscarriage of justice that had occurred and the glaring inconsistencies between sentences handed out to Jackie Lo Ah Fuh and the unfortunate policeman. After a short walk along the track from Mile 11 and an inspection of the overgrown POW camp sites, the Australians left for Jesselton and home: Simpson and MacFarlane with enough material for a radio documentary and Jackson with a swag of recommendations.

The Australian government honoured his promises: 22 Certificates of Appreciation; 58 demands for cash; 67 monetary rewards totalling almost $37,000; and pensions to the widows of all those executed and those who had died in gaol. The lump sums ranged from $5650 for Katherine Lagan, who had four children to support, to $2150 for Halima binte Amat and Halima binte Binting, who had no dependants. Rewards for assistance varied from $15 to Gumbaiu, of Kampong Kaporing, who took food to Sticpewich and Reither, to the Goh brothers, who received around $900 for harbouring the escapees at near Mile 11. Civilians gaoled for their underground activities received in excess of $600 each. As the police had their own pension system, they and their dependants were not eligible for compensation from the Australian government. On the advice of Richard Evans, who was concerned that relatives would sponge off the widows and

The children of Ernesto Lagan

Chang Siew Ha, widow of Soh Kim Seng, and her children

Jackson with local helpers at Sapi

Jackson rewarding a helper at Sapi

Jackson (second right) in 1950, on his return visit. Kulang is far left

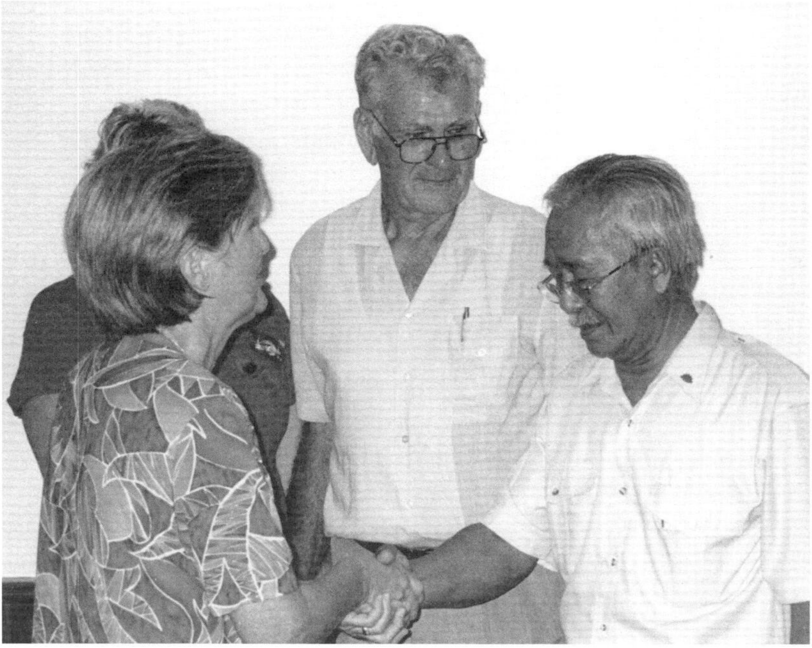

Kulang's son, Tuan Haji Kangawan Kulang, with the author and Jack Carter, brother of POW Perc Carter, who had given Kulang a photograph for safe-keeping as the POW column passed by

leave them penniless, their lump sum money was paid in the form of a monthly pension. Paddy Funk, who had been beaten up and sentenced to six-years' imprisonment wanted no reward or compensation. Like his brother Johnny, all he asked for, and received, was $500 to help with medicines and medical treatment. [for a full list of payments, see Honour Roll]

Certificates of Appreciation were also given to the many local people who had joined the guerrillas or served directly with SOA, all of whom had been paid a salary of $75 a month by the Australian army. In addition, Daiman bin Barano, an SOA runner who was wounded in 1943 and was still on crutches, received a lump-sum pension of $2150. To make sure that the payments were getting through, and to check on the recipients' well-being, in 1950 Jackson returned to Sabah, where, on discovering that Mu Sing had a son from a previous marriage, he organised a trust fund of $1525 to pay for his education.

Jackson's report on his 'Borneo Mission', compiled from scores of interviews with local people and survivors, was released in August 1947 and covered 88 closely typewritten pages. The original draft, which included details not appearing in the official version, covered even more. Although his official account was far more emotive and detailed than anything previously published in the Australian newspapers, its circulation was limited and it contained nothing new regarding the actual fate of the prisoners of war. Any information at all was virtually impossible to obtain: the Australian government had decided to 'protect' POW families, believing that details of what had happened to the prisoners would only add to the relatives' sorrow and suffering. Consequently, with SOA's hierarchy desperate to keep the truth about the rescue debacle from leaking out to anyone, least of all the press, the Sandakan story soon became enmeshed in a conspiracy of silence.

There was no enquiry into the loss of the Sandakan prisoners, let alone the reasons for the failure of Operation Kingfisher. By the end of 1945, this mission no longer officially existed, all mention of it having been expunged from SOA's compiled, but unpublished, official history. When questions were finally asked by one of the paratroopers in 1947, Australia's General Blamey, to whom SOA had been answerable, deliberately suppressed the truth by claiming that it was all General MacArthur's fault. According to Blamey, just as the paratroopers were about to launch their rescue mission, the American General refused to supply the necessary aircraft, resulting in the cancellation of Operation Kingfisher. With all paperwork to prove otherwise locked away under a thirty-year secrecy ban, it was not until 1998, with the release of the book *Sandakan A Conspiracy of Silence*, that this lie was finally exposed. When the work of the recovery, inquiry and war crimes teams was finally over, their mountain of paperwork was also filed away in government archives. With no way of gaining access to any details, the relatives of the POWs had to make do with whatever they had: small, pathetic piles of mementos; fading photographs and precious letters sent home before Singapore's fall; brief, impersonal postcards from the POW camp, some of which were delivered long after the sender was dead; a few yellowing news clippings and, for the luckier ones, relics recovered from the camps which could be identified to an individual owner. The grieving Australian relatives certainly had no idea that, in Borneo, families struggling to begin their lives all over again were also mourning the loss of their menfolk.

Once the payments had been made and the certificates distributed, Australian officialdom forgot all about the people of Sandakan for the best part of fifty years. A proposal put forward by MacAlister Blain in Australia in 1947 to construct some kind of memorial was considered, but nothing came of it, probably because the British had already erected a memorial in Sandakan in September the previous year. Honouring the estimated 280 local people who had died at the hands of the Japanese, it was unveiled by the Governor General of Malaya and British North Borneo, Malcolm McDonald.

Hollywood then became involved, with a black-and-white movie entitled *Three Came Home*, a story of survival under the Japanese, based on Agnes Keith's best-selling book of the same name. Actress Claudette Colbert, who landed the role of Agnes, refused to put foot in Borneo, so Lillian Funk was hired as a stand-in for the film star for scenes that were shot on location in Sandakan.

It was Lillian's husband Johnny who was responsible for a memorial to honour the thirteen members of the underground who had either been executed or died in gaol. Unable to obtain any support from the British government, Johnny raised the $2180 needed for a large marble slab placed over the mass grave in Kuching, where they had been reburied. On it are inscribed their names and the words:

> *In memory of the eight gallant men of all races who, loyal to the cause of freedom, rendered assistance to Allied prisoners of war at Sandakan camp, and were executed in Kuching on March 2, 1944, and also the five who died in prison for the same cause.*

A few years after the war ended, the local Chinese Chamber of Commerce erected a large commemorative stone at the entrance to the Chinese Cemetery in Sandakan, where the bodies of those executed on 27 May 1945 had been reburied by Australian soldiers. A substantial memorial was also unveiled at Petagas, to remember Albert Kwok and his men, killed or executed as a result of the Double Tenth uprising. However, it was not until the early 1960s that a memorial to honour **all** those who died in Sabah became reality. Built on a small hill in the village of Kundasang, this project was the result of several years of effort by a New Zealander, SOA's Major G S 'Toby' Carter. Horrified to discover at the cessation of hostilities that so many had died in Sabah, while he was in Sarawak taking part in what he considered to be an interesting war, Carter had begun a campaign in the late 1950s to establish a memorial to all those who had suffered and died at the hands of the Japanese. With the general public having little idea of what had occurred during the war years, the reaction to Carter's proposal was one of general apathy. However, after a great deal of lobbying and fund-raising, which included exerting considerable pressure on the British and Australian governments, the Kundasang War Memorial Gardens were dedicated to the memory of the Sabah, British and Australian war dead.

Unfortunately, there were problems with the provisions put in place to maintain the memorial, which covered a large area and was spread over four levels. Although the Sabah government injected some $500,000 into the refurbishment of the memorial in 1995, by 2004 the entire complex had been reduced to a virtual ruin by years of neglect, exacerbated by acts of vandalism. However, before it deteriorated beyond salvation, Mr Sevee Charuruks of Kota Kinabalu undertook its restoration as a retirement project. Six years later, it is a showpiece, its crumbling walls, dilapidated architectural features and weed-choked gardens lovingly and carefully restored to a state which far surpasses their original glory. The beautifully landscaped gardens, each with its distinctive national focus, are a magnificent tribute to all who lost their lives. In recognition of the importance of Mr Charuruk's work, the Australian government has provided substantial financial support and presented him

Sevee Charuruks

The Pool of Contemplation, Kundasang War Memorial

with a Certificate of Appreciation, while the British government has honoured his efforts with an MBE.

Gort Chester was also honoured: by the British with a Distinguished Service Order (DSO) and Order of the British Empire (OBE), and by the United States with a Medal of Freedom. He survived the war and was apparently setting up business again in Tawau, his last recorded address, when ill health sent him to seek medical treatment in Jesselton, where he died in August 1946 at the age of 47. His grave in the old European Cemetery in Kota Kinabalu is marked by a granite headstone erected by his friend Nick Combe, who also selected the epitaph: 'Pioneer of Victory in Borneo, 1943-45 And a Most lovable Man'. His death was regarded by the British Army as 'civilian' until 2005, when historian Lynette Silver and Michael Chin, a resident of Kota Kinabalu, located sufficient documentary evidence to prove that he had died in Jesselton Hospital from blackwater fever: a complication of the malaria he had contracted while on the run with Python. In 2006 the Commonwealth War Graves Commission accepted that his death was war-related and added him to their official records. His rank was also raised from major to lieutenant-colonel, his temporary rank at the time of his death.

Headstones for Stookes and his three European companions are also in this cemetery. Their bodies were never found, so the four headstones serve as memorial markers. All five men are commemorated at Keningau where a large memorial, funded by the Chinese Chambers of Commerce, the governments of Sarawak and British North Borneo, and relatives of the deceased, was erected near the airport.

The efforts of other Sabahans to preserve the memory and sacrifice of prisoners of war has been considerable. In 2004, two local women walked along the east–west highway linking Sandakan to Kota Kinabalu (Jesselton) to raise awareness of the Sandakan story, a tribute followed up by members of the Sabah Society and others, who marched from Sandakan to Ranau in August 2005. Six months later, trekking specialist Tham Yau Kong, and his team of Dusun jungle experts, joined forces with Lynette Silver to retrace and open up the last section of the original route cut by Willie and Kanak, from Bauto to the Last Camp at Ranau, much of which had been 'lost' for six decades. In early 2008, while exploring the river in the vicinity of the Last Camp, Tham met the owner of the land, Dr Othman Minudin. On learning of the site's historical significance, Othman and his wife, Dr Lungkiam binte Dambul, rejected overtures by the Malaysian Government to buy it for a substantial sum of money, generously

Keningau Memorial

Memorial to those executed on 27 May 1945, Sandakan

Tham Yau Kong

Double Tenth Memorial at Petagas

Heroes' Grave, Kuching

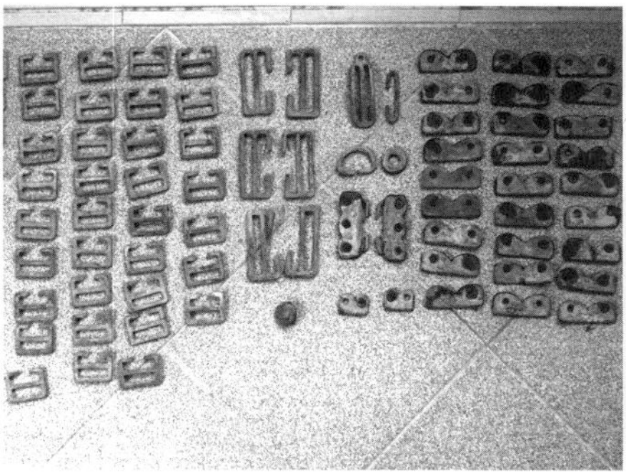

The brass items buried by POWs at the Last Camp, Ranau

Neil and Lynette Silver with helper, Benedict, following the discovery of the POW cache

Brass webbing fittings and the button

offering to put aside a large portion of the land as a memorial park in perpetuity. Using money raised through Lynette Silver and Tham Yau Kong, they co-ordinated the erection of a rock-and-granite memorial, funded by trekkers and relatives of the POWs who had died there.

In August 2008, while working on this project with Othman, Lungkiam and Tham, Lynette and her husband Neil located and uncovered many relics, including the cache of brass fittings and the tunic button buried by the POWs sixty-three years previously. The resultant publicity, generated by a series of on-going articles by journalist Kan Yau Kong in Sabah's *Daily Express*, greatly raised the profile of the Sandakan story, and the importance of the Last Camp site in particular. The press coverage also helped to ensure a large crowd of local people joined POW relatives to witness the unveiling of the memorial by Datuk Masidi Manjun (Sabah's Minister for Tourism, Culture and Environment), Lynette Silver and Dr Othman on 27 August 2009 – exactly 64 years after massacre of the last fifteen prisoners of war.

Neil Silver, Lynette Silver, Dr Lungkiam, Dr Othman and Tham Yau Kong at the Last Camp Memorial, 2008

With the Last Camp Memorial marking the end of the death marches now in place, and with funding from the Sabah and Australian Governments to help preserve the site, the original owners have taken on the responsibility for further improvements: a bamboo and atap hut where the original POW hut stood and a commemorative pavilion alongside the commemorative area, to educate the public and to display the relics recovered, including makeshift weapons that the prisoners had hidden among the roots of the large tree.

Not far from Ranau is the village of Nalapak, where the management of Sabah Tea Gardens has completed two memorial projects honouring individual Australians with special connections to the area. The first, in 2007, was to name a hill for an Australian POW, Alan Quailey, who died at this spot while on the first death march. A commemorative area was also created, featuring a large rock, to which a granite memorial tablet explaining the site's significance has been secured, along with visual material. The second initiative was to name one of the Estate's tourist accommodation cottages in honour of John 'Lofty' Hodges who, after rescuing Botterill, Moxham and Short, helped nurse them back to health at their base at nearby Silad. The cottage was officially named on 27 April 2010 in a special ceremony, attended by Lofty's son Ken, relatives of Australian POWs, local people and dignitaries.

Although numerous private and public memorials have been erected in Australia and England since the late 1980s, all focus entirely on POWs. The first memorial to acknowledge the sacrifice of local people is at Ranau, where there is a cairn of river rocks, funded by an Australian ex-service organisation, close to the site where Australian POW Neil Cleary died. Often erroneously referred to as the 'Cleary Memorial', the Ranau Memorial was unveiled in 1985.

On the other side of the Ranau plain, at Marakau village, is the grave of Adihil bin Ambilid, who died in 1997 at the age of 104. The following year, the Australian army recognised his bravery in

Quailey's Hill Memorial, Sabah Tea plantation

The Sandakan Memorial

caring for Sticpewich and Reither by unveiling a brass plaque to his memory. Barigah lies in a far more modest grave at his village.

The Sandakan Memorial Park, developed and maintained with funds supplied by the Australian Government, opened in March 1999. The inscription on the memorial, written in English and Malay, enshrines the memory of all who suffered and died at Sandakan, Ranau and on the death marches. However, as the Park occupies part of the of the original B Force compound at the Mile 8 camp, it is generally regarded locally not only as a purely POW memorial, but also as an Australian one; a perception reinforced on the day the Park was opened, when the presence of Joseph Wong and Sini, two of the central figures of the Sandakan underground, was not officially acknowledged.

This unfortunate beginning, which attracted adverse local criticism, has been countered to some extent by the Sabah Tourism Board and the Sandakan Municipal Council, which initiated a Sandakan Day commemoration in 2003. The first service was held at the Park in late May that year, but the date was subsequently changed at Lynette Silver's suggestion to 15 August – the anniversary of Japan's surrender in 1945 and the execution of Sandakan's last prisoner of war. The service, organised by the Council, is supported by local community and service organisations, as well as the Australian Government, and attracts a growing number of visitors from Australia.

However, the greatest tribute to the people of Sabah has not come from any government or organisation but from relatives and friends of the prisoners of war and ordinary Australian citizens. Apart from donating almost RM 500,000 ($170,000 Australian) to commission and install stained glass Windows of Remembrance and Friendship Windows in St Michael's Church, these benefactors are the sole source of income for the Sandakan Memorial Scholarship Scheme, a 'living memorial' established in 2005 by the Silvers to help educate talented but underprivileged students from remote Kadazandusun villages. People from this ethnic group provided food and shelter for the prisoners on the death marches and at Ranau. (Details of these two projects, and the Last Camp Memorial are available on www.lynettesilver.com.) Since 2005, several documentaries have been made on the stained glass windows and the Sandakan Track, all of which have helped raised the profile of the Sandakan story.

Although the year 2010 marks the 65th anniversary of the end of World War II and the liberation of Sabah from occupying forces, the scars left on members of local and POW families remain very much in evidence. That many folk are still trying to come to terms with this tragedy, more than sixty years on, is demonstrated by increasing numbers of people who attend the Anzac Day and Sandakan Day commemorations held at the Sandakan Memorial, undertake treks along the Sandakan Track, and flock to view the stained glass windows. For some, the passage of time has not lessened their sense of loss: the hurt and pain run far too deep. While the wounds are less raw for others, the many people profoundly affected by the events of 1942–45 can take comfort in the knowledge that, although Sabah was a place of immense suffering during the Japanese occupation, it also produced some of World War II's finest heroes.

Epilogue

Lest we ever forget

St Michael's Church, Sandakan
24 April 2008

It is late afternoon on the eve of Anzac Day, the day put aside each year by Australians all over the world to remember their war dead. However, a low buzz of excited anticipation runs through the crowd packed into this heritage stone church, for today is not one of solemn reflection, but of joy. Relatives of the prisoners of war and the people of Sandakan are here to celebrate a very special friendship; forged by men of different races, colours and creeds in the darkest days of World War II. This is a friendship sealed in blood – the unbreakable bond of blood brothers. It is a priceless legacy, and one that soon will be commemorated by the unveiling of two beautiful stained-glass Friendship Windows, set above the north and south doors.

It is fitting that the only building still standing that has any connection to the prisoners of war is the focus of today's events. The significance is not lost on the POW relatives, for St Michael's has changed very little since 1942 or, indeed, in the past 100 years. The governor in his ostrich-plumed hat no longer graces the vice-regal pew, but the metal clips that held his official standards are still in place. So is the altar where Bert Walker and his bride made their vows at 'the wedding of the decade' in 1929; the pulpit where countless sermons have been preached; and the stone font where Bert's daughter Pauline was baptised. Apart from various concessions to creature comforts, it is almost as if time has stood still, were it not for one outstanding new feature – the magnificent stained-glass Windows of Remembrance.

Unveiled in 2005 at an equally impressive ceremony, the windows are not simply a memorial to the prisoners who perished at Sandakan, Ranau or on the death marches. They are also, most importantly, a thanksgiving to the people of Sabah who risked, and gave, their lives to help them. The reaction from the local community to this gift, funded entirely by families and friends of the prisoners of war, was overwhelming. It had been sixty years since Harry Jackson's visit: sixty years since anyone had bothered to say 'thank you'.

Flag parade, unveiling of Friendship Windows

Melvyn Funk, flag bearer for Sabah

The 'Friendship' panel, stained glass window

Neil and Lynette Silver present a Plaque of Appreciation to Kaingal

Sabah Heroes. Domima, Justina Chin (representing her father, Sini) and Kaingal

Many of the donors, now seated in St Michael's Church on this warm April afternoon, have now travelled many thousands of kilometres to express their gratitude to the people of Sabah. Such overtures would have been made many years ago had the story been more widely known, but it is only recently that they have discovered that the tragedy of Sandakan's POWs is one they share with local people. They understand only too well the sorrow of a child deprived of the love and support of a father, and the feelings of helplessness of a widow left to struggle on alone. They know the heartache of waiting for news; of clinging to hope when all else has gone; of the emptiness when the inevitable must finally be accepted. However, the belated discovery that they are not alone, and that they are part of a much wider 'Sandakan family', has been a liberating and rewarding experience for most.

The people of three nations, split asunder by war, are now united in a common bond. It is time to look to the future, to celebrate the ties that bind. The organ music swells to a crescendo and the congregation stands as the clergy, robed in crimson and gold, move slowly down the aisle, followed by visiting and local people, proudly bearing the flags of Malaysia, Australia, Great Britain and Sabah. After representatives of all three countries unveil the windows, and young Kadazandusuns perform traditional dances of celebration, a leather-bound Book of

Friendship is presented to the people of Sabah. Enshrining the names of those known to have helped the prisoners, it will be displayed in the POW Chapel at the rear of the church, on a marble-topped Table of Honour, inscribed with the immortal words of the great English poet, Lord Byron.

For there are deeds that should not pass away,
and names that must not be forgotten.

The focus now shifts from the general to the specific, as Plaques of Appreciation are presented to three of Sabah's finest heroes: Domima who, as a twelve-year old girl, left food for the six starving prisoners at Paginatan; Kaingal, who helped save the lives of three of the escapees at Ranau; and Sini, the Boy Scout who put his duty to his King, his country and his fellow man above all else, and was awarded two medals for his outstanding bravery.

Dignified and unassuming, these three elderly people are the last remaining survivors of the many Sabahans who so willingly and selflessly extended the hand of friendship to strangers in distress. As their names are announced, the entire congregation rises to its feet, in thunderous and spontaneous applause.

Brotherly love knows no limit to its endurance, no end to its trust.
Brotherly love still stands when all else has fallen.

Heroes' Roll

Note: the spelling of some names varies from document to document

Sandakan Underground

Arrested at Sandakan, not tried:
Koram bin Andaur, Corporal (escaped)
Mananai, Puloro (tortured and released)
Wong Yun Siew (released after feigning insanity)

Arrested and tried at Kuching

Shot by firing squad (2/3/1944):
Abin, Sergeant
Azcona, Felix Junior
Funk, Alexander
Heng Joo Ming
Lagan, Ernesto
Matusup bin Gungau
Singh (Mannan), Jemadar Ojagar
Wong Mu Sing

Sent to Outram Road Gaol, Singapore:

Mavor, Gerald	15 years
Taylor, Dr James	15 years

Imprisoned in Kuching:

Allan, D R	1 year
Amat	1 year
Amigau bin Hassan	8 years
Apostol, Lamberto	10 years
Aruliah, Samuel	3 years
Chan Ping (Ah Ping)	4 years
Chan Tian Joo	6 years
Chang, Henry Ting Kiang	6 years
Chin Chee Kong	8 years
(Edmund Kong, Chin Piang Syn/Sini)	

Damudaran, Mr M	15 years
Foo Seng Chow	5 years
Funk, John Simon Jr (Johnny)	4 years
Funk, Patrick H	6 years
Goh Tiek Soong (Teck Sing)	1 year
Goh Tiek Tshi (Teck Chai)	1 year
Gorokon, Police Constable	4 years
Guriaman, Inspector Samuel	8 years
Jakariah	5 years
Kai, Police Constable	1 year
Kassim bin Jumadi	2 years
Kassiu, Police Constable	6 years
Laband, Dr J F	1 year
Lai, 'Peter Raymond' Kui Fook	12 years
Lau Bui Cheng (Bueh Ching)	2.5 years
Leong, Peter	7 years
Lumatop, Police Constable	4 years
Majinal, Dick	7 years
Mavor, Gerald	15 years
Mohamet Salleh bin Madang	12 years
Ng Ho Kong	10 years
Ngui Ah Kui	2.5 years
Phillips, A E	3 years
Raymond, Peter (see Lai)	
Sastroh	2 years
Sidek bin Simoen	5 years
Soh Kim Seng (Ah Tu)	8 years
Surat Min bin Jumadi	2 years
Tahir, Police Constable Mohamed	3 years
Tang, Felix	4 years
Yangsalang, Sergeant-Major	15 years
Yong Cha Ming	10 months
Yusup (Yusof/Usop) Basinau, Jemadar	15 years

Died in Outram Road Goal:
Mavor, Gerald (5/5/1945)

Died in Kuching Gaol:
Amigau bin Hassan
Kassim bin Jumadi
Kassiu, Police Constable

Sastroh
Sidek bin Simoen
Soh Kim Seng (Ah Tu)

Fined:

Cohen, Mrs Moselle Y	(later killed)
Hu Li Tsia	$50
Khoo Siek Choo	$1000
Kwan Choo Ming	$2000
Kwan Ming Ming	$1000
Lo Hoi Chee	$2000
Wong Wee Ming	$2000
Yan Sec Chan	$1000

Escaped from Kuching Gaol:
Surat Min bin Jumadi

Escaped from penal servitude:
Funk, Paddy

Civilian executions

Executed at Mile 1.5, 27 May 1945:
Chan Tak Wah (clerk, Harrison and Crosfield)
Chan, Thomas (former Chinese Consulate staff, firewood merchant)
Chong Wai Cho (Basel Church school teacher, Editor Sandakan Chinese Overseas Daily)
Dominic, Pongolo Stanislaus (retired Deputy Assistant Commissioner of Customs)
Fung Bak Ming (member, China relief Fund)
Fung Shong Kong (Chief Clerk, Finance Commissioner)
Funk, Alfred (Partner, Funk and Sons)
George, K A (Inspector, Sandakan Sanitary Board)
Ho Shu Fah (Merchant, member of China Relief Fund)
Jappar (trader)
Khoo Kim Cheng [Yau Kam Chung] (Chip Loong & Co, Chairman of China Relief Fund)
Kong Su En, Lieutenant (Chief Clerk and BNB Volunteer Force)
Kong Su Leong (wireless operator)
Kwan Lok Ming (Man Woo Loong & Co, Chairman, Chinese Chamber of Commerce)

Kwan Yun Hin (Member of Legislative Council, partner of Man Woo Loong & Co)
Lee Seng Lok (trader)
Lew Kew Chong
Linck, Mrs (wife of German doctor)
Lee Sah Che, Dr (Japanese language censor, Chungking news)
Ng Shea Wah (member, China Relief Fund)
Ng Tai Yong (building contractor)
Pang Thau Fen (Government clerk)
Patel, M S (pharmacist, Manager Sandakan Dispensary)
Tam (wireless operator)
Tao, Stella (Chinese school teacher from Shanghai)
Voon Thau Yin (teacher, St Michael's School)
Voon Yin Chong (Chief Clerk, Public Works Department)
Unidentified Indian (doctor)

Executed at Mile 17, 28 May 1945:
Foo Chi Ming
Pereira, Andrew
Watson, Richard

Shot by Hosotani Naoji at Mile 1.5, 27 May 1945:
Sui Chong
Ten Pek

Others:
one unidentified Chinese at Mile 1, early June 1945
two unidentified Chinese at Mile 9, June 1945

Others who helped:

The following people are known to have helped prisoners of war at Sandakan, Ranau or on the death marches, or to have served with Australians who were operating behind the lines

Abbott, Mr
Abdullah bin Giter
Abing bin Luma of Sapi
Abu Bakar Tan
Adihil (Godohil) bin Ambilid, of Samaang
Ajak, Headman Andong
Akui, Headman of Paginatan

Ali, Mandor, Police Constable
Ali bin Salleh, Sergeant,
Aluidin bin Abin, of Sapi
Ambiau, of Muanad
Ambrose Dumpagnol (Samuel Dumpugnol Ambrose)
Amir, of Ranau
Amit of Sapi
Ampun, PC 596
Andu bin Patrick
Ansangan, of Ranau district
Apuk
Aruliah, Samuel
Asadi bin Ajan
Atayde, Pascual
Aubin, of Ranau area
Ayuh (Dusun mandor)
Azcona, Felix Snr
Balinti, of Ranau
Barigah Katus, Headman of Batu Lima
Batingi of Ganagana
Bauto's headman
Bazan, Tagima Theresa (formerly Mrs Azcona)
Bintang binte Udung (Mrs Abin)
Brown, Mr G
Buang bin Saban
Buang of Sapi
Burih of Paginatan
Cha Chin Nam
Chan Tian Joo
Chang Siew Ha (widow of Soh Kim Seng)
Chin Ah Tak, Kapitan Cina of Ranau
Chew, Leonard Thiam Boon
Chin Kin Choi of Mile 15.5
Chin, brother of Kin Choi
Chin Sang, Secret Agent
Choi Hee and Family
Chong Kwey
Chow, Henry Fook On
Chow Yee Soo
Chu Li Tsia
Cohen, Mrs Moselle
Dahlan, of NBT Coy

Daiman bin Barag, Secret Agent
Deekee, Richard of NBT Coy
Dewa, Secret Agent
Domima binte OKK Akui
Foo Seng Chow
Funk, Dimitiria (Dimit) Macaria Mananai
Funk, Helen Cecilia
Funk, John Simon Snr
Funk, Lillian Rose
Funk, Magdalena (Maggie)
Galitang, of Ranau
Galunting, of Muanad
Gambaiu, of Ranau
Gangau, of Ranau district
Gantuang, Police Constable, of Ranau
Ganung, of Ranau
Gapar bin Lalil, Secret Agent
Geronsi, of Ranau district
Gesikin of Ranau
Ghani bin Akub
Gileh (Dusun mandor)
Gilenki of Lansat
Gilintang, school teacher of Ranau
Gilong of Ranau
Ginsising, school teacher of Ranau
Ginssas bin Gangass
Go To Sang
Gontamas of Ranau
Gopakau of Ranau
Guak, of Bundu Tuhan
Guak, farmer of Kaparingan
Gumbaron villagers
Gundi, Headman of Tapaan
Gunting, Headman of Batu Lima
Halima binte Amut
Halima binte Binting
Harima binte Amat
Hassan bin Sirajan
Hikandoa, of Ranau
Ho Ah Lee, of Bongawan
Hosina
Hussin bin Ulan, of Telupid

Ikul, of Ranau area
Ingurru of Ranau
Ishmael bin Inshe, Police Constable and Secret Agent
Ismail bin Awang Raman, of NBT Coy
Jahil, PC249
Jaimi, Edmund of Ranau Government Station
Jaimi bin Ginsund
Jakarullah Korludin
James, Andrew, Dresser of Ranau
Jamin, of Ranau area
Janan, of Matang
Jenny bin Sarudin
Jones, Arthur, of Mile 11
Jonit, Police Constable
Kabairu, of Ranau
Kai, Police Constable
Kaingal (see Suamin bin Gadalip)
Kalbin bin Mait
Kalindai, of Ranau
Kambatang, of Kandowai-an
Kanak of Muanad
Kangas, of Gana Gana
Kanon bin Garfu, Secret Agent
Kantong, of Batu Lima
Kassim bin Jumadi
Kasui, Police Constable
Katus, Baregah, Headman of Batu Lima
Keith, Agnes
Keith, Harry
Kemansi villagers
Khalid, Secret Agent
Khoo Heng Hong
Khoo Siek Chiew
Kimin bin Magador, of Ranau District
Kulang, Headman of Muanad
Kuniwau
Kuting Main, of NBT Coy
Laduma (Ladooma), of Batu Lima
Lagan, Katherine (Kathleen) E
Lai, Gabriela
Lai, Phoebe
Laidlaw, Dr A

Laip, of Muanad
Lasa
Latif bin Ahmad, Secret Agent
Lewah binte Mandalus
Limbaan bin Kumporo (Zimban/Gimbalan)
Liminggo, Police Constable, of Ranau
Liu, Mabel
Liu Tse Shia, Dr
Lo Hoi Tshi
Low, Richard
Magador, of Batu Lima
Main of NBT Coy
Mananai, Agnes Batai
Mananai, Puolo (Flores)
Manoulong (Mangalong), of Sapi
Mansia, of Ranau
Manso, Haji
Matang village, near Ranau
Mavor, Mrs
Mentod, Police Constable (guerrilla)
Merasin, headman of Melinsau
Mohamet Salleh Salunti bin Madang, of Sinarut
Mohamed Tassim, of NBT Coy
Mohommed Salleh
Mumian, Headman
Munjong bin Yahya
Mustapha bin Datu Harun
Ng, Peter Kam Wah
Ng Peng Keong
Omar, of NBT Coy
Omar, of Sapi
Onsi (Unchi/Onchi), Headman of Kemansi
Oteh bin Burog
Pardi bin Dulbar
Pastor, Monica
Patuk bin Gijiran, of Marakau
Pelula of Paka
Polinoh, Secret Agent
Quadra, Alberto
Quadra, Bernard
Raman
Raschid, Abdul (Padua, Loreto)

Rice-Oxley, Major
Rijan
Ropoi, Police Constable
Rowe, Michael Wati
Rumbai, headman of Pinawantai
Rusman, of Mile 11
Sagan bin Haji Arst, of Sapi
Sahat, Mandor
Saidin, of Ranau area
Saliam (Salium), of Sapi
Salium, of Muanad
Salunda bin Gambuai, of Sumaang
Samak of Meninghatan
Sampura, PC 610
Sapan (Sagan), of Sapi
Serong Usup, Secret Agent
Sherman, Winfield, Secret Agent
Sigindai, of Ranau area
Siluntai, of Ranau
Sin Tshau
Sin Yen
Singh, Police Corporal Pritam
Singki, of Ranau
Siti binte Jakariah
Smith, Governor Robert
Solom, PC 196
Sompik (Indonesian mandor)
Stookes, Dr Valantine Alexander (executed at Keningau 1945)
Suamin bin Gadalip (Kaingal/Kabinbgal) of Kaparingam
Sumping, of Batu Lima
Surap, of Ranau
Tamanis, Secret Agent
Taylor, Celia
Teo Kim Chin
Tima, of Ranau
Tsen Kui Foh
Tshu Khi
Udang Taha
Wales, Mrs Anna
Wands, Dr H
Watson, Richard
Willie, Bede Soemole

Willie, Francis
Willie, James
Willie, Thomas Francis
Wong Bow Sang
Wong Chee Kan
Wong Hiong
Wong Mui Yin (widow of Heng Joo Ming)
Wong Tse Thau
Wong Wei Ming (Wai/Wee Man)
Wong Yee Choy
Wong Yin
Yap Sian Chui
Yee Sing Kee
Young, Simon
Zamen, Mohamed
Zimban bin Dittuan, of Sumaang

SOA agents/helpers:

The following names appear in Australian archival documents

Operation Python (Labian Point area)
Abok bin Pusu, Police Constable (killed)
Chang Fatt
Chin En Foo (killed)
Chin En Sung (Michael Chan – killed)
Fernandez, Floranzia
Ismail bin Andan
Lim Keng Fatt (killed)
Prali, Headman of Tungku
Samudi, Police constable (killed)
Willie, B S
Yan Cheong

Operation Agas 1 (Sandakan area)
Amat, of Sapi
Askali, headman of Sungei Sungei
Chang Su Yin (guerrilla, Chinese Chamber of Commerce)
Ho See (guerrilla, Volunteers)
Hussin bin Ulan, of Telupid
Ali bin Jandar, Mandor

Haji Abdul Raja (Abdurajap), of Jambongan
Kulang, of Muanad
Mohamed Salleh, Pangeran of Trusan
Mukor, headman of Paitau
Munjong bin Yahya, boatman (also guerrilla)
Mustapha, Datu bin Harun (later Sabah's 1st Yang di-Pertua Negeri)
Odun, Panglima of Sugut area
Ogi, Panglima of Mumiang
Panjam, of Sapi
Sabrang
Semak, of Menginhatan
Tan Tek Bak (also guerrilla), storeowner of Musa Island
Tsen Yin San, (Kudat Chamber of Commerce)
Willie, B S
Willie, James

Operation Agas 2 (northern Sabah)
Abdul Rahman, Police Constable of Tanjong Batu
Andjong Ajak, headman of Ulu Bengkoka
Chit Singh, small landholder of Tanjong Batu
Daud, Mandor of Kudat
Ejip, of Mattunggong
Eshak, Police Constable of Telega district
Koloh (killed at Pitas)
Lim Sui Wei, of Lokopas
Matahir, Haji of ulu Bengkoka
Mitoh, of Rampayan
Muallamat and others, of Kudat
Mustapha, Datu of Taritipan
Mustol, of Pitas district
Nuang, from the islands
Ussoff (Yussoph) of Pitas, Sergeant
Sawad, headman of Tegaman
Serip Taha, of Kota Belud
Tan Kah Kee (guerrilla section leader)
Tan Tek Bah, of Lokopas
Tsen Sen Yen, of Pingan-Pingan

Operation Agas 3 (Ranau area)
Adjong Ajak, headman of Pitas
Ampun, Police Constable 596

Chin Ah Tak (Kapitan Cina, Ranau administration)
Gelintang (Ranau Schoolteacher, administration)
Gilenki, headman of Lansat
Gimbahan of Ranau
Ginsiang (Dresser, Ranau administration)
Jahil, Police Constable 249
Jaimi, Edmund (Head of Ranau administration)
James, Andrew (Dresser, Ranau administration)
Jonit, Police Constable
Mandor Ali
Mentod, Police Constable (local guerrilla, shot in wrist, arm amputated)
Sampura, Police Constable 610
Salunti, of Sinarut
Solom, Police Constable 196
Wong Yse Thau (dresser, Ranau administration)

Operation Agas 4 (Tawau area)
Abdul Kadir (Baju)
Ali bin Jandar, Mandor
Ali Marden, of Semporna
Bachee, J D, of Semporna
Bangkuran village (Mostyn-Lahad Datu area)
Blaauw, Dr Chu Leong
Gata, Headman Sungei Taman
Guru Awang Besar, of Semporna
Ishmael bin Inshe, Police Constable
Jalalah, Headman of Mostyn,
Karino, Mrs, of Mostyn (Japanese – helped Dr Blaauw)
Koram bin Anduit, Sergeant
Lieu Kui Chin
Lim Pik Chu, of Semporna
Manup, B, of Sabalik Island
Mohamed Salleh, of Sabalik Island
Nurl, of Semporna
Pritam Singh (ex Sandakan Constabulary)
Sahat, Mandor, of Semporna
Sherman, Winfield
Sidek, of Sabatik Island
Sin Pio, of Mostyn
Titingan, of Sungei Taman

Ulu Serudong, Headman of
Willie, B S

Operation Agas 5 (Lahad Datu area)
Buaya, Headman of Talesai
Chan Fatt
Chin Sang
Fernandez, Florianzia
Ismail bin Andan
Khalid (interpreter)
Majit
Polinoh
Prali, Headman of Tungku
Tamanis
Yan Cheong

Operation Agas 3 subdivision (Stallion 4 – Kimanis Bay)
Ali bin Jandar, Mandor
Ho Ah Lee

Operation Stallion (Brunei Bay)
Dewa
Gapar bin Dalil
Latif bin Ahmad

Attached to SOA for special duties:
Ambrose, Samuel Dumpagnol
Willie, Thomas

North Borneo Volunteer Force, B Company, Sandakan

Some of those serving when the Japanese arrived

Officers:
Hunt, Lieutenant H F
Kong Su En, Lieutenant
Parnell, Captain Henry Rupert Carlton
Walker, Lieutenant Herbert James

Lieutenant Michael Edge and Jamadar Ojagar Singh, members of the BNB Constabulary, were also the Volunteers' instructors.

Men:
Apostol, Lamberto
Aruliah, Samuel
Azcona, Felix
Chan Wai Yuan, Private
Chang, Henry (Chang Ting Kiang)
Chow Chan Kuen
Chow Yuk Chung
Funk, Alexander
Funk, Lance-Corporal John Simon Jnr
Funk, Patrick
Ho See
Ja'affar Hussein
Khoo Siak Chiew, Corporal
Koh Soon Hock (Soon Fook), Gunner
Koh Yong Sing, Lance-Corporal
Kong Su En
Lagan, Ernesto (No. 1129)
Lim Kuan Poh
Lim Toi Chi, Private
Lo Ah Fuh (Jackie - collaborator)
Lo Hoi Chee
Lo Kwok Chuan, Gunner
Ng Peng Keong
Olaybal, D
Pang, Corporal Mark
Quadra, Bernard (No 1119)
Robert, Anthony P
Singh, Pritam
Talip bin Supian
Tan Thien Kai, Private
Wong Hoi Chuen, Gunner
Wong Wei Ming (Wai Man), Corporal
Yap Man Siu (Stephen), Lance-Corporal

Australian POWs

Arrested and detained at Kuching

Died in Kuching, before trial:
Keating, Sapper Edward (11/2/1944)

Transferred to POW camp, owing to lack of evidence:
Lander, Sergeant Colin

Tried and found guilty

Shot by firing squad:
Matthews, Captain Lionel (2/3/1944)

Sent to Outram Road Gaol Singapore:

Blain, Sergeant Alistair	1.5 years
Davis, Sapper Roy	1.5 years
Davis, Private Stanley	2 years
Graham, Corporal Thomas	1.5 years
Holly, Sergeant Ray	1.5 years
James, Staff Sergeant J	1.5 years
Jensen, Sapper Carl	2 years
Marshall, Sapper Donald	4 years
Martin, Private Frank	3 years
McMillan, Corporal J	1.5 years
McDonough, Sergeant William	6 months
Mills, Corporal C	2 years
Rickards, Corporal J	6 years
Roffey, Corporal W	1.5 years
Rumble, Private Thomas	6 months
Small, Corporal Arnold	1 year
Stevens, Sergeant Alfred	6 years
Wells, Lieutenant Roderick	12 years
Weynton, Lieutenant Gordon	8 years

Died in Outram Road Gaol:
Davis, Sapper Roy (13/10/44)
Marshall, Sapper Donald (11/8/44)
Small, Corporal Arnold (9/11/44)

Sent to Kuching POW Camp from Sandakan:
Brown, Captain Robert
Morrrison, Lieutenant J
Poole, Lieutenant John
Rae, Captain Vernon
St John, Lieutenant Harold
Weston, Sergeant Joe

POW attempted escapees:

Tried and sent to Outram Road Gaol:
Allen, Private Edward
Brown, Private Miles Pierce
Carr, Private Matthew
Fairey, Lance-Corporal William
Jacka, Driver M
McWilliams, Private Bruce
Minty, Private Allan
Morris, Private Norman
New, Lance-Corporal Frederick
Shelley, Driver Jeffrey
Trackson, Lance-Corporal Herbert
Young, Private Keith (Bill)

Sent to Outram Road for punishment:
Darlington, Private James

Died in gaol:
Allen, Private Edward (10/7/43)

Died in Changi POW hospital, after transfer from gaol:
Fairy, Lance-Corporal William (5/4/44)
Shelley, Private Jeffrey (29/10/44)

Escaped from Berhala Island to Tawi Tawi:
Blow, Lieutenant Rex
Butler, Private Rex (killed 18/8/1943)
Gillon, Lieurenant Leslie Miles
Kennedy, Private R James
McLaren, Private Robert Kerr
Steele, Captain Ray
Wagner, Lieutenant Charles (killed 21/12/1943)
Wallace, Warrant Officer Walter

SOA (Australian and British) behind the lines

Operation Python: (* Captured and executed)
Brandis, Sergeant William *
Broadhurst, Captain Douglas

Chester, Major Francis George (Gort)
Chew, Warrant Officer Alexander
Cottee, Sergeant Lindsay
Jinkins, Major William Thomas
McKenzie, Sergeant Donald George*
Neil, Sergeant Stanley
O'Keefe, Captain Edward
Olsen, Sergeant Frederick Gordon
Rudwick, Lieutenant Alfred John (Jack) *
Woods, Lieutenant Lloyd James

Operation Agas 1:
Chester, Major Francis George (Gort)
Greenwood, Sergeant Graham
Harlem, Lieutenant Donald Alfred Lawrence
Hollingsworth, Lieutenant Harold Henry
Hywood, Corporal Amos William Carson (Skeet)
Kelm, Signaller Adolph Victor
Neil, Sergeant Stanley
Norton, Signaller Harry
Olsen, Sergeant Frederick Gordon
Russell, Sergeant William Allen Campbell
Sutcliffe, Major D S (Jock)
Thompson, Warrant Officer N W
Wong Sue, Sergeant Jack

Operation Stallion 4 sub-party:
Chester, Major Francis George (Gort)
Hywood, Corporal Amos William Carson (Skeet)
Wong Sue, Sergeant Jack

Operation Agas 2:
Alexander, Sergeant Gerard Beltrand
Carmody, Sergeant Martin Albert
Combe, Major R G P N (Nick)
Lange, Sergeant Keith
Ma'Aruff bin Said, Sergeant
May, Captain W K S
McDonough, Corporal Ernest
McKeown, Sergeant Edward
McLean, Captain Roy
McMaster, Lieutenant J

Miller, Sergeant W G
Mongan, Lieutenant Frank
Nash, Sergeant George
Watts, Sergeant Jeffrey Godwin

Operation Agas 3:
Forster, Major J A (Indian Army)
Gore, Sergeant Eric William
Grinham, Sergeant Leslie Arthur
Hodges, Sergeant John Allen (Lofty) Hodges
Hywood, Corporal Amos William Carson (Skeet)
McNeale, Sergeant Jack Part
Nicholls, Captain Henry William
Ripley, Flight-Lieutenant Geoffrey Charles
Wallace, Sergeant Norman Alexander

Operation Agas 4:
Blow, Major Rex
Campbell, Warrant Officer C A
Halsey, Captain J A
Hibbard, Stoker (RAN, attached)
McLeod, Sub-Lieutenant (RAN, attached)
Neville, Seaman (RAN, attached)
O'Brien, Sergeant A A (AIF, attached)
Schinckel, Signaller Barragwanath (Barney)

Sub-party to check intelligence:
Blow, Major Rex
Schinckel, Signaller Barragwanath (Barney)

Operation Agas 5:
Haley, Signaller Francis
Herps, Sergeant Douglas Thomas
McLaren, Captain Robert Kerr (Jock)

Compensation and Rewards

Note: Spelling of names may differ

Aruliah, Samuel	$631	
Adihil	$180	
Ambiau	$137	
Amit	$35	
Andu bin Patrick	$281	
Apostol, Lamberto	$631	
Azcona, Felix Snr	$637	
Barigah Katus	$168	
Bazan, Tasiana Theresa	$535	(remarried widow of Felix Azcona)
Burih	$69	
Chan Ah Ping	$672	
Chang, Henry	$446	
Chang Siew Ha	$4188	(widow of Soh Kim Seng)
Chan Tian Joo	$637	
Chin Chee Kong	$677	(Chin Piang Syn/Sini)
Chow Yee Soo	$233	
Chu Li Tsia	$137	
Dahlan	$69	
Damian bin Barag	$2150	(SOA agent, wounded)
Dekee, Richard	$69	
Foo Seng Chow	$631	
Funk, John Simon Jnr	$500	(medical expenses only)
Funk, Patrick	$500	(medical expenses only)
Funk, Magdelene	$3400	(widow of Alex)
Galunting	$103	
Gambaiu	$15	
Ginssas bin Gunsass	$137	
Goh Tiek Soong	$897	(Tek Sen/Sing)
Goh Tiek Tshi	$957	(Tek Chai)
Gunting	$267	
Gusman	$637	
Halima binte Amat	$2150	(widow of Wong Mu Sing)
Halima binte Binting	$2150	(widow of Matusup)
Hussin	$99	

Ismail bin Awang Raman	$69	
Jakariah	$651	
Jenny bin Sarudin	$69	
Jones, Arthur	$637	
Kantong	$134	
Kulang	$137	
Kuting Main	$69	
Laduma	$134	(Ladooma)
Lagan, Katherine	$5650	(Kathleen/widow of Ernesto)
Lai, Peter	$631	
Lai, Phoebe	$137	
Liap	$137	
Magador	$134	
Mahomed Tassim	$69	
Mandor Salleh	$637	
Mananai, Puolo	$240	(paid to his widow)
Manoulong	$69	
Ng Ho Kong	$672	
Ngui Ah Kui	$631	
Omar	$69	(NBT Company)
Omar	$69	(Sapi)
Onsi, Orang Tua	$99	(Onchi/Unchi)
Pardi bin Dulbar	$103	
Raman	$69	
Sagan	$69	
Saliam	$123	(Salium)
Salleh	$631	
Sagan	$69	(Sapan)
Siti binte Jakariah	$230	
Sumping	$134	
Surat Min	$637	
Wong Mui Yin	$2250	(widow of Heng Joo Ming)
Wong Mu Sing's son	$1524	
Wong Wai Ming	$254	(Wee Man/Wei Man)
Wong Yun Siew	$231	(Joseph 'Pop' Wong)
Young, Simon	$69	

Bibliography and References

Printed books:

Aiken, A, *In Time of War*, Scotland, 1980.

Archer, John Beville, *Lintang Camp,* Kuching, 1946.

Bhar, Supriya, *Sandakan One Hundred Years 1879–1979*, Sabah, 1979.

British North Borneo Chartered Company, *Views of British North Borneo with a Brief History*, London, 1890.

British Government, *Hansard*, London, 1892.

Casino, Eric, *The Jama Mapun: A Changing Samal Society in the Southern Philippines*, Manila, 1976.

Chin, Daniel 陈东和（日军侵占北婆罗洲血泪史），沙巴华文作家协会, Kota Kinabalu, 2004.

Church of St Michael and all Angels, Sandakan, *75 Years on Elton Hill, The History of St Michael's Church Sandakan, North Borneo*, 1963.

Cunningham, Michelle, *Defying the Odds*, Melbourne, 2006.

Evans, Stephen R, *Sabah (North Borneo) under the Rising Sun Government*, Singapore, 1990.

Firkins, Peter, *Borneo Surgeon, The Story of Dr James P Taylor*, Perth, 1995.

Firkins, Peter, *From Hell to Eternity*, Perth, 1979.

Gorlaski, Robert, *World War II Almanac*, London, 1981.

Hall, Maxwell, *Kinabalu Guerrillas. An Account of the Double Tenth 1943*, Hong Kong, 1962.

Hatton, Frank, *North Borneo Explorations and Adventures on the Equator*, New York, 1886.

Hill, Elton, *Elton Hill Diary* (reprint of diary 1888–1913), Hong Kong, 1976.

Imperial War Graves Commission, *The War Dead of the British Commonwealth and Empire, Labuan Memorial and War Cemetery Registers*, London, 1960.

Keith, Agnes, *Land Below the Wind*, London, 1939.

Keith, Agnes, *Three Came Home*, London, 1948.

Leong, Cecelia, *The First 100 Years*, Sabah, 1982.

Lim Shau Hua, Julitta, *From an Army Camp to a Teachers' College*, Kuching, 1995.

Lucas, Celia, *Prisoners of Santo Thomas*, London, 1975.

McGregor, John, *Blood on the Rising Sun*, Perth, n.d.

Padasan, John M, *Sabah History in Pictures, 1881–1981*, Sabah, 1981.

Pollard, Elizabeth, *Kuching Past and Present*, Kuching, 1972.

Pryer, Mrs W B, *A Decade in Borneo,* London, 1893.

Richardson, H, *One Man War: the Jock McLaren Story*, Sydney, 1957.

Sabah Tourism Promotion Corporation, *Lest We Forget 1945–1995, Commemorating 50 Years since the End of World War II*, Sandakan, 1995.

Sarda, James and Wong, Danny, *Spirit of Borneo, Martin and Osa Johnson's Journey 1920 & 1935*, Kuala Lumpur, 2009.

Silver, Lynette Ramsay, *Sandakan A Conspiracy of Silence*, Sydney, 2004 and Kota Kinabalu, 2008.

Smith, Kevin, *Borneo Australia's Proud but Tragic Heritage*, (privately published), Armidale, 1999

Tanaka, Yuki, *Hidden Horrors: Japanese War Crimes in WWII*, Boulder, Colorado, 1996.

Treacher, W H, *British Borneo: Sketches of Brunei, Sarawak, Labuan and North Borneo*, Singapore, 1891.

2/19th Battalion Association, *The Grim Glory of the 2/19 Battalion A.I.F.*, Sydney, 1975.

Wallace, Walter, *Escape from Hell*, London, 1958.

Whelan, F G, *Stories from Sabah History*, Hong Kong, 1968.

Wigmore, Lionel, *Australia in the War of 1939–1945: The Japanese Thrust*, Canberra, 1957.

Young, Bill, *Return to a Dark Age*, Sydney, 1991.

Newspapers, Articles, Journals

Note: Many of the articles cited in newspapers below contain inaccuracies, and should not be used as source material without further checking.

Advertiser, 12 Mar 2007

Air Force News, Mar 1999

Anglican Historical Society Journal, June 2009

Argus, 17 Sept 1945; 21 July 1947

Australasian Post, 6 Oct 1983; 1 April 1989

Australian, 15–16 June, 25–26 July 1992, 25 Feb 1995; 28–29 Oct 2006

Border Mail, 26 Apr 2007

Borneo Bugle, March 2006

Borneo Bulletin, 10 Aug 1985

Borneo Post, 29 Sept 1998; 13 Feb 2005; 29 April 2007; 15 July 2007

British North Borneo Herald, 1, 16 May 1939; 3 Sept 1939; 16 Oct 1941; 16 Jan 1942

Brunei Times, 24 Nov 2006; 21 Dec 2009

Bulletin Magazine, 25 Apr 2006

Canberra Times, 6 Feb 1995; 30 Aug 1998

Daily Express, 8 May 1982; 4 Jan 1998; 20 Sept 2004; 15 May; 23, 28, 30 Aug; 6, 9, 13 Sept; 3, 9, 12 Dec 2003; 18 May 2004; 21 April 05; 22, 28 May 2005; 7, 21 Aug 2005; 8 Jan 2006; 9, 16, 23, 30 April 2006; 19 Nov 2006; 26, 29 Apr 2007; 6 May 2007; 22 Jul 2007; 15 Sept 2007; 15 May 2009; 16, 23, 28, 30 Aug 2009; 6, 9, 13 Sep 2009; 22 Nov 2009

Daily Telegraph, 31 Dec 1998; 6 Apr 2008;

Herald (Melbourne), 7 July, 22 Aug, 11 Sept, 13 Oct, 17 Nov 1945; 19, 20 Nov, 4 Dec 1947

Manly Daily, 23 Sep 2008

New Sabah Times, 28 Aug 2009

New Straits Times, 16, 19 Aug 2005

New York Times, 20 Oct 1882, 15 April 1883

News Weekly, 16 Oct 2009

North Borneo News, 25 Dec 1952; 1, 8 Dec 1953

North Shore Times, 5 Apr 2006; 19 Jul 2007; 11 Jul 2008; 28 Aug 2009

Outpost Magazine, Jul–Aug 2006

People Magazine, 17 Jan 51; 27 Aug 1952

QANTAS Magazine, August 2005

Reveille Magazine, Sept–Oct 2008

Rhymie Abdul Rahman, Damit Rebellion (translation in SP)

Stand-To, Journal of ACT Branch, RSS&AILA, Vol 8, No 5, Sept–Oct 1963 (Article by Rex Blow)

Star (Malaysia), 7 Aug 2005; 29 Aug 2009

Still Serving, Annual Magazine of the Ex-Services Association of Sabah, Dec 1970

Sun Herald, 17 April 1988; 25 July 1993; 9 July 1995

Sunday Mirror, 23 Aug 1959

Sunday Telegraph, 9 July 1995

Sydney Morning Herald, 11 Oct 1945; 3, 4 Jan, 6 Feb, 12, 15 Mar, 6, 8 April 1946; 21 Nov 1947; 7 Jul, 14 Aug 1995; 13 Sep 2003; 19 Apr 2006; 24 April 2008; 28 Aug 2009

Table Tops (AMF Troop Newspaper), 18, 22 Sep 1945

Tumut-Adelong Times, 8 Jul 2005

Vic Eddy, Journal of Eighth Division Signals Association, Vol 65, March 1996 (article by Rus Ewin)

University of Queensland Law Journal, The Tokyo War Crimes Trial, A.J. Mansfield

West Australian, 26 Jul 2007

Wong, Dr Danny, *The Funk Brothers* (reprinted in *Daily Express* 20 Sept 2006)

Young, May (account of escape to Australia – copy in SP)

Documentaries:

ABC Compass programme, *Windows to Sandakan*, April 2009

Film Australia, *Return To Sandakan*, 1995

Sixty Minutes, *Secret Heroes*, 26 Jun 2005

Sunday Programme, *A Long Walk through Hell*, April 2006

Documents in the Public Record:

Abbreviations:

NAA ACT: Australian Archives, Canberra, ACT
NAA NSW: Australian Archives, Sydney, NSW
NAA VIC: Australian Archives, Melbourne, Victoria
AWM: Australian War Memorial, Canberra, ACT
SP: Silver Papers

Note: Some of the names against file numbers have been changed to give a clearer indication of the contents.

National Australian Archives, ACT:

Natives, Compensation to, A1838/1 1464/1/4

Plan, Operational, Relief of POWs, A5954 265/6

POW Borneo Information on, A 1067 IC46/12/1

POW Borneo, Information on CP78/24 1914/16/89/271

POW, Relief of Australian, A5954 676/9

Special Operations Australia (SOA), Operational Files, A 3269 Items:

A1 Agas 1

A2 Agas II

A3 Agas III

A4 Agas IV

A5 Agas V

A5a Agas Intelligence Reports

A7 Python

A 22 Kingfisher
A28 Operations, BNB
A31 Geographical Information, Static report BNB
H1 SRD Intelligence reports, Correspondence AIB
H4 SRD Organisation
H9 Intelligence Summaries
H13 SRD Projects
J1 Intelligence Reports Group A
J2 Progress Reports Group A
J3 Progress Reports, Group A
J26 Progress Reports
J31 Sectional Reports
K3 Group B progress report
M1 Planning
M3 AIB Monthly Status Reports
07 History of SOA – Organisation
O8 History of SOA – Operations
012/13/14 Operations of AIB GHQ SWPA
V9, V10 Consolidated Status reports
V16 32 2nd Echelon Missing personnel
V17 Tracing and Recovery of SRD POWs
V18 Rescue of Allied POWs
V19 Report on Investigations Australian and Allied POWs – 9 Aust Div Area
War Graves Registration Sheets, A8234
War Crimes Trials:
Hayashi Yoshinori and others, Trial of, A 471/1 80779
Murozumi H, and others, Trial of, A 471/1/80776
Yamawaki and others, Trial of, A 471/1 81956
Webb Report, Publication of, A 1067/1 UN 46/WC/17

National Australian Archives, Victoria:
Army Minister, Statement by, regarding BNB POWs MP 742 255/15/1291
Bodies, Recovery of 109, MP742/1 132/1/529
Casualty Reports (of other POW), by Campbell, B 3856 144/1/244
Casualty Reports, (of other POW) by Braithwaite, Campbell, B 3856 144/1/246
Compensation, Claim for, MP742/1 66/1/796
Compensation, natives, MP742/1 66/1/572
Documents, Mass Grave, Sandakan B 3856/0 Item 144/14/140
Department of War Graves Services' Reports MP742/1 132/1/529

Japanese Policy re wounded, MP 1582/7 Item 144
Jackson, Lt-Col H, Report by, MP 742 328/1/32
Laband, Statement by Dr, MP749/1 44/431/101
9 Div Report on Investigations BNB, B 3856 145/4/147; B3856/0 144/1/255
Nominal Rolls, Internees and POW, B 3856 140/1/41
POWs, Borneo, B3856 144/1/372
POW Casualties, B3856 145/4/137
POW, Contact Inquiry Unit 3, MP 729/8/0 44/431/101
POWs, Died Borneo, B3856 144/4/84
POW, Information on, MP729/8 44/431/101
POWs, Loss of, MP 742 51/1/269
POWs, Missing, Borneo, B 3856 144/1/235
Rayson, Dr, Statement by, MP 742 336/1/153
Red Cross, Lists Malai [sic] to Borneo since 1/4/44, B 3856 144/1/21
Red Cross Cables re above, B 3856 144/1/22,26,27
Red Cross Transfers, B 3856 144/1/30,32,113,115
Taylor, Dr, Statement by, MP897/1 156/19/152
War Crimes Investigations, 1945-1949, MP 375/14
War Crimes Investigations/Trials
Series MP 742 Files 336/1/
153: Sandakan, Ranau (including statements by POWs)
252: Kempeitai Sandakan
258: Sandakan Death March, Trial of Nagahiro Maseo and Others
268: Massacre at Ranau, Goto and others
314: Trial of Hayashi, Y, and Others
343: Affidavits, from Members of AMF (parts 1 & 2)
606: 2nd Death March, Takakuwa, Watanabe
614: War Criminals, nominal rolls
636: Affidavits (parts 1 & 2)
707: Hoshijima, Susumi
786: War Crimes Act 1945
838: Trials, Rabaul
1113: Trials of Major War Criminals, Tokyo
1016: Diary, 1 Australian War Crimes Section
1180: Baba, Lt-Gen and others
1182: Last PW/Crucifixion, Sandakan
1319: Baba, Lt-Gen Masao
1416: Sandakan, 1st March
1470: War Crimes, Borneo, General (incl. additional Sticpewich Statement)
1548: Rudwick and others, Execution of

1697: Hosotani, Trial of (murders at 15 mile)
1698: Ikada and others (cemetery massacre)
1715: Murozumi and others (incl. statement by Botterill re Toyoda)
1731: Beppu and others (Ranau massacres)
1806: Yamamoto and others (1st march)
1811: Civilians Yamamoto and Katayama
1830: Suzuki, Cpl
1840: Ueno, Cpl
1846: Yunome, Civilian
1854: Matthews, Wells and others, Torture of; Matthews murder, Kuching
1943: Ill-treatment, Kempei-tai
2121: Yamawaki and others
2093: Yamamoto Shoichi and others (1st march)
B3856 144/14/140 Diary of Tom Burns
B 5569/1: Hayashi Yoshinori and others
5569/1 NN: Hoshijima
MP742/1 132/1/465: Massacre of 23 POW (Sandakan)
MP375/14 WC 18,19: Murder of Unknown PW (Sandakan)
" WC 20: Murder, Crucifixion
War Criminals, 1945-47 MP 1395/2
War Graves Recovery, B3856/0 114/1/235
Webb, Sir William, Report by, AWM226 8A
Wells, Report dated 16/5/49, MP 897/1/0 156/19/152
Wells, Weynton, Affidavits, MP897/1 156/19/152
Wong, memoirs of Mr, MSS1492

National Australian Archives, NSW:
Compensation, natives SP459/1/ 434/1/1727

Australian War Memorial Collection, ACT
Abe Soichi and others, trial of (1st march), AWM54 1010/3/116
Agas Patrol report, AWM54 779/3/82
Allen, Driver, report of Death (Outram Road), AWM54 554/11/1
AWGU 8, AWM52 21/2/9
AWGU 23, AWM52 21/2/24
AWGU 31, AWM52 21/2/32
Baba, Gen, Trial of, AWM54 1010/3/88
B Force Activities (Wells), AWM54 554/3/1
Blow and McLaren, PR story, AWM54 779/10/1
Bombing restrictions, AWM54 779/13/12
Borneo, General Report 1945-46, AWM54 1010/1/5

Borneo Mission, Report by Lt-Col H Jackson, AWM 84/231 Item 21
Braithwaite, Richard, Death March from Sandakan, AWM76 15434
Campbell, Owen, Interrogation, AWM54 1010/1/2
Campbell, Owen, Statements, AWM54 1010/4/27
Chan, Chi To, ex-Sandakan, Preliminary Interrogation, AWM54 779/3/8
Darling, Captain, Report on Investigations by, AWM54 779/4/5
Darling, Captain, Report on Investigations by, AWM54 1010/9/111
E Force, Report on, by Major Fairley, AWM54 554/6/1
Funk, Helen, Statement, AWM54 1010/4/55
Funk, Paddy, Account of Experiences, 3DRL 7408
Fukushima, Maseo, Trial of, AWM54 1010/6/5
Hammer's Report, re Guerrillas at Sulu, AWM54 519/2/8M
Hayashi, Noshinori, Trial of, AWM54 1010/6/89
Hoshijima, Trial of AWM54 1010/3/46
Hoshijima, Pencil Sketch of, 3DRL 7914
Intelligence Reports, AWM54 779/3/97
Investigation Report, AWM54 1010/9/12
Jackson, Harry, statement, Private Records, AWM PR 86/144
Japanese ID's of Officers, NCOs on 1st march, AWM54 779/3/5
Japanese, Interrogations of (various), AWM54 1010/4/134
Japanese Interrogations, conducted by Capt Brereton, AWM54 779/3/4
Japanese Interrogations, by 163 Language Detachment, HQ I Aust Corps, AWM 54 779/3/38
Japanese POW Interrogation reports, 24 Corps, ATIS, AWM54 779/3/39
Japanese, outline of plan re release of POWs (August 1945), AWM54 555/2/3
Japanese, statements by, AWM54 1010/4/158
Japanese, statements by, relating to 1st march, AWM54 779/3/5 and AWM 54 1010/6/59
Japanese, statements by, relating to Massacres and other murders and Ranau, AWM54 1010/4/174
Japanese Sworn Statements, AWM54 1010/4/158 Pts 1-18
Kitamura, Kawakami, Suzuki, Trial of, AWM54 1010/6/105
Maffey, Dr, Report by, MS S051
Maps, Borneo Camps, AWM54 779/13/5
Massacre, Sandakan AWM54 1010/9/99
Mort, Captain, Report by, AWM54 779/3/82
Moxham, William, Statement, AWM54 1010/4/107
Murozumi, Hiseo, Interrogation of, AWM54 1010/9/99

Natives, Special Reports and Interrogations of, AWM54 424/4/7
9th Division Area, Report on Investigation, Allied and Aust POW, Aug-Nov 1945, AWM54 779/1/25
9th Division Report, AWM 54 1010/9/111
Official History Files, Sandakan (including Braithwaite article), AWM76 B434
Overall, John, oral history tape
Photographic Collection, Sandakan
Photographic Reports, AWM54 621/2/15
POW, Allied, Borneo, Collated Information, AWM54 779/3/81, 779/3/97
POW, Allied, Kuching, report by Lt Abbott, AWM54 779/3/103
POW & Internees, Report of Investigation, AWM54 779/1/25
POW Camps, Far East, Locations of AWM54 779/13/13
POW Camps, Messages, Reconnaissance and Photographic Interpretation Reports, AWM54 424/4/15
POW Contact and Inquiry Unit, Report by Captain Mort, AWM 54 554/3/2
POW Liaison Office, Report by Captain McKinnon, att. to 9 Div, AWM54 779/1/16
POWs, Recovered, Interrogation of, AWM54 779/3/8
POW, Report of, at Brunei, Miri, Kuching, AWM54 779/1/17
Sandakan Force, AEME Activity Report, October 1945 AWM54 314/2/7
Sandakan, Massacre at AWM54 1010/9/99
Short, Nelson, Statement, AWM54 1010/4/129
Simpson's Report, AWM54, 773/4/11
SRD Intelligence Reports, XIII-28, Sandakan, AWM54 627/4/16 Part 18
Steele, Captain Ray, Report by, AWM54 627/4/16
Sticpewich, Affidavits, Stat Decs, by, AWM54 1010/4/174; 134
Sticpewich, Collected information, interrogations etc AWM54 779/2/16
3 Aust PW&I Unit, AWM54 554/3/2
26 Australian Infantry Brigade, Yamamoto, trial of, AWM54 1010/3/116 and 1010/6/59
War Criminals, Sentence Register, AWM26 15
Watanabe and Takakua, Trial of, AWM54 1010/3/94; 1010/6/59
Watanabe Genzo, Interrogation, AWM54 779/3/14
Webb, Sir William, Report by, AWM226 8A
Wong, Memoires of Mr, MSS 1492

Australian Broadcasting Commission Archives
Six from Borneo, transcript of Radio Documentary, and Tapes, 1947. Unedited tape transcripts *Australia under Nippon*, including interviews with K Botterill, J Braithwaite, R Braithwaite, O Campbell, S Davis, J Hodges, K Mosher, N Short, R Steele, H Trackson, recorded by Tim Bowden, 1983.

State Library, NSW:
Transcripts, International Military Tribunal For the Far East (Tokyo War Crimes Trials), including Evidence of Botterill, Moxham, Sticpewich, Wells, Weynton; Statements by Japanese officers and guards; Japanese Policy, Jesselton Revolt, Kuching Camp, Labuan Camp

Other government agencies:
Registrar of Births, Deaths, Marriages in Tasmania, Australia; New Zealand; Sabah

Private Collections, Correspondence:
Apostel, Lamberto, Statement by (SP)
Blanche, Bruce, correspondence with (SP)
Blow, Rex (SP)
Cottee, Len (Operation Python, SP)
Dominic family's *Clan Reunion Dec 2004*
Ewin, Rus (Ewin Papers)
Fu, Rev Clarence, correspondence with (SP)
Fullford, Major R, account of wartime and post-war experiences, *Picking up the Pieces* (SP)
Funk Family Papers, Melvyn Funk (SP)
Funk, Grace, correspondence
Funk, John, Obituaries, printed in *Time & Tide* and *Sydney Morning Herald* (SP)
Funk, Lillian, unpublished manuscript *The Wind Can Change* (SP)
Funk, Melvyn and Olga Puckett (née Funk), account of experiences (SP)
Funk, Melvyn, correspondence (SP)
Hodges, John 'Lofty' (SP)
Hooley, Ray, Ruston-Bucyrus Expert, Machinery and Engine Collector (Private Correspondence, SP)
Hywood, Skeet, Statements relating to Agas I, Agas III (SP)
Johnstone, Charlie, Diary of (copy in SP)
Korum, Cpl, Statement by (SP)

Lai, Bryan (re Peter Lai – copy in SP)
Lee, Peter, Diary (copy SP)
Marshall, Ron, Obituary, 2/18th Btn Association Newsletter, No 106, July 1996
Muller, Brigadier-general Henry J (Los Banos- SP)
Pang, Bart (re Mark Pang - SP)
Parker, Captain Herbert J (Los Banos - SP)
Pereira, Albert, correspondence, phone interview (SP)
Puckett, Olga, correspondence with (SP)
Rance, Bill, RAAF Flight Log Book, 35 Squadron, April 1945
Rance, Stan, statement regarding movement of C-47s to Morotai (SP)
Ringler, John M (Los Banos)
Robinson, Graeme, Photographs, Memorabilia from 31 AWGU (Robinson Papers)
Santos, Terry (Los Banos – SP)
Short, Nelson, Diary of, and Statement of Experiences (SP)
Silver, Lynette, *Fate of Dr V Stookes* (SP)
Singh, Anup, account of wartime experiences, family papers
Southwell Memoires (of Kuching camp, SP)
Steele, Report by Capt Ray, Steele Private Papers (SP).
Walker, Herbert Peter, war diary, photographs, personal papers (Patterson Papers)
Wallace, Norm (SP)
Wells, Rod (extensive correspondence, SP)
Wong, Joseph, statement
Young, Bill (paintings, sketches of Sandakan Camp, Outram Road Jail)

Interviews:

Ex-POWs: Keith Botterill, Owen Campbell, D Carment, Eric Davis, Stan Davis, Rus Ewin, Frank Gaven, Carl Jensen, Jim Millner, Ken Mosher, Nelson Short, Ray Steele, Herb Trackson, Rod Wells, Bill Young.
Specialists: Ray Battram (War Graves Recovery), Ted Boyd (9th Division, Sandakan Force), Brian Burke (water, boiler engineer), John Chapman (Paratroop Regiment), Jack Eaves (Royal Marine assigned to rescue mission), Denis Emeron-Elliott (SOE, SOA an British Secret Service), Bill Garing (Air Force command), Harry Jackson (Borneo Mission), Cyril Hutchings (steam expert), Skeet Hywood (ex-SOA), J 'Lofty' Hodges (ex-SOA), Sir John Overall (Paratrooper CO), Eric Pierce (water, boiler engineer), Tony Ramsay (wireless expert), Hal Richardson (McLaren's biographer), Graeme

Robinson (photographer, War Graves Recovery), Norm Wallace (ex-SOA), Yoshi Tosa (all Japanese translations)
Civilians: Aki Lagan, Sevee Charuruks, Peter Chew, Chin Chee Kong, Domima Akoi, Grace Funk, Melvyn Funk, Bryan Lai, Dr Lungkiam binte Dambul, Dr Othman Minudin, Alice Ng, Bart Pang, Pauline Patterson, Olga Puckett, Anup Singh, George Stookes, Suamin bin Gadalip (Kaingal), Tham Yau Kong, Joseph Wong, Martin Wong, Yumpil bin Yaron, Zudin

Subject References

Note: Each of the Sandakan survivors, including those removed from the camp, has made a number of general statements. These statements include various testimonies at the trials of Hoshijima, Yamamoto, Baba, Watanabe, Takakuwa as well as ABC radio interviews. The reference 'statement of', in the following notes, includes all statements made by the deponent.

Sabah's History 1875–1905:
Books: Bhar, BNB Chartered Company, Evans, Hatton, Hill, Keith's *Land*, Leong, Padasan, Pryer, Treacher, Whelan
Newspapers: *Brunei Times*, 24 Nov 2006, 21 Dec 2009; *New York Times*, 20 Oct 1882, 15 April 1883

Documents: various Charters, copies in SP; *Hansard*, 23 June 1892
Private papers: Dominic family

Sabah's History 1905–1942:
Books: Bhar, Evans, Firkins' *Surgeon*, Hill, Padasan, Sarda and Wong
Newspapers etc: *Borneo Bugle*, March 2006; *BNB Herald*, 1, 16 May 1939; *North Borneo News*, 25 Dec 1952, 1, 8 Jan 1953
Private papers: Dominic family, Walker

Civilian Life under Japanese occupation:
Books: Evans, Firkins' *Surgeon*, Hall, Keith, STP Corp
Newspapers: *Daily Express*, 15 May 2009
Documents: Steele Rpt
Interviews: Chin, Pang
Private papers: Dominic, Funk, Puckett, Walker

Voyage on *Yubi Maru* :
Books: Firkins' *Hell*, Silver, Tanaka, Young

Statements/Documents: Botterill, Braithwaite, Burns Diary, Carment, Davis S, Jackson Rpt, Maffey, Sticpewich
Interviews: Botterill, Davis E, Davis S, Wells, Young

Sandakan/Movement to Mile 8 Camp:
Books: Evans, Firkins' *Hell*, Keith, Wallace, Young
Documents/Statements: B Rpt, Burns Diary, Jackson Rpt, SRD files, A22, A31; Sticpewich, Wells, photographs, maps
Statements/Interviews: Botterill, Wells, You

Sandakan POW Camps, July 1942–September 1943:
Books: Silver, Wallace, Young
Documents: B Rpt, Burns Diary; Jackson Rpt, Lee, SOA/Intelligence Reports, Maps (see A22 and Hoshijima trial also), aerial photographs; sketches of Compound by Unknown Artist and Young, Steele Rpt, War Crimes files re treatment at Sandakan, 23/31 WGU records, Webb Rpt
Statements: Botterill, Braithwaite, Campbell, Davis S, Fleming, Helen Funk, Maffey, Nagai, Rayson, *Six from Borneo,* Sticpewich, Trackson, Wagner, Wells
Interviews: Botterill, Davis E, Davis S, Ewin, Millner, Wells, Young

The Camp Water and Electricity Supply:
Interviews: E Davis, Wells, with technical advice from Burke and Pierce

Wireless construction:
Documents: Jackson Report; Funk papers, Wells papers
Interviews: Chin, Davis, Wells

Airfield Construction/Treatment:
Books: Firkins' *Hell*, Silver, Wallace, Young
Documents/Statements: B Rpt, Botterill, Braithwaite, Campbell, Fleming, Hirota Nobuo (AWM 54 1010/4/174), Maffey, Moxham, *Six from Borneo*, Sticpewich, War Crimes Trials re treatment at Sandakan, Yamawaki (papers relating to, MP 742 336/1/1416)
Interviews: Botterill, Davis E, Young

The Sandakan Underground:
Books: Evans, Firkins' *Hell*, *Surgeon*, Keith, Tanaka (re uprising in Dutch Borneo), Wallace, Wigmore
Articles/Newspapers: *Daily Express*, 20 Sept 2004 (Funks); *Borneo*

Post, 29 Sept 98 and *Star*, 7 Aug 2005 (Tahir); Wong
Documents/Statements: Apostel, B Rpt, Carment, Funk J, Funk P, Jackson Rpt, Jackson statement, Koram, Laband, Lai, *Six from Borneo,* Sticpewich, Taylor, War Crimes Trials re Sandakan & Matthews, Wells, Weynton, Wong
Interviews: E Davis E, Milston (re Matthews biog), K Mosher, Wells

Local personalities:
Books: Casino, Firkins' *Hell*, *Surgeon*; Keith's *Three;* Silver; STP Corp; St Michael's Church
Newspapers: *Daily Express* 15 May 2009
Documents: Jackson Report
Private papers/correspondence: Blanche; Chin family; Funk family; Lai; Ng; Pang Family; Pereira family; Anup Singh; Walker; Willie family; Young

Early Escapes:
Books: Firkins' *Hell*, Silver, Young
Documents/Statements: B Roll (notations), B Rpt, Burns Diary, Jackson Rpt, Laband, Lai, Sticpewich, Trackson, SRD file V17, War crimes File MP742 336/1/1740
Interviews: Trackson, Young

Outram Road Jail:
Books: Firkins' *Surgeon*, McGregor, Silver, Young
Statements: Trackson, Wells
Interviews: S Davis, Jensen, Wells, Young

The Wireless and Transmitter:
Books: Silver, Wallace
Documents/Statements: Apostel, B Rpt, Funk J, Jackson Rpt, Wells, Wong
Interviews: Ramsay, Wells

E Force to Sandakan Camp:
Books: Keith, Richardson, Silver, Wallace, Wigmore
Documents/Statements: Blow, B Rpt, Campbell, E Rpt, Jackson Rpt, Koram, POWs Borneo (NAA VIC), Steele Rpt, Short Diary
Interviews: Campbell, Gaven, Richardson, Short, Steele

E Force & Wallace Escapes/Shooting of McKenzie and Harvey:
Books: Richardson, Silver, STP Corp, Wallace
Newspapers: *Borneo Post*, 29 Sept 98; *Star*, 7 Aug 2005

Documents/ Statements: Blow, B Rpt, Funk P, Jackson Rpt, Koram, Lee Diary, Steele Rpt, Tahir, War Crimes MP742 336/1/153, AWM54 1010/4/174; War Graves Records

British POW Experiences:
Documents: Burial records, Nominal rolls, Johnstone, Lee, War Crimes File MP 742 336/1/1470

The Sandakan Incident, Trials, Execution:
Books: Evans, Firkins, Goodwin, Wallace
Documents/Statements: see Sandakan Underground refs and War Crimes trials; Apostol, Helen Funk, Laband, Lagan, Laidaw, Chang, Chin, Funk, Khoo, Singh, Tahir, Taylor, Wells, Weynton, Wong
Interviews: Chin, E Davis, Wells
Private papers: Funk family, Lai

Double Tenth Uprising:
Books: Evans, Hall, Silver, Whelan
Documents: SRD Files A7, O8, O10

Operation Python/Fate of Brandis, Rudwick, McKenzie:
Documents: SRD Files A7, O8, O12, O13, O14, V7, V16; War Crimes Files 1470,1548 (NAA VIC).
Interviews: Cottee

SOA Operations in BNB (All Agas Missions, incl. Kingfisher):
Documents/Statements: SRD files A1, A2, A3, A4, A5, A5a, A22, A28, A31, A32, 37, H1, H9, H10, H13, J1, J2, J3, J26, J31, K3, M1, M3, N1, V9, V10, V16, V17, V18, V19.
Interviews: Cottee, Hodges, Hywood, Russell, Wallace

Sandakan Camps, September 1943–August 1945:
Documents/Statements: Botterill, Braithwaite, Campbell, Moxham, Short, Sticpewich, various POW and Investigation Reports, SOA Intelligence Reports, Maps, War Crimes Files re Sandakan
Interviews: Botterill, Campbell, Short

The 1st March:
Documents/Statements: Botterill, Jackson Rpt, Moxham, Sticpewich (NB: some is hearsay), Webb Rpt, Investigation Files, SRD A1, A5a, H1,J1, J2, J3, J26, M3, V9, V10, V16, V17, V19 and War Crimes Files relating to march
Interviews: Botterill

Paginatan and Ranau Camps:
Documents/Statements: Botterill, Moxham, Short, Sticpewich, Intelligence information in SRD Files A1, A5a, various POW and Investigation Reports, Webb Rpt, WGU Records, War Crimes Files relating to Ranau Camps
Interviews: Botterill, Short

The 2nd March:
Documents/Statements: Braithwaite, Campbell, various POW and Investigation Reports, Jackson Rpt, Aki Lagan, Short, SOA files (see previous entry, for 1st March), Sticpewich, War Crimes Trials relating to march, Webb Rpt, Yumpil bin Yaron, Zudin

Sandakan Massacres:
Documents: War Crimes Files re Last POW, Crucifixion, Massacre 23

Events leading to Collapse of Operation Kingfisher:
Books: Silver
Documents: Reports and signals etc in A3629 A1 viz: A8, 15, 2, 29–32, 34, 36 (A, F, G, L, M), 37 (A-C, H, M, N); File A5a, reports of 4, 16, 30 April 45 & 11, 20, 21 22 May; file V5 Schedule of current operations
Interviews/statements: Overall (*Canberra Times* 6 Feb 1985, 30 Aug 1998; AWM oral history tape; statement at 1993 paratroopers' reunion dinner); Chapman

Operation Kingfisher – Failed Rescue Mission:
Books: Silver
Newspapers: Various – see November/December 1947; *Canberra Times,* 6 Feb 1995; *Australian*, 25 Feb 1995; *Daily Telegraph*, 31 Dec 98; *Air Force News*, March 1999
Documents: A3269 A, A2, A5a, H1, H9, H13, J1; A663/1 O148/2/470, A5954 256/6, A5954 676/9, data extraction re C47 maintenance sheets
Private papers: Bill Rance, RAAF Flight Log
Correspondence/interviews: Chapman, Emerson-Elliott, Stan Rance

Operation Kingfisher – naval evacuation ships:
Books; Aiken (contains transcripts of documents held in Pro London, including admiralty 202/327; Force X Landing Craft flotilla)
Interviews/statements: Eaves

Kingfisher cover-up:
Documents: for evidence of, see A3269 A22 (all 'working' paperwork, signals, RAAF and RAN instructions, movement orders, intelligence summaries, memos etc are missing; Official SOA History A3269 O8 (no reference to Agas problems Oct 44-Mar 45; vital material in A3269 A1, 5a, 7, H11 not included)
Correspondence/Interviews: Emerson-Elliott, Garing, Overall

Los Banos Mission:
Books: Lucas
Documents: Statements by Muller, Parker, Ringler, Santos

War Crimes Trials:
Books: Silver
Documents: See various crimes in NAA VIC, NAA ACT and AWM

Kuching prisoners:
Books: Cunningham (Australian officers' experiences)

Fate of Civilians, SOA agents:
Books: Evans, Hall, Silver, STP Corp
Documents: See Agas files I-V
Correspondence: Lai, Pang, Christine Willie
Private papers: Funk family

Collaborators, British and Japanese:
Documents: For arrest list of 32 Japanese collaborators in Sandakan area, plus list of British collaborators, and all Japanese and Allied collaborators in other zones see Agas operational files I–V. Also 9 Division Report and Jackson's Report

Post-War Investigations:
Books: Silver, STB
Documents: See various files relating to investigations, Jackson, War Graves Units, Missing POW; Stookes
Private papers/correspondence: Blanche (re Stookes); George Stookes

Preserving the memory:
Books: Silver (2008 edition)
Newspapers: *Borneo Post* 13/2/05, 29/4/07, 15/7/07; *Daily Express* 3/12/03, 9/12/03, 10/12/03, 18/5/04, 21/4/05, 22/5/05, 28/5/05, 7/8/05, 21/8/05, 8/1/06, 9/4/06, 16/4/06, 23/4/06, 30/4/06, 19/11/06,

26/4/07, 29/4/07, 6/5/07, 22/7/07, 15/9/07, 16/8/09, 23/8/09, 28/8/09, 30/8/09, 6/9/09, 9/9/09, 13/9/09, 22/11/09; *New Straits Times,* 16/8/05, 19/08/05; *Star* 29/8/09; *Advertiser*, 12/3/07; *Anglican Historical Society Journal*, June 09; *Australian*, 28–29/10/2006; *Border Mail*, 26/4/07; *Bulletin Magazine,* 25/4/06; *Manly Daily*, 23/9/08; *News Weekly*, 16/10/09; *North Shore Times*, 5/4/06, 19/7/07, 11/7/08, 28/8/09; *Outpost Magazine*, Jul–Aug 06; *QANTAS Magazine*, August 05; *Reveille Magazine*, Sept–Oct 08; *Sydney Morning Herald,* 13/09/03, 19/4/06, 24/4/08, 28/8/09; *Telegraph*, 6/4/08; *Tumut-Adelong Times*, 8/7/05; *West Australian*, 26/4/07
Documentaries: *Sixty Minutes*, 'Secret Heroes', 26/6/05; *Sunday Programme*, A Long Walk through Hell, April 2006; *Compass ABC* 'Windows to Sandakan', April 2009
Documents: Service forms for Unveiling of Windows of Remembrance and Friendship Windows
Private papers: Records of development and opening of Sandakan Memorial Park, 1995–1999; Sabah Society march to Ranau, 2005; Sandakan Memorial Windows Projects, 2003–2008; Sandakan Memorial Scholarship Scheme, 2005–2010; Last Camp Memorial, 2006–2009; Sandakan Track development, 2005–06; Quailey Hill Memorial, 2007; Lofty Hodges Cottage 2009–10 (all in SP). See also Memorial Projects, www.lynettesilver.com and www.sandakan-deathmarch.com
Documents: Compensation files

Index